VERDICTS ON
Lawyers

Other Books by the Editors

RALPH NADER

Unsafe at Any Speed (1965, expanded edition in 1972)
Whistle Blowing (1972, edited with Peter Petkas and Kate Blackwell)
Corporate Power in America (1973, edited with Mark Green)
You and Your Pension (1973, with Kate Blackwell)

MARK GREEN

With Justice for Some (1971, edited with Bruce Wasserstein)
The Closed Enterprise System
(1972, with Beverly C. Moore, Jr., and Bruce Wasserstein)
Who Runs Congress?
(1972, updated in 1975, with James Fallows and David Zwick)
The Monopoly Makers (1973, editor)
*The Other Government: The Unseen Power of Washington
Lawyers* (1975)

VERDICTS ON
Lawyers

EDITED BY

Ralph Nader
Mark Green

Thomas Y. Crowell Company

ESTABLISHED 1834   NEW YORK

The publisher thanks the *Harvard Law Review* for permission to quote from Stone, "The Public Influence of the Bar," 48 *Harvard Law Review* (1934), copyright 1934 by The Harvard Law Review Association; and *The New Republic* for permission to quote from Kempton, "The Washrooms of Power," Aug. 3, 1973, copyright © 1973 The New Republic, Inc.

Designed by Jack Meserole

Manufactured in the United States of America

LIBRARY OF CONGRESS CATALOGING IN PUBLICATION DATA

Main entry under title:

Verdicts on lawyers.

Includes bibliographical references and index.
1. Lawyers—United States—Addresses, essays, lectures.
I. Nader, Ralph.   II. Green, Mark J.
KF298.V47   340'.0973   75-23292
ISBN 0-690-01006-0
ISBN 0-690-01667-0 (pbk)
        3   4   5   6   7   8   9   10

To law students who pursue justice as their highest calling

Ralph Nader

An Overview

THE struggle for legal supremacy in a society lies in the tension between raw power and just law. In our legal system the periodic beacons of justice's triumph have served to mask the frequent exclusion of the many by the few who block ready access to the law. There is a lengthy obstacle course to be run in order to attain justice. Sequentially, it involves the exercise or securing of *rights*, the access to competent *representation*, and the obtaining of effective *remedies* in a relative context of acceptable economics and expeditiousness. Beneath these formidable barriers—historically insurmountable for the vast majority of Americans—is a myth whose repeated invocation cloaks its hollow reality. That myth is equality under the law.

Let us ask a simple question of the kind rarely heard at law schools or bar association meetings. How many citizens have practical access to the legal system, whether to defend their rights or to advance their causes? Very few, say the available studies. Very few, say lawyers or active citizens who have observed and tried to work with the three branches of government on issues relating to consumer complaints, housing, health care, taxes, government services, occupational and environmental diseases, corporate abuses, and the legal industry itself. When compared with the exclusionary realities of the administrative and legislative forums, the judicial forum appears, and is, more accessible for individualized justice. The essays in this volume focus heavily on the courts and how the legal profession has avoided squaring its duty of service to all with its monopolistic status under the law. This focus, then, is modest; the contributors have bitten off less than they can chew. For the problem of exclusivity applies with greater latitude to the legislative and executive forums of government, where the most sweeping and serious decisions of public authority are initiated and implemented.

At the crossroads and at the ramparts of the legal system stands the legal profession. It has often been said that the health of a profession can be gauged in part by the scope of dissent that is tolerated within its ranks. This easy assertion does not apply to the lawyers' world. Internal dissent and criticism of the profession as a whole has been frequent, factual, and incisive. There have been landmarks of criticism, from Roscoe Pound's famous speech seventy years ago to a startled American Bar Association to the academic self-examination of the 1930s in the legal literature to the emergence of an activist-lawyer movement since 1965. Such criticism has been a measure, not of the health, but of the sickness of the profession and its resilient ability to stonewall critics via little concessions to a small, circumscribed legal services program by the federal government.

An endemic malaise of lawyers is that 90 percent of them serve 10 percent of the people. Their deployment is highly skewed to available retainers—a kind of retainer astigmatism. They reject the vast majority of their potential customers—a long-standing "law-lining" much as banks and insurance companies red-line urban areas. This is not simply a matter of avoiding a lesser remuneration, it is a choice in favor of that affluent class whose legal and illegal interests are often directly adverse to the bottom 90 percent of the citizenry. If one represents large land-lords, drug companies, and local industry, one finds little room in the office files for cases on behalf of tenants, patients, and local citizens critical of industry. This maldistribution of lawyers in a highly legal-istic society fortifies powerful interests at their most vulnerable inter-face with their victims or complainants—that is, when the legal system is supposed to decide conflicts or policy on the merits rather than due to deep pockets or political influence.

Conceptually, lawyers, with their exclusive licenses, are on shaky ground. Professor Karl N. Llewellyn gave a good description of the situation back in 1933:

> For the men of law are a monopoly, and monopoly is subject to regu-lation. The ground for monopoly is that it makes possible better service; this holds of the bar. The condition of monopoly is that it serve; this does *not* hold of the bar. If it were gas or transportation these men of law were furnishing, the established policy and rule would be service to all comers on demand and no refusal, at fixed and reasonable rates,

by state compulsion. The bar, man by man or firm by firm, set their own fees, choose among clients, and leave the bulk of needed service unperformed—the poor man's case. The bar purport moreover to exist as a profession. A profession is a line of work in which, so long as he who professes it can eat, his job is service.

Law is a profession in theory, and a monopoly in fact; a monopoly not merely by force of skill and brain but established and maintained by law. Only through lawyers can the layman win in fact the rights the law purports to give him.

Both before and after Llewellyn's observations, lawyers have indeed had it both ways. As officers of the court, they are susceptible to the imposition of professional duties, such as representing the indigent. Where the courts have instructed attorneys to represent the improvident, the quantitative significance compared to the need has been *de minimis,* though some pioneering cases of general impact, such as *Gideon* v. *Wainwright,* have been reassuring. But what of other professional duties implicit in the "officer of the court" status and Canons of Ethics? Here the courts have been unimaginative. The bar associations have been mostly inert. The most highly touted one of them all—the Association of the Bar of the City of New York—has sat sphinx-like while massive "sewer service," probate court injustice and other more parochial abuses proliferated to the benefit of lawyers and their clients. But even parochial abuses were treated with myopic indifference.

Such behavior, practiced throughout the country by bar associations, highlights the active use of the law to oppress innocent people. Denying many people practical access to the law is a condition which is almost always associated with the use of the law itself as an instrument of injustice. Years ago, a candidate for the governorship of the Brazilian state of Pernambuco was more blunt. He issued his campaign slogan—"To my friends, facilities; to my enemies, the law." The defensive orientation of reform lawyers in American legal history—e.g., when the NAACP's Legal Defense Fund defended victimized blacks in court—has sharply framed this criminal, unconstitutional, or otherwise abusive use of the law by both state and corporate institutions. Recognition of major rights—electoral, civic, procedural—has resulted from such litigation and the legislation it provoked into enactment.

But deeper, broader advances of structural justice require an *offensive* capability by people in varying roles—as consumers, as taxpayers, as workers. The highly publicized ad hoc courtroom victories should never become a substitute for a quantitatively significant change in the use and output of the legal process related to the case's holding; so a *Gideon* requiring the provision of lawyers is one thing, but the legislative appropriation of funds to actually provide such lawyers to accused felons is quite another. This test in turn emphasizes the need for more enduring mechanisms of legal reform which shift the distribution of legal services. Only then will the major challenges to the legal profession animate the required changes in the clients and causes that practitioners assume.

It is easier to recognize these challenges—many are discussed in succeeding chapters—than to ascertain how the legal profession can connect up with important and enduring civic reform. It is a characteristic of public dialogue that instruments of change receive less attention than the desired changes themselves. Consider, for example, the encompassing problems of governmental and corporate accountability. While people discuss and approve of the need for both institutions to be more open, fair, efficient, farseeing, and sensitive, there is almost no attention placed on how to achieve these attributes. Should there be voluntary consumer checkoff systems installed on utility bills and various contracts of adhesion to support full-time consumer action groups whose directors are elected by contributors? Should consumer class actions, court-awarded attorneys' fees, lawsuits by state attorneys-general on behalf of defrauded citizens, and other means of challenge and recovery for the great unrepresented be actively promoted? Should there be more reversion of electoral decision-making to the initiative, referendum, and recall? Should government bureaucracies and their officials be accountable directly to the citizens aggrieved by their decisions through a right of action based on a fiduciary principle that goes well beyond the customary ministerial/discretional distinction? Should alternative economic forms, such as consumer cooperatives, be treated equally by the government in its credit-extension and other supportive practices that are now overwhelmingly directed toward investor-owned, profit corporations? Should a new federal chartering authority redesign the duties of the large corporation toward its constituencies?

These are not exactly issues of prime political attention. Not yet, anyway. Yet they represent age-old problems with new exacerbations of serious import for most people. Lawyers represent the catalytic profession that draws upon other professions for public policy-making. Furthermore, as the profession that commands high posts within the three branches of government, the lawyering fraternity merits an inside audit.

VERDICTS ON LAWYERS evaluates the fraternity as advocates before the bar of justice. The authors represent practitioners, scholars, active reformers, journalists, and government officials who, not being strangers to controversy, have watched, pondered, and, for the most part, experienced that of which they write. Many were brought together in a conference of public interest lawyers designed as a counterpoint to the simultaneous August 1973 meeting of the American Bar Association in Washington, D.C. The conference considered the legal system from a consumer's perspective. This was an important touchstone from which to proceed. For the consumer of the law is the measure of a legal system. With the ultimate beneficiary constantly held uppermost in mind, the duties, roles, and behavior of the "trustees" (the lawyers) can be more realistically appraised.

And appraised they are in this book with a candor that can produce a searing quality of enlightenment. There has rarely been a more forthright description of a municipal court than that given by Detroit judge Justin Ravitz. Coupled with Jack Newfield's sobering reporting on some of the dregs of the New York City courts, these chapters call for radically improved methods of selecting judges and regularly monitoring the courtrooms of the land. Even at more refined levels of the judiciary, John Schmidt says much when he writes that "as a practical matter, federal district judges are appointed by the senior senator of the president's party from the state involved." But before that political step is taken, various bar associations, typically dominated by corporate lawyers, initiate their informal clearance process. This can be often construed as an appointment process whereby the bar associations are encouraged to suggest a list of candidates by governors or presidents. The American Bar Association has become a virtual partner, except for a few episodes, with presidents regarding the screening of U.S. Supreme Court appointments—as John MacKenzie subsequently discusses.

Bar associations have played a highly instrumental role in entrenching the law and legal system as a favored cohort of special-interest clients. Their committees help write state and federal laws or stop others from being enacted. As Mark Green points out in the chapter on the ABA, these committees are riddled with conflicts of interest between the lawyers' corporate clients and their supposedly independent participation on antitrust, patent, insurance, environment, tax, public utility, and other ABA committees. Regularly, chairmen of these committees become leading candidates for appointive office, such as Antitrust Division Chief in the Justice Department.

The professional imprimatur of their status within the ABA is a politically recognized asset. It permits governors and presidents to say that the candidate is "highly respected by his professional colleagues" instead of having to explain that he was highly rewarded by his clients. The patina of professionalism covers the reality of a career committed to corporate advocacy.

As a price-fixing guild, the bar association has suffered a recent setback: the June 1975 *Goldfarb* case declaring that coercive minimum fee schedules violated the antitrust laws. During the argument before the U.S. Supreme Court, counsel for the Fairfax County Bar Association urged upon the justices a "learned profession" exemption to the price-fixing prohibition that more mundane businesses must observe. A unanimous Court rejected the contention—but millions of consumers had already been overcharged throughout the country by the minimum-fee-schedule ploy.

In *Goldfarb,* the High Court altered one professional practice. There are many others in need of substantial revision and reform.

When consumers present grievances against their lawyers, it falls to the bar associations to decide whether to investigate and recommend disciplinary action by the courts. A system where lawyers pass on lawyers can institutionalize with some facility the practice of mutual back-scratching. Even the pretense of a self-policing structure is mocked by the absence of staff and resources for the bar associations' appointed mission. As Garbus and Seligman write, "Beyond this self-protective attitude on specific cases is a greater structural problem: Bar Associations have rigged the disciplinary process so that it barely can function at all."

In recent years, ABA leaders have explicitly affirmed the duty of the bar to support efforts at making legal services available regardless of the clients' ability to pay. But ambiguities filled their statements in the late sixties and early seventies. Is the obligation on the collective bar or on individual lawyers? Who pays for these services—the general taxpayer or lawyers donating their time and contributions? Canon 2 of *The Code of Professional Responsibility* does little by way of clarification when it says that "a lawyer should assist the legal profession in fulfilling its duty to make legal counsel available." The last decade has been faithful to the bar's desire to have the taxpayer, primarily through the Office of Economic Opportunity, pay for legal services for the poor.

Marna Tucker, in her evaluation of the ABA's efforts later in these pages, gives credit where credit is due, but is careful to make some important observations:

"The ABA public service programs provide opportunities for those relatively few lawyers who wish to participate in such work. But there has been little response from the legal profession as a whole. The ABA's programs, including the *pro bono* work of the private bar, have for the most part allowed the activities of some lawyers and law firms to make all the others look good. In the final analysis, only a handful of exceptional attorneys are attempting to meet the vast needs of the public and to atone for the general failure of the bar to service the non-rich public. The majority of funds used to operate these programs do not come directly from the average lawyer's pocket. These programs are paid for in large part by government, foundations, and other private and public sources."

Ms. Tucker notes the difference in results to the public which can flow from imposing duties on each lawyer rather than on the bar as a whole. She recommends a tithing system for lawyers, a public service internship program for law school graduates, and other mechanisms to focus responsibility on the individual practitioners.

Most lawyers fail to go beyond passive tolerance of government-funded legal services for clients they would never consider taking in the first place. In the early years of the Republic, citizens formed volunteer fire departments and, without any hoary jargon about learned professions, assumed the civic duty and personal risk of fighting fires affecting their neighbors' property and safety. Lawyers might reflect upon this continuing example of civic duty when they take umbrage at suggestions that along with their monopoly and professional pretensions there should be a much greater fulfillment of what Roscoe Pound called the "primary purpose of public service." Real income of lawyers has been increasing sharply since 1960, which should make some of these suggestions of public service more acceptable. Yet such suggestions are rarely heard. Instead, attorneys who tell their brethren at bar association meetings how to increase their billings ("Come right out at the beginning and sock him [the client] hard," declaimed one such pitchman at an ABA annual meeting) speak to packed and attentive audiences.

Hypocrisy being the bar's major consistency throughout the generations, the challenge by Dean Monroe Freedman to the profession's professions—their *Canons of Ethics*—provokes outrage among the fraternity. Smudging the cosmetic canons which give lawyers their paper conscience gets the dialogue down to fundamental issues. Freedman describes these issues as revolving around the bar's ability to discipline lawyers who inform ordinary citizens of their legal rights and remedies while permitting and often participating in other forms of solicitation when it comes to attracting business clients. He has been a leader in challenging anti-solicitation rules as they apply to non-fee cases and in forging a process of overdue rethinking—a challenge which has helped prod the American Bar Association to consider revising the *Code of Professional Responsibility* as it relates to advertising by lawyers. It is also likely that the Supreme Court will be asked to rule on a pending challenge to the bar's blanket restrictions on forthright lawyers' advertising as a corollary to the *Goldfarb* decision.

However encouraging are recent judicial decisions directed at clipping some of the guild's rules and encouraging competition between lawyers, the basic power thrust of the legal profession is against meaningful restructuring of the ways lawyers can do their work. After losing court battles to stop group legal services, the bar, through the ABA, strove to make closed-panel plans an unethical practice. The establishment was willing to go along with group services if the members of the group were free to patronize outside lawyers rather than only group staff lawyers, for what would assuredly be higher-priced services at higher insurance premiums. Jim Lorenz draws on his own experiences in California to show how the bar in that state tried to take control of the group legal service movement and develop a lucrative middle-class market for cartels of attorneys. There are signs that such a drive is slowing if not retreating, in part because of a pertinent amendment to the Labor-Management Relations Act and the consequent drawing back of the ABA in early 1975 from its previous year's action against closed panels. But from another corner comes pressure to Balkanize the profession into sublicensed specialties, as Jerome Hochberg asserts in his essay. This trend will increase prices and decrease competition while leaving the status of the important general practitioner heading in the direction of its counterpart in medicine.

It would be incomplete to attribute all of the opposition to accessible legal delivery systems to the legal profession. Lawyers representing business are agents who use the derivative power of corporations as well as their own. This convergence of influence is seen in the determined opposition against class-action liberation not merely before the courts but more generically before the Congress and the White House. Consumer class-action rights are procedural; they are a volume response to volume abuses in an economy where giant sellers market to thousands or even millions of people. The contribution of class actions to judicial efficiency, win or lose, is noteworthy, apart from being a means of hurdling the dual barriers of expense and unawareness by those defrauded of their rights to legal redress. As pointed out in the section by Beverly Moore, Jr., and Fred Harris, the specious arguments against consumer class-action rights for the people are not limited to corporate counsel. Judges have resorted, they note, "to a wide variety of legal sophistries." To complete the circle, Joseph Califano aptly frames the vision of the big-business lawyer at the seat of political power: "The Washington lawyer rarely litigates cases; rather, he tries to appoint judges." Or, one might add, become one himself.

The near-destruction of the OEO legal services program in the fifth year of the Nixon Administration is illustrative of the expansive strategy by powerful opponents when they are successfully challenged in the courts: Simply move to political forums, in this case the White House and Congress. Anyone who wishes to sense the deep-rooted animosities toward the goal of equal access to the legal system should read the congressional hearing record on the illegal regime of Howard Phillips, appointed head of OEO in 1973 by Nixon to dismantle the agency and, in particular, the legal services program. Phillips reflected the desires of entrenched local and state interests, both governmental and corporate, which did not want to tolerate any further the "law reform" or "institutional" lawsuits brought by the poverty lawyers. The disclosures in the courts of massive official and business illegalities were upsetting to these elites. Their rage spilled by proxy onto the floor of the House of Representatives on the night of June 21, 1973, during the debate on a bill to establish a Legal Services Corporation as a successor to the OEO legal program. It was a debate and vote which separated the autocrats from the democrats, regardless of their customary party affiliation.

The Legal Services Corporation survived congressional assaults and, in a modest fashion, began operations in mid-1975. But the turmoil over providing lawyers for the poor during the past decade indicates how opponents expand their strategic use of power far beyond the courts and far beyond the formal confines of the three branches of the legal system. Specifically, the behavior of the Justice Department under Nixon reflects this political misuse or abuse of appointees, agencies, and the law. Ramsey Clark clearly pinpoints these derelictions and offers valuable suggestions to make the Justice Department produce justice.

The essays in VERDICTS ON LAWYERS valuably expose lawyer abuses and prescribe remedies. But what is not addressed is how to jump the gap from abuse to remedy. What is the sparkplug to trigger and accomplish the reform of the legal profession?

The only satisfactory answer must be the public, a *sine qua non* for any long-range change in this country. When citizens concerned about the high cost of lawyers, their unavailability, and their frauds begin to systematically pressure bar associations and legislatures, the legal profession will never be the same.

A publicly inspired reform of the legal system has historical antecedents with which to encourage future innovations. Organized farmers and organized workers, in the populist-progressive and union movements respectively, represent political and economic power which have translated their programs into the formal system of law—legislation, administrative rule-making, and judicial decisions. More recently, civil rights advocates and environmentalists from the outside jolted or persuaded the formal rules and practices affecting them to change. *Outside* coalescence of civic interests, as in the consumer and women's rights efforts, found their expression *inside* the legal system. Recently, it has been seen that to sustain their principles in practice requires a perpetuation of that external presence, recalling the revolutionary insight "The price of liberty is eternal vigilance." Vigilance by whom? Certainly the reference was not to the appointees or the delegates of the public, but to the public itself.

How do you energize and mobilize citizens around this issue? Educative efforts—such as this volume, John Tunney's Senate hearings, and a recent spate of television programs on the trouble with lawyers —are a necessary beginning. If activist citizens can picket nuclear power plant sites or school buses, it should not be impossible to get them interested in a profession that has failed to deliver them justice. Toward that end, Public Citizen in Washington, D.C., is developing for citizen groups a report on what unresponsive bar associations won't do, and what responsive bar associations either are doing or should be doing to provide improved legal representation. For example, some of the latter include: a disciplinary program with nonlawyer participants, full-time staffs, and public proceedings; a conflict-of-interest rule to discourage the corporatization of supposedly independent bar committees; a *pro bono publico* program that is more than token; a system to encourage informational and accurate advertising by lawyers; a system to encourage inexpensive prepaid legal insurance plans to interested citizens; and a judicial selection and review process that shatters the lockhold of a few politicians and bar leaders.

Other forms of consumer self-help on a grander scale are needed.

Consider, for example, the rise of consumer cooperatives. Genuinely run by their owners, they would help reduce the amount of merchandising deception and monopolistic practices of giant chains. These coops would also be a political force behind a consumer advocacy agency, much as the largest food chains were against such legislation in the Congress. By rebuilding the neighborhoods economically, consumer cooperatives could prevent many of the injustices and neglects which now proliferate in city slums. Their interest in expanding consumer services through consumer cash flow could lead these cooperatives to establish group legal services for their members and counteract attempts to limit them or take control of their operation. Informing their members of both pocketbook and more general economic issues would enhance a more knowledgeable response at election time—including more successful programs for equitable treatment of cooperatives by government.

In discussing the impact of such extralegal institutions, the distinction between practical access and legitimate power needs to be remembered. Having access does not ensure a fair outcome; it does not guarantee that the bias or corruption of the forum itself will be changed or even disclosed. Moreover, as F. Raymond Marks has noted in a recent paper, there is a resistance by many people to using lawyers even when they are available without charge (prompted, for example, by fears of landlord or employer retaliation). Pointedly, access can be an illusory attraction for reformers without a parallel recognition of the need for common communities and common constituencies to engage the civic culture in a daily and capable manner.

In the next few years, the roots of the democratic system will be more clearly seen as the true roots of the legal system. Under pressure and manipulation, under corruption and purchase, the legal system that is grafted lightly onto a democracy will not be sustained. Quite promisingly, there may well be more public interest law firms, more student-funded public interest research groups, and more consumer-operated civic institutions based on checkoff systems placed on monthly utility bills, contracts of adhesion, and other widely communicated instruments. The career of full-time citizen may spread to involve, hopefully, many thousands of Americans working with millions of part-time citizens. For the political, economic, and legal subcultures in our country to radiate more justice, opportunity, and humanity, the civic duty must become an expected norm for the citizenry.

Beyond these enabling structures for a just society is the reassertion of individual conscience and responsibility. The need for conscience in lawyering is what Califano, Pertschuk, Morrison, Rabinowitz, and Smyser were discussing in their treatments of the lawyer as advocate, as lobbyist, as prosecutor, and as government and corporate counsel. One appropriate place for anticipating the individual conflicts between conscience, role, and client is the law school. This volume of writings should be read and pondered by law students while they have the time and freedom to think about what kind of roles they wish to dedicate their careers around and how they will resolve these conflicts by prevention, avoidance, or confrontation. It has been said that law schools are places where students become sharp by becoming narrow. But as I elaborated in the April 1973 *Harvard Law School Bulletin*, students can help make them places where they become fosterers of broader visions and ways to pursue the quest for justice—the lawyer's highest calling. The gathering of facts and judgments in this book can help illuminate the tangible horizons of the profession so that the ranks of the few, who are working for these kinds of change, can be swelled by the many who are on the way to the bar. The result could be a renaissance for the legal profession, which could well use it.

Contents

Contents

VI Judges: Sketches from Detroit, New York City, Chicago

All professions are conspiracies against the laity.
—GEORGE BERNARD SHAW

I

The ABA and the Organized Bar

*Mark Green**

The ABA as Trade Association

HERE IS IN LAWYERS a political itch, the yearning to do more than polish off an error-free stock registration. As far back as 1878, the American Bar Association's second president, James Broadhead, proudly said, "The members of our profession . . . have always exercised a greater influence than all other classes in the community combined." [1]

As the professional organization of lawyers, it is hardly surprising that the ABA has political interests and impact. Since the creation in 1936 of its House of Delegates—the ABA's parliament, it today has 318 representatives from various local, state, and national bar groups—the Association has adopted more than 600 resolutions relating to federal legislation and national issues. When it speaks it does so with authority. Its membership is 190,630 lawyers (as of early 1975), or one-half of the profession; it has 21 sections, 69 committees, an annual budget of $16 million, and a staff of 360, including a six-person, $190,000-a-year lobbying office in Washington, D.C. And ABA leaders prominently ride the public-private shuttle: Among its former presidents are a president of the United States (William Howard Taft), three justices of the Supreme Court (George Sutherland, Charles Evans Hughes, and Lewis Powell), and a special prosecutor (Leon A. Jaworski).

The ABA also exerts its influence in less visible ways, especially through its committees and sections, which have become a kind of farm system for government jobs. "Holding high office in the ABA is virtually a prerequisite to an important position in the Treasury or IRS," says Thomas Field, a former Treasury lawyer who now directs a public interest tax group, Tax Advocates and Analysts. The Nixon Administration's first commissioner of the Internal Revenue Service, Randolph Thrower, was a former chairman of the ABA's Tax Section. So is the current IRS commissioner, Donald Alexander. The past chairman of the

* MARK GREEN IS AN EDITOR OF THIS VOLUME AND DIRECTOR OF THE CORPORATE ACCOUNTABILITY RESEARCH GROUP IN WASHINGTON, D.C.

3

Securities and Exchange Commission, Ray Garrett, Jr., once directed the ABA's Section on Corporation, Banking, and Business Law. For one memorable period in 1971–1972, the two federal officials in charge of the nation's antitrust policy—Miles Kirkpatrick, chairman of the Federal Trade Commission, and Richard McLaren, head of the Justice Department's Antitrust Division—were both former chairmen of the ABA's Antitrust Section.

But how does the ABA exercise its political power? As ABA leaders and publications are quick to point out, the Association is a professional society dedicated to legal and social betterment, and surely not a trade association promoting its own interest. "The Bar . . . is guided by a desire to serve the country and not itself," we are told by two ABA presidents thirty years apart;[2] more specifically, the ABA notes that members of Congress "recognize generally that the views of these bar associations do not represent 'selfish interest' or 'pressure group interests.' "[3] But there is more to the picture than contributing professional talents to the cause of good government. Those who have watched the Grocery Manufacturers of America struggle to defeat food-adulteration legislation will not be astounded by the ABA's illustration of how public service and self-service do not always overlap.

Prominent and visible? Yes, the ABA is that. But for whom? And for what?

"Originated as it was in the wake of the decision in *Munn* v. *Illinois*," wrote Professor Edward Corwin about the beginnings of the ABA in 1878, "the Association soon became a sort of juristic sewing circle for mutual education in the gospel of *Laissez Faire*."[4] During the 1920s, the ABA criticized the 1890 Sherman Antitrust Act as "unsound [and] uncertain," and condemned the income-tax amendment as an "encroachment on private wealth." With the election of Franklin D. Roosevelt, the ABA of Social Darwinism and Spencer's *Social Statics* flowered into full bloom. There was the repeated fear that the New Deal aimed more to revolutionize the American Way rather than preserve it. As a consequence, the ABA militantly opposed nearly all New Deal measures.[5]

Nor did moderation characterize its performance in the 1950s. An ABA presumably committed to the Bill of Rights and the Rule of Law was at times indistinguishable from Senator Joseph McCarthy. In 1950 the House of Delegates voted to expel from the ABA any lawyer "who is a member of the Communist Party of the United States or who advocates Marxism-Leninism" and urged that all those who would become lawyers should take a loyalty oath as a condition of practice.[6] In 1953, still imitating its perceived enemies in order to defeat them, the ABA urged the profession to disbar any Communist lawyers (but at the same session, at least, the ABA did pass a resolution condemning book burning). Such intolerance, as well as later ABA criticism of Supreme Court decisions in free speech–Communist cases, led to Earl Warren's resignation from the Association in 1959.*

At a time of major shifts in race relations, the nation's association of lawyers did not take the lead in integrating schools and public facilities in the 1950s. Outgoing ABA president Frank Holman had warned in 1949 that "the easiest way to sell each new step toward statism has been to work on the emotions of the people through some catch phrase like 'social justice,' or 'economic equality,' or 'racial equality.' " [7] In fact, there is no mention of this subject or of the 1954 *Brown* v. *Board* decision, perhaps the most important Supreme Court decision of the past century, in the 1954 to 1956 ABA annual reports. Instead, the ABA rejected a resolution in 1956 calling for either willing or court-ordered compliance with the Supreme Court's anti-segregation rulings.

Instead of a concern over social issues, the Association revealed a keen solicitude for its public image. It carefully monitored the media for comments adverse to lawyers and swooped down "to rectify them" when the ABA's name was taken in vain—such as when a 1952 television show alleged that a murderer was an ABA member because an ABA medallion was found on him. In 1953 the ABA's Standing Committee on Public Relations could report that "persons in a position to know say that the active interest of many members of the bar as well as ourselves has had its influence on [movie] scriptwriting." [8]

While the 1950s ended with one critic concluding that "the A.B.A. could merge with the Daughters of the American Revolution without any drastic revision of its credo," [9] such an appraisal seems outdated today. For

---

* The Association's anti-Communist ethos was still in evidence by 1974, when it refused a resolution urging the abolition of the House Committee on Internal Security, which was formerly the House Un-American Activities Committee (HUAC). One prominent opponent of the resolution said that it represented "the sort of lethargy that permitted the take-over of the Kerensky Government in Russia and the Weimar Government in Germany."

in the past decade, as the ABA has increased its membership some 50 percent, it has grown less stridently conservative and more modestly liberal. Instead of a Frank Holman there are the Bernard Segals and Robert Meserves and Chesterfield Smiths, ABA presidents who understand that you cannot approach the problems of our third century with the practices of the first. Instead of table-pounding, laissez-faire, America First militancy, there are the calm and cautious and civilized statements of polished spokesmen.

In the past decade, for example, the ABA has supported the direct election of the president, the Twenty-fifth Amendment providing for presidential inability and vice presidential vacancy, the equal rights amendment, legal services for the poor, the Freedom of Information Act, and a clutch of proposals to improve the functioning of the courts; it has also opposed such things as the Federal Trade Commission's inefficiencies and criminal penalties for consensual sexual activity, marijuana use, or campus riots. All admirable positions, to be sure, but interesting largely because of how they contrast with the ABA of the recent past. A modern bar committed to the public good could hardly come out against legal services or even manufacture plausible arguments for more court delays. From this eluvium of proper positions, however, there is the persistent aroma of noblesse oblige, decorous advocacy for well-meaning but safe policies, for change but nothing earthshaking or boat-rocking, especially not to the interests of lawyers or most of their clients.

Is the ABA a trade association for lawyers and the status quo?

Former judge Simon Rifkind, now a prominent New York City attorney, described part of the problem.

> I do not know a group of people with whom I would rather play and work and drink than lawyers. But once they are formed into an organized body . . . they are not conspicuous, either for imagination or for bold reform. When they meet in an aggregated body, it seems the cautious which are, of course, characteristic of the profession, and the fears which are, of course, the attributes of a great many of the practitioners, reinforce each other so as to create a wall . . . so that you cannot break through and make progress. Inside that wall they just worship the status quo.

The ABA itself provides substantial support for the trade-association thesis. As John Tracey in the ABA's Washington office admitted, in reference to a proposal to increase legal fees, "It's clearly easier to mobilize the bar on a bread-and-butter issue like this than on public interest issues." After actually proposing a constitutional amendment in 1953 to limit the graduated income tax to 25 percent of income "to end confiscatory federal taxation," the ABA within the past decade has:

- Continued the struggle for improved benefits for self-employed persons (like lawyers), which, judging by emphasis in the ABA's Washington newsletter, was the major legislative issue of the 1960s.

- Promoted a bill to permit lawyers to practice before federal agencies without having to obtain special admission or take a special admission examination (and, in a rare appeal, the membership was urged to write and call their Congressmen).

- Promoted a bill to remove fixed maximum limitations on attorneys' fees in federal departments and agencies (inviting the membership to send in examples of unreasonably low rates).

- Opposed a proposal which would have expanded the role of title companies in home closings while curtailing the role of lawyers.

- Opposed a proposal which would have sharply reduced legal fees at some Department of Housing and Urban Development mortgage closings.

- Opposed a bankruptcy reform that would have avoided lawyers and contested proceedings by putting bankruptcy into an executive agency.

- Urged that the business and sale of insurance be exempted from the proposed Uniform Consumer Sales Practices Act and Consumer Protection Act of 1970.

- Urged that patents arising out of government-financed research should go to private industry, not the government which funded their development.

- Opposed the Consumer Credit Labeling Act.

- Opposed the Fair Packaging and Labeling Act.

- Opposed citizen suits to help enforce environmental quality standards.

That the Association's policies are not unrelated to its economic interest is apparent. Consider, for the most obvious example, the ABA position on one of the most critical issues challenging the existing structure and income of the legal profession today—no-fault auto insurance.

They may hate themselves in the morning, but the lawyers keep resisting the no-fault proposals. Crash litigation is a nuisance to everyone —except lawyers, for whom it produces 16 percent of the gross legal product. So, in 1969, the ABA's House of Delegates came out against no-fault and for the "fault" system because of "the moral values which underlie the almost instinctive feeling that persons guilty of wrongful conduct" should pay.

The ABA again took up the problem in 1972 when it created a Special Committee on Automobile Insurance Legislation. The committee's composition gave a hint of the care and objectivity that went into developing the ABA's position. All ten people who have served on the committee have been engaged in and collected fees from auto negligence cases, the very type of litigation they have been asked to consider abolishing.

Although ABA president Robert W. Meserve privately confided in 1972 that he hoped the ABA would take no position on this controversial issue, the Association declared itself "opposed to any federal 'no-fault' insurance legislation" that year.[10] In a memorable display of institutional loyalty, Meserve then became the Association's major witness against Senator Philip Hart's national no-fault plan. Meserve stoutly argued his group's position, but with more than a little defensiveness. "This is not a matter of lawyer protection, he said, "it is a matter of client protection." This did not entirely convince Senator Frank Moss, who wondered whether "a little bit of the economic factor does creep in when the lawyers in the House of Delegates take this attitude." [11]

But perhaps the ABA could not really control itself on no-fault (and on prepaid legal services, as Jim Lorenz explains in Part III)—these being issues where all the laws of self-preservation were pushing one way. Yet even when the pressure is not as great, the ABA has displayed its preference for self-serving policies.

The best example of this is the ABA's sections and committees. Here Congress and the ABA have much in common: Each is a bulky body which has delegated policy-making responsibility to smaller, more specialized committees. Unfortunately, the parallels do not stop there. Just as many members of the House Banking and Currency Committee, for example, have significant financial holdings, so the ABA sections are marred by systematic conflicts of interest. The following are some recent chairmen, with their major clients, of eight ABA committees and sections:

- Committee on Aviation: Harold L. Russell, Eastern Airlines

- Committee on Railroads: James N. Ogden, VP and general counsel, GM&O R.R. Co.

- Committee on Public Lands and Land Use: Terry Noble Fiske, Colorado Contractors Association

- Committee on Environmental Controls: Evans Brasfield, Humble Oil and General Motors

- Section on Antitrust Law: Thomas M. Scanlon, IBM and Shell Oil

- Section on Insurance, Negligence, and Compensation Law: G. Robert Muchemore, VP and general counsel, Mutual of Omaha Insurance

- Section on Natural Resources Law: Northcutt Ely, Gulf Oil

- Section on Public Utility Law: F. Mark Garlinghouse, AT&T

Such conflicts are not merely theoretical, as a focus on four ABA sections reveals:

Antitrust Section: In 1969 the ABA's Antitrust Section created a Special Committee on Consumer Legislation to analyze pending consumer class action legislation, which the committee did with critical relish in a report it sent the Senate Commerce Committee. It ridiculed consumer class actions as unwise, unnecessary, and inefficient, a burden to the courts and a potential bonanza to *plaintiffs'* lawyers. But unmentioned was the potential benefit to *defendants'* lawyers and their clients—perhaps because all nine members of this special committee were defense lawyers handpicked by section chairman Frederick Rowe, general counsel of the Grocery Manufacturers of America and a name partner in the large corporate firm of Kirkland, Ellis, & Rowe. The stacking was a little too obvious even by ABA standards, and journalists and congressmen discredited the report into oblivion.

A freshly chastised Antitrust Section shortly thereafter did adopt a new policy against the establishment of ad hoc committees. Existing committees, whenever possible, would make recommendations on pending legislation. It was a change long overdue—and short-lived, for in 1972 the section's leadership casually appointed two new "special committees" to evaluate the two most controversial antitrust issues of the year: Senator Philip Hart's industrial-deconcentration bill and Senator John Tunney's consent-decree bill. In all, section chairman Julian von Kalinowski appointed seven special committees, leading one reform-minded member of the section, Gerald Kandler, to lament that his "worst fears about special committees have been confirmed, since the members appointed to serve all appear to be from the so-called 'establishment' of the section and clearly do not represent a cross-section of the 7,500 dues-paying members."

The special committees studying the Tunney and Hart proposals both recommended against the legislation. This can hardly be surprising, given the section's prior history: It has supported businesses' right to deduct "treble damage" penalty payments from their taxable income, has opposed legislation to permit government and private suits for damages and injunctions under the Clayton Act, has resisted attempts to raise the maximum fines that can be levied against individuals under the Sherman Antitrust Act, and has tried to defeat legislation that would enlarge the Federal Trade Commission's rule-making power.

On the other hand, the section has risen at least twice above its normal behavior, once to oppose a plan to exempt joint newspaper publishing ventures from antitrust provisions and once to urge the Senate Judiciary Committee to withhold action on a bill that would have partially exempted soft-drink bottlers from antitrust enforcement. The Antitrust Section's bottlers position so surprised one skeptical Judiciary Committee lawyer that he speculated, only half-jokingly, "Maybe one reason they opposed it was that they were getting fees from that litigation."

There have been some attempts to democratize the Antitrust Section. Former government antitrust lawyer and section member Jerome Hochberg wrote Antitrust Section chairman Fred Rowe after the class-action report was released:

> For too many years this Section and the Association as a whole have been run by a clique of attorneys who represent entrenched interests in the various communities across the United States without regard to the views or concerns of other attorneys, both members and non-members. The procedures for running the organization are undemocratic and are geared so as to make it almost impossible for individuals with contrary views to be heard and gain acceptance for their position.

Hochberg suggested a variety of reforms and even got the section chairman to begin circulating a quarterly report to the members. In the end, however, he was rebuffed; the Jacobs case helps illustrate how and why. Ephraim Jacobs is a highly respected Washington lawyer who was in line to become the Antitrust Section's representative to the ABA House of Delegates. But Jacobs was also a lawyer for plaintiffs in an antitrust case that challenged some of the major drug companies. A defense lawyer for one of the drug firms, who was sitting on the Antitrust Section body choosing nominees for the House of Delegates post, eliminated Jacobs from consideration. Jacobs and his colleagues decided not to launch an all-out fight for this largely honorific post, but they came to understand who was running the antitrust show.

Section on Patent, Trademark, and Copyright Law: A former member of this section's Copyright Division complained that "if people ever wear two hats, they were it [sic] there. The lawyers all represent proprietary interests, not the interests of users." On the pending copyright issues, the proprietary interests always prevail, he said. This member, essentially the only representative of user interests, eventually quit. "I was just a foil for them."

Within the section's Patent Division is a small clique called the Tuesday Group. The group first drafted what came to be called the "Scott Amendments"—proposals which sought to legalize many patent practices now prohibited under the antitrust laws—and then convinced Senator Hugh Scott to introduce the package to Congress. One member of the Tuesday Group was attorney Arthur Seidel, from a Milwaukee corporate law firm whose clients (like Du Pont and General Electric) had a keen interest in seeing the Scott Amendments passed. As chairman of the Patent Section's committee dealing with the Scott Amendments, he urged his fellow committee members to lobby for the measure. ("This education of senators does not seem to be within the purview of our committee, but I trust many of you can devote some personal efforts along such lines," he wrote in a memorandum.)

The chairman of the Patent Section in 1973–74 was Theodore Bowes, former member of the Tuesday Group, former general patent counsel at Westinghouse Electric, and presently executive director of Intellectual Property Owners, Inc. (IPO), a group which objects to the "whittl[ing] away at the rights of patent owners." Bowes showed some irritation at public criticism of his patent advocacy. "Nothing in the Scott Amendments," he said, "was intended to or would expand the patent monopoly, as even a casual reading would make plain." Not many would agree with him. Among the doubters are forty law professors (who sent a petition to the Senate Subcommittee on Patents, Trademarks, and Copyrights), former ABA president Bernard G. Segal, Senator Philip Hart, and former Justice Department antitrust chief Richard McLaren—all of whom understood that expansion of the patent monopoly is precisely what the Scott Amendments intended. In a private letter to Hart, McLaren warned of the ongoing antitrust cases which would have to be dropped if the bill became law; these included the prominent patent case *United States* v. *Westinghouse–Mitsubishi*, a case that could not have escaped Bowes's attention, given his past position with Westinghouse. Bowes personally lobbied on Capitol Hill to delay action on the Hart and Administration reform proposals. He offered, instead, his own Patent Section's bill, which he presented as "the ABA bill." In fact, the ABA House of Delegates never approved his proposal.

Westinghouse, the Tuesday Group, IPO, the ABA, the Patent Section—Ted Bowes is a man of many hats. Patent reformers on Capitol Hill are not pleased with his versatility. "The ABA and the American Patent Law Association," said a Senate antitrust subcommittee lawyer, "are the two groups consistently throwing monkey wrenches into all serious efforts to reform the patent system."

Natural Resources Section: The subcommittees comprising this section have been recently headed by lawyers whose clients read like a Sierra Club enemies list. William Forman, chairman of the Hard Minerals subcommittee, represents Anaconda Copper and U.S. Gypsum; Charles Wheeler of the Oil Subcommittee represents Cities Service; Terry Noble Fiske of the Public Lands and Land Use Subcommittee is the lawyer for four associations of contractors and realtors, and his subcommittee's vice chairman is from a firm representing American Smelting and Refining, Johns-Manville, and Standard Oil of California.

In 1973 the Natural Resources Section sent the ABA House of Delegates a package of four complicated resolutions. The first noted that there would be a serious energy crisis and urged Congress to undertake long-range planning. Appreciating the lawyer's role as a midwife to new government projects, the section offered to "tender [the ABA's] good offices" to be the appropriate bodies for the "drafting and implementation of legislation designed to maximize supplies of energy. . . ." A second resolution made the same offer on non-fuel minerals. A third recommended that the government vigorously protect the contract and property rights of investors who have placed their money overseas. The fourth resolution had to do with control of the international seabed. Its importance was explained by Jonathan Adler, an environmental lawyer from California:

The final resolution is an insidious combination of motherhood, apple-pie and an audacious attempt at such a massive raid on the resources of the international seabed beyond the territorial limit that it prompted three dissents from members of the section's marine resources committee. . . . The resolution opposes admirable efforts by the State Department, in a draft treaty on deep sea resources, to recognize a "common heritage of mankind" in the oil, gas and minerals which technology is beginning to make recoverable from the deep seabed, and to establish a comprehensive international regime for their exploitation which would benefit non-coastal nations in addition to coastal nations and highly-developed technologies. It would preserve for American sovereignty, and thus for American corporations, resources of the so-called "continental margins" extending beyond the continental shelf hundreds of miles out to sea. . . .

This resolution was produced, observed Adler, by a Marine Resources Subcommittee whose chairman represents Chevron and whose predecessor was a lobbyist for the American Petroleum Institute. Comprising the section's eight-person ruling council is an Oklahoma law professor, three attorneys from firms representing Humble Oil, Kaiser Steel, and other gas and oil companies, and four corporate general counsels from Marathon, Humble, Shell, and Texaco.

Tax Section: This unit is clearly one of the ABA's most influential. It regularly sits down with the Treasury officials and congressional leaders to convey its opinions on pressing tax problems. On May 21, 1973, for example, nine leaders of the Tax Section met with ten Treasury representatives to cover an agenda of fifteen tax issues.* The obvious intimacy between the public and private sectors displayed at these sessions is extraordinary, but not rare. Thomas Field, the former Treasury lawyer, recalls that his boss invariably used to ask whether proposed Treasury actions had been screened by the Tax Section. "They had an advance veto on proposals," said Field.

The deliberations of the Tax Section clearly have an impact beyond that of the usual private association. Most often it is an impact favoring their private clients, argued Hofstra law professor Stuart Filler, a section

* As summarized by a Tax Section memorandum, the subjects ranged from "Suits to Compel Action by the Treasury or Internal Revenue Service" ("Mr. Asbill [the recent section chairman] asked whether the Committee might be helpful to the Treasury") to the "Status of Proposed Revenue Ruling on Prepayment of Feed Expenses" ("The Treasury would be interested in participating in the meeting of the section's committee on agricultural problems with the IRS on its drafts on a ruling re-payment of feed expenses") to a final discussion of "The Federal Advisory Committee Act" ("It would be disastrous if the Treasury could not get reactions and intelligence [at these private sessions] without public meetings").

member. "They very rarely take off their client hats as members of the ABA," he said.

Occasionally this devotion to clients can lift Tax Section members above even the imperatives of self-interest. The corporate pension issue is an example. For years lawyers had debated the question of how much money a taxpayer should be able to deduct as a contribution toward a tax-deferred pension plan. The tax code has traditionally treated the self-employed (like lawyers) more strictly than corporate officials in this matter. Then one Tax Section subcommittee proposed a plan that would equalize the benefits by imposing a ceiling of $10,000 for pension-plan deductions; in general this would have restricted corporate pensions and aided lawyers. "But this was overwhelmingly defeated on the floor of the Tax Section," recalls Filler. "The attorneys were pressured by their corporate clients to vote against it. People who would have been for it as lawyers were against it as retained counsel."

The Tax Section's behavior does not fool insider-critics. As a former Treasury tax legislative counsel and former Tax Section participant has commented:

> The Tax Section is "business" and not "charity." It is not really surprising that the Section cannot be said to be fulfilling any obligation to the public—and I don't think it has even recognized such an obligation. . . . I think it should change its character. It goes without saying that it should not be used to further narrow interests of clients. It does so today even though in less crude fashion than in the good old days. . . .
>
> Had I concluded that the Section and the ABA were amenable to change, I think I might have continued to burrow from within. I concluded, erroneously I hope, that the battle was not to be won. . . .

Ex-ABA president Chesterfield Smith has disagreed that self-dealing is a problem. "A section is financed by its own dues and all work is done by individuals who, of their own volition, band together to further a common purpose," he wrote the author of this article. "Their interest in the subject matter is self-evident and fully disclosed." Smith referred to a conflict-of-interest resolution passed by the ABA's Board of Governors in August 1972. It requires that "every effort should be made to obtain representation of differing views" in section appointments and that any section members involved in a recommendation or report to the House of Delegates should reveal any client interest they have in the issue. Occasionally, the Association has acted affirmatively to create balance, as it did in 1970, when it formed a Special Committee on Environmental Law with representatives from both industry and environmental lawyers. But judging by the onesidedness described in the no-fault, patent, antitrust, natural resources, and tax situations, as well as by the non-disclosure of client interests, the ABA resolution seems a paper tiger.

Smith went on to insist that, anyway, "no policy is a policy of the American Bar Association until it has been adopted by the House of Delegates. The Sections only recommend to the House." This is really no more persuasive than if Carl Albert insisted that House floor activity is the only thing that matters, not what the Ways and Means Committee does. ABA sections, like congressional committees, shape legislative proposals with their "expert" hands so that their respective Houses often just follow their lead. In addition, sections (like Patents) often deal directly with congressional committees, despite an ABA policy against doing so.

It is not only at the section level on self-interest issues, but at the House of Delegates level on human-rights issues, that the ABA still has much to be modest about. Chief Justice Warren Burger told the ABA's ninety-seventh annual meeting in Washington, D.C., in August 1973, "I think it is apparent . . . the Association is the voice of progressive development and it is the hands and feet of progress." Despite the chief justice's organic metaphor, the ABA occasionally still gets caught in the undertow of its historic conservatism.

Genocide: On December 9, 1948, the UN General Assembly unanimously adopted the Genocide Convention, making the destruction of any national, ethnic, racial, or religious group, as such, a crime under international law. President Truman submitted the Genocide Convention to the Senate in 1949. When the ABA's House of Delegates voted to oppose it that year, however, the chairman of the Senate Foreign Relations Committee announced he would not call the treaty up for a vote unless the ABA approved it.

There the matter rested for twenty years, until President Nixon resubmitted it to the Senate in 1969. It had become something of a diplomatic embarrassment that the U.S. had stood nearly alone among world powers in refusing to sign a convention against genocide. But apparently the ABA wasn't embarrassed, for at its 1970 winter meeting the House of Delegates voted 130–126 to continue its opposition. Opponents wove a web of hypothetical horrors—such as the spectacle of

American prisoners tried for genocide under international auspices in Hanoi, which the treaty would in no way permit—to successfully ensnare the genocide pact, arguments which the Senate Foreign Relations Committee later found to be without merit.

Beyond procedural obstacles were emotional salvos. One ABA delegate invoked his son in Vietnam. "The last time [he] called . . . he was somewhere on the Cambodian border. He is fighting communism there," the delegate said, adding in a non sequitur that he was not about "to support a kangaroo trial of the decent young manhood of this country." Another lawyer expressed his opposition with, for the ABA, unusual candor: "We wouldn't be in this country if we hadn't committed genocide. That was the only way we established this country, by getting rid of the Indians. It was a matter of life and death between the white man and the Indians. The white man survived." All this consternated the ABA president at the time, Bernard Segal, who warned that "the Association and the organized bar are on trial . . . the question is whether this Association, and through us the legal profession in the United States, can come together in support of an international commitment to root out genocide." [12] It couldn't.

War: Having failed to come out against genocide, the ABA was hardly prepared to support the antiwar movement. At the 1971 annual convention a group of New York lawyers proposed a resolution calling for immediate withdrawal from Vietnam (later modified to read withdrawal "as soon as physically and logically possible"). A past head of the ABA's Law Student Division declared that "we all have a moral responsibility in this day and age not to avoid the issue. Vote for the resolution or against it, but don't avoid it by saying we don't have jurisdiction. Young people of this nation deserve an answer from you." Louis Pollak, former dean at the Yale Law School, saw the issue as "whether we, as lawyers, are going to be blind to what we know as citizens." But former ABA president John C. Satterfield saw it differently:

[T]he Communists reached ruthlessly for domination of Southeast Asia and ultimately the free world. Communism must be fought somewhere, and for some foolish reason I prefer it be fought in Vietnam rather than in Yazoo City, Mississippi, or Boston, Massachusetts. . . . Our boys are giving their lives in our defense, and the defense of our lives, our children and grandchildren, and not for some foolish matter.

The resolution lost, although the ABA did create a special study into the president's war-making powers.

Hunger: The ABA in 1970 also refused to come out ringingly against hunger. The proposal, like the ones dealing with marijuana and consensual sex, came from the Association's new Individual Rights and Responsibilities Section, a sort of institutional nest for ABA liberals (it has 3,777 members; Corporation, Banking, and Business Law has 29,707 members). Since hunger and malnutrition were major problems in America, the section reasoned, there should be (a) a national income supplement plan, (b) an improved food stamp program, and (c) a national center for family planning and population research.

But the House of Delegates turned them down, largely because it was supposedly not within the ABA's competence to pass such a measure. One former Association president labeled it a "sociological" problem. "Certainly we can't through this section go into all facets of our civilization." Another warned that it was not "germane" to the ABA, and that "if this Association starts running all over the lot, we will lose all the reputation that we have gained." Which were odd appeals coming from a group with committees on pollution, drug abuse, atomic energy, and communism, and which presumably felt it germane and within its competence to urge at this same 1970 meeting that the president of the United States declare an annual "Family Day, USA," with the goal of "focusing [the] spotlight upon the merit, the worth, and the contribution of the ideal family and its members in building and motivating our Nation. . . ."

Bert Early, the ABA executive director out of the coalfields of West Virginia, vigorously denies that the ABA is some stodgy trade association. "Anyone who says that just doesn't know anything about the ABA," he insists. "We spend ninety-six cents out of every dollar on educational and public service, for projects on minority law students, criminal justice, housing, a [proposed] National Institute of Justice, Youth Education for Citizenship, legal rights for the mentally disabled, prison reform; those are not the things that pretzel-twisters are doing." This is true, as far as it goes. For Early stresses what the ABA *staff* does, not the political position taken by the ABA's House or sections. These positions do not lead commentators to confuse the ABA with Common Cause.

First, the Association avoids promoting issues against its own economic self-interest. It will take up issues like presidential succession, firearms control, "law explorer posts" for the Boy Scouts, and even marijuana, but not the distribution of wealth and income or the high cost of lawyers. It spends untold hours attacking a handful of "disruptive lawyers" but fails to study the dilatory tactics of big corporate law firms. At its 1972 annual meeting the ABA recommended "the *immediate* establishment of a Commission on the Review of the National Policy Toward Gambling" but withdrew from consideration an earlier proposal by its Criminal Law Section for a Presidential Commission on White Collar Crime.

Second, when it is progressive, the ABA seems to rush in where others already have trod. It is a follower, not a leader. It has shown an obvious reluctance to inaugurate or even actively participate in the major social issues of its time. Of the major movements of the past decade—civil rights, consumer, antiwar, feminist, and tax reform—in none has the ABA played a leading or serious role. As a result, one has come to expect it to be largely a procedural technician on issues of law enforcement or an advocate of lawyers' benefits, but not, in Martin Luther King's phrase, a drum major for justice.

Instead, and third, there is often timidity and inconsistency. It came out early for an independent legal services corporation but refused to choose between the Nixon and Mondale versions of *who* should appoint the corporation's board, which became the nub of the controversy. It came out for a Consumer Protection Agency but refused to choose between the varying Holifield and Ribicoff versions of the CPA's jurisdiction. The ABA announces that it favors a conversion to the metric system *if* Congress thinks it's necessary, and then the change should be voluntary, not coercive. (With a similar resolve by our Founding Fathers, we might still be British.) Its sections condemn consumer class actions because they (allegedly) clog the courts without equally condemning auto negligence cases which *do* clog the courts.

Former ABA president and now justice Lewis Powell once explained that the Association was wary of controversial social issues like "the Civil Rights bill, aid to education and the Economic Opportunity Act" because its membership had many varying opinions. "The Association's responsibilities relate primarily to the legal profession," he added, "and these could not be discharged if our membership were lost, fractionated or embittered by involvement in political controversy." [13] This argument failed to persuade professors Vern Countryman and Ted Finman in *The Lawyer in Modern Society*, their 1966 text on the legal profession:

> Mr. Powell's test for whether the ABA should abstain from activity on an issue is one that would seriously divide the membership. . . . If the ABA, in

order to preserve itself, should avoid issues that might cause deep division within its membership, what of the individual lawyer? In his case, too, self-preservation can be urged as a reason for avoiding positions on various issues.[14]

Still, unlike most unions or trade groups, the ABA does not promise to reward the obedient with campaign gifts or punish the wayward with a loss of votes. Most of its staff budget supports projects for minority law students, prison reform, legal rights for the mentally disabled. Thus it adds a dash of good works to its defense of the status quo, and it has the good sense to elect leaders, like Chesterfield Smith, who are more liberal and sensitive than the association. In so doing, the ABA has repaired its traditional obstructionist image and shown itself to be more than merely twisters of pretzels.

But it has not taken the big step—moving away from a fretful concern with its own well-being to a serious exploration of how it could use its power to advance the cause of legal justice. Fred Rodell, the rakish Yale law professor, has written that "while law is supposed to be a device to serve society . . . it is pretty hard to find a group less concerned with serving society and more concerned with serving themselves than the lawyers." Ultimately the most discernible common cause of the ABA is the needs of its lawyers and those clients whose interests they regularly attend.

*Marna S. Tucker**

Pro Bono ABA?

A S THE DEMAND for legal services accelerated in the past decade—in response to the poor and, more recently, the middle class—the bar in general, and the American Bar Association in particular, could hardly afford to sit nonchalantly on the sidelines. It is part of the professional credo that lawyers not only make money but do justice, and if the legal system fails, the blame surely falls on those who operate it. The bar's original view of how it could best serve the public, then, has been altered considerably over the past hundred years, and particularly over the past decade. But what has not changed very much is the bar's view of who should be providing the service.

At first, the profession saw its public responsibility only in terms of providing better skills and honest lawyers, for a century ago legal incompetence and corruption held center stage. The founding of the first "modern-style" bar association, the Association of the Bar of the City of New York, was a reaction to a thirty-year era of decadence and vice for the New York bench and bar. In 1870, 235 of the 4,000 lawyers in New York City organized to protest the Tweed regime and widespread political and judicial corruption. The Association fought the Tweed ring head on, only to have its charter rejected by a hostile legislature. The continuing struggle eventually brought about the downfall of the regime, the impeachment of two judges, and the resignation of a third. But, most importantly, the Association established a sense of public confidence at a time when most lawyers were considered scoundrels. On the occasion of the Association's creation, Samuel J. Tilden said that the bar should organize for two objectives: "The one is to elevate itself—to elevate its own standards; the other is for the common and public good." [1]

This fledgling Association sought to guarantee a minimal competence

* MARNA TUCKER IS IN PRIVATE LEGAL PRACTICE IN WASHINGTON, D.C. SHE IS THE FORMER PROJECT DIRECTOR OF THE ABA PROJECT TO ASSIST INTERESTED LAW FIRMS IN *Pro Bono Publico* PROGRAMS AND IS CURRENTLY A MEMBER OF THE ABA HOUSE OF DELEGATES FROM THE DISTRICT OF COLUMBIA.

and a high moral character in lawyers—desirable goals, to be sure—but it did not address the problem of access to lawyers by the public. The modern notion of access to lawyers for those who needed them was about as topical as mink breeding and fallout shelters are today. There was then an unarticulated premise that professional pursuit and the public interest were synonymous. The magical hand of laissez-faire, it was assumed, would govern the market for lawyers as justly as it had governed the market for goods.

Half a century passed before the bar acknowledged that it owed something more than mere professionalism to its paying clients, that more than some "invisible hand" was needed to insure justice. It was after World War I that legal aid as we know it began to flourish. In 1920 Reginald Heber Smith, the founding father of the legal aid movement, delivered perhaps the most ringing call to public responsibility ever issued to the American Bar Association:

> If we were to take command of the moral forces which are now stirring throughout the nation, we shall find public opinion ready to fight staunchly at our side. Let us assume that leadership by declaring here and now, that henceforth within the field of law, the mighty power of the organized American Bar stands pledged to champion the rights of the poor, the weak and the defenseless.[2]

Smith's challenge, elaborated in his book, *Justice and the Poor*,[3] had a profound impact on the organized bar. In the twenties the ABA created a Special Committee on Legal Aid, with none less than Charles Evans Hughes as its chairman. Then came a Standing Committee on Legal Aid, and a recommendation by the ABA that every state bar association appoint such a committee. Most members of the bar at that time supported legal aid societies; it did not occur to them that they themselves had any *obligation* to represent the poor. A spirit of noblesse oblige prevailed. Work contributed to indigent clients was laudable; but the lack of a contribution to indigent clients was not deplorable. Private practice represented those who paid; legal aid supposedly represented those who couldn't.

Advocates who sought to stimulate the bar to generate and support an increasing number of legal aid societies welded a missionary zeal to an understanding of the bar's more pecuniary interests. As Earl Johnson, a former Office of Economic Opportunity legal services director, has written:

The men who went out in the field to sell legal aid to the local bars soon learned that flowery speeches about equal justice and the moral responsibility of the bar did not produce new legal aid societies. What sold lawyers were documents that stressed the practical advantages of the legal aid office. A legal aid society will keep undesirable non-paying clients out of the private practitioner's office . . . ; a legal aid society will educate people who haven't used a lawyer before about the value and necessity of lawyers which will increase the business of private attorneys; a legal aid society offers an opportunity for younger members of the profession to gain valuable experience; and a legal aid society builds the public relations image of the bar with the general public.[4]

Although the bar came to recognize the practical benefits of legal aid, it maintained a useful and continual watch over legal aid lawyers. Client income limits and eligibility standards discouraged the commercial practice of law, and the ban on solicitation of business insured that legal aid programs would not compete economically with the practicing bar. Charity was one thing, competition quite another. Thus, the bar came to recognize its responsibility to provide legal representation for all, regardless of ability to pay, so long as this representation did not disrupt business-as-usual.

The profession's attitude has not changed in the decades since, but it has become far less crass. Consider, for example, the central role played by the ABA in efforts to add a legal services component to the Office of Economic Opportunity in the early 1960s.

At that time a maverick legal assistance movement began, independent of the bar-supported legal aid societies. It was unwilling to attack symptoms yet ignore causes. So, unlike the traditional legal aid movement, these new lawyers wanted not merely to provide equal justice for the poor but also to reduce poverty—a social and economic, as contrasted to a strictly legal, goal. The Ford Foundation and the President's Committee on Juvenile Delinquency of the Department of Health, Education, and Welfare provided funds for experimental programs that decentralized social services, including legal services, in the ghetto. The new programs moved legal assistance out of a single "downtown" facility and into the din and dirt and crime of poverty neighborhoods. Not surprisingly, the new movement was unaffiliated with the organized bar, which continued its comfortable attempts to represent the poor.

Many of the same lawyers involved in the neighborhood experiments were responsible for the inclusion of legal services in the OEO War on Poverty; the latter evolved from the former. Jean and Edgar Cahn, for example, who coauthored the 1964 *Yale Law Journal* article which was the blueprint for neighborhood legal services,[5] became special assistants to R. Sargent Shriver, the OEO director.

The early planning stages of OEO legal services efforts progressed without any participation by the organized bar. As a measure of the bar's complacency, the simple fact was that no one thought to include it. The ABA moved quickly to include itself when it heard about the plans, reflecting the sympathetic attitude of Lewis Powell, ABA president in 1964–65. Powell, moreover, was not dragged unwillingly into the OEO legal services movement. His priorities during his term as ABA president included an expanded effort by the bar to assist the poor. In the months before he assumed the presidency, he would regularly confer with Bert Early, the executive director of the ABA, about strategies to modernize the legal profession. These ideas included group practice, legal insurance, and more extensive use of non-lawyers, ideas which now, a decade later, are just beginning to enter the mainstream of ABA thinking.

It would have been far easier for Powell to lead the ABA in a crusade *against* OEO. Certainly that had been the desultory history of the medical establishment's reaction to programs for group insurance. Lawyers were already letting him know what they thought about the "socialized practice of law." Aside from such philosophic problems, there were personal risks Powell would have to take to produce an ABA endorsement, plus operational risks. The proposed program was, in fact, an unknown quantity. Nevertheless, in January 1965 another key Powell adviser, John Cummisky, along with William McAlpin and Edgar and Jean Cahn, worked out a series of understandings about the role of the ABA in the future operations of the program.[6] They satisfied Powell that the goals of the ABA and OEO were compatible. He then set about to secure ABA endorsement of the proposed legal services program—no mean feat by itself, much less accomplishing it within the month available before the February 1965 House of Delegates winter meeting.

The ABA House of Delegates has never been known for its speedy deliberations, as even the least controversial of notions can disappear in the arduous process like a ripple in a wave. Still, Powell persevered. He personally drafted the resolution that went to the House, and began a personal campaign to enlarge the base of support for the resolution to include virtually every member of the top power structure in the ABA. Rarely have so many been enlisted so quickly in the ABA. Everything went like clockwork—and on February 7, 1965, John Cummisky introduced the pro-OEO resolution to the ABA House of Delegates. The powerful phalanx of supporters made their speeches, and the resolution, *mirabile dictu,* passed unanimously. But John Cummisky, for one, was not surprised.

> The majority of the delegates favored the resolution because they knew legal aid required more money for much-needed expansion. The rest of them knew that if the Federal Government was set on starting a legal services program, the ABA had better be involved in the formulation and administration of the program. It was a bit of the carrot and the stick. In effect, they had no alternative.[7]

In fact, the rank and file of the ABA lacked sufficient time to form an opinion either way about OEO legal services. The ABA voted in response to Powell's personal campaign and to the leadership which supported him. The endorsement was really a vote of confidence in Powell, not in the OEO, which explains the uneasy relationship that later existed between the OEO and the rank-and-file bar. The original ABA support of the OEO has been seen as "leadership heavy," not accurately reflecting the concerns of the local bar associations. Because the operations of OEO legal services programs were to be strictly local, the local bar associations were bound to be affected, if not ultimately threatened, by their challenging presence.

In reality, the OEO legal services program would have undoubtedly taken root and grown even without an ABA endorsement. Local bar associations and communities would have rushed to the federal trough for funds to start or expand programs. ABA endorsement, however, legitimized the program. By it the organized bar had effectively diverted the attack on the program from the issue of whether the federal government should be funding such programs at all—the "socialization" of the profession—to lesser issues surrounding the way the program should be implemented. Those persons who wished to develop OEO programs in communities with hostile bar associations found a serviceable ally in the ABA leadership. "Hell, even the ABA is for it," could be said to local obstructionists, and no doubt was. It was the reassurance of ABA support, for example, that allowed E. Clinton Bamberger, Jr., the first director of the OEO legal services program, to stand before a packed meeting of the Bar Association of Baltimore City in December 1965 and announce that the OEO would fund legal services programs with or without approval by the local bar association. "This is not a program for lawyers," he said, "it is a program for poor people—and disapproval by the organized, or the disorganized bar will not preclude approval by OEO." [8]

As for the private bar, it did not seriously oppose OEO legal services offices once they began appearing across the country. If anything, there was relief that someone was assuming the burden of the profession's responsibility to provide representation for the poor. So the bar responded to the OEO program as it had to the legal aid programs of fifty years before: Yes, the bar has an obligation to provide legal services regardless of the client's ability to pay, but the mechanism for providing the services should not interfere with the economic security of the private bar. From the bar's perspective, the major difference between legal aid of the 1920s and legal services of the 1960s is that the latter shifted the financial obligation of legal representation of the poor from the shoulders of the profession to the shoulders of the general taxpayer.

This shift, however, has actually involved the organized bar in poverty lawyering more than ever before. What had once been thought by some lawyers as a way to provide more service to the poor with less direct involvement by the private bar has become, in fact, the medium that has caused the organized bar to address issues such as the ability of government-paid lawyers to sue government agencies; the independence of lawyers to engage in full representation of their clients' interests, including legislative activities; and the right of legal services lawyers to engage in political activities on their own time. The ABA leadership has consistently supported and actively lobbied for expansion of the responsibilities of legal services lawyers, for their independence from political pressures, and for their unhampered ability to provide full and effective representation of their clients, much to the consternation of some local bar associations.

As the experience with the OEO legal services program demonstrates, the ABA can provide conservative respectability for new trends and experiments in professional growth. This is hardly the "cutting edge" of change, but that is the way the ABA wants it. Instead of promoting controversial reformulations of the profession, the Association appears more comfortable in supporting programs for improvement of the system of justice, or providing administrative support for volunteer lawyer programs, or running programs that involve an exchange of ideas or studying improvements in the delivery of legal assistance. This is reflected in its present roster of public service activities.

Among these programs are: the Commission on Correctional Facilities and Services,[9] the Young Lawyers Committee on Drug Abuse,[10] the Young Lawyers Free Legal Aid Program to Disaster Victims,[11] the Special Committee on Housing and Urban Development Law,[12] the Criminal Law Section's program to formulate minimum standards of criminal justice,[13] the Council on Legal Education Opportunity,[14] the Consortium on Legal Services and the Public,[15] and the Section on Individual Rights and Responsibilities' *Pro Bono* Project.

The *Pro Bono* Project, to take one instructive example, was conceived by the Section on Individual Rights and Responsibilities under the leadership of its chairman, Jerome Shestack. Funded initially by the Ford Foundation, the Project sought to encourage and stimulate *pro bono* work by private law firms. The ABA leadership accepted the Project with the condition of a limited mandate—to work only with firms "interested" in *pro bono* work. During its first two years, the Project functioned primarily, and quite modestly, as an informational clearinghouse. As the ABA became reassured that the Project held no hidden "revolutionary" dangers, it began to support this effort more actively. By 1973 it had been adopted as one of the "pet" projects of the 1973–74 ABA president, Chesterfield Smith, who was a member of the section council when the Project commenced.[16] Finally, on July 1, 1973, the Project transformed into a new Special Committee on Public Interest Practice. (In the arcane world of the ABA hierarchy, the creation of a special committee reflects the increased status of an official Association project.) The new special committee was assigned to design a role for the organized bar in *pro bono* activities and to develop special projects pursuant to that defined role, such as public interest law firms, fellowship programs, and resource facilities, as well as revisions of outdated ethical restrictions.

The ABA public service programs provide opportunities for those relatively few lawyers who wish to participate in such work. But there has been little response from the legal profession as a whole. The ABA's programs, including the *pro bono* work of the private bar, have for the most part allowed the activities of some lawyers and law firms to make all the others look good. In the final analysis, only a handful of exceptional attorneys are attempting to meet the vast needs of the public and to atone for the general failure of the bar to service the non-rich public. The majority of funds used to operate these programs do not come directly from the average lawyer's pocket. These programs are paid for in large part by government, foundations, and other private and public sources.

While the ABA deserves praise for its support and encouragement of various public service activities, it has only recently adopted the position that public service is a professional obligation of each lawyer, rather than only of the bar as a whole. The ethic of the personal obligation was approved in August 1975 by the ABA House of Delegates. Former president Chesterfield Smith, again well ahead of his membership, has been an ardent and frequent advocate of imposing a duty on each lawyer to perform public service work. And the Special Committee on Public Interest Practice recommended such a position to the ABA leadership. As a voluntary association, the ABA is limited in the enforceable demands it can make on its individual members. But, given the fact that only lawyers can practice law, the public, at whose sufferance this monopoly exists, can demand its quid pro quo.

As the spiritual leader of the profession, the ABA has a unique obligation to acknowledge and fulfill this public claim. The bar must take steps to enforce the professional duty on each individual lawyer to provide representation or to make sure that representation is provided to all who seek it. The present notion of a "collective responsibility" to provide representation does not translate into the individual lawyer's responsibility. Everybody's business can become nobody's business. A collective duty is no duty at all when each lawyer can point to someone else who should be doing the job. It is no longer an adequate response, if it ever was, for the bar to assume that legal aid and legal services should handle the private bar's share of the burden of representing the poor. The time has come for a breakthrough as important as Reginald Heber Smith's in *Justice and the Poor.*

There are several ways of placing an affirmative obligation upon the individual lawyer to donate services to the indigent. The *Code of Professional Responsibility*, for example, could be revised to make a serious and clear statement of professional obligation.

Canon 2 of the code now provides "a lawyer should assist the legal profession in fulfilling its duty to make legal counsel available." The code places a collective duty on the legal profession to make counsel available. The Ethical Considerations of the code, on the other hand, place the ultimate responsibility on the individual lawyer to provide legal services to those unable to pay. EC 2-25 elaborates:

> The basic responsibility for providing legal services for those unable to pay ultimately rests upon the individual lawyer. . . . Every lawyer, regardless of professional prominence or professional workload, should find time to participate in serving the disadvantaged. The rendition of free legal services to those unable to pay reasonable fees continues to be an obligation of each lawyer, but the efforts of individual lawyers are often not enough to meet the need.

Ethical Considerations, however, are merely "aspirational in character." As such, they are not enforceable standards, but are "objectives toward which every member of the profession should strive." [17]

Although it is clear from the canons that the legal profession accepts responsibility for providing public service representation, EC 2-25 provides few guidelines concerning the extent, nature, or form of the profession's public interest responsibilities. And lack of specific guidance on how to satisfy this duty has reinforced the notion of buck passing.

Now needed are mechanisms to convert duty into reality. A tithing or taxing system on each lawyer could require that a percentage of each lawyer's time or income be devoted to representing those who need, but cannot afford, legal representation. A tithing system would no longer allow the individual attorney to escape his or her public responsibility. Certainly, some lawyers are better equipped than others to perform particular types of public service work, just as some lawyers prefer to do that type of work and others do not. A realistic concern for both clients and lawyers alike leaves no other choice than to allow a lawyer the option of whether to do the actual work or to provide the financing for a surrogate who wants to do it.

The reaction of the organized bar to systems of tithing or taxing can be expected to be less than enthusiastic. Nobody likes to be told he has to do something. The idea grates on the lawyer's sense of independence. Moreover, it grates on his income. Requiring a lawyer to provide representation or funds to provide representation raises several issues, some constitutional in scope.

A case illustrating some of the difficulties involves the District of Columbia Bar (Unified Bar). The Criminal Justice Act[18] provides funds to pay attorneys appointed to represent indigent defendants in the federal court system. Partially as a result of these funds, a corps of experienced criminal defense attorneys developed who regularly accept court appointments. Due to a series of political intrigues, the U.S. Congress cut the requested appropriation for 1974 in half. When the funds ran out in February 1974, Chief Judge Harold Greene of the Superior Court and Chief Judge Gerard D. Reilly of the D.C. Court of Appeals notified the members of the D.C. Bar that funds would not be available to pay attorneys who had performed services in reliance on the CJA payment. Moreover, funding for the fiscal year 1975 remained unresolved, and it looked as though no funds would be forthcoming. In a letter to the president of the bar, the chief judges stated:

> The Supreme Court has consistently held that criminal defendants are entitled to counsel whenever imprisonment is a possibility at the disposition of a case. There are presently 16,282 indigent defendants per year, or approximately 54 per day, in the criminal and juvenile branches of the Superior Court for whom such representation must be provided. The Public Defender Service is able, with its staff, to represent about 16 of these defendants daily. Thus, 38 attorneys per day, every day, including Saturdays and holidays, must be found if the criminal justice system of the District, and with it law enforcement in the Nation's Capital, are not to come to a halt, with virtually incalculable consequences.[19]

The D.C. Bar's position on a program of appointed, uncompensated counsel was outlined in an earlier letter from President Charles Duncan to Chief Judge Greene:

> The *Code of Professional Responsibility*, which governs our conduct, prohibits an attorney from handling a legal matter which he knows or should know that he is not competent to handle (DR 6-101) (A) (1). . . . [T]he constitutional rights of the defendants themselves almost certainly would be seriously jeopardized if they were represented by inexperienced counsel who were unfamiliar with the criminal law and its many procedures.
>
> On the other hand, if assignments in indigent cases were limited to those attorneys, estimated to be about 700, who have had criminal trial experience, it is obvious that extreme burdens would be placed on them, as they would be required to devote as much as one-third to one-half of their professional time to uncompensated legal services; this in turn would raise due process and other constitutional objections.[20]

Nevertheless, the chief judges went ahead and initiated their program appointing uncompensated counsel. And in reply the D.C. Bar filed a lawsuit[21] to compel funding of the Criminal Justice Act, and to enjoin the appointment of inexperienced counsel in criminal cases. The experienced criminal trial lawyers refused to accept further appointments, as negotiators continued behind the scenes to get Congress to appropriate funds.

Critics of the bar have said that "if the client was going to pay $100,000, the lawyer would become experienced damned quickly." They view the bar's reluctance as a protection of the majority of lawyers who would rather spend their time earning an income than providing a public service.

Those sympathetic to the bar insist that the D.C. Bar wants to insure fair payment for services and a decent livelihood for practitioners who choose to represent those who cannot afford to pay. The bar seeks the funding of these activities by bringing suit and pressuring Congress to appropriate the funds. They note that the D.C. Bar was the first bar association in the country to issue a statement to its membership that the "District of Columbia Bar (Unified) regards it as the individual duty of each member of the legal profession practicing in the District of Columbia to provide, within the attorney's field of competency, public service representation to insure that such representation is provided to all who legitimately seek it." [22]

The familiar pattern again emerges—the bar supporting a movement which will lead to other lawyers doing the work that the majority of the bar does not want to do. But this time the support is clothed in a different canon. Here, the bar admits in rare candor that lawyers specialize and that few are competent generalists. There is a notable absence of high-sounding principles and a refreshing display of reality.

The D.C. Bar illustration involves a crisis in the criminal justice system. In the civil area, a requirement to perform public service representation would probably not evoke the competency argument. Public service practice, if one follows the recently adopted definition of the ABA, is:

> Legal service provided without fee or at a substantially reduced fee, which falls into one or more of the following areas:
>
> 1. *Poverty Law:* Legal services in civil and criminal matters of importance to a client who does not have the financial resources to compensate counsel.
>
> 2. *Civil Rights Law:* Legal representation involving a right of an individual which society has a special interest in protecting.
>
> 3. *Public Rights Law:* Legal representation involving an important right belonging to a significant segment of the public.
>
> 4. *Charitable Organization Representation:* Legal service to charitable,

religious, civic, educational and governmental institutions in matters in furtherance of their organizational purpose, where the payment of customary legal fees would significantly deplete the organization's economic resources, or would be otherwise inappropriate.

5. *Administration of Justice:* Activity, whether under bar association auspices or otherwise, which is designed to increase the availability of legal services or otherwise improve the administration of justice.

This scope of practice is sufficiently broad so that most lawyers could competently handle cases sufficient to meet their public service obligation. Predictably, if a "time or taxing" system is imposed in the civil law area, much of the controversy will focus on how much time or money is fair. The larger question, however, looms. Who should bear the cost of the system of justice? The bar? The public? The litigants?

Beyond the tithing system is the view that legal practice is a public utility, with licensing requirements similar to those placed upon public utilities. In their 1972 book *The Lawyer, the Public and Professional Responsibility*, F. Raymond Marks, Kirk Leswing, and Barbara A. Fortinsky, who are proponents of this system, recommended that lawyers be required to certify periodically that they have operated their licenses with balanced programming for the public good.[23] And when they don't, just as when broadcast stations don't, the license renewal would be denied.

Still another way for the organized bar to implement its duty to the public would be through a bar-sponsored internship program in the area of public service—similar to a medical internship. Each law graduate could be assigned for a year to a public service program, such as a public defender's office, an OEO legal services program, a public interest law firm, or a private firm with a *pro bono publico* department. The benefits to the public and the bar are obvious—increased service, more involvement of the older bar in supervision, and the development of a healthy competition among the private bar for *pro bono* departments to help recruit the most outstanding law graduates. Perhaps the greatest benefit would be the sensitization of the legal profession as a result of each lawyer having gone to "boot camp."

Some of these suggestions might strike bar elders as unworkable, if not dangerous. What is truly dangerous, however, is intransigence in the midst of swirling change. The organized bar can become a professional buffalo, an endangered species killed off by new circumstances, if it ignores a growing pressure for it to respond to those who need lawyers rather than merely those who can afford to pay for lawyers. The thesis that members of the private bar should cease shifting the public service mantle to surrogates and accept it themselves is novel only to those who have lost sight of what it should mean to be a member of the legal profession. Roscoe Pound stated the profession's true function succinctly:

> There is much more in a profession than a traditionally dignified calling. The term refers to a group of men pursuing a learned art as a common calling in the spirit of public service—no less a public service because it may incidentally be a means of livelihood. Pursuit of the learned art in the spirit of a public service is the primary purpose.[24]

*John P. MacKenzie**

Of Judges and the ABA

THE WORST THING ever done by the American Bar Association's Standing Committee on the Federal Judiciary, the ABA's official judge-picking body, was to stand by silently while the Senate nearly confirmed G. Harrold Carswell for the Supreme Court, although the committee had evidence that Carswell had deceived the Senate at his confirmation hearing. One of the best things the committee ever did was to signal its disapproval of, and thus prevent, the nominations by President Nixon of Mildred L. Lillie and Herschel H. Friday to the same high court.

These contrasting episodes, one in 1970 and the other in 1971, had contrasting sequels. After the committee's cooperation with the Nixon Administration in the Carswell case, it was promised that Attorney General John N. Mitchell would consult it before suggesting any future Supreme Court nominees to the president. Yet in the aftermath of the Lillie-Friday episode, the Administration in effect fired the committee, denying it henceforth the guarantee of an advance look at potential nominees. So the poorest performance in two decades of the committee's existence was rewarded with the most treasured prize of powerful lawyers: access—access to the Supreme Court nominating process—while one of the committee's finest hours resulted in a loss of that privilege.

By rewarding the ABA in inverse proportion to the quality of its performance,[1] the Administration betrayed its own purpose in dealing with the association so intimately in the first place. The affiliation was not designed by the Administration to obtain the most highly qualified candidates for the nation's highest courts, but rather was designed to engineer public consent to nominees without regard to quality. The ABA was expected, especially after Carswell, to acquiesce in any Supreme

* JOHN MacKENZIE HAS BEEN A STAFF WRITER ON THE *Washington Post* SINCE 1956, AND ITS SUPREME COURT REPORTER SINCE 1965. HE IS THE AUTHOR OF *The Appearance of Justice* (1974).

Court choice the Administration might wish to make. Despite its loss of favor and despite the burns suffered from being too close to the Administration on some Supreme Court appointments, the ABA continues to hope that someday the White House or the Justice Department will restore the bar's lost influence on the selection—not merely the confirmation—of Supreme Court justices.

What is this ABA committee, working so quietly yet so visibly influential in the judicial selection process? Are its members qualified to wield the power they wield or the power they seek? Are they representative of the organized bar, and if so, is the organized bar representative of the legal profession in such matters? What is the proper role of "the legal profession" in choosing justices and judges? These and other questions have been asked with increasing frequency throughout two decades of growing ABA influence.

The ABA's role in Supreme Court selections seems to date back to 1916, when seven ABA presidents or former presidents, including William Howard Taft and Elihu Root, signed letters saying that Louis D. Brandeis was "not a fit person" to sit upon the highest bench.[2] Although the seven men did not have the power to speak for the Association, and did not even constitute a majority of the living ex-presidents of the ABA, nevertheless they appeared to represent the established bar. Indeed, according to A. L. Todd's book on the Brandeis fight, the turnout of professional horsepower was the bar's most impressive display of opinion in Washington on any subject, not merely judicial selection, up to that time. Thus 1916 may be the birthdate of the ABA's more general lobbying role in Washington.

In more modern dress the ABA judicial selection arrangement dates from the closing days of the Truman Administration. Then Deputy Attorney General Ross Malone, later a general counsel to General Motors, established a program of referring candidate names for the district courts and the circuit courts of appeals to a special ABA committee. The Eisenhower Justice Department actually put such a plan into effect under Deputies William P. Rogers and Lawrence E. Walsh. Attorney General Herbert Brownell wanted to reserve the Supreme Court for the president's exclusive domain but was crossed up by President Eisenhower himself, who told a press conference that the successor to Justice Sherman Minton would of course be checked with the ABA.[3]

In practice the Supreme Court procedure proved unsatisfactory by any measure. Often the ABA committee would be given only a matter of hours to render an opinion on the president's choice, too short a period of time for an investigation or for anything but an uneasy acquiescence. Meanwhile the ABA waxed more powerful over the years with lower courts, chiefly because something like genuine advance consultation did take place.

The ABA's influence grew another cubit with the advent of the Kennedy Administration. Like other new regimes, the early Kennedy days were marked by what Assistant Attorney General Burke Marshall later admitted was "inexperience, lack of information, or overdependence on the judgment of others" in judicial selection.[4] The fledgling Administration was happy to join the bar in a mutually reinforcing operation. The ABA got the prestige and power of being the Administration's confidant on judicial matters. In return, the bar's favorable opinion would bolster an otherwise uncertain nomination, especially one from the Administration's own ranks. Second, and perhaps more important in light of the realities of the selection process, the ABA was a handy tool for the executive branch when it was under pressure to nominate someone it didn't want to nominate.

The beginning of wisdom about federal judicial selection is to understand the aggressive role of United States Senators and the relatively defensive role of the executive branch in the process. Turning the shield of senatorial courtesy (whereby the Senate will refuse to confirm a nominee who is obnoxious to the Senator from his home state) into a sword, senators frequently take the initiative in proposing names for district judgeships within their states and for their states' apportionment of judges for the circuit court of appeals of their regions. It is the thankless task of the Justice Department, usually the deputy attorney general's office, to resist the bad nominations and encourage better ones. Not infrequently the deputy's office, bereft of an articulable reason for opposing a given proposed nominee or worn out from dealing with legislators who will not listen to reason, has been forced to fall back upon the professional opinion of the ABA committee. Often this has provided the grateful bureaucrat with a colorable reason that will pacify the importuning legislator.

The ABA committee has operated under fairly rigid ground rules for evaluating prospective judges. Whether by force of circumstance or the committee members' predilections or both, the standards have been most unyielding for district court nominations; strict minimums of trial experience were established. Another restriction on the committee, this one imposed by circumstance, has been the raw material the evaluators could work with. The committee ordinarily would not propose names to a senator or president, but rather would have the passive function of passing on the qualifications of those who were proposed. The common denominator of those proposed was that all were politically acceptable to someone, which did not mean that a candidate was per se unqualified, but it provided a built-in bad start for the committee. Often the requests to screen judicial candidates who were politically acceptable but professionally questionable came in clusters for the same vacancy, forcing the committee to pass judgment wholesale on the legal crowd around a senator.

Whether or not the committee needed all the autonomy it received from the ABA, and whether or not the committee required all the secrecy it sought to impose upon its deliberations, the fact is that over the years the group of twelve men, serving rotating terms, exercised a closely held sovereign power on behalf of the organized bar. Not all the committee members have been widely known bar leaders, but each enjoyed the confidence of the ABA president who appointed him, or at least the confidence of someone with the ear of the president. The committee has produced its share of recent presidents, including Bernard Segal of Philadelphia, Leon Jaworski of Houston, Robert Meserve of Boston, and Lawrence Walsh of New York. Nothing in the committee's charter requires it to be the all-male, all-white group it has been without exception since its formation. Despite the proclamations of the ABA's president for 1973–74, Chesterfield Smith of Orlando, Florida, that the Association would be a more open place for lawyers of diverse backgrounds and interests, no women and no blacks were appointed by him to this highly prestigious subgroup within the ABA.[5] The exclusiveness of this club has cost it dearly in credibility and will continue to do so until some of the lines are broken.

Over the years the Standing Committee on the Federal Judiciary has been careful in exercising whatever political influence it had, judiciously picking its spots to stand firm and fight over nominations it disapproved.

The first major battle was over Irving Ben Cooper, sponsored by House Judiciary Committee chairman Emanuel Celler in 1961. The ABA lost that long confirmation fight, but learned how to fight for another day. In 1965 its committee bitterly contested the nomination by President Johnson, at the urging of Senator Edward M. Kennedy, of the Kennedy family retainer, Francis Joseph Xavier Morrissey. The fight bruised President Johnson, who was bitter over what he deemed the committee's elitism and preference for "Wall Street lawyer" types over graduates of hard-knocks law schools. In retrospect, the 1965 Morrissey controversy was the dress rehearsal for the confirmation fights of 1968, 1969, and 1970 and the selection controversy of 1971.

On one occasion the ABA played into the hands of its opponents. When Abe Fortas was nominated in 1968 to succeed retiring Earl Warren as chief justice during the waning days of the Johnson Administration, it developed that the committee's investigation of Fortas had been largely delegated to Jaworski. Yet his claim to objectivity was compromised by his history of association with the fortunes of President Johnson. This encouraged Senator Robert P. Griffin of Michigan to question the quality of advice the committee could give the Senate in supporting the nominee.

None of these attacks, bruises, and wounds apparently injured the ABA committee in the estimation of Deputy Attorney General Richard G. Kleindienst. At the ABA's 1969 convention, Kleindienst calmly announced that President Nixon would not nominate anyone rated "not qualified" by the ABA committee.[6] The pledge, which went far beyond any previous expression of willingness to cooperate with the ABA, did not extend to Supreme Court nominations, which the president considered his own territory.[7] But it amounted to what Kleindienst candidly admitted was a "veto power" over lower federal court appointments. Later recognizing the legal implications of that admission, the Administration denied that such governmental power had in fact and irrevocably been delegated to the private group. The proof of the pledge, however, was in its keeping, and the president kept the pledge at least until late 1973, when Attorney General Elliot Richardson and his deputy, William Ruckelshaus, withdrew from its stark terms while continuing to work closely with the committee.

Mr. Nixon's reservation of authority for Supreme Court nominees was asserted promptly with his appointment of Chief Justice Warren E. Burger, who easily won ABA endorsement for confirmation. The ABA was again relegated to passing on a fait accompli in investigating and taking a position on the nominations of Clement F. Haynsworth, Jr., and G. Harrold Carswell. Walsh, who was chairman during this period when not on leave in Paris as a member of the Administration's team at the Paris peace talks, felt frustrated in trying to get a candid opinion from the bar over a nomination already made and likely to be confirmed. This is not an excuse for the committee's failure to recognize or acknowledge that Carswell was unqualified, a fact brought home by other leading members of the bar, but it unquestionably proved to be an institutional handicap.

Another institutional handicap was self-imposed. The committee's rules gave it the choice of finding a Supreme Court nominee "highly qualified" or "not qualified" at all. During both the Haynsworth and Carswell fights, the committee had no mechanism for damning with faint praise. Too late the committee adopted a middle category labeled "not opposed," a potential warning to the appointing powers that a nominee need not be unfit to fall short of hearty committee support. Had this category been available, it very likely would have been applied to Carswell. There might also have been some sentiment for applying it to Haynsworth, at least after his confirmation became embroiled in a battle over ethical standards. Thus, the committee supported Haynsworth and refused to change its mind, despite a meeting to reevaluate its position in view of Haynsworth's admitted failure to remove himself from a case where he owned stock in a litigant and accusations that he should have disqualified himself in other cases.*

The story of the Carswell case begins on the night of January 26, 1970, when George Harrold Carswell of Florida, a judge of the United States Court of Appeals for the Fifth Circuit, received two visitors in his Washington hotel room. Carswell was there to await the morning's opening day of confirmation hearings by the Senate for his nomination to the Supreme Court. The two visitors, Charles A. Horsky of Washington and Norman P. Ramsey of Baltimore, were there as members of the ABA committee. Their mission was to clear up a few matters before reporting on Carswell's fitness to the Senate Judiciary Committee.

---

* Still another handicap lay in the nature of the reporting system the committee had adopted for itself. Even a cursory reading of the committee's formal reports on Haynsworth and Carswell, on the one hand, and Lewis F. Powell, Jr., and William H. Rehnquist, on the other, will show that the committee developed a format for detailed reporting that in the future should elevate its own investigatory standards.[8]

The ABA committee had all but wrapped up its investigation of the nominee and was preparing to report that Carswell should be confirmed. Although Carswell's lack of qualifications for so high a post were widely known, the committee's unfinished business did not relate to this aspect of his fitness, but to other factual matters. For example, what was the role, if any, that Carswell played in the conversion of a public golf course in Tallahassee to a private country club in 1956, just when the federal courts were demanding that such public facilities be desegregated? Although the ABA committee portrayed itself as an investigating body, and although the Federal Bureau of Investigation had failed to explore this aspect of Carswell's career, a band of resourceful civil rights lawyers had uncovered documentary evidence linking Carswell to the transaction. They turned the incorporation papers for the Capital City Country Club over to Ramsey and Horsky, who on the evening in question confronted the nominee with them. Carswell then acknowledged that he had indeed been an incorporator of the club. Within hours, the ABA committee dispatched its letter to the waiting Senate Judiciary Committee. The letter said the nominee was qualified and should be confirmed.

This event alone would suffice to mark the low point in the history of the ABA's role in the selection and confirmation of justices and judges. Previously a journalist had discovered that Carswell had given a speech in a Georgia political campaign in 1948 proclaiming his "firm, vigorous belief in the principles of white supremacy." [9] Appropriately and promptly, Carswell had repudiated the speech and said he could not picture himself making it. The country club conversion understandably raised the question whether Carswell's racism died in 1948, sometime after 1956, or not at all. Whatever Carswell told the ABA committee members in the interview, they apparently accepted it, paving the way for fairly smooth hearings.

The committee's default, however, did not stop with this event. It then added to the crime of insensitivity the sin of gross negligence, to put it mildly. For its members stood by and said nothing while Carswell misled the Senate, to use another euphemism.

Next morning, with the country club story prominently displayed in the newspapers, Carswell was given his opportunity to explain. Gently prodded by Senator Roman L. Hruska, whose expressed hope that mediocrity would have representation on the high court seemed about to bear fruit, Carswell responded in this fashion:

> I read the story very hurriedly this morning, Senator, certainly. I am aware of the genuine importance of the facts of that. Perhaps this is it now. I was just

going to say I had someone make a phone call to get some dates about this thing. This is not it. [Noting a paper on the desk.] I can only speak upon my individual recollection of this matter. . . . The import of this thing, as I understand it, was that I had something to do with taking the public lands to keep a segregated facility. I have never had any discussion with any human being about the subject of this at all. That is the totality of it, Senators, I know no more about it than that.

SEN. HRUSKA: Judge Carswell, it was sought to make of you a director in that country club. Did you ever serve as a director?

JUDGE CARSWELL: No, sir, nor in any other official capacity.

SEN. HRUSKA: Did you ever attend any of the director's meetings?

JUDGE CARSWELL: Never.

SEN. HRUSKA: Were you an incorporator of that club as was alleged in one of the accounts I read?

JUDGE CARSWELL: No, sir.[10]

In an apparent attempt to be helpful to the witness, Hruska repeatedly suggested ways in which Carswell might have been innocently involved as an incorporator. Was the witness familiar with the club bylaws or the articles of incorporation? "No, sir." Well, perhaps the stock he received carried the designation "incorporator"? "Perhaps," said Carswell, "I have no personal recollection." [11]

When it came the turn of Senator Edward M. Kennedy to ask questions, the senator held in his hand what appeared to be copies of the documents. "Did you in fact sign the letter of incorporation?" he asked pointedly. This time the nominee replied, "Yes, sir. I recall that." What did he recall about that? the senator wanted to know. "They told me when I gave them $100 that I had the privilege of being called an incorporator. They might have put down some other title, as if you were a potentate or something. I don't know what it would have been. I got the one share and that was it." [12]

Next day the inquiry was further thrown off the track of Carswell's racial views in this exchange with Senator Birch Bayh of Indiana:

SENATOR BAYH: Yesterday, as I recall, you said the purpose of this, to your knowledge, was to build a clubhouse?

JUDGE CARSWELL: Clubhouse or club facilities, I suppose they had in mind a swimming pool, tennis courts, the usual thing.

SENATOR BAYH: Since you have looked at the documents, I suppose—

JUDGE CARSWELL: Senator, I have not looked at the documents. I didn't mean to leave that impression with you. The documents speak for themselves. I couldn't begin to tell you what the documents say.[13]

Asked by Senator Kennedy whether he had had any idea whether the club was going to be open or closed to Negroes, Carswell replied, "The matter was never discussed."

"What did you assume?"

"I didn't assume anything. I assumed that they wanted one hundred dollars to build a clubhouse. . . ."

"When you signed this, and you put up the money and you became a subscriber, did you think it was possible for blacks to use that club or become a member?"

"Sir, the matter was never discussed at all."

"What did you assume, not what was discussed?"

"I didn't assume anything. I didn't assume anything at all. It was never mentioned." [14]

Not only did the ABA not come forward to refute Carswell's testimony, but the committee compounded its misfeasance when, on February 21, it met to reconsider its stand on the nominee, discussed the question of his candor with the Senate—and reaffirmed its support.[15]

Why did the committee fail in this manner? One answer—there being no official answer from the committee—might be that it did not view Carswell's testimony as basically deceitful. If so, it was a question for the Senate committee, not the ABA committee, to judge, and the evidence in the ABA's possession should have been made available to supporters and opponents on an equal basis. Another possibility is that while recognizing the impeaching quality of its own evidence, the ABA felt that opponents would use it as a red herring. Again, the ABA's view of its evidence would not have relieved it of the obligation of disclosure. Or perhaps, realizing the potential impact of the evidence, the ABA opted for suppression lest it prevent the confirmation of a nomination that did not deserve to be defeated. If this were the case, it would only magnify the misjudgment the ABA committee made on the nomination's merits.

Although the Association, its committees, and its sections are private bodies, the public function of its committee on the judiciary gives it a public duty. The public is entitled to know more of the innards of its investigation not only because of the committee's role as adviser to government, but more importantly because if its near-monopoly on certain investigative capabilities. Only the FBI can elicit the kind of cooperation from the nominee and other sources of information that is available to the ABA committee. The public could not readily confront Carswell with the country club documents. And the Senate, as representative of the public, was deprived of the full use of the documents as a basis for inquiring into the possible continuing existence of racial prejudice in the mind of the nominee.

If the ABA was severely restricted under the ground rules that obtained before 1970, the new understanding of that year imposed intolerable restraints on the Nixon Administration. Attorney General Mitchell pledged to await the ABA committee's judgment *before* submitting any name to the president for a future Supreme Court vacancy. But this president had already made clear that Mitchell—whom Mr. Nixon deemed superbly qualified for the high court—was to be a major source of input for prospective nominees, on occasion the only source.[16] (Alas, Mr. Nixon told newsmen in 1969, Mitchell would not consider being appointed to the Court.) And what if Mitchell and Nixon should quickly reach at least tentative agreement on a nominee? To keep his promise with the ABA, Mitchell would have to obtain the president's agreement to withhold the nomination pending a check with the ABA,[17] a process which, after the embarrassing disclosures about Carswell, would have to take some time. In fairness to Mr. Nixon—to the presidency—this is too self-limiting a procedure for a process in which time can be so critical.

This particular ABA-Administration arrangement carried with it the seeds of the misunderstanding that was to follow. The exchange of letters among Walsh, Segal, and Mitchell included Walsh's observation that the process of checking out names under consideration by Mitchell might not be conducted in airtight secrecy. A good investigation, said Walsh, simply would involve too many people. Walsh apparently did not lament this fact. Rather, he welcomed it as a potential added source of information for the committee and a consequent reduction in the chances for embarrassment from belated disclosures. It later appeared that somewhere in the Administration this feature was not perceived as a virtue. Probably the demurrers came from the White House staff, since Mitchell displayed an understanding somewhat similar to Walsh's.

This relatively open procedure worked well, except perhaps from the White House perspective, since it aborted nominations that would have been bitterly opposed and probably soundly defeated in the Senate. Within hours of the ABA's inquiries to the outside world in 1971, a list of six candidates was known to many newspapers. For example, the *Washington Post* learned the six names before 3 P.M. on October 13,

1971,[18] and was able to begin gathering information from Little Rock, Arkansas, and Los Angeles on the two prime candidates, Herschel Friday and Mildred Lillie.

In addition to smoking out expected civil rights opposition and permitting its evaluation, the daylight made it possible for such investigators as Laurence E. Tribe of the Harvard Law School to investigate Mrs. Lillie's record on the appellate bench in California. His analysis, a devastating statistical summary of a dismal judicial record, could thus be completed in time to appear in print in time for the ABA's consideration, though too late of course for the half-committed White House. This kind of information, along with vibrations from elsewhere in the bar across the land, combined to make it highly unlikely that the ABA committee would support Friday and certain that it would oppose Mrs. Lillie. Learning this, the Administration turned to other candidates, and the ABA's final vote, while damaging to the Administration, was a formality. The Administration then resorted to recruiting two qualified men, Powell and Rehnquist, enabling the president to beam with pride on national television. The Administration seized upon the publication of the original list of six names and the committee's action concerning Friday and Mrs. Lillie as the reason for severing the ties of prior consultation that had bound them.

The action of the ABA's judiciary committee, though correct, was remarkable. Few who remembered the Carswell episode would have been willing to predict what the committee did. Many assumed its tolerance for mediocrity to be endless. To many it seemed that the expectations for a Supreme Court nominee had sunk to a new low—a situation in part fomented by the ABA, yet altered by its Friday-Lillie performance.

The committee's performance was all the more remarkable when one measures the risks it undertook in displeasing the Administration. Much has been said by way of complaint about the "access" to high government officials enjoyed by members of the "establishment" bar, of which the committee has almost a charter membership. Chairman Walsh, for example, has been criticized for intervening on behalf of International Telephone & Telegraph Corporation at a critical point in litigation aimed at divesting ITT of important and arguably illegal corporate acquisitions. Unquestionably, Walsh was able to trade on years of goodwill in government to gain the attention of Kleindienst and obtain a postponement of the government's planned appeal against ITT in 1971. The specific vehicle was a Walsh proposal for an Administration-wide restudy of conglomerate mergers, going over the head of the Justice Department's

Antitrust Division. But the fault for what happened lay not with Walsh, who made the proposal, but the Administration, including President Nixon, who accepted it in one form or another. Ultimately, the ABA committee's accomplishment is all the more remarkable because Walsh took the risk, in leading the committee to the action it took, of losing that favor and access.[19]

Curiously, the Nixon-ABA relationship was severed at the moment of Nixon's fall from power. On August 9, 1974, his last full day in the White House, Nixon made the only federal court nomination of a person rated not qualified by the committee. He nominated Thomas J. Meskill, a former two-term Republican congressman, lame-duck governor of Connecticut, and loyal Administration supporter, to the U.S. Court of Appeals for the Second Circuit.

The committee, which had lobbied successfully for many months to forestall the nomination after beating back an earlier candidate proposed by Senator Lowell P. Weicker (R.-Conn.), resolved to go to the mat on the nomination and oppose confirmation for the first time since Morrissey a decade earlier.

The ABA's opposition was primarily responsible for the eight-month delay between the nomination and a final floor vote in April 1975. Joined by the Association of the Bar of the City of New York, the ABA took the position that in addition to being unprepared for the work of the important court, which handles appeals from the New York, Connecticut, and Vermont federal courts, Meskill as governor had been implicated in some unsavory dealings with political friends in state leasing matters. A number of investigations by the bar and the FBI failed to turn up evidence of downright wrongdoing, although the evidence indicated an awareness or at least due notice of improprieties and a lack of sensitivity on Meskill's part.

The ABA itself unwittingly became an issue in the Meskill fight. It belittled Meskill's brief career as a lawyer by noting the apparent insignificance of the cases the nominee listed as his most important. Supporters of Meskill were able to turn that criticism into something approaching a plus, portraying the Association as an elitist, Wall Street–oriented trade group. More damaging to the ABA, and more helpful to Meskill, was the serious overstepping by the ABA committee and by Walsh, now president, in testimony before the Senate Judiciary Committee. In an uncharacteristic moment of unguarded speech, Walsh suggested in his testimony that Meskill's refusal to discuss the leasing matters with bar representatives reflected on his "candor" and that similar silence by other figures in the leasing scandal indicated consciousness of wrongdoing. This brought countercharges from Senate Republicans that the ABA itself was unfair and even a rebuke from Senator Kennedy that Walsh had gone too far. Kennedy and other Meskill opponents then were forced to go out of their way to say that they disavowed the extreme position taken by the ABA and they urged the Senate not to be diverted by a side controversy over the Association.

The final vote on the Senate floor was 54 to 36 for confirmation. The ABA had been instrumental in mustering the most votes against a circuit court nominee in the memory of Senate veterans (roll call votes themselves being a rarity in the judicial confirmation process), but had suffered from its own backlash—to what extent, only time would tell.

There is enough in all this to breed both suspicion and confidence in the ABA role in judicial selection. Surely too much power resided, even if temporarily, in private hands when the Administration gave the ABA a veto power over lower court judgeships. Yet even this is not all bad when one considers the particular Administration the committee was dealing with at the time. It was a Justice Department almost totally lacking in the requisite skill and the requisite will for high-quality Supreme Court appointments. As for the lower courts, the Administration may have been still more inadequate, so that the delegation of much of its work to the ABA was a redeeming feature of the selection process. Imagine sending an FBI agent to find out what Professor Tribe knew about Mrs. Lillie when what was needed was a lawyer in the executive branch who was willing to face up to her demonstrated inadequacy for the Supreme Court! The agents did not visit Professor Tribe at Harvard to intimidate him, although the visit easily and carelessly seemed to have that effect.

What should lawyers do if they are unhappy about the ABA's influence? The answer is obvious: Lawyers must organize. It's not enough to sit around and stew about the undue power or lack of representativeness of the established bar organizations. Justice Powell, for all the denunciation of Ralph Nader in the Chamber of Commerce memorandum he wrote while in private practice,[20] never suggested a move to close the courts to Nader. He said the Chamber should equip itself to litigate in the Nader manner.

If lawyers do organize on the occasion of a future Supreme Court appointment, they might find themselves enjoying an advantage over the formally organized bar. Where the choosing of judges is concerned, the ABA simply lacks the institutional capacity to speak for anything you might call the "conscience" of the bar, but non-committee lawyers, such as those who did so much to bring down the nomination of Carswell, may find that it is they who have the larger constituency.

Martin Garbus
*& Joel Seligman**

Sanctions and Disbarment:
They Sit in Judgment

WATERGATE was a disaster for the reputation of America's lawyers. With the exception of three men—H. R. "Bob" Haldeman, Jeb Stuart Magruder, and Dwight Chapin—every principal figure involved was an attorney.

Along with the highly publicized obstruction of justice and perjury convictions were the well-publicized efforts of state bar associations to cleanse themselves. By January 1975 G. Gordon Liddy, John Dean, Charles Colson, and former vice president Agnew had been disbarred. Egil Krogh, Jr., had been suspended from practice in Washington State. Disciplinary proceedings had been launched against John Ehrlichman, Herbert Kalmbach, Robert Mardian, former California lieutenant governor Edwin Reinecke, and Donald Segretti. Former president Nixon had resigned from the bar of California under threat of disbarment and has attempted, unsuccessfully so far, to resign from the New York State bar.

Adding to the impression that the American bar is a vigilant self-policeman have been recent highly publicized speeches by Chief Justice Warren Burger. He has argued that the failure to train trial lawyers in courtroom skills has helped bring about "the low state of American trial advocacy and a consequent dimunition in the quality of our entire system of justice." Burger was especially vehement in urging the profession to deal with uncivil and ill-mannered lawyers. He castigated "adrenalin-fueled" attorneys who appeared to think that "the

* MARTIN GARBUS, A PRACTICING NEW YORK CITY TRIAL LAWYER, IS AUTHOR OF *Ready for the Defense* (1971), ASSOCIATE DIRECTOR OF THE AMERICAN CIVIL LIBERTIES UNION, AND A MEMBER OF THE NEW YORK STATE BAR ASSOCIATION'S SPECIAL COMMITTEE ON LAWYERS AND THE COMMUNITY. JOEL SELIGMAN IS A WRITER AND RECENT LAW SCHOOL GRADUATE WORKING WITH THE CORPORATE ACCOUNTABILITY RESEARCH GROUP.

zeal and effectiveness of a lawyer depends on how thoroughly he can disrupt the proceedings or how loud he can shout or how close he can come to insulting all those he encounters—including the judges." In November 1973 the chief justice called for a special license system for trial lawyers to purge incompetent advocates and generally raise ethical standards.

In stark contrast to the expulsion of some—by no means all—convicted felons and the occasional high-sounding words of legal elders is the reality of bar disciplinary proceedings. Self-regulation has collapsed.

There are, for example, about 50,000 lawyers in New York State. Between 1957 and 1972, disciplinary action—reprimand, censure, suspension, or disbarment—was taken against 810 lawyers, or some 54 a year. In the Bronx and Manhattan, where some 32,000 attorneys practice, 10 were disbarred in 1973. One attorney, found to have suborned perjury, was merely suspended for eighteen months; another, who filed a fraudulent tax return, was merely censured. In 1972, bar associations disciplined 357 lawyers, or roughly one-tenth of one percent of the nation's 380,000 practicing lawyers.[1]

This means, law professor–sociologist Jerome Carlin has concluded, that only about 2 percent of the attorneys who violated generally accepted ethical norms were even processed by disciplinary machinery.[2] In many jurisdictions, less than one complaint in 100 results in admonition, censure, resignation, suspension, or disbarment.[3]

Disciplinary mechanisms are "a scandalous situation that requires the immediate attention of the profession," said the American Bar Association's Special Committee on Evaluation of Disciplinary Enforcement, chaired by retired United States Supreme Court justice Tom Clark, in 1970. "With few exceptions, the prevailing attitude of lawyers toward disciplinary enforcement ranges from apathy to outright hostility. Disciplinary action is practically non-existent in many jurisdictions; practices and procedures are antiquated; many disciplinary agencies have little power to take effective steps against malefactors." The Clark committee found that in some instances disbarred attorneys are able to continue practice in another location; that even after disbarment lawyers are reinstated as a matter of course; that lawyers fail to report ethical violations by their brethren; that in many communities disciplinary agencies will not proceed against prominent lawyers or law firms and that, even when they do, no disciplinary action is taken; and that state disciplinary agencies are undermanned and underfinanced, many having no staff whatever for the investigation or prosecution of complaints.[4]

In sum, if the purpose of court and state bar association disciplinary proceedings is to assure the public high standards of diligence and propriety, self-regulation is a nearly complete failure—an embarrassment for a profession which brags that the integrity of its practitioners "is the very breath of justice." [5] How has the failure of disciplinary proceedings come about? What can be done about it?

Centuries ago in England, a lawyer who misbehaved was subject to a disbarment proceeding which really was a disbarment. In a public ceremony, the wayward barrister would be physically thrown over the wooden railing—"the bar," and hence the term "disbarment"—that separated the judges' and lawyers' half of the courtroom from the spectators'. Disbarment was a frequent and obviously painful occurrence.

The custom of expelling profligate lawyers, though not the public ceremony, was initially adopted in the United States. Pre–Revolutionary War efforts to organize attorneys into self-regulating associations had substantially succeeded in establishing high professional standards when the American Revolution set off a wave of hostility against all exclusive groups. By the time Jacksonian democracy hit full stride, the organized bar had been virtually eliminated. State legislatures, warning against the creation of new elites, reduced the requirements for the practice of law to the barest minimum. Indiana, for instance, established the constitutional right of *any* man of good moral character to be admitted to the bar. Bar organizations disappeared or degenerated into social clubs.

These organizations, however, arose again after the Civil War, when extensive corruption of both the courts and the bar reached such excesses that political reform became imperative. "To regain their lost leadership in public life," said one legal historian, "selected groups came together to 'maintain the honor and dignity of the profession' as their primary object, and, incidental to this, to do 'whatever needed to be done.' " "Whatever needed to be done" primarily meant the establishment of standards of professional conduct. This among other reasons led to the formation of the American Bar Association in 1878.[6]

Since 1908 the ABA's *Canons of Ethics*—after revision in 1969 called *The Code of Professional Responsibility*—have been the most widely adopted standard of legal conduct. The present code sets a scrupulously high tone. Phrased both in terms of Ethical Considerations, which are considered "aspirational" (e.g., a lawyer should assist in maintaining the integrity and competence of the legal profession), and specific disciplinary rules (e.g., "A lawyer shall not engage in conduct involving dishonesty, fraud, deceit, or misrepresentation"), *The Code of Professional Responsibility* is intended to be both "an inspirational guide to the members of the profession" and "a basis for disciplinary action when the conduct of a lawyer falls below the required minimum standards in the Disciplinary Rules." Although several of the Disciplinary Rules have been criticized as mere subterfuge to fortify the position of the most prominent law firms—such as those prohibiting advertising and soliciting clients—they are generally rigorous, designed "to avoid even the appearance of impropriety." Under the code, a lawyer must not represent conflicting interests or charge an excessive fee. He must be adequately prepared to represent each client zealously. He must help protect the public from those who are not qualified to be lawyers. He must report violations of Disciplinary Rules by other attorneys, assist in preventing unauthorized practice by those who are disbarred or suspended, and never personally engage in conduct that is prejudicial to the administration of justice.

But standards are mere exhortations without an enforcement mechanism. The courts and bar associations are supposed to review lawyers' professional conduct and performance. Under usual procedures, local bar associations initiate investigations and process complaints, with the ultimate responsibility reposing in state courts. Disciplinary proceedings are often prosecuted by a local grievance committee and tried by a referee appointed by the courts.

It is here, at the enforcement level, that self-regulation breaks down.[7] There is a tendency for a member of the disciplinary agency to go to a friend and say, "Look, Joe, why don't you take care of this before it goes any further?" Even in the largest associations, where there is presumably less intimacy, lawyers have proven utterly incapable of disciplining each other. Attorneys and judges generally refuse to report instances of professional misconduct. They will not testify against each other. There is a strong tendency to treat serious misconduct complaints as private disputes between attorney and client. Typically, an attorney accused of charging a grossly excessive fee or even stealing a client's money is exonerated when he returns the misappropriated funds. The general impulse is to protect a brother at the bar—even a knavish one—rather than protect the public.

Beyond this self-protective attitude on specific cases is a greater structural problem: Bar associations have rigged the disciplinary process so that it barely can function at all.

Virtually no state bar adequately finances disciplinary agencies. Robert Lees, the head of the Philadelphia Bar's disciplinary panel, had to abort an investigation of an ambulance-chasing scandal when his bar association cut his funding. "To the extent that the allegation is generally made that it's very difficult for a profession to police itself," acknowledges Lees, "I would have to say that the results of that investigation indicated that there was a lot of substance to that charge." Yet without funds, there is no systematic or regularized review of lawyers' behavior. There is no professional staff, only volunteer lawyers who lack the time and interest to thoroughly investigate complaints. There is no record keeping. The whole process becomes haphazard and fortuitous.

Disciplinary proceedings are usually launched when a client complains to the local bar about his attorney. Occasionally an investigation is undertaken on the basis of an adverse item about a lawyer in a newspaper which comes to the attention of the bar. This means that attorneys who join their client in unethical behavior are rarely investigated. Lawyers without individual clients—those who work directly for the government or corporations—are practically exempt from any review.

Almost as self-defeating as underfinancing is secrecy. "To protect the reputation of the attorney" accused of misconduct, many states keep confidential the existence of a disciplinary proceeding until a trial has been held, the charges have been found sustained, and the record filed in the court having disciplinary jurisdiction. Secrecy invariably leads to abuse, allowing the doyens of the bar to bury the misconduct of their fellow doyens. Grave charges against members of the "establishment" bar tend to be dismissed out of hand or result only in a gentle admonition. In either event, the conduct of the errant attorney, and his judges, is never made public at all.

Procedural rules further cripple the process. The Clark committee found that a cumbersome review process results in an inordinate time gap between the inception and conclusion of disciplinary proceedings. "It is not unusual to find jurisdictions with procedures involving six or seven stages, including three adversary hearings, before final action on a complaint can be taken." The full process can take more than five years!

Some jurisdictions do not provide their disciplinary committees with subpoena power. Thus, misconduct investigations may neither compel witnesses to testify about a lawyer's conduct nor require production of written records. Again and again they are required to take the accused attorney's word for it—yet the accused attorney doesn't have to talk at all. In 1967 the Supreme Court ruled that no attorney need testify against himself at a disciplinary hearing nor may he be punished for not testifying.[8] The problem is that few jurisdictions responded to this decision by allowing disciplinary investigators to gather evidence from other witnesses by granting them immunity from criminal prosecution, as is commonly done in state and federal courts. The result is a lawyer's *Catch-22*. The more serious the misconduct, the harder it is to investigate. Accordingly, minor ethical lapses often are ignored because the bar association knows worse conduct cannot be pursued. Really heinous behavior is not penalized because the bar lacks the tools to prove it. In point of fact, only felony convictions readily result in bar discipline.

And many jurisdictions make it difficult to punish felons as well. Although a felony must be proved beyond a reasonable doubt, only a few jurisdictions—such as New York—automatically suspend an attorney convicted of a serious crime. Few jurisdictions make conviction of a crime conclusive evidence of guilt for purposes of the disciplinary proceeding. There is a real possibility that an attorney convicted of a serious crime in a court of law will be found not guilty in the subsequent disciplinary proceeding, especially given the weaknesses of grievance-committee investigators and evidentiary rules. Several bar associations further undermine enforcement by prohibiting the disciplining of an attorney until he has exhausted all his criminal appeals, which can take three to five years, *and* until he has completed all disciplinary proceedings, which can take another three to five years. This proved too much for the Clark committee:

> The public is unable to understand these apparently inconsistent results and concludes that the bar is not interested in maintaining high standards. . . .
>
> The public is unable to comprehend why an attorney convicted of stealing funds from a client can continue to handle clients' funds; why an attorney convicted of securities fraud can continue to prepare and certify registration statements; why an attorney convicted of filing a fraudulent income tax return can continue to prepare and file income tax returns for clients; why an attorney convicted of conspiracy to suborn perjury can continue to try cases and present witnesses; why an attorney convicted of bribing officials of an administrative agency can continue to practice before that very agency; or why an attorney convicted of a serious crime of any nature can continue to hold himself out as an officer of the court obligated to uphold law and to support the administration of justice.

The cumulative effect of underfinancing, secrecy, lax procedures, and self-protective rules is the thorough insulation of the largest and most prominent law firms from any scrutiny whatsoever. As Orville Schell, a past president of the prestigious Association of the Bar of the City of New York, put it: "We don't get the fat cat." He might have been even more accurate if he had said, "The fat cats refuse to get themselves." For most bar associations are dominated by the most successful local attorneys. They have transformed judicial ethics into a sleazy system of self-protection under which the leaders of a local bar assume the grave mantle of self-regulation and moral leadership and then wink at most improprieties they encounter.

It is a vulgar reflection on American jurisprudence that corporate law—the field with the most lucrative fees; the field that attracts the law's best and brightest—has evolved into the field with some of the lowest ethical standards. Recently Professor William Cary, the dean of American corporate lawyers, reflected on this decline.[9] "Are we never shocked?" he wondered. He recited a long litany of abuses: corporate lawyers going to any lengths to deflect shareholder challenges; corporate lawyers advising clients to buy another firm in the same industry "so that it can trump up an antitrust defense" against a tender offer; corporate lawyers amending the company's charter so there may be no shareholders' meeting without an 80 percent quorum; corporate lawyers serving as directors of corporations they advise, thereby, in Cary's view, surrendering their independence and ignoring their fiduciary responsibility. "Already conflicts of interest abound," warns Cary, "yet everywhere corporate lawyers are rushing to be part of 'the deal.' They are no longer simply issuing an opinion as would a solicitor acting independently in England. They are involved in all business aspects." Worse yet, corporate lawyers have adopted the morals of the marketplace. *In S.E.C. v. National Student Marketing Corporation*, the Securities and Exchange Commission sought an injunction against White and Case, a prominent Wall Street firm, to stop them from "making false and misleading statements and omitting to state material facts [when filing] annual and other periodic reports" on behalf of their client (a case undecided as of mid-1975). More recently, the Second Circuit Court of Appeals let the corporate bar know that its patience was wearing thin. After holding that an attorney who prepares a legal opinion letter which turns out to be "wrong" may be held liable in an SEC enforcement action, the court roundly condemned the practice of lawyers who act as shields for their clients' misdeeds.[10]

If it's not the corporate lawyers, who, then, does get disciplined? "It is the lawyer serving the poor and the middle class who is cited most often by ethics committees for advertising, ambulance chasing and using lay intermediaries as methods of getting business," says the *Yale Law Journal.* In other words, those lawyers who don't pay dues to the local bar association, those outside "the club," are the ones that get punished. The point should not be overstated. These attorneys aren't monitored much either. Yet it is discouraging to read that 54 percent of the complaints to the New York Bar in 1970 concerned "neglect," a catch-all category that generally covers the malefactions of the small attorney, and less than 1.5 percent concerned "conflict of interest," the category that would include a prevalent sin of Orville Schell's "fat cats." [11]

Equally discouraging is the grievance-committee punishment of anti-establishment lawyers. Consider three cases.

In September 1972 two attorneys opened a legal clinic in a Los Angeles suburb, claiming that it would lead to reduction in the cost of legal services to middle-income persons. The lawyers had devised a systemic approach for handling basic legal problems, making extensive use of prepared kits and paralegal assistants. The national and local press contacted the two, who granted interviews to such publications as *The Christian Science Monitor* and *Newsweek.* Shortly thereafter, the Bar Association of the State of California charged both with violation of the anti-advertising rule, and, as a result of that violation, with acts involving "moral turpitude and dishonesty." [12] In so doing, the bar association elevated an alleged infraction of a much-criticized ethical rule into a seemingly criminal act.

Equally indefensible is the case of a young Kentucky attorney, Daniel T. Taylor III. Taylor represented blacks and civil rights activists in a very hostile local environment. During a highly charged murder trial, Taylor accused the presiding judge of calling him a "dirty son of a bitch." At the subsequent disciplinary proceeding, the judge denied that he had done so. Although Taylor presented a spectator at the trial who said the judge's lips had formed these words, the bar association's Board of Governors recommended that Taylor be suspended for *five years.* Ultimately the Kentucky Court of Appeals imposed a six-month suspension. [13]

Finally, there is the case of Philip Hirschkop. In the ten years Hirschkop has been a member of the bar in the Commonwealth of Virginia, at least a dozen separate disciplinary investigations have been commenced against him. Not once has an infraction been proved. Yet for the preponderance of his career, the threat of censure or suspension has hung ominously over him.

What are the sins of Philip Hirschkop? He is a cofounder of the Virginia American Civil Liberties Union and a past member of the National Board of the ACLU; he is widely known for his writings and teachings in the field of civil rights and civil liberties, and for, as he calls it, "constitutional litigation." His cases have struck down all the interracial marriage laws in the United States; brought about sweeping changes in the Virginia prison system; and achieved the release of H. Rap Brown when he was originally arrested in Virginia.

Hirschkop has not become popular for his pains. In his most celebrated run-in with the Virginia State Bar, Hirschkop was hauled before a local grievance committee without the normal opportunity to refute by letter the charges brought against him or without the State Bar apparently even investigating the complaints it made. On this occasion, Hirschkop was charged with three improprieties during his defense of a liberal prison administrator who had been charged with "willful misconduct in office" by a state prosecutor, shortly after a conservative governor inaugurated a program to roll back the reforms of his predecessor. The principal allegation was that Hirschkop had told reporters that his client and codefendants were "the good guys," contrary to a Virginia Bar Association rule which prohibits attorneys from "acquiescing" in the publication of their comments in a newspaper story concerning their client's case. For this remark, the Virginia State Bar attempted to disbar him. This, despite the fact that Hirschkop had steadfastly refused to answer reporters' questions about the merits of his client's case. Moreover, as Hirschkop demonstrated at the hearing which vindicated him, past governors of Virginia, lieutenant governors, attorneys general, assistant attorneys general, state attorneys, and judges have commented and acquiesced in publicity in numerous cases in which their offices were involved, without any similar disciplinary proceeding being launched against them.[14]

Cases like Taylor's and Hirschkop's cannot help but have a chilling effect on activist lawyers. Attorneys committed to defending minority or unpopular interests will know they do so at their peril. Currently, it is well known that grievance committees in the South regularly harass civil rights lawyers. Committees in the North almost as frequently threaten the William Kunstlers. This community of lawyers is small enough as it is without having to endure the risk that they might trigger bar retaliation if they prove too successful in their muckraking litigation.

How can disciplinary procedures better sanction unethical offenses without harassing unpopular lawyers?

Several reforms suggest themselves. Disciplinary enforcement must be adequately financed. There must be professional investigators reviewing the bar on a full-time basis. Procedures must be streamlined and sped up. Evidentiary rules should be rewritten to parallel those used in criminal court. Felons convicted of serious crimes should be immediately suspended.

The big question, however, is not rules. Nor is it money. It is structural. Who should administer the disciplinary process? [15] Or, more broadly, how can the public assure itself competent and responsible attorneys?

Consider four alternatives. The first would retain the disciplinary procedures in the hands of the courts and the bar associations. A second option would be to abandon licensing and disciplinary regulation altogether—i.e., anyone could practice after graduating from law school. The third would be to create a separate lay administration to supervise the discipline and ethics of legal practice. The final option would be an agency composed of lawyers *and* laymen to discipline attorneys.

Leaving things as they are just won't do. It is a great maxim of the law that no man should be a judge in his own case or in any case in which he has the least interest. This maxim identifies what is most wrong with self-regulation. Lawyers are incapable of enforcing tough rules which might ultimately be enforced against themselves. In the years since the Clark committee first began meeting, several states—including New York, New Jersey, California, Michigan, and Minnesota—have recognized this fact and reformed their procedures.

The second option, abandoning licensing and disciplinary regulation altogether, has certain theoretical attractions. It would lead to the abandonment of bad rules such as those prohibiting advertising and soliciting (thereby probably helping reduce the cost of legal services) and it would, of course, make impossible punitive use of grievance committee machinery. It would not eliminate ethical discipline entirely, since the criminal courts and regulatory agencies would hopefully become more aggressive against wayward lawyers. Still, on balance, deregulation raises more questions than answers. It would remove the only standard lawyers have for collective ethical conduct. It would open the door wide for more shysters and incompetents to parade as minions of justice. There would be no feasible way for potential clients to gauge the ethical standards of a particular lawyer. Ultimately the public might lose all faith in the legal profession.

Nor does the third alternative—delegating disciplinary oversight to a completely lay body—seem to be the answer. This approach emphasizes independent judgment, which is desirable, but the effectiveness of a purely non-lawyer group is difficult to predict. If it lacks a professional staff to counsel it in deliberations and investigations, it might be unable to unravel the more complex transactions of attorneys.

The fourth alternative seems best: the creation of an agency independent of the state and local bar associations, composed of a minority of lawyers and a majority of laymen, to establish and enforce standards of integrity and competence. Such a panel would possess both the ability and the independence to examine ethical questions long ignored by the legal profession—such as prosecutorial overzealousness, government or corporate conflicts of interest, or lawyer involvement in a client's business. A "mixed" panel would be less interested in professional "image" than an all-lawyers group, and it should help promote public confidence in the seriousness and objectivity of the disciplinary process—which in turn should increase the likelihood of complaints and suggestions from the public. Moreover, the existence of such a panel armed with its own staff would create a momentum to seek out areas appropriate for investigation, study, and public scrutiny, rather than passively await specific complaints.

It will no doubt prove difficult to convince the organized bar to adopt such a restructuring of the disciplinary process, but the recent experiences of two states suggest how this new approach can work.

A few years ago the Michigan legislature, reflecting a strong public mistrust of misbehaving lawyers, introduced a bill calling for lay control of the disciplinary machinery. Ethical standards had slipped so precipitously that even the Michigan Bar Association conceded that a thorough reappraisal of its disciplinary procedures was long overdue. The Michigan Supreme Court then interceded and on its own initiative established the State Bar Grievance Board, an independent professional board of review. Under the court's plan, two of the seven members of the board are laymen. A full-time staff (four lawyers, three investigators, and clerical help) reports to the board, and this staff, in turn, coordinates the activities of some two hundred volunteer attorneys who conduct investigations and serve on hearing panels. A yearly budget of $325,000 derives from $100-per-year dues levied on each state bar member.

In its first five years, the Michigan system has proven a tremendous success. By 1973 disciplinary actions (reprimand, suspension, or disbarment) had increased 400 percent. More importantly, by supervising investigative work of such a large number of volunteer attorneys (one out of every forty state bar members), the staff has both improved the quality of ethics investigation and generated a widespread awareness of professional standards in the legal community.[16]

In 1971 Minnesota adopted a similar approach. Each lawyer in the state is annually assessed $25 to fund a State Board of Professional Responsibility and a professional staff headed by highly regarded trial attorneys. Three laymen and eighteen attorneys presently comprise the board. All serious complaints are heard by one of four panels of five members—always including a lay member. The Minnesota board has ranged far beyond the activities of the traditional grievance committee. Not only does it review ethical lapses, it has also suspended or placed on probation attorneys whose competence is diminished by chronic alcoholism. It has issued several "opinions" which serve as "guidelines" for the conduct of lawyers in the state of Minnesota. Significantly, a majority of the first opinions dealt with fee disputes, conflicts of interest, and incurring debt on behalf of clients—areas of direct impact to the "consumers" of the "legal product" which the typical bar association has been reluctant to regulate.[17]

It is now clear the Minnesota and Michigan experiments have made a substantial difference. Citizen participation and centralized staff have put the bar on its good behavior. For the first time, a state has involved the public in the ethical rule–making process. Most importantly, lay participation has burst the myth that only lawyers are competent to judge the derelictions of other lawyers. As long as the organized bar was able to persuade the state legislatures and state supreme courts that only attorneys possessed the ability to hear evidence about legal improprieties, the bar was able to keep the process "within the family." Now the opposite has been proven true. As Michigan staff director Michael Franck found, "Laymen are as competent as lawyers in judging misconduct." This result should hardly seem surprising. When lay representatives need help on a difficult problem, they can receive it, like jurors, through "expert" testimony. Moreover, lay representatives on disciplinary committees have two advantages that ordinary trial jurors do not: They have their own staff and they have attorneys serving with them.*

Now that Michigan and Minnesota have shown the way, it is time for other states to go much further.

First, they should include not a minority but a majority of public representatives. There is a great danger that if the public has a mere minority voice it will become a rubber stamp for the lawyer majority or the staff, thereby compounding an evil by giving the appearance rather than the reality of lay involvement. Constantly outvoted, the lay minority might be cowed into acquiescence by a knowledgeable and articulate lawyer majority.

Second, state Boards of Professional Responsibility must assume a rule-making function. Ethical rules made by lawyers to regulate lawyers invariably protect the lawyers' financial interest. A predominantly lay body would reassess rules in terms of their public impact. They would worry, for example, more about the cost and availability of legal services.

Third, and most important, any "mixed" panel must be open to the public for it to be fully effective. Cloistered and hidden, even a minority of lawyers could exert an undue influence. Well-lit and well-known, the same attorneys would be more inclined to be commendable public servants.

The most telling criticism of the Michigan and Minnesota plans is that they have maintained excessive secrecy in the complaint and initial hearing stages. Since civil and criminal trials and their results are fully public, it is difficult to see why disciplinary proceedings should be kept secret. Secrecy defeats the deterrent of knowing that all unethical or wrongful conduct may be exposed to public scrutiny. Yet it can be honestly asked: Why should an attorney suffer the publication of an unfounded complaint? But an attorney should not suffer at all if a public hearing record demonstrates that the complaint was, indeed, unfounded. Procedural rules could guarantee that only complaints supported by a minimum of substantial evidence would be made public—which would make the process analogous to the secrecy of the grand jury and publicity of a trial *if* an indictment is handed down.

There is an important public interest in open proceedings. It is more essential to assure the public that the ethical proceedings which affect it

---

* By 1975 five other states—Colorado, Georgia, Maine, New Hampshire, and Washington—had added non-lawyers to their grievance boards.

are being conducted fairly and effectively than it is to assure lawyers confidentiality. This was the reason that the District of Columbia's grievance board recently recommended fully opening up all disciplinary hearings. Such a ventilation of the disciplinary process is necessary to assure the public that the integrity of a once "noble" profession has been restored.

II

The Canons of
Profits

*Mark Green**

The Gross Legal Product: "How Much Justice Can You Afford?"

WHAT DID Robert Vesco, Richard Nixon, Aristotle Onassis, and Ms. Delores Durham have in common in 1974? The high cost of lawyers.

When a television interviewer asked Robert Vesco, a fugitive at his luxury Costa Rican retreat, why he had contributed $200,000 to the Committee to Reelect the President, he replied, "It was cheaper than paying lawyers." In a form of legal aid for presidents, taxpayers contributed $300,000 toward Richard Nixon's legal expenses during his much-celebrated difficulties. Once out of office, however, the millionaire ex-president strained to foot the growing bill himself—aided by a Justice for Nixon Defense Fund (shades of Angela Davis!). Jacqueline Kennedy apparently spared no expense in retaining Paul, Weiss, Rifkind, Wharton & Garrison to file a counterclaim against photographer and privacy-invader Ron Galella. She won but her late husband Ari refused to pay the $400,000 bill. (The law firm sued, and settled for $225,000.) Delores Durham testified at a Senate hearing how she could not afford a lawyer to help her obtain car repairs under a warranty. "Do you know what attorneys' fees would be?" Senator John Tunney asked her. "I would think about $500 and I know I cannot afford that." [1]

It is, of course, difficult to sympathize with the financial burdens of the Vescos, Nixons, and Onassis'. But it is newsworthy that even they share the dilemma of most citizens: Rich or poor, crooked or innocent, Americans are paying more and more to lawyers today.

Justice has not always carried such a high price tag. In the Bible Aaron

* THE WRITER WOULD LIKE TO THANK JUDITH FRIEDLAENDER FOR HER VALUABLE ASSISTANCE IN PREPARING THIS ARTICLE.

spoke on behalf of Moses, yet there is no record of the receipt of even a minimum fee. Under the teachings of Confucius, who was a magistrate in the fifth century B.C., people in the government gave legal advice but were prohibited from taking money for doing so. The Cincian law of ancient Rome in 200 B.C. forbade advocates to charge any fees, which prompted the satirist Juvenal to later write, "Alas! a hundred lawyers scarce can gain, what one successful jockey will obtain." [2] Skipping two millennia, the top lawyer's income in Connecticut in 1789 was only $2,000. Of Philadelphia's 1,500 lawyers in the 1880s, less than one-third were self-supporting and no more than 100 earned over $5,000.[3] Beginning salaries for attorneys in New York City were $600 a year in 1910, $2,400 in the 1920s, $3,600 in 1949,[4] and still a modest $10,000 in 1967. In 1960 the average sole practitioner in America earned $7,080 and the average law firm partner $17,181—more than the average citizen, to be sure, but hardly enough to cover a second car, three weeks in Gstaad, or a Piping Rock membership.

The last decade, however, has seen an explosion in the Gross Legal Product (GLP) and the earnings of lawyers. The GLP, according to Bureau of the Census data, was $1.3 billion in 1950, $2 billion in 1955, $4 billion in 1966, and $9.7 billion by 1972 (which is the most recent data available); of this $9.7 billion, lawyers had a net profit of $5.2 billion.[5] Statistics vary somewhat on the average income of lawyers, but it is clear that the graph points sharply upward. Based on 1968 data, Robert Weil's *Census of Law Firms* estimated that the average law firm partner in America earned $39,000.[6] In 1970 the ABA reported that the average income of its members was $28,000 annually.[7] When the consulting firm of Daniel J. Cantor surveyed 4,908 attorneys in private practice in 1972, it found their median annual income to be $40,100.[8]

Such aggregate data obscures the reality that, economically speaking, there are two distinct legal professions in the United States today. Large corporate law firms on both coasts or in major urban areas generate vast fees and lush incomes; for example, the opening salaries of associates in New York City and Washington, D.C., now range from $16,000 to $22,500, while the average partner (based on 1968 data) earns $52,000 in New York City and $60,000 in Washington, D.C.[9] On the other hand, solo practitioners or small-firm lawyers in small towns—those who handle personal wills, divorces, and auto cases rather than corporate, antitrust, banking, or tax issues—have moderate incomes. In 1969–70 the median income in Iowa was $19,800, in Oklahoma $18,000, and in Georgia a slim $15,300.[10] But "take out the depressed fringe among small-town and solo-practice lawyers," observed *Forbes* magazine, "and the typical lawyer probably does as well as the average doctor." [11] And since doctors (as of 1973) average $49,415 annually, that is very well indeed.

This newfound wealth has several sources. In the past fifteen years business has boomed and busted, conglomerateurs have parlayed accounting rules into empires, government regulation has grown more complex—and lawyers have been needed at every stage, at every merger and every bankruptcy. And making sure that legal need converted into large fees have been the bar associations themselves. While their rhetoric is usually publicly spirited, as discussed earlier, occasionally the sound of candor cuts through the sanctimony. In 1960 the Illinois Bar Association boldly proclaimed, "The respect for the legal profession and its influence in the individual community will be raised when the lawyer occupies his proper place at the top of the economic structure." [12] At the ABA's 1966 annual meeting in Montreal, ABA-er William Fuchs told an appreciative gathering, "Come out and hit the client hard at the beginning. If you're going to bill a half-way rate on your first bill, you'll be at half-way rates for the rest of your career with that client. Come right out at the beginning and sock him hard." [13] In a film on how to increase billings, presented at the 1972 ABA convention in San Francisco as well as for local bar groups around the country, Texas attorney J. Harris Morgan lectured that "it is in the public policy of this country that you be prosperous." Prosperity, added Morgan, was at least $55,000 a year. And when Graham Bartlett, president-elect of the Tennessee bar, was asked in 1974 why his state association no longer published minimum fee schedules, he proudly announced, with an attitude Andrew Carnegie could only have admired, that they weren't necessary any more "because through surveys we have taken we knew that the income of the lawyers had been raised enormously!" [14]

All of which makes understandable the *New Yorker* cartoon of a distinguished-looking attorney and an anxious prospective client which carried the caption "You have a pretty good case, Mr. Pitkin. How much justice can you afford?"

In their time, minimum fee schedules had significantly promoted high legal fees. The idea of these schedules—which suggest that lawyers not charge less than a specified amount for various legal tasks—has been traced as far back as colonial times.[15] * The bar of Sedgewick County, Kansas, adopted one in 1872: Wills brought $10, uncontested divorces $25, and contested ones $50. Schedules flourished especially in the 1950s and 1960s, as lawyers began to worry about income slippage. "The gods help those who help themselves," said one proponent in 1959. By 1965 Philip Haberman, executive director of the Wisconsin State Bar, reported that "obviously and desirably a fee schedule will tend to increase the income of lawyers," adding that within eighteen months of the schedule's implementation in Wisconsin, "the overall net take-home pay of our lawyers . . . went up in excess of 10 percent." [17] Economist Richard Arnould corroborated this conclusion. "A lawyer in an area where some form of jurisdictional fee schedule exists makes, on the average, $3,500 more per year than a lawyer in an area where no schedule exists," he calculated.[18]

Minimum fee schedules therefore seemed merely a euphemism for what industrialists have long ached to do: fix prices to raise profits. That this practice was a criminal act under the antitrust laws if undertaken by auto makers or bakers did not deter the lawyers. By 1971, 34 states and about 800 local bar associations utilized minimum fee schedules. One survey found that in places where the schedules existed 52 percent of lawyers used them as one of the three major ways of determining fees, while 87 percent used them to some extent.[19]

As a result, one could not get a lawyer to handle an uncontested divorce for less than $250 in Denver or $600 in New Canaan; a simple title search earned a lawyer at least $150 in Birmingham, $300 in Columbus, and $350 in Jacksonville. While the probate of a will of an estate over $750,000 could cost $60,000 in fees in some areas, it went for

---

* Because of the unreliability of fee collection, six prominent attorneys in 1773, including Thomas Jefferson, Patrick Henry, and John Randolph, wrote the following:

> The Fees allowed by Law, if regularly paid, would barely compensate our incessant Labours, reimburse our Expenses, and the Losses incurred by Neglect of our private Affairs; yet even these Rewards, confessedly moderate, are withheld from us, in a great proportion, by the unworthy Part of our Clients. Some Regulation, therefore, is become requisite to establish Terms more equal between the Client and his Counsel. To effect this, we have come to the following Resolution, for the invariable Observance of which we mutually [commit] our Honour to each other. "That after the 10th Day of October next we will not give an Opinion on any Case stated to us but on Payment of the whole Fee, nor prosecute or defend any Suit or Motion unless the Tax and one Half the Fee, be previously advanced, excepting those cases only where we choose to act gratis;" and we hope no Person whatever will think of applying to us in any other Way.[16]

only $9,000, or one-seventh as much, elsewhere.[20] Minimum fee schedules, therefore, lead both to wildly divergent fees in different areas for similar services and to inflated fees. How inflated? Based on the projections of Haberman and Arnould, it would be fair to estimate that these fee-fixing compacts raised prices at least 10 to 15 percent and that they affected some 12 percent[21] of the $9.7 billion gross legal product. Using these calculations, one can conservatively estimate that lawyers overcharged clients by at least $155 million to $233 million annually.

Attorneys, of course, do not acknowledge this professional legerdemain. Lawyers are lawyers precisely because they forensically try to make flowers out of deserts, as they wax eloquent justifying what everyone knows is pure hokum. So they attempt to wrap minimum fee schedules in the toga of ethics and the public interest, though their rationales tell us more about the lawyers than they intend:

- *One ABA publication argues that "the profession will not attract and keep men [sic] of ability and high intellectual attainment unless an adequate financial reward is provided."* It is not self-evident that there should be a policy preference for talented people in law rather than in, say, medicine, architecture, business, or government; nor is it clear why clients should be compelled to be so charitable with their money, especially since lawyers already have more money than most of their clients.

- *Leroy Jeffers, president of the State Bar of Texas, has testified that fee schedules are "based upon costs and minimum earnings" and have "stabilized rather than inflated legal costs."* [22] If fee schedules are based on cost, it is difficult to understand why they vary as much as 600 percent between jurisdictions. "We find no evidence that the fixed fees were determined," wrote Richard Arnould and Robert Corley in the *ABA Journal*, "by multiplying the hourly rate by an agreed on time taken to perform the service. . . ." [23] Fees are based on what lawyers want to earn, not their costs. If the goal of schedules were merely to stabilize price, why wouldn't the bar offer *maximum* fee schedules instead of only minimum fee schedules?

- *Bar associations say these fees are mere suggestions.* Historically, undercutting the minimum would expose a lawyer to disciplinary action. Under the whip of criticism, however, the ABA issued an opinion in 1961 announcing the not well known fact that under Canon 12 "minimum fee schedules can only be suggested or recommended and cannot be made obligatory." But (a) most lawyers believe minimum fee schedules mean what they say; (b) few lawyers want to turn down an extra $3,500 a year; and (c) there is little incentive to offer a lower fee when canons against advertising and soliciting prohibit a lawyer from informing potential clients of the lower rates.

- *Higher fees will lead to a higher-quality representation.* It is improbable that the lawyer who scraped through law school, who doesn't like the law, who is not experienced, or who is simply no good will suddenly become a more competent and responsive lawyer because of a 10 to 15 percent fee hike. Yet even if high fees guaranteed high quality, some people want not Cadillacs but Vegas, expecting less by paying less because they can't afford more. If the marketplace only offered Cadillacs, a lot fewer people would drive. So, too, with the marketplace for lawyers.

- *Lawyers form a profession, not "a mere moneymaking trade," and it would be crassly commercial to permit price shopping and fee bartering.* Given what fee schedules obviously do, this argument appears developed by the same kind of people who called recessions in the 1950s "rolling readjustments." Since such schedules "were promulgated at a time when lawyers were expressing concern that their incomes were insufficient," notes the March 1972 *Harvard Law Review*, they "may *contribute* to a commercial image of the profession." [24] Rather than avoiding the taint of commercialism, the following passage from *A Lawyer's Practice Manual* seems to flaunt it: "If packaging is important for commodities, it certainly should be for the fee schedule. A fee schedule should be in an attractive folder, preferably evidencing a degree of dignity and substance. A black leather cover with gold lettering, or even a dignified, all-black cover, is more desirable than a plain, though neat, paper cover."

Lewis Goldfarb objected to the leather and gold lettering. In order to obtain a mortgage to buy a home in Fairfax County, Virginia, Goldfarb had to retain a Virginia attorney to conduct a title search. Nineteen lawyers quoted him a fee of $522.50 for the title search on his $54,000 home; all refused to go below it. "It is policy of this office," wrote one, "to keep our charges in line with the minimum fee schedule of the local bar association." But unlike thousands before him who had grumbled and paid, Goldfarb, then a Federal Trade Commission attorney, got Ralph Nader's Public Citizen Litigation Group to file a lawsuit in early 1973 against the Virginia state and local bar associations for illegal price-fixing under the antitrust laws—a lawsuit that reached our highest court.

On March 25, 1975, the Supreme Court building echoed with arguments about the lawfulness of lawyers. Appropriately, the Court chamber overflowed with an audience comprised largely of interested attorneys. After an hour and a half of argument, one sentence best summed up the controversy. Solicitor General Robert Bork, his voice easily filling the vast chamber, rhetorically asked why the antitrust laws should not apply to lawyers. "The answer is said to be the ethical responsibilities of the bar [but] one searches in vain for the connection between professional ethics and price-fixing for professional services." Many in the audience smiled at this compelling simplicity, and the Virginia State Bar never fully recovered. On June 16, speaking for a unanimous Court, Chief Justice Warren Burger found that "respondent's activities constitute a classic illustration of price-fixing." Although his opinion cautiously avoided saying that lawyers would always be treated like any other commercial enterprise, it did observe that here the bar's "activities resulted in a rigid price floor from which petitioners, as consumers, could not escape if they wished to borrow money to buy a house." [25]

In other words, the Court ruled that lawyers for decades had illegally overcharged their clients based on the rationale that they constituted a "learned profession" who deserved the money more than their clients.

Lewis Goldfarb is not alone in his distress over legal expenses at property closings. Real property and probate problems are the two consumer areas most frequently requiring use of a lawyer by the public. And they spotlight what's wrong with legal fees.

Few consumers appreciate why a lawyer who fills out forms for two hours at the closing of a $50,000 house deserves one percent, or $500, for his or her effort. It makes even less sense that for comparable work on a $500,000 estate a lawyer can earn one-half percent of the estate, which equals $2,500. This malady (also common to municipal bond lawyers) occurs whenever lawyers reap a fixed percentage of a corpus rather than a fee per hour. The bar explains that lawyers earn more as the value of the transaction increases because they are exposed to greater risk should an error be made. But since mortgage companies universally require a purchaser of land to obtain title insurance, the lawyer's liability is not what it seems to be.

Not only are real estate lawyers paid large fees for little work, but some collect for services not provided. A confidential report of the Virginia Bar Association found it not uncommon for Virginia real estate lawyers to pay a free-lance lawyer or paraprofessional $30 to $50 to do a required title search and pass the title certificate on to the client at a charge of $350 to $400. In other cases, a lawyer connected to a particular real estate development will have already searched title for the previous purchaser. Yet he charges the new buyer at the same percentage rate for the elaborate and time-consuming task of opening a file cabinet.

A situation of such easy money, perhaps inevitably, has led to scandal. A 1972 report by the Department of Housing and Urban Development and the Veterans' Administration found that "rebates, kickbacks, commissions, referral fees, however named, paid by title insurance companies, are common. . . ." [26] Typically, lawyers have connections to land developers, title insurance companies and/or brokers whereby clients are passed along and the profits shared. News articles have reported that title insurance companies will pay from 15 to 25 percent of the premium on a policy to the attorney who brings in a client to be insured.[27] The New York State Insurance Department estimates that consumers pay lawyers in the state $4 to $6 million annually in undeserved profits due to these title insurance kickbacks.

The *Washington Post* reported that some developers refuse to sell property unless the buyer agrees to deal with the attorney of the developer's choice.[28] From a project of 200 houses, in the estimation of several Virginia bar officials, the developer gets a kickback of some $16,000 from the lawyer. The lawyer gets $100,000 in fees, $80,000 for work already done and for which he has already been paid by a previous client. The bill rendered by the lawyer will not reflect that the client is paying compensation to the title insurance company, the builder, or the broker. Nor will the client know when the builder, having selected the lawyer, is pressuring him to overlook possible defects in title or other aspects of the sale which may be against the client's interest.*

* The Emergency Home Finance Act of 1970 contains a provision which allows (but does not require) the Secretary of Housing and Urban Development to establish standards governing the level of attorneys' fees in house closings—but this authority had never been exercised as of mid-1975. The Real Estate Settlement Procedures Act of 1974 made kickbacks in real estate transactions involving a federally mortgaged loan a federal crime.

The probating of wills presents similar opportunities for windfalls from legal work. In a recent year 100,000 Americans died and left estates valued at $60,000 or more; it cost $800 million to settle these estates—as opposed to the $150 million for funeral costs to bury those 100,000 individuals.

In probate, as in real estate, legal fees are determined as a percentage of the worth of the transaction—in this case, the value of the estate. Typical charges are 7 percent on the first $7,000 of the estate, 5 percent on the next $4,000, 4 percent on the next $10,000, 3 percent on the next $60,000, and 2½ percent on the remainder of the estate over $75,000. Once again, the amount of the fee has nothing necessarily to do with the amount of work exerted by the lawyer. As Leo Kornfeld, the former editor of *Trusts and Estates Magazine*, writes:

> In the main, the handling of moderate estates is a cut-and-dried affair. Much of the work is done by the lawyer's secretary, problems are solved gratis by clerks at the probate court, and very little of the lawyer's own time is consumed. The legal fees earned in probate and estate settlement work are more often than not quite astronomical in relation to the time spent by the lawyer on the matter. . . . It is the exception when a lawyer handling a $100,000 estate devotes more than 15 to 20 hours of his own time to the task. At that, I am probably being generous. The resulting legal fees work out to between $150 and $265 an hour—or higher.[29]

Some states have attempted to regulate probate and guardian fees by requiring that lawyers file a record of their fees with a court-appointed supervisor. But if the experience in New York is any general indicator, such regulation is easily avoided. In the seven years since the 1967 inception of the requirement, 20,000 of 100,000 cases failed to record the lawyer's fee; as a result, the New York State special prosecutor's office was opening an investigation into matters which *The New York Times* indicated "involved possible kickbacks of appointment fees to political figures." [30]

There are a number of possible solutions to profiteering probate lawyers. One is to take lawyers out of the probate system altogether. Judge William Haworth of Oklahoma told CBS investigators that 90 percent of probate legal work is unnecessary and that the rest could be done well enough by a legal secretary.[31] In Canada, a full-time, court-appointed lawyer serves as special guardian in all cases in which one is needed; there is no reason why probate should not be a court-financed process as well. The government effectively pays for some private legal services already, by allowing fees to be deducted from the estate before taxes are paid. It would be far more economical to finance the procedure through court-associated lawyers or an agency to supervise proceedings and provide arbiters. Finally, of course, both probate and real estate percentage fees should at the very least be replaced by hourly billing, to avoid windfall fees based on a few hours of work.

To corporate lawyers in big city law firms, minimum fee schedules and minimum percentages on estate work appear as relevant as wigs on British barristers. Those who daily toil for our largest corporations are not interested in squeezing out another $3,500 from unsuspecting clients. For they already obtain the kind of dazzling retainers that lawyers using minimum fee schedules can only dream about—a fact both George Smathers and Richard Nixon appreciate. "I'm going to be a Clark Clifford. That's the life for me," said Smathers gleefully in 1969 as he left the Senate for corporate practice in Washington. "A fellow with my background can make more money in thirty days out here than he can in fifteen years as a Senator." [32] When Richard Nixon was a mere corporate lawyer in New York City in the mid-1960s (he reportedly took a 33 percent cut in salary to become president at $200,000 a year), "he was struck by how easy it was, after all, for him to make money," according to the English authors of *The American Melodrama*.

> One story he told friends concerned a big corporation which came to him for advice about a plan to establish a division in France. They wanted his advice on the likelihood of political stability in France. Nixon, after some thought, told them simply that France would be stable while De Gaulle was alive, and he was much impressed to find that the clients were happy to part with twenty-five thousand dollars for this insight. [33]

Beyond such quotable admissions, hard information about the billings of leading corporate law firms such as Cravath, Swaine & Moore, Covington & Burling, or Kirkland, Ellis & Rowe are extremely difficult to obtain. Associates know almost nothing, beyond their ample annual salaries, about the balance sheets of their large law offices. And partners accord their billings a secrecy usually reserved for one's dalliances and income taxes—a secrecy which often extends to clients as well. Bills to regular clients at some firms are rendered as infrequently as once a year and are no more informative than saying "For legal services rendered from [date] to [date]." Few large corporate clients complain about such vagueness, and even fewer refuse to pay. Those that do are sometimes sued, but law firms shy away from this sort of thing. Among attorneys of means and stature it is considered gauche to sue over a fee—and foolish as well, since it could entail the disclosure of confidential information on the public record about a firm's billing practices. The bar reinforces this attitude of secrecy, explaining in a 1943 opinion that "suits to collect fees should be avoided. Only where circumstances imperatively require should resort be had to a suit to compel payment. And where a lawyer does resort to a suit to enforce payment of fees which involved a disclosure, he should carefully avoid any disclosure not clearly necessary to obtaining or defending his rights." [34]

Lawyers don't tell and bar groups don't study the size of corporate law fees. Still, due to disclosure requirements of the Securities and Exchange Commission, the Civil Aeronautics Board, and the Interstate Commerce Commission, as well as some investigative studies, one can assess preliminarily this gilt-edged corner of the profession.

In major city law firms of over 30 attorneys, which service those listed among *Fortune*'s top 1,000 companies, associates generally bill at $30 to $60 an hour and partners $60 to $150 an hour. The top unrebutted number mentioned is $250 an hour for (former judge) Simon Rifkind of Paul, Weiss, Rifkind, Wharton & Garrison ("and boy is he ever worth it!" adds an admiring associate at that firm).

With the legal meter running at these rates, enormous fees to business clients—fees passed on to the rest of us in the form of slightly higher product prices—are predictable. Several examples illustrate their magnitude. In 1971 First National City Corporation paid $2,210,000 in legal fees to Shearman & Sterling of New York City; Pennzoil United paid Baker & Botts of Houston $1,221,300; American Financial Corporation paid Keating, Muething & Klekamp of Cincinnati $1,159,730; of those companies filing so-called 10K annual reports at the SEC, at least twenty-five reported annual fees of over $500,000 to a law firm. [35]

CAB documents disclose that in 1973 Braniff Airways paid Arnold & Porter $524,206, Continental Airlines paid Hydeman & Mason $408,715, and American Airlines was billed $211,026 by Prather, Levenberg, Seeger, Doolittle, Farmer & Ewing to keep it out of trouble. On railroad matters, Lloyd Cutler and others at Wilmer, Cutler & Pickering, at $132 an hour, billed the United States Railway Association $268,146 in the first four months of 1974 for defending their client's constitutionality in court.

Covington & Burling represents the Penn-Central trustees during the bankruptcy proceedings of that floundering firm; and as creditors clamored for the railroad's money, C&B earned $890,633 and $301,000 out of Penn-Central's dwindling estate in 1972 and 1973.*

Why are billings so high? A lawyer doesn't have to be told in law school that you can charge a client worth $400 million more than one earning $40,000 a year. "There are so many zeros on the ends of the problems clients have," one Washington lawyer reported, that "when they're dealing in a $50 million business, what do they care about the fee?" [36]—a fee that is tax-deductible as well. And since both law firm and business firm realize that legal fees are usually such a small percentage of a business's costs, there is little resistance to big legal bills. This is especially true when the client's corporate life is at stake. Because an environmental lawsuit threatened to shut down Reserve Mining Company's iron-ore facility on Lake Superior, it gladly spent $5,854,658 for its legal defense between 1969 and 1974.[37] IBM reportedly is expending $20 million in its defense against the Justice Department's accusation that it is an illegal monopoly.

Legal proceedings can also get exquisitely complex and time-consuming. "This is a lawyer's dream," said a participant in the Penn-Central case. "It's like peeling an onion. For each skin of the onion you need a new lawyer." One SEC lawyer explained, in this connection, that "there's an enormous amount of duplication and make-work in bankruptcy cases. One lawyer writes a memo, numerous others review it, forty firms study it, and everybody petitions for compensation." [38] Aggravating complex proceedings is the built-in incentive for delay, since the more a lawyer works the more he makes. As one lawyer noted in an interview, "Antitrust is a game to private counsel. They think they can milk a client since they know it can take eight years for a resolution. They know no one will push them, so they take a free ride and travel around the country getting admissions and taking depositions. . . ." It should therefore be understandable when it takes the Federal Trade Commission a decade to stop Geritol's deceptive advertising or when it

* The size of such fees from a bankrupt organization has distressed some observers. ICC law judge John P. Dodge calculated what a reasonable hourly fee would be by comparing earnings of government and private lawyers and factoring in overhead and profit; he concluded it was $39 an hour, or less than one-half the fee charged by Covington's partners. In fact, for at least a three-month period in 1973, the ICC knocked down Covington's request for fees by 25 percent, from $125,347 to $95,000, because "the sum sought is not justified in light of the evidence at this time, particularly in view of the debtor's financial condition."

requires eight years for the Food and Drug Administration to persuade the peanut butter industry and their resolute lawyers to agree to a food identity standard.

Big stakes in complex proceedings, then, lead to big incomes. A 100-person law firm is likely to have an annual gross of some $10 million, which goes to associates in the form of fixed salaries and to partners according to their firm rank, work output, and client-getting abilities. The workers and rainmakers have been known to haggle over their respective partnership shares, each considering themselves the sine qua non of firm success, but this bartering occurs far from public view. Usually there is enough to go around so that disagreements do not escalate into wars.* The most renowned corporate lawyers—such as Clark Clifford for his lobbying and Simon Rifkind for his litigating—can easily earn up to half a million dollars annually. In Washington, D.C., reports John MacKenzie, "anywhere from one-fourth to one-half of a big firm's partners will reach six figures." [40]

With rewards like that, it is somewhat ironic that business attorneys have taken aim at the legal fees of a different target, one which, not uncoincidentally, encompasses those plaintiff lawyers whose mission it is to sue the clients of corporate lawyers.

Plaintiff lawyers—the best known are Harold Kohn and David Berger of Philadelphia, Abe Pomerantz of New York, and David Shapiro of Washington—often represent large classes of allegedly victimized individuals in antitrust or shareholders' derivative actions against business interests. Instead of a substantial fee per hour, they collect a large percentage of any settlement—*if* there is a settlement; and then they earn a reward only at the very end of their lawyering effort. If they should lose the case, they get nothing. To subsidize those cases they do lose and to keep up the payroll during the lean years between filing and settlement, plaintiffs' lawyers can earn huge fees in particular cases.

After a $5 million settlement of a shareholders' derivative suit against the Dreyfus Corporation in 1971, Abe Pomerantz, dean of the plaintiff's bar, asked for a $1.25 million fee, then turned down an offer of $900,000 by the settlement fund, and was finally awarded $750,000 by the court. In

---

* There has been a recent and stunning exception to this custom. Joel Dolkart, who was a senior partner in the prestigious New York City firm of Simpson, Thacher & Bartlett and who earned an estimated $150,000 to $200,000 annually, was criminally charged in October 1974 for walking off with a $1.5 million fee paid to the law firm. [19]

mid-1974 two San Francisco lawyers were awarded $3.2 million for seven years' work on a successful plaintiff antitrust case against the gypsum industry. Judge Alfonzo Zirpoli thought the award well deserved because the lawyers had recovered $67.6 million from the gypsum defendants "without benefit of an assist from the government" and because the price of fiberboard gypsum consequently fell 21 percent, saving American consumers $86 million a year. And in perhaps the largest antitrust class action ever, several major drug companies in 1970 agreed to pay $100 million for illegally fixing the price of tetracycline since 1954; the price then fell *90 percent*. For his six years and 35,000 hours of work, attorney David Shapiro and his law firm earned over $4 million.

Such fees have outraged judges and defense counsel. Judge Edward Lumbard of the Second Circuit Court of Appeals has written, "Obviously the only persons to gain from a class suit are not the potential plaintiffs, but the attorneys who represent them." [41] Several lawyers protesting the award of a large fee asked whether the Federal Rules of Civil Procedure "[were] designed to foster the interest of injured class members or to make millionaires of lawyers." [42] Judge Simon Rifkind, too, was concerned about bloated legal rewards. "Courts need [not] . . . compete with casinos by offering bonanzas that turn lawyers into millionaires overnight," [43] he complained.

To be sure, there are abuses. Plaintiffs' firms can reap inequitably large fees due to the probate syndrome: A percentage of a large sum can reap windfall profits far beyond the hours worked. In one recent class action *(City of Detroit v. Grinnell Corp.)* plaintiff counsel David Berger won a $10 million settlement and a $1.5 million fee, which came to an exorbitant $635 an hour—although a higher court overturned this fee. There is also the temptation, as years of litigation slip by, to abandon the client's long-term interest for the guarantee of at least some immediate fee. Writer Nick Kotz summarized this dilemma: "Private attorneys too often find it in their own financial interest to settle cases rather than to engage in protracted litigation with powerful industries." [44] Unethical plaintiff counsel can also engage in a kind of invisible bribe. In a recent massive bankruptcy case involving many plaintiff lawyers in New York City, one plaintiff attorney asked defense counsel to designate him the lead lawyer for all claimants, in return for which he would settle on favorable terms. Thus, the lawyer would sell out the interests of his client in order to garner the bulk of any class action settlement fee.

Still, at $250 an hour, watching former Judge Rifkind intone against large legal fees is not unlike Elmer Gantry denouncing sin. Students of legal economics agree that, over time, the fees and income of corporate defense counsel easily exceed the fees and income of their plaintiff counterparts—or, as a perhaps-piqued Harold Kohn put it, plaintiff's counsel would be quite willing to receive "one half of the fees for winning the case that the defendant's counsel get for losing it." [45] Judges regularly review fees in major class actions, which can usually discourage abusively large fees. A study in the *California Law Review* of fee awards in nineteen large civil antitrust cases demonstrated that compensation was not excessive: In only five of nineteen did lawyers earn over $40 an hour, and in only two did they earn over $60.[46] And one of these was the famous *TWA* v. *Hughes* case in which the Wall Street firm of Cahill, Gordon, based on a $7.5 million fee, netted an average hourly rate of $128.

Plaintiff fees labor under the double notoriety of being paid in one big lump and being publicly judged in court. Corporate defense fees, on the other hand, are paid periodically and privately, a situation not designed to arouse public curiosity or criticism. So while we should carefully monitor plaintiff fees for abuse, it would be good for business counsel, as well, to begin to scrutinize their own unexamined economic excesses.

High prices for any product or service are a costly burden in America today. But paying too much for soft drinks and bicycles is one thing; paying too much for lawyers is quite another. Usually there are substitute products for the soft drinks and bicycles of our lives. There is no substitute for legal justice. When citizens can no longer afford justice, a democratic society loses a part of its legitimacy.

Studies indeed indicate that lawyers have become an expensive entry barrier to justice. On the basis of various research projects conducted in the 1930s and 1940s in New Haven, Columbus, Chicago, and New York City, and by the U.S. Army, legal historian James Willard Hurst concluded in 1950 that "by a conservative estimate there was unsatisfied need for legal services among 'at least one third of all our citizens.' " [47] In 1965 Jerome Carlin and Jan Howard, analyzing the retention of lawyers in California, Texas, Iowa, Missouri, and Ohio, found that two-thirds of lower-class families had never employed a lawyer as compared to one-third of upper-class families; they noted that 70 percent of all lawyers represented clients with median incomes over $10,000, a category including less than 10 percent of our population.[48] A study commissioned by the American Bar Association reported in 1974 that one-third of all families surveyed had never used a lawyer, while another third had taken only one problem to one lawyer.[49] When the survey asked respondents if "the legal system favors the rich and powerful over everyone else," 56.8 percent agreed and 38.8 percent disagreed; when questioned whether "most lawyers charge more for their services than they are worth," 62 percent said yes and 29.5 percent no. "A regular civil trial today, with or without a jury," argues circuit court judge Shirley M. Hufstedler, "is beyond the economic reach of all except the rich, the nearly rich or the person seriously injured by a well-insured defendant."

Delivering reasonably priced legal justice will be far from easy. On the issue of excessive fees, especially, it is unlikely that bar "self-regulation" will be a tenacious watchman of the public interest. True, the *Code of Professional Responsibility* says that "A lawyer shall not enter into an agreement for, charge, or collect an illegal or clearly excessive fee," but this injunction alone has obviously proven inadequate. Going somewhat further, bar rules could require a lawyer to mention fees at the initial meeting with the client; one survey showed that while 80 percent of all the clients wanted lawyers to discuss fees in the first interview, at least 36 percent of the lawyers didn't. Personal legal expenses could be tax-deductible, like medical expenses. Fee arbitration boards comprised of lawyers and laymen could hear lawyer-client disputes over fees and resolve disagreements in public rulings—especially in those documentable situations, not discussed in this article, when lawyers simply steal from their clients.

Three final alternatives are all of sufficient importance that subsequent chapters by contributors Freedman, Lieberman, Lorenz, Moore, and Harris will explore them in more detail.

First, to the extent that courts require lawyers to do things that legal secretaries or state boards can readily do, clients pay something for nothing, or a 100 percent overcharge. Instead of this legal featherbedding, we need the expanded use of paraprofessionals, no-fault settlements of auto accident cases, no-fault divorce and adoption cases before statewide boards, and more *pro se* appearances (appearances by the interested party without a lawyer) before administrative agencies like zoning, unemployment compensation, or liquor control boards.

Second, bar restrictions against advertising and soliciting conspire with minimum fee schedules to discourage the availability of lower fees. These "ethical" restrictions should be dropped by the bar before the Justice

Department again stirs itself to file suit against this patently anti-competitive restriction.

Finally, consumer groups, if not the legal profession, must promote and implement low-cost legal services such as prepaid group services and class action rights. Rather than the traditional technique of "fee for service," these forms can deliver inexpensive legal services by reaping the efficiencies of group practice.* Instead of a thousand union members separately searching for lawyers they can afford, let them join together to hire on salary a panel of their own attorneys; instead of a thousand consumers each suffering because $100 fraud doesn't justify a $500 lawyer, let them merge themselves into a collective lawsuit to seek justice as a commonly victimized class. The efficiencies of low-cost operations are a matter of course in business, and cannot long be kept from a profession merely because its members like to be at the top of the economic structure. Before lawyers suffer the obloquy of medical colleagues who fought prepayment plans as "socialistic," they should begin to appreciate the difference between doing well and doing good.

---

* Savings for consumers can be dramatic. While an uncontested divorce can cost $300 in most areas, it cost $182 under Wisconsin Judicare, $58 under Colorado Rural Legal Services (CRLS), and $38 under Upper Peninsula Legal Services in Michigan (UPLS). A bankruptcy can easily cost $500 today, but under the Wisconsin plan it goes for $226, and for only $181 and $45 respectively under CRLS and UPLS.[50]

*David Riley**

The Mystique of Lawyers

HE BIG EVENT in second grade was going to the police station. The policemen were very nice to us. They smiled and explained things and showed us a jail cell that I was afraid to stand in for very long. Then they showed us the electric chair. I remember that the most: dark steel, leather straps, square, silent. It was where you would go if you disobeyed the law badly enough.

The big event twenty years later during the 1971 May Day antiwar protest was to get arrested. It meant we had broken the mystique of the law instilled in us from the beginning of our middle-class upbringing. When a policeman dragged me by the hair to the paddy wagon and bonked me on the head before throwing me in, I knew that the law was only human.

There's another way to break the mystique of the law: Go to law school. There you learn about the faulty reasoning of judges and lawyers, the prejudice of juries, and how Supreme Court decisions can veer and zigzag according to the makeup of the Court and the mood of the country.

But most citizens do not go to law school or get arrested in antiwar demonstrations. One way or another, they do go to the police station in the second grade, and though they may sometimes lose respect for individual policemen, lawyers, and even judges, their inner reverence for the law remains unshaken. This is especially true in a country whose Constitution is a sacred document, enshrined in our National Archives, where 750,000 Americans pay homage to it every year.[1] People's reverence for the rule of law depends upon their belief that law is a higher entity: a body of thought, based on universal truths tested through the ages, by which we are all bound to act for the common good.[2] If everyone

* DAVID RILEY IS A WRITER WHO GRADUATED FROM GEORGE WASHINGTON UNIVERSITY LAW SCHOOL, HAS WORKED WITH LAWYERS, WRITTEN ABOUT THEM, AND BEEN A CLIENT.

stopped and calculated whether to obey every specific law, we would have chaos.

The problem is that while we all instinctively carry on this great tradition of the Rule of Law, we also live our daily lives. Rather than ponder this great tradition, we think about suing the builder over the roof that leaks. Law has a dual nature: On the one hand, it is the noble tradition of transcending our selfish petty needs; on the other, it nags, scratches, and yells to get the leaks fixed—to accomplish our selfish petty needs over the other guy's. Judges sit on elevated platforms, and are called "Your Honor." And they get up in the morning and put on underpants, and if they yell at their spouse on sentencing day, someone might spend a couple of extra years in jail.

The law's dual nature contributes to the layman's ambivalent attitude toward the law and lawyers. We know the law is a precious spirit among us, and we sense that lawyers have a special connection to that spirit. We select them to write our constitutions, and elect them to run our governments. We rely on them at every step in our business dealings, as in the constant refrain "I'll have to check with my lawyer first." Yet we also distrust lawyers. We think of the legal profession as an honored tradition, and we think of individual lawyers as shysters out to make money off our troubles.[3]

Watergate was one of the most dramatic examples of our ambivalent attitude toward the law and lawyers: to root out corruption among lawyer-officials at the highest level of government, we relied on judges and lawyers acting as special prosecutors. With every new revelation of wrongdoing, just as many commentators commended our legal system for uncovering the evil as condemned it for its corruption. While Watergate defendants tarnished the image of the legal profession, Watergate prosecutors and judges enhanced it. And like most developments in government, Watergate increased the power and influence of lawyers, whose services are ever more in need as our political machinery gets ever more complex.

The lawyers' dual role in our culture creates a social and personal mystique around them that is almost never looked at critically, either by lawyers or by sociologists.[4] Everyone knows lawyers play a very important role in our society, and people have a gut feeling that this is a good or a bad thing. But few look at how that role is played and what's good or bad about it. The law is researched *ad nauseam* by students, teachers, and practitioners. Every self-respecting law school fills a thousand law review pages a year with articles bearing titles like "Some Aspects of a Preliminary Analysis of Section 14b of the National Labor Relations Act, as Amended by the Eightieth Congress, and its Effect on Collective Bargaining in North Carolina." Some articles have a broader scope than this, some narrower.

Meanwhile important matters go unexamined. The closer a topic gets to an honest look at the role of lawyers in our society, the less research is done on it. When lawyers have looked at the legal profession, it has almost always been image polishing or figuring out how to make more money while serving the public interest.[5] Beyond the image and the retainer fee problems, the social role of lawyers is an undiscovered field for investigation. This article on the mystique of lawyers is a little push of the plow in that fallow field so long covered by the bar's verbal blanket of bovine solid waste.

"An order as old as the magistracy, as noble as virtue, as necessary as justice," is how D'Aguesseau described the legal profession in law texts.[6] Lawyers are generally very practical people, but that doesn't keep them from expressing in such soaring phrases their esteem for their profession, which they tend to look upon as a secular priesthood. Even Justice Oliver Wendell Holmes, about as unsanctimonious a jurist as the law could ever expect, once told the Suffolk Bar Association: "If we are to speak of the law as our mistress, we who are here know that she is a mistress only to be wooed with sustained and lonely passion—only to be won by straining all the faculties by which man is most likest to a god." [7]

Holmes didn't explain what he meant by that; he didn't have to for the Suffolk Bar Association. The priestly mantle of lawyers comes from being the profession in charge of interpreting the higher law that we all live under. At least since Thomas Aquinas called law that part of the mind of God discoverable by the right reason of man,[8] the most distinguished interpreters of the law have seemed to sit as God's righthand men, dispensing the social wisdom of the mind, as doctors dispense the wisdom of the body and ministers the wisdom of the spirit.

These three ancient "learned professions"—law, medicine, and divinity—all have a mystique about them. Their practitioners' business is not just to make a buck, but to serve us all by dispensing wisdom and virtue, which they swear to do according to a higher standard of conduct than we hold ourselves to in our self-seeking daily lives. The word "profession" comes from the Middle English "profess," meaning bound by a vow, originally applied to religious orders. And a "layman" is one of the laity, or in its Greek origin one of the people, as distinguished from the clergy.[9] A professional professes to have some special knowledge that others lack and to offer it to us for the benefit of the whole community, or—that mystical phrase—in the public interest.

We laymen put the most precious things we have—our liberty, our livelihood, and our lives—in the hands of professionals. We trust them to cure our cancer, win our freedom, save our eyesight, get our divorce, keep us sane, and absolve us of our sins. We give them the power of God to make, ruin, and even end our lives.

Of the three original professions, medicine is the most purely scientific, by its nature less involved in the ordering of society than the law. Over the last hundred years since the Industrial Revolution, religion has declined and commerce has become our cultural motif. As a result, the social power of the ministry has shrunk to a fraction of what it was, and the lawyers—whose work affects all aspects of our commercial, political, and personal lives—have become the top priestly class in social power.

During the colonial era, lawyers played a key role in the political organization of the country (thirty-three of the fifty-six signers of the Declaration of Independence were lawyers). Then there was a populist reaction to the prominence of lawyers. Kentucky debated a constitutional amendment barring the existence of the legal profession, and Indiana passed one that said any man of good character could practice law.[10] Other states lowered the standards for admission to the bar and established the popular election of judges.

After the Civil War the bar grew in power as lawyers played a key role in organizing the business structure of the country and inventing the trusts. Lawyers also began to organize into associations, and to raise the standards of training and, at least on paper, the ethical conduct of the bar. Though the image got better, the reality in some ways got worse: Many of the best lawyers became the captives of their own creation, the corporation. Justice Louis Brandeis and Chief Justice Harlan Stone made their well-known criticism that the profession had become, in Stone's harsh assessment, "the obsequious servant of business." [11] Even as Stone spoke, though, lawyers were playing a key role in the New Deal's efforts to curb the excesses of capital. Up through the contemporary civil rights and ecology movements and Watergate, the profession has, in its most publicized work, kept its split personality of being prominent both in reform movements and in conserving the status quo.

Today we live with the legacies of the colonial, populist, and industrial eras. Lawyers continue to wield disproportionate power in society,[12] and continue to be distrusted by many. But popular resentment against them has had only a limited political effect, partly because the bar's most visible work is also its most appealing to the public: courageous attorneys dramatically prosecuting criminals or defending the persecuted in public trials. Meanwhile, the work of the vast majority of lawyers on behalf of business is mostly hidden in the confines of law firms and corporate house counsel offices, where contracts are drafted, corporate structures are designed, government agencies and legislatures are influenced, and other unseen legal and illegal fixes flash along the telephone lines to keep the wheels of society rolling.[13]

The law and its practitioners have always played a particularly central role in American life. As Tocqueville wrote long ago, "Scarcely any question arises which does not become, sooner or later, a subject of judicial debate." [14] So accepted is the prominent role of lawyers that, as Anthony Lewis pointed out, no one even noticed that one of the country's greatest political crises, the impeachment of Richard Nixon, was conducted in courtrooms and in Congress by lawyers who decided the procedures, dug for the evidence, argued the prosecution and defense, and, in our lawyer-dominated legislature, voted to decide the outcome. According to Lewis:

> Americans have been turning political issues into questions of law and the Constitution for so long that we no longer realize how unusual that is. The reach of the federal government and the states, the right to limit slavery and then protect the freed blacks, the power to tax and spend—all these and a hundred other great political problems have been tested in terms of law in our history.
>
> No other country does such things. Just now the British have had what they call a "constitutional" dilemma: whether Prime Minister Heath should resign after an inconclusive general election. But no one in Britain would have dreamt of putting the question to a court. . . .[15]

Having made social issues into legal ones, we then conclude that lawyers are best qualified to handle them. When Senate majority leader Mike Mansfield thought about whom to appoint to the Senate Watergate

Committee, his first decision was that all its members should be lawyers (and they were).[16] Somehow legal expertise was considered essential for senators investigating the political morality of a president and his reelection campaign.

The mystique of lawyers, like most mystiques, is based partly on truth and partly on myth. The truth lies in the fact that lawyers' special knowledge of the Constitution and the legal system *is* relevant to political decisions about the ordering of society. The myth, an exaggeration of the truth, lies in the way that specific expertise somehow becomes a general wisdom about human affairs. In fact, wisdom may be limited by the experience of lawyering, as Thoreau believed:

> Statesmen and legislators, standing so completely within the institution, never nakedly behold it. They speak of moving society, but have no resting-place without it. . . . Webster never goes behind government, and so cannot speak with authority about it . . . his quality is not wisdom, but prudence. The lawyer's truth is not Truth, but consistency or a consistent expediency.[17]

Lawyers are dispensers of law more as a practical commodity than as an age-old wisdom; they practice law more as a livelihood than as a profession. The nobler notions of law and lawyers in our minds have a definite psychological and financial effect on us, but they are not the basic reality of our legal system.[18] The reality is that the mystique of lawyers converts into the income of businessmen. Like other professionals, lawyers make money by being part of an honored profession that stands for something nobler than making money. True, some lawyers do practice law as a profession in the sense of working for the public interest. There is a long tradition of public service in the bar. But for every Brandeis or Darrow or Kunstler who gives up profitable private practice for public interest work, there are thousands of lawyers who earn their livelihood dispensing their special knowledge to private interests for the highest fees they can get, and do little else, as Mark Green's essay, "The Gross Legal Product," elaborates.[19]

Just as lawyering in America today is basically a livelihood, so the law is basically a commodity through which we measure our status and regulate our relations. Virtually all lawyers agree that law is not synonymous with justice, that some laws are just and others unjust, and still others become unjust because of changed conditions or the way they are administered. Justice Holmes offered this dry-eyed definition of the law: "The prophecies of what the courts will do in fact, and nothing more pretentious, are what I mean by the law." [20] Seen in this way, the law, like money, is a commodity through which power, justice, and chance regulate our affairs. Sometimes justice is done, often power prevails, and chance always affects what happens. The law as practiced is no more noble than a commodity, which is defined by Webster as "that which affords convenience or profit, esp. in commerce," or "an element of wealth, an economic good." [21]

Lawyers object to this view of the law on the ground that the adversary system is a higher value which rises above the economic vagaries of society and must be perpetuated at all costs—most of them paid by clients. Under the theory of the adversary system, the two opposing lawyers vigorously present their version of the truth within the rules worked out; out of that clash, the real truth will emerge and justice will be done, or the closest we can come to it. Lawyers, it is assumed, are not to be concerned with the final truth and justice of the matter, which is the direct concern of only judge and jury. Lawyers thus play an essential but conceptually secondary role in this roundabout process of finding truth and justice, which may be, as Churchill once said of democracy, the worst system except all the others that have been tried.

Lawyers in the adversary system can thus rise above judgments about the justness of their clients' activities which they protect and promote, though it doesn't raise them above living off the fees generated by those activities. When environmental activists criticized the tactics of General Motors lawyers in pollution matters a few years ago, established lawyers like Lloyd Cutler and Abe Fortas objected that any association of attorneys with the merits of their clients' positions endangers the right of everyone, however unfavorably viewed in the public eye, to be vigorously represented by an attorney.[22] The argument equates activists criticizing lawyers who represent GM (with a gross income greater than most countries and a legal staff of hundreds) with Senator Joseph McCarthy in the fifties criticizing lawyers who represented persecuted, pallid leftists (who as a result had trouble finding anyone to represent them).

The obvious problem with such reasoning is that it ignores the social context in which the adversary system operates. Lawyers have long practiced this kind of social ostrich-ism.[23] If they hadn't, they might see that the social conditions necessary for the adversary system to produce justice do not exist in the United States. The one undeniably necessary condition is that the two opposing sides be relatively equal in strength.

"Obviously, if one side is much stronger than the other, a correct determination will not come out of the conflict but only the answer that power can impose," a criminal lawyer explains. "Anything that tends to build up one side as opposed to the other, or anything that tends to weaken one side, is detrimental to the adversary system." [24] Our legal profession's manning of the adversary system is extremely detrimental to it: We provide topnotch lawyers for some, mediocre lawyers for others, and none at all for most—as contributors Tucker, Conyers, and Lorenz make clear. If the profession were to provide counsel with roughly equal qualifications and resources for everyone, it would take a complete restructuring of the bar, undoubtedly with sharp limits on the amount lawyers could make.

But providing equal counsel would be only one step among many toward equality before the law. There is the far deeper problem of equal economic and political power to influence the making and administering of the laws that operate in adversary proceedings. Even before such proceedings have a chance to operate formally, the effect of economic power on the legal system can be crucial:

- When Chicago's steel companies said it would take eight years to comply with the city's air pollution law, the Air Pollution Department gave the companies the eight-year variance they wanted, citing, as usually happens in such cases, the industry's economic importance to the city: "Over 100,000 persons are directly dependent upon these companies for their livelihood. . . . [S]teel operations . . . add nearly three billion dollars to the Chicagoland economy." [25] This legal decision, based on a controlling economic factor, was made in administrative hearings before the matter ever got to an adversary proceeding in court. If it had gotten there, the result would have been not a strictly legal contest between two relatively equal sides, but a clash in a legal setting between the economic power of the industry and the political power of the city government.

- When William Vanderbilt's worth was discovered after his death to have been grossly underappraised, the New York City tax commissioners tried to force the Vanderbilt estate to make good on what it owed the city. The Vanderbilts' lawyer informed the city that if it pushed his clients too hard, they would simply switch their holdings to nontaxable securities—and thus impoverish the city's tax base. The dispute predictably ended in compromise and never reached the courts.[26] Again economic power dictated a legal decision that was made outside an adversary proceeding, as happens daily in huge areas of legal work done out of court, reflecting the unequal power of the parties in dispute. When Vanderbilt sues Vanderbilt or Jones sues Jones, then the sides may be relatively equal, and the adversary system can operate fairly. But it does not operate fairly when Vanderbilt and Jones both face New York. Then the same rules apply to situations with vastly different underlying, and often controlling, economic and political realities. As the British put it, "The courts are open to all—like the Savoy Hotel." [27]

The economic setting has at least as much effect on criminal law as civil. The effect of poverty and unequal opportunity on crime and law enforcement in the ghetto has been repeatedly documented. A policeman says it's hard to be a law officer in the ghetto "because we send the kids to school and teach them about rights and then put them back in the neighborhood. I think we either ought to get rid of these neighborhoods or stop teaching these kids about their rights." [28] After conducting exhaustive studies on how to improve our criminal justice system, the National Crime Commission "doubts that even a vastly improved criminal justice system can substantially reduce crime if society fails to make it possible for each of its citizens to feel a personal stake in it." [29] In other words, the legal system will not work as it's supposed to—to deter crime—unless the economic and political systems work as they're supposed to—to provide equal opportunity.

You have to isolate the adversary system from the social conditions that shape it to believe there is equality before the law. Though the social foundation for it does not exist, the adversary system remains deified. Lawyers tend to enshrine it and the legal system in general, like an isolated icon on a special shelf in their minds. They see the law as perhaps affected by "social policy considerations," but not as an integral part of the social system. [30]

If lawyers really saw law as an integral part of society, they would have to take social justice as seriously as they take legal reasoning. That might bring about a real revolution; at least it would help us look a lot harder at the social injustice of a system that treats the unequal equally before the law—in the name of justice. The system operates on the same theory that the robber barons used in claiming the mom-and-pop store on the corner had the same right to crush them as they had to crush it.

This legal laissez-faire attitude leaves the mystique of the law and lawyers intact in the minds of laymen. The mystique shrouds from our view the law's social injustice, while it emblazons in our minds the law's noble phrases. As the late chief justice Earl Warren once described it:

> Over the entrance to our Supreme Court Building in bold letters are chiseled the words, "Equal Justice Under Law." How wonderful it would be if we could in honesty say that we had achieved that great objective. However, so long as any Americans are living in abject poverty in squalid slums; so long as any child is denied an education; so long as opportunities to develop are denied to any segment of our society; so long as there is more than one class of citizenship and anyone is denied the right to participate in the affairs of his government; in short, so long as we fail to treat others as we would have them treat us, we cannot say in honesty that we actually have achieved equal justice under law.[31]

The mystique of lawyers applies to their personality as well as their role in society. The personal mystique of lawyers, like the social one, is based partly on truth and partly on myth. It is true that lawyers' training and experience develop independence of mind, skepticism, ability to reason, articulateness, and other intellectual virtues of value to clients and to society. The myth, an exaggeration of the truth, lies in the way these specific qualities are expanded to endow a lawyer's whole personality with more trustworthiness. In fact, the opposite may be true if we accept Plato's belief that the lawyer

> . . . has become keen and shrewd; he has learned how to flatter his master in word and indulge him in deed; but his soul is small and unrighteous. . . . from the first he has practiced deception and retaliation, and has become stunted and warped. And so he has passed out of youth into manhood, having no soundness in him; and is now, as he thinks, a master in wisdom.[32]

The useful traits of lawyers, like independence of mind and articulateness, are mainly technical, neutral virtues, not substantive qualities. They are the tools of the mind and have little to do with its disposition, which determines how the mind is used. If lawyering develops the technical virtues of the mind, it can also induce a negative disposition of the spirit among its practitioners—a disposition to be money-minded, contentious, and emotionally and ethically unaccountable for their actions. Some lawyers develop that disposition more than others, of course; some mix their negative disposition with a sense of fairness and other positive qualities.[33]

But the negative disposition remains something of the model lawyer's trademark. Money, being central to society, is central to law. In law school students flock to the standard four credit courses in commercial transactions and tax law that develop moneymaking skills. They stay away in droves from the minor two credit courses in jurisprudence, social policy, and ethics that develop a sense of justice. Professionals like doctors and plumbers make money by knowing how to manage bodies and pipes; lawyers make money by knowing how to manage money, which is why Veblen felt they typified man's primitive, predatory, pecuniary instincts. Success in the legal profession, he wrote, is "accepted as marking a large endowment of that barbarian astuteness which has always commanded men's respect and fear." [34]

A second well-known occupational hazard of lawyers is their tendency to become contentious, and to develop such associated traits as being arrogant, deceitful, and punitive. Chicago law dean Soia Mentschikoff tells the wives of first-year law students: "Your husbands are going to change: their personalities are going to change in law school. They'll get more aggressive, more hostile, more precise, more impatient." [35] Law school develops an imperious impatience toward people with cobwebs in their minds. The constant atmosphere of contest and debate puts a premium on one-upmanship and a zero value on modesty. Law school is the one place of learning where an appropriate "I don't know" is almost never heard in the classroom, out of fear of professorial ridicule and the need to display the appearance of competence and confidence. Law schools like the one I attended are one of the few secular institutions where the professor teaches the equal rights of man from a raised platform. The contentious, imperious atmosphere of the law leads to experiences like that of Henry Miller, who describes how laws "aggressively insist that the aggressive should be aggressively eliminated, thus establishing the right by means of outwronging the wrong-doer." [36]

For all the blaming the law does, the practice of it often has the curious subterranean effect of relieving both lawyer and client from a full sense of responsibility for their actions. Many lawyers serve the function of carrying the guilt of their clients who want their lawyer to assuage the dim thought in the back of their mind that they may have done something wrong. "The only satisfied client," says David Riesman, who has practiced and taught law, "is the one who has convinced himself—with your help—that *you* are the thief, the conniver, the guilty party." [37] In the rough-and-tumble of our adversary process, lawyers may also act out their clients' hostility for them, dishing out the nastiness the client feels toward the other side. This both rattles the opponent and calms the client, who gets his licks in without having to express his anger himself.

But clients also act out for their lawyers, who get the psychic or financial benefit of promoting their clients' actions, without having to suffer the political or legal consequences of them. Clients may risk their liberty or even their lives crusading for a cause, while their lawyers can feel they are working for the cause by speaking in courtrooms that they walk out of free to go home every night.[38] In another arena, corporate lawyers personally benefit from promoting their clients' lucrative businesses, but don't personally suffer from the anti-business hostility of the public or politicians. Though lawyers may not be identified with clients in the public mind, that does not keep them from identifying with them in their own minds, as several writers suggest.[39] Lawyers may subconsciously identify with clients who get back at their wives in divorce suits, swindle the masses in a business deal, or take on the establishment. Lawyers are nuts-and-bolts men and naturally skeptical of such psychological speculation. But as practitioners of the law—whose every aspect is highly symbolic, from the judge's robes to the very concept of legal sanction—lawyers should know that all action has a symbolic side to it, including their own.

Having it both ways—identifying with clients when it benefits them but not when it doesn't—applies to lawyers' accountability for their ethical conduct too. The profession promotes the idea that it disciplines itself, but in fact it doesn't. Under the ABA's self-policing code, lawyers are accountable to their own consciences as the "touchstone" for guiding their conduct. Many lawyers do have a sense of their responsibility as professionals to a certain standard of conduct. But when attorneys' consciences fade, almost no disciplinary action is taken to enforce the code, except in well-publicized cases like that of Spiro Agnew and high-level Watergate criminality, as Chapter 4 has elaborated.

Self-accountability is a noble notion. In fact it is the basis of the inner respect by individuals for the rule of law that society needs to function. It is the essence of the spirit of the law that spiritual leaders like Confucius and Gandhi, after careers in law, came to emphasize in their teaching as the internal discipline that supersedes external law.[40]

Thus it is that many lawyers, so caught up in the worldly ways of practicing their profession, are prime violators of the best in the tradition of law. Practicing law can minimize their emotional and ethical accountability to themselves. Though the whole purpose of the law is to temper man's meanness and teach us to accommodate each other's desires, law is taught in an imperious, competitive atmosphere, and practiced with a premium on money-hungry contention and strife.

The work of the lawyers, charged with keeping society running smoothly, cultivates in them and in us qualities that keep us at each others' throats. The profession, identified through history with passing on the highest reason and nurturing the nobility of man, often in practice encourages our lowest instincts. That is why Jesus told the lawyers they were no better than the Pharisees, but they were too busy manipulating his words to hear what he said:

> Alas for your lawyers! You have taken away the key of knowledge. You did not go in yourselves, and those who were on their way in, you stopped.
> After he had left the house, the lawyers and Pharisees began to assail him fiercely and to ply him with a host of questions, laying snares to catch him with his own words.[41]

Periodically people get fed up with lawyers and eliminate them. The conquering barbarians did it in Rome, the American populists did it, and the Communists have done it (so far with success in the relatively young revolutions of Cuba and China). Thomas More abolished lawyers in his Utopia, and Yale law professor Fred Rodell largely urged it in the 1930s. Jeremy Bentham made more modest proposals in eighteenth-century England and succeeded somewhat in simplifying and de-mystifying the law.[42]

But two thousand years of history show a pattern of reforming the law and sometimes eliminating lawyers, and then having them and their evils grow up again. If we are destined to repeat that pattern, it must be because lawyers and their ways, however objectionable, reflect something deep in us. It is after all our money that they are minding, our fights that they are waging, and our actions for which they assume the burden of guilt, as much as we assume theirs. We have struck a bargain with the lawyers that benefits us both—if seen in our limited perspective of getting along in the world, without fundamentally changing it. We go on fighting and grabbing, largely unaware of other ways of being. We think it inevitable that people be as grabby as we are. Our economy, based on that assumption, is serviced by lawyers who help keep us stuck on this level of living, while the noble phrases of the law remind us that we can transcend it.

Lawyers stride across our social landscape with one hand toward the sky and the other in the gutter. But whatever we say about our lawyers, we can also say about ourselves. Most of our law, like most of our life, is learned and practiced in a mundane manner, sugared over by a vague sense of our own nobility, which we would rather believe in than act on. But if we are ever to have social peace that is more than fleeting, we will have to haul our "impractical" ideals of justice and charity down from the sky as we reach for them with our feet cemented in the ground. We will need not a mystique about our ideals, but a workable belief in them as *practical* standards, thoroughly livable in our everyday lives.

*Monroe H. Freedman**

Advertising and Soliciting:
The Case for Ambulance Chasing

RNEST GENE GUNN, a five-year-old boy, was seriously injured as a result of negligent driving attributed to John J. Washek. Shortly after the accident, an adjuster from Mr. Washek's insurance company visited the boy's mother at their home. The adjuster told her that there was no need then to retain an attorney because the company would make a settlement as soon as the boy was out of his doctor's care; if Ms. Gunn was not satisfied at that time, she could retain an attorney and file suit.

The boy's injuries were sufficiently severe to require a doctor's care for twenty-three months. At the end of that time Ms. Gunn made repeated efforts to reach the insurance company adjuster, but without success. She then retained a lawyer, who promptly filed suit for her. Ms. Gunn's boy never did have his day in court, however, because the attorneys for the insurance company successfully pleaded a two-year statute of limitations.[1]

A case such as the Gunns' raises two important issues of professional responsibility, neither of which has ever been adequately confronted by the organized bar.

If counsel for the insurance company did not know of the adjuster's actions, then it would not have been unprofessional to raise the defense of the statute of limitations. A client is entitled to have the benefit of the presentation of any lawful defense.[2] But it would have been entirely proper—indeed, ethically required—for counsel at least to have urged the company to forego pleading the statutory bar because of the unjust

* MONROE FREEDMAN IS THE DEAN AND PROFESSOR OF LAW AT HOFSTRA UNIVERSITY LAW SCHOOL. HE IS CHAIRMAN OF THE LEGAL ETHICS COMMITTEE OF THE DISTRICT OF COLUMBIA BAR, A MEMBER OF THE BOARD OF DIRECTORS OF THE AMERICAN CIVIL LIBERTIES UNION, AND THE AUTHOR OF THE TEXTBOOK *Contracts* (1973) AND OF *Lawyers' Ethics in an Adversary System* (1975), FROM WHICH THIS ARTICLE IS ADAPTED.

circumstances of the case.[3] Moreover, an attorney would be justified in refusing to accept a retainer in such a case because, contrary to popular belief, an attorney has no obligation to take a case (as distinguished from continuing in a case already underway) that would require acting in a way offensive to his or her personal judgment.[4]

Yet what if counsel was, in advance, aware of (or prompted) the adjuster's actions? For a lawyer to participate in a scheme to trick a lay person out of effective representation of counsel would constitute counseling or assisting the client in fraudulent conduct in violation of DR 7-102(A)(7) of the *Code of Professional Responsibility*.[5] There is some reason to believe, however, that it is not uncommon for some lawyers, acting alone or in connivance with insurance adjusters, to take advantage of claimants' ignorance and to mislead them into foregoing legal rights. Yet it is rare that a lawyer has been disciplined for such perversion of professional knowledge and skills.

On the contrary, bar discipline has worked to *restrict* lay persons' knowledge of their rights and their access to legal redress. For example, not long after Ms. Gunn had lost her fight to overcome the effects of the insurance adjuster's deceitful actions, the Committee of Censors of the Philadelphia Bar Association undertook a $125,000 investigation—not of insurance adjusters, but of "unethical" solicitation of clients by plaintiffs' lawyers. The resulting report recognized the need on behalf of plaintiffs "to counter the activity of [insurance] carriers' adjusters," but casually suggested that the problem could be dealt with "by the exercise of restraint on the part of carriers." [6] The report also acknowledged the propriety and "social value" of automobile-wrecking companies listening to police calls in order to be the first to arrive at accident scenes to carry off the damaged vehicles, but it found "no justification" at all in a similar effort directed toward protecting the legal rights of the injured people.[7]

The basis for disciplinary action that interferes with lawyers' efforts to advise people of their rights is, of course, the ABA code strictures against advertising and solicitation.[8] Those provisions continue long-standing rules against maintenance, champerty, and barratry—commonly referred to as ambulance chasing or stirring up litigation.

A common justification for such rules is that advertising would lead to abuses such as false and misleading claims. Why lawyers would be more prone to engage in that kind of dishonesty, however, than are sellers of other services or of commodities has never been articulated. Nor has it been explained why it is feasible to regulate the size and content of professional cards and building directories, which is done now, but impossible to regulate false and misleading advertising by lawyers. On the other hand, the principal purpose of the anti-solicitation rules is clear: the limitation of competition among lawyers. One illustration involves a case permitting a bar association to advertise its lawyer-referral service in a newspaper.[9] The court expressly justified its decision on the ground that the real evil in advertising is competition among lawyers, which is not present when the bar advertises as a whole.[10]

It is not surprising, therefore, that a number of leading critics consider the anti-solicitation rules unrelated to professional ethics, but rather, as Harvard law professor Andrew Kaufman calls them, "the rules of a guild." [11] That is, they are directed against competition rather than for the maintenance of moral standards in the public interest. Other authorities have also emphasized the effect of those rules in protecting established lawyers and large firms from undesired competition from young lawyers and small firms.[12]

Still, there are those who object that advertising for clients would "degrade the profession," and the ABA code informs us that "history has demonstrated that public confidence in the legal system is best preserved by strict, self-imposed controls over, rather than by unlimited, advertising" [13]—although no historical reference is provided to support that assertion. Similarly, the Philadelphia report noted earlier suggests that solicitation of clients in violation of the rules has led to intense public dissatisfaction with the bar.[14] In fact, the opposite may be true—that is, that dissatisfaction with the bar stems in major part from lawyers' aloofness, and from their failure to reach out to those whom they claim to serve.

For example, in a survey conducted by the two law professors at the University of Edinburgh for the Law Society of Scotland, people were asked whether they would resent or welcome an attorney who approached them to offer legal services in six situations (e.g., if you were in an accident; if you were considering buying a house; if you were going into a new business venture; etc.). The study revealed that less than two percent of the people in the survey would resent an attorney's contact, while about half would welcome the unrequested offer of services by an attorney in all six cases.[15] The least well educated people were those who, most of all, would welcome being solicited by attorneys. The study concludes:

> The extraordinarily high proportions of people who would welcome the solicitor's initiating contact on the different situations we have posed must

seriously question many commonly held assumptions about the correct stance for members of the profession. Taken with the data noted which showed that few members of the public have adequate knowledge of the services solicitors could provide, and would like to know about these (i.e., want more advertisement), there is a coherent and very emphatic call for a more active and positive legal profession.[16]

It seems, therefore, that nobody is in favor of solicitation except the public. One is left wondering in whose eyes, and by what standard of ethics or esthetics, the profession would be "degraded" by responding to that public need. Those who object to solicitation of clients are typically unaware that the ABA strictures against this are themselves only minor exceptions to the more fundamental rule of professional responsibility expressed in Canon 2 of the *Code of Professional Responsibility*: "A lawyer should assist the legal profession in fulfilling its duty to make legal counsel available." The code thus recognizes an affirmative obligation of the profession to provide access to the legal system—and that access, presumably, is for the benefit of all people, not just a select few.

The solicitation limitation appears in the *Code of Professional Responsibility*'s Disciplinary Rules. Rule 2-104 reads, in part: "A lawyer who has given unsolicited advice to a layman that he should obtain counsel or take legal action shall not accept employment resulting from that advice. . . ." Rule 2-103 says: "A lawyer shall not recommend employment as a private practitioner of himself, his partner, or associate to a non-lawyer who has not sought his advice."

Those rules appear on the first reading to be broad and absolute. But they are practically meaningless—at least for a particular class of lawyers and clients—because of special exceptions to the anti-solicitation rules. For example, Rule 2-104 provides further: "A lawyer [who has volunteered advice] may accept employment by a close friend, relative, [or a] former client. . . ." This refinement means that those who are accustomed to retain lawyers, say for their tax or estates work, and those who have attorneys as relatives and friends, are the kind of people who can be solicited despite the rule. As to that socioeconomic class of people, there is no impropriety in solicitation. In addition, consistent with DR 2-104, many lawyers take a tax deduction for membership fees in country clubs, on the ground that such fees are an ordinary and necessary business expense—i.e., a means for discreetly soliciting business. One prominent federal judge resigned from several exclusive clubs upon going to the bench because, he told friends, he no longer needed to attract clients.

Another approved device for soliciting clients is the law list, such as in the impressive volumes of *Martindale-Hubbell*. This is purely and simply a self-laudatory advertisement, euphemistically called a "card" and directed to potential clients. Yet not every attorney is permitted to advertise his or her professional autobiography, prestigious associations, and important clients in *Martindale-Hubbell*. One must await an invitation from the publisher to apply for an "a" rating, which can be achieved only upon submission of favorable references from sixteen judges and attorneys who have themselves already received an "a" rating. For all other members of the profession, *Martindale-Hubbell* is a closed book.

A similar service is *The Attorneys' Register*. Its brochure boasts that the register holds a certificate of compliance from the American Bar Association and explains that "the primary purpose of *The Attorneys' Register* is to continue to be a valuable forwarding medium aimed at securing SUBSTANTIAL legal business for our listees. . . ." (The word "substantial" is written in capital letters throughout the brochure.) Further, it offers the attorney "an opportunity to be recognized in association with other reputable members of the Bar," and the publishers promise that they will do "everything they properly can to encourage active forwardings to our listees." The brochure also provides a partial list of "important corporations which . . . have requested, and will receive, a copy of our current edition . . . for use when seeking qualified . . . counsel." The list contains about a hundred corporations, including Abbott Laboratories, American Sugar, Continental Can, Du Pont, General Electric, and U.S. Plywood—corporations that will look for the attorney's name and qualifications in the paid advertisement in the register. In addition, the register is distributed free to "a careful selection of banks and trust companies, important industrial corporations, insurance companies, financing institutions, and the like, who are believed to be prolific forwarders of SUBSTANTIAL legal matters."

That is the way solicitation is done by lawyers seeking to represent those of wealth and privilege, such as John J. Washek's insurance company. Ambulance chasing may be reprehensible, but corporation chasing carries an ABA seal of approval. The problem of impropriety arises, of course, only for those who seek to represent that other socioeconomic group typified by the mother of Ernest Gene Gunn or, say, by tenants as distinguished from landlords, or by consumers as distinguished from manufacturers. For such unsophisticates—that is, for those who are most in need of being aggressively informed of their rights—the organized bar, through its disciplinary actions, discourages any realistic access to the legal system.

Imagine, for example, the following situation. A woman arrives at a metropolitan courthouse holding a small boy by the hand. She speaks almost no English at all. She is intimidated and confused by the imposing surroundings. All she knows is that she is required to be someplace in that building because her son has been arrested or her landlord is attempting to evict her family. People brush by her, concerned with their own problems. Then a man appears, smiles at her, and asks in her own language whether he can help her. Through him, she meets and retains the man's employer, a lawyer who guides her to the proper place and who represents her interests. In my view, that lawyer should have been given a citation as Attorney of the Year. Instead, he was prosecuted as a criminal, convicted of the misdemeanor of soliciting business on behalf of an attorney, subjected to disciplinary proceedings, and censured by the court.[17]

If the profession has an obligation to "[fulfill] its duty to make legal counsel available," strictures against advertising and soliciting are precisely the wrong way to go about it. Instead, attorneys have a professional duty to stir up litigation when they are acting to advise people who may be ignorant of their rights to seek justice in the courts. As expressed by one authority;

> We must . . . discard . . . the assumption of Medieval Society, that a lawsuit is an evil in itself. It is hard to see how either the legal profession or our court machinery can justify its existence, if we go on the assumption that it is always better to suffer a wrong than to redress it by litigation. . . . If we have so little confidence in the process of law as to think otherwise, we shall do well to consider a fundamental overhauling of our system.[18]

Fortunately, there is authority that the legal system exists to be used by people, and that people who need legal advice are entitled to have it. Indeed, the new ABA code at one point makes such advice a matter of professional duty: "The legal profession should assist laymen to recognize legal problems because such problems may not be self-revealing and often are not timely noticed." Advice regarding legal rights is therefore held proper when it is "motivated by a desire to protect one who does not recognize that he may have legal problems or who is ignorant of his legal rights or obligations." [19] At the same time, however, the code properly condemns the instigation of litigation that is intended "merely to harass or injure another." [20]

The code does suggest that an attorney should not solicit a client solely for the purpose of obtaining a fee.[21] When the lawyer's motives are mixed, however—that is, when the attorney acts with both a proper motive (to provide needed advice) and an "improper" motive (to obtain a fee)—it is the proper motive that is determinative. For example, during the New Deal period, an organization was formed called the Liberty League, a group of lawyers opposed to such New Deal innovations as the National Labor Relations Act. The league published advertisements expressing its view that the act was unconstitutional and offering to represent anyone who wanted to litigate against it. In Formal Opinion No. 148, the Committee on Professional Ethics of the American Bar Association held that the lawyers' activities were not only professionally proper but "wholesome and beneficial." And the committee made it clear that the propriety of the advertisement would not be affected by a motive on the part of the lawyers to serve the interests of fee-paying clients:

> . . . We need not assume that these lawyers were actuated solely by altruistic motives. It would be extraordinary indeed if some of the lawyers in the list do not have some clients whose rights may be adversely affected by the legislation which the lawyers condemn, but their right to organize and declare their views cannot for that reason be denied, and no ethical principle is thereby violated.

So even though an attorney may receive compensation, the solicitation of a client is not unethical if the client might otherwise have failed to vindicate his or her legal rights.

This discussion leads to one conclusion: The *Code of Professional Responsibility* takes a schizophrenic position on solicitation and advertising. On the one hand, it is good to advise people of their rights, even if a fee might result. On the other hand, there are some lawyers, for some clients, who had better not try to do it. One result of that inconsistency in the anti-solicitation rules has been that bar association disciplinary committees have been using it to harass public interest lawyers—even those working without fees from clients—who represent unpopular clients or causes.

In part because of that particular abuse of the rules, in 1971 the Stern Community Law Firm in Washington, D.C. (of which I was then Director), decided to challenge the anti-solicitation rules as applied to non-fee cases. The test case related to child adoption. The District of Columbia then kept a larger proportion of its homeless children in public institutions than did any other American city. The D.C. institutions were notoriously overcrowded and understaffed. In the view of the Stern Firm, these conditions owed to arbitrary rules and bureaucratic policies and practices relating to adoption and foster care. For example, potential adoptive parents had been turned away or discouraged because they were single, because both parents were working, or because they were white and seeking a black child.

The adoption agencies contended, on the other hand, that there were no such adoptive parents available and that no such arbitrary rules or practices existed. It therefore became essential to demonstrate that potential adoptive parents were in fact available but were being arbitrarily rejected, despite the agencies' claims to the contrary. In order to produce such adoptive parents, we published a Public Interest Legal Opinion in newspapers and magazines, and over radio and television, to advise members of the community of the need for adoptive parents, the invalidity of the restrictive rules, and the availability of free legal services to establish the rights in question.

A second Public Service Legal Opinion published by the Stern Community Law Firm related to our efforts to have the Food and Drug Administration declare certain toys as hazardous to children and to provide that earlier purchasers could return any such toys for a full refund. The Stern Firm brought an action against the Secretary of HEW on behalf of Consumers Union and the Children's Foundation to compel the FDA to take appropriate action; and it did, barring over three dozen dangerous toys, declaring them to be capable of killing or maiming children. But the FDA then failed to issue regulations providing for a refund for the return of the toys. So the firm published a Public Service Legal Opinion setting forth the names and manufacturers of the toys found by FDA to be hazardous and advising purchasers that they were entitled immediately to return the toys for refund.

Predictably, some members of the bench and bar complained to the Committee on Legal Ethics and Grievances of the Bar Association of the District of Columbia. Although the committee began with an attitude hostile to the idea of advertising, the members changed their views in the course of lengthy consideration of the issue. As a result, the committee wrote the first Bar Association opinion in the country approving solicitation of clients by public interest lawyers serving without fees. In its opinion, the Legal Ethics and Grievances Committee held that solicitation of clients by the Stern Firm was "consistent with the spirit and letter of the *Code of Professional Responsibility*" and "in keeping with the highest responsibilities of the legal profession." Fred Graham commented in *The New York Times* that "for a profession that has forbidden lawyers to wear tie clasps bearing their state bar emblem or to send Christmas cards to prospective clients on the ground that such activities were unethical 'advertising,' the activities approved in the new ruling are unprecedented."

In fact, the Supreme Court has held in a series of cases of major importance that "ethical" restrictions must give way to constitutional rights. The First Amendment protects solicitation both because of an attorney's freedom of speech and because of a client's right to petition the government for redress of grievances.[22] *NAACP* v. *Button* considered solicitation of clients in the context of efforts by the NAACP to recruit plaintiffs for school desegregation cases.[23] The organization called a series of meetings, inviting not only its members and not only poor people, but also all members of the community. At these meetings, the group's paid staff attorneys took the platform to urge those present to authorize the lawyers to sue in their behalf. The NAACP maintained the ensuing litigation by defraying all expenses, regardless of the means of a particular plaintiff.

Virginia contended that the NAACP's activities constituted improper solicitation under a state statute and fell within the traditional state power to regulate professional conduct. In 1963, however, the Supreme Court said that "the State's attempt to equate the activities of the NAACP and its lawyers with common-law barratry, maintenance and champerty, and to outlaw them accordingly, cannot obscure the serious encroachment upon protected freedoms of expression." The Court concluded: "Thus it is no answer to the constitutional claims asserted by petitioner to say, as the Virginia Supreme Court of Appeals has said, that the purpose of these regulations was merely to insure high professional standards and not to curtail free expression. For a State may not, under the guise of prohibiting professional misconduct, ignore constitutional rights." [24]

In *Brotherhood of Railroad Trainmen* the next year, the Supreme Court considered the question of solicitation in a case where a union's legal services plan channeled all or substantially all of the railroad workers' personal injury claims, on a private fee basis, to lawyers selected by the union and touted in its literature and at meetings. The Court again upheld the solicitation on constitutional grounds, despite the objection of the two dissenting justices that by giving constitutional protection to the solicitation of personal injury claims, the Court "relegates the practice of law to the level of a commercial enterprise," "degrades the profession," and "contravenes both the accepted ethics of the profession and the statutory and judicial rules of acceptable conduct." [25]

In the *United Mine Workers* case the Supreme Court dealt with the argument that *Button* should be limited to litigation involving major political issues and not be extended to personal injury cases. The Court held in 1967 that "the litigation in question is, of course, not bound up with political matters of acute social moment, as in *Button*, but the First Amendment does not protect speech and assembly only to the extent that it can be characterized as political. 'Great secular causes, with small ones are guarded. . . .' " [26]

Finally, in its 1971 *United Transportation Union* decision, the Court reversed a state injunction designed, in Justice Harlan's words, "to fend against 'ambulance chasing.' " [27] In that case a union paid investigators to keep track of accidents; to visit injured members, taking contingent fee contracts with them; and to urge the members to engage named private attorneys who were selected by the union and who had agreed to charge a fee set by prior agreement with the union. In approving that arrangement, the Court reiterated that "collective activity undertaken to obtain meaningful access to the courts is a fundamental right within the protection of the First Amendment." What is important to bear in mind, however, is that (1) the attorneys in question were not in-house counsel for the union, but were private practitioners; (2) the attorneys earned substantial fees; (3) the cases were not "public interest" cases in the restricted sense, but were ordinary personal injury cases; and (4) the attorneys were retained as a result of the activities of "investigators" paid by the union. Their job was to find out where accidents had occurred, to visit the victims as promptly as possible, to "tout" the particular lawyer, and, if necessary, to take the victim to the lawyer's office to get a contingent fee contract signed.

We began with *Gunn* v. *Washek*, and it is an appropriate case with which to close. If lawyers are to take seriously the overriding rule expressed in Canon 2, the bar will have to reverse the pattern illustrated by *Gunn*. First, we must vigorously discipline attorneys who abuse their training, skills, and status by misleading or exploiting unrepresented lay people. But, second, we must encourage, rather than forbid, lawyers to seek out people, like Ms. Gunn, who have legal rights and who may be ignorant of them or be deprived of access to the legal system.

In short, we should recognize that when Ernest Gene Gunn was injured by John J. Washek, the legal profession failed doubly in its duties when an insurance adjuster rather than a plaintiff's attorney was the first to call on Ms. Gunn.

*Jethro K. Lieberman**

How to Avoid Lawyers

VOIDING LAWYERS is a vast ambiguity, at once a hope, a plea, a paradox.[1] It is an old utopian dream to avoid lawyers by simply doing away with them. In America, however, there has been a much more pragmatic approach for the poor and the middle class: High fees make the retaining of legal counsel prohibitively expensive. The paradox is summed up in the contradictory attitudes we may all hold: Any number of disadvantaged people may believe as fervently as they know God is their friend that the lawyer is an unscrupulous rascal bent on gouging the helpless. Yet these same people could find no greater happiness than for their children to go to school to become—lawyers.

We despise lawyers and we are proud of them. We would prefer to do without lawyers, and we encourage them because we need them. This paradox—which David Riley closely examines—brings great tensions. To relax them we must recognize the necessity of operating on both ends at once: Legal services must be made both more accessible and also less necessary.

To learn this lesson we must first know why it has not happened previously. In the nineteenth century, at least prior to the Civil War, the practice of law was wide open, like all professional practice. If most states prescribed some period of study or apprenticeship, there was no strict adherence to formalities; it took very little to become a practicing attorney. No one was required to go to school, though law schools did exist. Bar examinations in the modern sense were unknown. A few questions might be asked of the prospective attorney, but little was expected by way of answer. Salmon P. Chase, appointed to the Supreme Court by President Lincoln in 1864, took an examination in Maryland in 1829 before a state judge, who wanted Chase to pursue his studies one more year. But Chase had other ideas, having already managed "to go to

* JETHRO K. LIEBERMAN IS A LAWYER, LEGAL AFFAIRS EDITOR OF *Business Week* MAGAZINE, AND THE AUTHOR OF SEVERAL BOOKS, INCLUDING *The Tyranny of the Experts* (1970) AND *How the Government Breaks the Law* (1972).

the Western country and practice law," and he persuaded the judge to swear him in.[2] Lemuel Shattuck summed up the prevalent attitude in 1850 toward the practice of all professions when he said of doctors in his *Report of the Sanitary Commission* of Massachusetts: "Anyone, male or female, learned or ignorant, an honest man or a knave, can assume the name of physician and 'practice' upon any one, to cure or to kill, as either may happen, without accountability. It's a free country!"[3]

The increasing freedom of access to the profession during much of the last century did not mean that the law itself was accessible to laymen. Lawyers were a class apart.[4] In a nation where the common law ("unwritten," judge-made law) was important, one could not simply go to a codebook to know what that law was. The intricacies of pleading before the courts were sufficient to forestall the complete amateur from attempting to bring a case. Moreover, in a time when the prevailing belief was that judges did not "make" the law but "applied" preexisting eternal law to concrete cases, there had to be some class from which to draw judges with the proper sensitivity and training for this delicate task.

Following the Civil War, the American economy began to grow and diversify to an unprecedented degree. Local businesses became national businesses; markets expanded; competition, for a time, intensified. Professionals of all sorts awakened to problems and prospects. They perceived the problems as the growth of bothersome competition and the decline in standards and quality of service. The prospects were the converse: reducing competition and raising standards. Many professionals, other than lawyers, also saw the opportunity, as voiced by an Illinois druggist in the 1890s: "Some provision should be made so that upon passing the examination as a registered pharmacist [an assistant] cannot immediately start a drug store. This business of making it easy for young men to pass an examination and immediately start in business is what is hurting us."[5]

So the states began to license professionals—mostly at the professionals' behest, beginning with lawyers and doctors. The movement toward occupational licensing became so overblown that at a single session of the Wisconsin legislature about twenty years ago, caterers, canopy and awning installers, cider makers, coal dealers, dancing school instructors, egg breakers, frog dealers, labor organizers, meat cutters, music teachers, and beer coil cleaners tried but failed to require themselves to be licensed.[6] About the same time in California, grass cutters, billing themselves as "maintenance gardeners," also sought licensing, but the bill did not pass.[7]

Lawyers began their monopolization early. The first bar association, the Association of the Bar of the City of New York, was founded in 1870; the American Bar Association was organized in 1878. The formation of such associations arose in part from the general instinct that people with common interests ought to come together to share them. Many local bar associations today are little more than social groups, but the original associations were formed partly in response to rising competition by laymen. By the 1880s, according to the legal historian James Willard Hurst, "competition from outside the profession began to figure as a material element in the economic situation of the bar." [8] During the next half century, the practice of law grew to serve the increasingly national—or at least interstate—character of business. Such organizations and professions as title-guaranty companies, collection agencies, trust companies, banks, and certified public accountants became intimately engaged in business traditionally the domain of lawyers. The bar responded to this competition with a doctrine called "unauthorized practice of law," which has been used to justify the use of legal sanctions against others to maintain inviolate the territory of lawyers.[9]

In 1914, the New York County Lawyers Association established a committee on unlawful practice, which sought to ferret out and eliminate the practice of law by laymen, whether acting individually or through lay agencies. Not until the Depression, however, did the organized bar actively embark on its mission to search and destroy its competition. In 1930, the American Bar Association formed its committee on the unauthorized practice of law. Within ten years, 400 such committees were inaugurated throughout the country. Their exuberance belied the claim that these were not vigilante actions. A compilation of all court cases dealing with unauthorized practice prior to 1930 required 98 pages; in seven years following the stock market crash, such cases consumed 838 pages.[10]

The bar sought to control unauthorized practice in a variety of ways: by filing suit to enjoin laymen from acting like lawyers and by entering into treaties with other professional groups that divided up the market. Many such treaty organizations exist to this day: The ABA has ten so-called National Conferences (for example, the National Conference of Lawyers and Collection Agencies), and each exposes the inefficacy of antitrust law enforcement. Agencies of the government also helped separate lawyers from non-lawyers. Banking commissions, for instance, with power over collection agencies, could prohibit them from engaging in law practice. And most importantly, the courts claimed for themselves the exclusive governmental power to regulate the practice of law. As the justices of the Massachusetts Supreme Judicial Court declared in 1932: "No statute can control the judicial department in the performance of its duty to decide who shall enjoy the privilege of practicing law." [11]

The apotheosis of this doctrine of unauthorized practice may be the famous struggle between the bar and real estate brokers in Arizona in the late 1950s and early 1960s. To consummate a deal, real estate brokers there, as in many other states, would simply fill in the blanks of already printed forms widely used in the state. This practice represented a threat to consumers, said the State Bar of Arizona, which sued to enjoin a number of companies from such harmful pursuits. As a result, the Arizona Supreme Court decided to exclude real estate brokers and land title company officers from preparing "by drafting or filling in the blanks, deeds of conveyances of any kind, forms of notes, mortgages, contracts for sale of real estate," and many other documents.[12] Nor could the decision be annulled by the state legislature, said the supreme court, because the decision construed the state constitution as conferring exclusive power to the courts to decide who could practice law and who could not. A bitter political fight subsequently led to a constitutional amendment specifically permitting real estate salesmen and certain others to fill in those blanks.

This emphasis on who can do "legal" work has tended to mask an extremely important point—that a goodly portion of what lawyers do is simple, if not mechanical. This is practice by boilerplate. It occurs in numerous areas: simple real estate contracts, divorce, wills, adoption, various kinds of litigation, among others. As Jerome Carlin has written in his classic work, *Lawyers on Their Own*:

> Most matters that reach the individual practitioner—the small residential closing, the simple uncontested divorce, drawing up a will or probating a small estate, negotiating a personal injury claim or collecting on a debt—do not require very much technical knowledge, and what technical problems there are are generally simplified by the use of standardized forms and procedures.[13]

But the layman who seeks to publish forms for his brethren may find himself in considerable difficulties. Consider the well-known case of Norman F. Dacey, whose best-selling *How to Avoid Probate* caused a stir several publishing seasons ago when the New York County Lawyers' Association managed to secure, temporarily, an injunction against Dacey, his publisher, the distributor, and one of the bookstores that sold his controversial volume.

Dacey, not a lawyer, was a Connecticut resident. Operating under the name National Estate Planning Council, he had published a thirty-page pamphlet containing forms for wills, which he had used in conjunction with advice he gave individual clients. A Connecticut court enjoined him from further distribution of the pamphlet and from giving specific advice as though he were a lawyer.[14] So he enlarged the pamphlet into a full-fledged book—55 pages of text and 310 pages of forms with accompanying instructions—which was published and distributed throughout the United States.

Enter the New York County Lawyers Association. Acting under a statute expressly permitting any bar association in the state to sue to enjoin the unauthorized practice of law, the association succeeded in having Dacey held in criminal contempt, fined $250, and sentenced to thirty days in jail. Dacey, the publisher, the distributor, and the bookstore were stopped from further distribution and sale of material purporting to give legal advice to the public. There was no showing that Dacey gave specific advice to specific people; he was convicted only of writing and contracting to publish a book.

The New York State Appellate Division (the intermediate appellate court) upheld the injunction, saying that purchasers "in a sense . . . are solicited as his clients" and noting that Dacey received a "fee" in the form of royalties. In the grand adverbial manner of the appellate courts that know what result they wish to reach even if they do not know quite how to get there, the court stated: "It would be senseless to permit a person who is not an attorney to engage in the business of selling and distributing particularized legal advice to the public on a wholesale basis when he would not be permitted to do so on an individual basis." [15] (Of course, "bona fide" publishers of legal forms do practically what Dacey did all the time.) The court ignored the question whether, if Dacey had been an attorney, the outcome might have been different, since the danger of someone's misusing a form would be the same. In the end it didn't matter. The New York Court of Appeals, the state's highest court, reversed without opinion—presumably because it understood the purpose of the First Amendment—and the book is now sold openly.[16]

If the unauthorized-practice battle often seems absurd when fought against other professionals or laymen, it must seem all the more absurd when, though characterized somewhat differently, it is fought against lawyers themselves.

At the turn of the century, it was argued with some truth that since the lawyer-client relationship is fiduciary, not commercial, the free enterprise rationale of businessmen had to be replaced. As a substitute for the self-regulating market principle, lawyers embraced the principle of the self-regulating profession. Ethics would replace money as the moving force in the world of lawyers.[17]

What began as simple ethical standards have become Talmudic in scope. Glosses on business cards are typical. The New York State Bar Association ruled that the use of blue paper stock for business cards is impermissible. But I have been unsuccessfully urging the same bar association to declare unethical the custom of title companies' giving a kickback of 15 percent of the cost of title insurance to real estate attorneys (a practice subsequently outlawed by the legislature).[18]

It is understandable why laymen might not be able to see how the substitution of ethics for money has greatly changed things. Consider, on the one hand, the great Samuel Williston's withholding of evidence from the other side on behalf of his client in a civil suit, and on the other hand the attorney who works for a salary to save a group client the cost of large contingent fees. Had Williston been condemned and the salaried attorney applauded, any concern we might have had over the potentially dangerous course of professional ethics would be theoretical. Yet when Professor Williston withheld from the other side evidence he knew to be true but damaging to his client, he was not condemned. Quite the reverse: His conduct was justified as the work of a skilled advocate ably aiding his client by obscuring the issues. The salaried attorney, however, was enjoined from continuing his union affiliation because he was acting unethically simply by virtue of his affiliation.[19] Half-truths are ethical but low fees are not. Ethics is not as obvious a science as it might seem.

The problem of the salaried lawyer—whose low-cost office routine irritated the featherbedders of his profession—deserves closer attention. A decade ago the United Mine Workers in Illinois hired an attorney for an annual fee of $12,000 to aid its members primarily in the area of workmen's compensation law. A letter from the union to the lawyer stated in part: "You will receive no further instructions or directions and have no interference from the District, nor from any officer, and your obligations and relations will be to and only with the several persons you represent." Union members were not obliged to see this attorney, and he announced that each member was free to seek outside help. The attorney's work consisted largely in preparing proper papers for submission to the Illinois Industrial Commission whenever an injured employee or his next of kin wished to prosecute a claim. Most of this paperwork was apparently perfunctory: The attorney rarely spoke to his clients; he simply filled in the blanks. During the first three years he won more than three million dollars for his clients, and his annual salary was vastly smaller than the contingent fees other members of the bar would have charged for similar successes.

Yet this arrangement enraged the local bar. In 1966 the Illinois State Bar Association succeeded in enjoining the union from conducting its legal assistance program on the ground that the canons of ethics prohibited the "unauthorized practice of law by any lay agency," i.e., the union.[20] Here is ethics at its worst: Lay agencies don't practice law, people do, and this particular person was an attorney. The Illinois Supreme Court momentarily enshrined this example of unethical ethics as law, although the U.S. Supreme Court later upheld the union.[21]

This case and subsequent ABA activity over unauthorized practice reveal how lawyers and their associations strive to retain jurisdiction over anything that remotely smacks of legal work. But their exclusive grip is slipping. When knowledge becomes routine, when problems can be solved mechanically, and when a large population makes feasible techniques of mass production, a natural monopoly of skill is sure to be challenged by a host of competitors.

The lawyers' battle over the unauthorized practice of law, then, is ultimately the response of a monopolist to the inroads on his market made possible by new production techniques. When the public hears lawyers plead for their continued control over mechanics, for their right to be paid for legal featherbedding and expensive techniques, it is no wonder the desire is strong to avoid lawyers.

To bypass successfully the hurdle of "unauthorized practice" requires a many-pronged approach. Four possible solutions follow:

1. *Effective small claims courts can make it possible to avoid lawyers.* Most lawyers are familiar with the evolution of the independent arbitrator in the early part of this century. Despite determined resistance from the courts—which did not appreciate what they considered an encroachment

on their jurisdiction—the principle became recognized that two parties may agree to submit future disputes to private arbitrators rather than to courts. This principle—that there are often substitutes for expensive specialists—can be applied to lawyers.

The small claims court is the only regular judicial forum in which lawyers are regularly (though not completely) avoided.[22] The simplified procedures enable most people to argue their own cases before judges in hearings that take no more than several minutes. The entire process, from first filing of claim to the verdict, normally takes from one month to six weeks. These courts can be used to press any claim for money owed or damage or injury that can be measured in monetary terms. From the individual's perspective, shoddy repairwork, lost laundry, failure to honor a warranty—any of the annoyances consumers can suffer—can be resolved simply and inexpensively at the small claims court.

But there are problems. Most important is the "jurisdictional limit"— the amount above which a small claims court will not hear a case. Although small claims courts vary among states, it is clear that half the states impose maximum limits of from $300 to $500 (thirteen states have a $500 limit, twelve states a $300 limit). The others range from a high of $3,500 (the magistrates' courts in Missouri) to lows of $100 (in Georgia, Kansas, and Wyoming). Seven states have a sliding scale, at the upper end of which small claims courts share jurisdiction with other courts. Plaintiffs, in other words, can choose their procedures in those states.

To make small claims courts more effective, it seems obvious that the jurisdictional limit must be raised in many states—as a first approximation, at least in those twenty-eight states with limits below $500. Suits to recover damages for the failure of dealers to honor warranties covering major appliances and automobiles can involve more than the low limits imposed in many states, although the factual dispute is simple enough for a small claims court to resolve.[23]

Installment creditors have traditionally used small claims courts as cheap collection agencies. Poor consumers are often victimized through these courts because of ignorance and the difficulties of proving the shoddiness of the product. New York City corrected this problem by prohibiting partnerships and corporate entities from pressing these claims directly or indirectly.[24] But this remedy may be overbroad, because it assumes that consumers are never dishonest. Small proprietorships may have legitimate claims against people who do not pay their bills. Litigation

TABLE OF JURISDICTIONAL LIMITS OF
SMALL CLAIMS COURTS[25]

$3,500	$3,000	$2,000	$1,500	$1,000
Missouri[1]	Tennessee	New Mexico[1]	Delaware	Alaska
				Illinois
				Maryland

$750	$500	$400	$300	$250
Connecticut	Arizona[2]	Massachusetts	Alabama	Mississippi
District	Arkansas[2,3]	Oklahoma	Hawaii	Vermont
of	California		Iowa[4]	
Columbia	Colorado		Michigan[1]	
	Indiana		Minnesota[1]	
	Kentucky[2]		Montana	
	Louisiana[1,2]		Nevada	
	Nebraska[1]		New Hampshire	
	New York		North Carolina	
	Oregon[2]		Rhode Island	
	Pennsylvania[1]		Virginia[2]	
	South Dakota[1,2]		West Virginia	
	Wisconsin			

$200	$150	$100
Idaho	Ohio	Georgia[1]
Maine	Texas	Kansas
New Jersey		Wyoming
North Dakota		
South Carolina[1]		
Utah		
Washington[1]		

[1] Limit varies with geographic region within the state.
[2] Jurisdiction at upper limit concurrent with other courts.
[3] Limits may be different for certain classes of injuries.
[4] Both parties must consent at upper limit.

is a two-way street, and some rule short of a prohibition against a class of plaintiffs should be found.

Lesser though real problems reduce the effectiveness of small claims courts. Many states require a case to be thrown out of court if the consumer has sued a corporation in the wrong name—an easy mistake to make since retail store names, for example, are not always the same as the parent corporation's name. Provided that the defendant is named clearly enough, such as "Honest Abe's Discount House, 10 Maple Street," there can be no legitimate claim that the defendant thought the suit was against someone else. Some states permit removal of the small claims suit to another court if the defendant asserts a counterclaim that is in excess of the jurisdictional amount. The right of removal should be strictly limited to counterclaims directly related to the plaintiff's claim. Otherwise wealthy defendants can on their own easily counterclaim an impecunious plaintiff into a more expensive forum. The use of lawyers in the small claims court should be further restricted. Often, corporations are required to appear only through lawyers, but there is no manifest reason why an appropriate executive could not appear. After all, the time consumers spend in court is not compensated, even when they are victorious. Collecting a judgment can be extremely difficult for a successful plaintiff. The use of penalties, like treble damages, at least against corporate defendants, should be considered where there is delay in payment or where the plaintiff must resort to the process of the sheriff or marshall.

There is finally the problem of convenience. Small claims courts should be open on weekends and evenings, and communities should experiment with "circuit riding" small claims courts—judges and aides who travel with some regularity to different parts of the city and to different parts of suburbia.[26]

2. *If paraprofessionals can do it, they should do it.* There is no reason that lawyers with seven years of higher education, including three of specific legal training, must be required to do much of the mechanical work of law. Doctors have their nurses, dentists their hygienists, the armed forces their medical corpsmen; and many lawyers have secretaries who are quite adept at filling in blanks. There is no reason the lawyer should not admit to what is going on anyway and welcome a "legal assistant" to his office.

In fact, in many professions, including law, the paraprofessional has begun to take over the more mechanical tasks previously arrogated to the overtrained and licensed professional.[27] The profession must now establish the preconditions for the successful employment of what, for want of a better term, are being called "paralegals." These include developing a curriculum to train them and cutting back on the traditional notion of unauthorized practice to permit the paralegal to practice his or her trade. The paralegal should be employed in every area of legal practice—in the private law firm, in the legal aid office, in the corporation, in government, in the courts.

Some of these preconditions are being fulfilled. A number of schools,

Columbia and Minnesota for example, have begun training programs.[28] Graduates of these programs usually have two destinations: the law firm, where they will be able to take on a variety of functions generally performed now by junior attorneys and even legal secretaries; and the legal aid office (and in all too few areas so far, the small claims courts), where they will begin to function immediately like attorneys, conducting interviews and preparing papers to solve many of the routine but critical problems of the poor.

So far, paralegals themselves have not become a separate licensed class. Now the lawyers who hire them, supervise them. But pressures may build for some sort of regulation, if for no other reason than that in time paralegals may realize that a closed guild will be as beneficial to them as it has been for scores of other occupational groups. The second step toward creation of a submonopoly will come with the realization that paralegals need not work exclusively as employees for lawyers. There is every reason to suppose that paralegals will form, if permitted, companies or firms to supply services to lawyers, such as the drafting of wills and the like. It is only one more step to the paralegals' providing these services directly to the public. When this happens, demand for regulation and control cannot be far behind.*

3. *And if machines can do it, they should do it.* For the best of the paralegals, their status is likely only a way station on the road to becoming a lawyer. There may thus be a tendency for the paralegal class to stabilize at the lower end of ambition and talent. If the paralegal becomes nothing more than a paperpusher, a bureaucrat of forms and affidavits, a filing clerk who has some magic words at his or her command, he or she will be stifled by inertia and boredom. The legal profession will seriously err if it seizes upon the paralegal as a handy repository for drudgery.

Here, as elsewhere in modern life, the machine appears. First used as an aid in billing and accounting, the computer and allied machinery are now invading the domain of substantive law. A computer service presently operating has the full text of federal and some state statutes, court decisions, and tax and other regulations. This system permits the researcher to find his material in minutes, rather than the hours that conventional legal research takes.[30] Another company does complete

---

* California has already begun to consider professional status for the paralegal. The state bar has tentatively recommended the adoption of a Certified Attorney Assistant Act, which would set educational requirements, accredit schools, and mandate a written examination—a sort of sub–bar examination—to be administered, of course, by the bar.[29]

indexing of depositions and other material in litigation on an overnight basis, thereby saving secretaries and clerks from the tedium of cataloguing.[31] Still another firm is experimenting with computer-drawn legal papers, like complaints and wills.[32] The use of these machines is to be encouraged, as the paralegal becomes not merely a research assistant and clerk, but a genuine legal administrator, bringing law to many whom the present individualized, nonadministrative system is too expensive to reach.*

4. *Reduce the need for legal services by changing the laws.* Avoiding lawyers is an important way to make justice less expensive; another is the avoiding of law itself. The arbitrator helps replace the expensive, time-consuming, and cumbersome lawsuit. Workmen's compensation boards help avoid equally lengthy litigation. There is every reason to believe that in the large realm of accident law generally, innovative insurance programs can be devised to compensate victims without the need for the usual round of complaint and answer in court. No-fault automobile insurance is one manifestation of this thought, but only one, and it is important to convince lawyers to stop fighting this trend and to direct their energies instead toward devising better programs, preferably plans that would cover all accidents.[33]

Such proposals make many lawyers anxious. Reduce our workload just as our numbers are swelling? (The U.S. Department of Labor in 1973 estimated that new legal jobs will number 14,500 annually to 1980; each year the law schools graduate some 30,000.) But imaginative legislative approaches might bring the demand for and supply of legal services into a more socially efficient equilibrium—by doing away with the inequities in law that give rise to the need for these services in the first place and by encouraging prepaid legal insurance plans which could employ many excess lawyers for those who now cannot afford them. One has only to point to the ideas of "cooling-off" periods for contracts and the repeal of the holder-in-due-course doctrine. Giving a consumer three days within which to cancel an already signed contract permits the potential victim of unscrupulous salesmen to bypass trouble and hence bypass lawyers.[34]

As a specific step toward the general goal of better utilizing lawyers, a public interest law firm or a private foundation or the government itself should appoint a working panel to investigate specifically what areas of

---

* Another method of making legal services more accessible—by spreading the cost through prepaid legal insurance—will be considered in detail by Jim Lorenz.

legal practice are amenable to takeover by paralegals, what areas of conflict and coordination can be better served by nonlegal solutions, and what simple legislative changes can be made in the law to permit lawyers to represent clients more effectively. The panel will also have to decide what the legitimate limits of unauthorized practice should be; anything that takes existing business away from lawyers will simply not do as a standard. And all of us, lawyers and laymen alike, must spread the word that we as a nation can no longer tolerate the monopoly the legal profession holds on our everyday lives. The true ethics of a profession is service for the needs of all people. We will begin to practice these ethics only when the bar thinks more about service and less about the bar.

*Jerome A. Hochberg**

The Drive to Specialization

U NDER THE GUISE of progress toward quality legal services, the legal profession is steadily implementing programs called specialization, certification, and mandatory continuing legal education (CLE). CLE can require that every member of a state bar attend courses or lectures on legal topics. The ostensible purpose is to increase the competence of lawyers by enabling them to stay abreast of current developments in the law. *Certification* is an act of the state or other appropriate authority that attests to a lawyer's quality and/or competency, either generally or with respect to a specialized area of law. Certification may simply vouch that an attorney has completed a required CLE course, has passed a test, had a minimum of experience in a particular field of law, or a combination of such qualifications. *Specialization* is a process of formalizing the tendency of many lawyers to confine their practice either partially or wholly to a particular area of law— whether it be substantive (labor, tax, matrimonial, etc.) or procedural (trial practice). Presently, lawyers can of course voluntarily choose to concentrate in particular fields. Specialization plans being developed and implemented would regulate the process and impose requirements for specialist designation. Specialization, CLE, and certification, it should be noted, often function in tandem. Specialty designation may require certification and CLE may be necessary to either qualify or continue as a specialist.

This new movement springs in part from the fact that consumer groups, leading jurists, and the unrepresented middle class have begun to voice criticism of the quality and cost of legal services. Chief Justice Warren Burger's response to this crisis in legal services has been to decry

* JEROME A. HOCHBERG IS AN ATTORNEY IN WASHINGTON, D.C. HE FORMERLY SERVED WITH THE ANTITRUST DIVISION, U.S. DEPARTMENT OF JUSTICE, FROM 1961 TO 1973. HE IS CURRENTLY CHAIRPERSON OF THE DIVISION OF ANTITRUST, TRADE REGULATION AND CONSUMER AFFAIRS OF THE DISTRICT OF COLUMBIA BAR.

incompetent representation and inadequate training for young lawyers[1] —and to propose variants of these three programs. He has been joined in this criticism by Chief Judge Irving Kaufman of the Second Circuit Court of Appeals.[2] ABA President Lawrence E. Walsh encouraged the movement in an address to a conference on the subject held in 1974 in Colorado, stressing the importance of specialization as a way the legal profession can better serve the public. At a June 1975 ABA Conference on Specialization held in Chicago, Arthur Lewis, chairman of the ABA Special Committee on Specialization, endorsed the regulatory approach for specialization. Although the ABA Special Committee on Specialization has urged caution, bar organizations around the country are proposing their own plans. With such august sponsorship, it is clear that a process has started which may take the entire profession toward some form of mandatory continuing legal education, certification, and specialization.

Already many states have embarked on such programs. Iowa and Minnesota, for example, now require all attorneys to participate in CLE by attendance at approved courses and programs.[3] The Iowa program requires mandatory attendance of every attorney admitted to practice in the state for a prescribed number of hours in a course accredited by a regulatory commission. They must also pay for the administration of the program and submit proof of satisfactory attendance to the commission. Failure to comply can mean suspension of the right to practice. Minnesota's CLE program mandates 45 hours of schooling over a three-year period to keep one's license to practice law. Its purpose is to train lawyers, not educate them, the latter being the law school's function. A board of continuing legal education has been created which will be an arm of the Supreme Court of the state. There are neither group exemptions nor a grandfather provision available. The cost for these programs and the regulation of the whole program will be borne by lawyers.

Certification and specialization efforts, usually accompanied by either a CLE or specialization program or both, are also well advanced. Thus in California, among other requirements, a test must be taken and passed before certification in a specialty is awarded. To achieve certification a lawyer must be in practice for five years and substantially involved in the specialty for which he or she seeks certification. He or she must establish educational experience in the specialty involved and take a written exam on the subject. The lawyer must also show continuing involvement in the specialty and educational experience via CLE to be re-certified, a process that occurs every five years. The program is voluntary in that the specialist can practice in other areas and non-specialists are free to practice in the specialty areas. In referral situations, however, a lawyer cannot represent a client without the permission of the referring lawyer on any matter other than the one for which he received the referral. Under specialization, then, if Lawyer X referred a certain matter to Lawyer Y, Lawyer Y could do nothing else for that client without the prior permission of Lawyer X.

California's requirements for certification for the criminal law specialty include references from four attorneys already practicing in the specialty, at least three of whom were assisted by the applicant in the trial of a case. The lawyer must have participated in five felony trials and five other trials, spent one-third of his time in three of the preceding five years on criminal matters, and had 60 hours of CLE in the specialty in the previous five years. Similarly, workmen's compensation specialization certification requires a hefty 300 appearances in workmen's compensation forums in the preceding five years. If one meets all of these rigid requirements and passes the test, then the lawyer can advertise via a law list or the yellow pages as being a specialist with certification by the State of California. Older lawyers who have been substantially involved in one of the specialties in the past ten years are automatically granted certification as a specialist without having to meet any of these requirements.

New Mexico, on the other hand, offers all attorneys the opportunity to assert up to three specialties by merely affirming concentration of work experience in these fields. New Mexico has listed over 60 areas of specialization in which an attorney can, effectively, self-certify his own competence.

In a more narrow proposal for certification, the licensing of trial lawyers has gotten a recent and prominent push. Chief Justice Burger seeks ". . . specialist certification to limit admission to trial practice. . . ." He contends "from one-third to one-half of the lawyers who appear in the serious cases are not really qualified to render fully adequate representation" and deplores the fact that qualifications to act as an advocate are more casually considered than for licensing electricians.[4] Chief Judge Kaufman laments "the growing number of instances of poor legal representation . . ." and quotes Chief Judge David Bazelon, of the Court of Appeals for the D.C. Circuit, characterizing some attorneys as "walking violations of the Sixth Amendment."[5] Judge Kaufman urges additional law school legal training as a prerequisite for admission to the federal courts.[6]

This plan, however, has encountered serious criticism. Many law schools have opposed the proposal because of the great expense required to supplement curriculum and the rigid inflexible course requirements that it would impose on law students. Federal Judge Jack Weinstein of the Eastern District of New York, one of the jurisdictions which Judge Kaufman's plans encompass, has challenged the proposal as "elitist." Rather than restrict admission, he urges that a member of any state bar be admitted to any federal court.[7] Dean Soia Mentschikoff notes that graduating lawyers today are brighter than the older lawyers, yet the California plan would certify older lawyers without testing and the Burger-Kaufman plan might exclude the bright young lawyers from the courtroom.[8] Professor Philip B. Kurland, noted constitutional law expert at the University of Chicago Law School, has turned the Burger-Kaufman charge full circle. Says Kurland:

> And it may be, too, that a case is poorly tried because of the inadequacies of the judge rather than counsel. For certainly the judiciary—whether state or Federal—is not, as it should be, made up of the most competent lawyers. It is, rather, a group chosen by politicians as a reward for political services. Of course there are exceptions. But on the whole there is a greater proportion of incompetent judges than of incompetent counsel.[9]

Finally, many judges feel inadequate performance by attorneys stems from poor factual and legal analysis, not ignorance of how to move the admission of a document into evidence or similar shortcomings. The latter is easily learned; the former is not—the Burger-Kaufman plan notwithstanding.

Specialization, certification, CLE and trial advocacy licensing all have a certain plausibility. They can assure clients that the lawyers who serve them have been trained and approved for the task. They can lead to greater lawyer efficiency, which in turn can result in cost savings passed on to clients. So much for theory. In fact, these programs construct new and formidable barriers to free and open competition in the market for legal services. They reduce the supply of lawyers in critical areas, which will, if the medical specialties provide any analogy, lead to *higher* fees charged, not lower ones.

Consider, again, the Burger-Kaufman proposal. It suggests a solution that creates a new licensing barrier when lawyers seek to move from the law office to the courtroom. Licensing is a means to exclude, and to create, a monopoly, not simply a declaration of competency. Indeed, licensing procedures of many professions and activities are coming increasingly under the critical glare of the Antitrust Divison of the Justice Department.[10] Yet here are the chief justice and the chief judge of the leading federal circuit spearheading a drive that further frustrates competition for a group already under attack for a variety of practices that offend traditional antitrust principles.

The anticompetitive effects of specialization can be illustrated by the California plan. It requires five years of experience in the specialized field, a test for certification, and continuing course work to retain certification. Older lawyers are certified without meeting those requirements, which, to say the least, detracts from the announced intention to insure competence. Proponents argue that a lawyer need not apply for certification to practice in the specialized area and those who are certified can practice in other areas. But what judge will appoint a non-certified lawyer to defend an indigent criminal? What lawyer will risk referring a tax matter to any but a certified tax authority? The barriers are there and just as firm and formidable as if the plan were universal and mandatory.

Indeed, once a lawyer acquires his certificate of specialization, he can be expected to display it on the wall of his office and raise his hourly rates commensurate with his new and protected status. Consumers, without adequate information, are at a disadvantage when the subject of fees arises. Faced with a perceived (although not necessarily an accurate) need for the assistance of a specialist, the client is even less likely to exert what little bargaining power he or she may have.[11] While bar officials regularly proclaim that reduced costs are a purpose of specialization programs such as California's, a paper prepared by Richard H. Zehnle, under the auspices of the American Bar Foundation, suggests otherwise.

> But will the price of legal services really come down? Their experience with specialization in medicine must make the public wary of "reduced expense" through specialization in the legal profession. . . .
> . . . Will attorneys tend to specialize in more lucrative and exotic fields where identification of expertise may be easier for both attorney and client, thus neglecting an avowed purpose of specialization, namely, the greater delivery of legal service to the general public? Are we not much more likely to find eager specialists in "tax aspects of mergers and acquisitions" than in landlord-tenant relations?

Which members of the legal profession will really benefit from specialization controls? Already established specialists through grandfather certification? Members of prestigious firms who can easily afford the required legal education to qualify for certification and/or recertification? If high standards are adopted to avoid the risk of defrauding the public, is there not a danger of driving less affluent attorneys from public service?[12]

The medical profession is a cogent example of how control by a profession over the means of entry and the methods of practice can create competitive barriers resulting in higher prices and inadequate delivery of services.[13] Economist Elton Rayack describes the way in which specialization within the AMA has produced competitive battles between different types of specialists and between general practitioners and specialists.

> Specialty restrictionism has been a factor contributing to a decline in the number of GP's [general practitioners]. Authorities who have studied the causes of the decline invariably point to restrictions on hospital privileges as one of the key factors discouraging students from pursuing a career in general practice. Recent studies also indicate that specialists are increasingly taking over the functions of general practitioners since families are turning toward specialists for basic medical care as well as specialized services.[14]
> . . . Another undesirable effect of hospital medical staff restrictionism is that the non-certified specialist and GP tend to be barred from the better teaching hospitals.[15]

Instead of hospital privileges read, for example, courtroom privileges.

Just like the AMA then, the American Bar Association seeks to play a major role in the formulation of the industry's structure and regulation so as to benefit its members first and the public second. This is to be expected, for the ABA is a trade association of businessmen who sell legal services. Expected, but not endorsed. It is especially troubling that proposed programs for CLE, certification, and specialization are being developed and administered by the legal profession itself. Some state programs authorize a few laymen to sit on operating commissions, but the overwhelming majority of plans involve only lawyers. The self-interest of lawyers to establish rules to favor themselves can again be best appreciated by noting how doctors have kept their supply down and their incomes up.

The problems raised by CLE, although not as strikingly anticompetitive and anticonsumer as certification and specialization, are still substantial. For example, what courses are acceptable and what ones are not? Who can be excused from attendance, if anyone? Will government attorneys, perhaps thousands of miles away, who are members of the bar of such states, be required to return for these courses on a regular basis, and at whose expense? How many course hours and individual courses will be necessary to accommodate the thousands of lawyers who are members of the bar of such states? How does attendance for a few hours a year guarantee absorption of worthwhile knowledge, let alone competence—especially since even an ABA Conference on Specialization acknowledged that there was a lack of knowledge about "the pathology of incompetence"?[16] Most to the point, won't the added expense to attorneys and the lost time away from fee-paying work at the office be passed on to consumers in the form of higher fees? This cost can be significant: a typical bar of 7,000 lawyers would require 105,000 instructional hours each year under plans such as Minnesota's. While acknowledging such problems, Roger Brosnahan, president of the Minnesota Bar, believes that the administrative body that will regulate the program can deal with all of these issues.[17] But Paul Wolkin, director of the American Law Institute–American Bar Association Committee on Continuing Professional Education, predicts differently. "What may likely come about is that ten or fifteen hours a year of required professional education for all will entail big business for some continuing legal education entities, rote programming for others, and an exercise in frustration for most." [18]

The administrative burden of operating these plans is also great. The Minnesota plan, since it envisions no general exemptions, will require a considerable administrative structure to evaluate each application seeking relief from mandatory CLE. Without an exemption, lawyers face suspension or placement on restricted status, a penalty that constitutes deprivation of property. John Wirt, director of Minnesota's Continuing Legal Education program, has indicated that he sees problems with respect to who shall administer the program, given the limited available time of most lawyers. Moreover, Wirt asks who will nominate those who will supervise such programs and how will they be nominated? [19]

Plans for CLE, specialization, and certification can also restrict the free movement of lawyers from one area of the profession or geographical area to another. Lawyers will fear to take on different assignments lest they lose their specialty certification. The new law school graduate will have to choose carefully what kind of practice to enter. If the newly minted lawyer seeks a change after a few years at the bar, he or she can suffer a penalty since certification requires a full five years at the specialty.

Government lawyers or lawyers employed by a corporation may be deterred from moving to private practice or vice versa. The fortuitousness of one's first job after law school may encase lawyers in a permanent wrapping. Inflexibility replaces mobility.

The barriers created by specialization and certification can as well limit the number of attorneys who can serve a particular clientele. There may be fewer attorneys available to appear in court; thus, the occasional criminal defense lawyer who otherwise engages in a civil practice will probably stop his occasional representation. If the certification movement becomes mandatory or if the licensing procedure envisioned by the Burger-Kaufman proposal is enacted, serious Constitutional questions will be raised about an individual's right to pick an attorney of his own choice.[20]

A final concern over the drive to specialization is its tendency to narrow the learning and outlook of lawyers. As New Mexico's 60 plus specialty areas indicate, the number of technical specialties seems almost boundless. Dean Mentschikoff argues that competence requires broader, not narrower, knowledge. As an example, she cites a Florida plan that establishes specialties in wills, in trusts, and in probate—but not one under the broader rubric of estate planning.[21] If lawyers view their work through a narrow prism, they may neglect valuable concepts arising in other contexts. In short, they may see just the trees, not the forest. Rather than improving competence, specialization may be doing the opposite.

Whatever the value of formal specialization programs, it is important to note that many lawyers in the United States already specialize voluntarily. The trend is increasing and, given the American passion for detailed, organizational solutions to complex social and economic problems, it will probably continue. There are, to be sure, public benefits from such informal specializing. A tax lawyer can more easily and quickly come to grips with a consumer's tax problems. A lawyer unschooled in the tax code might make a costly mistake or reach the right result but only after expending far more time. And time is the basis for most lawyers' fees. The same principle applies in many areas of law—antitrust, labor, estate planning, admiralty, patents, divorce—to name just a few.

Accepting de facto specialization, however, is not to condone formal specialization—which can fix in cement mini-monopolies throughout the legal profession. Instead, there is a need for generalists to stray into specialized areas and challenge accepted doctrine with different insights. New ideas are a constant necessity in a dynamic economy—and legal system.

Meaningful competition, however, even in a market structured competitively, can be realized only if consumers are fully informed with respect to that market. "A prerequisite for the effective operation of any market," writes Rayack of the medical profession, "is that the consumer has considerable knowledge concerning the nature of the product so that he can make a rational choice in attempting to maximize his satisfaction." [22] He then goes on to point out that in the delivery of doctors' services it is the physician who possesses the knowledge and the consumer who remains in total ignorance.[23] Similarly, New Mexico's approach has been criticized because of the lack of adequate consumer information to guide clients to appropriate attorneys.

Consumer-sponsored information in the form of handbooks on lawyers in each community offers one way to provide needed information. It enables lawyers to engage in a general or specialized practice, with the public fully informed of the benefits and costs. The most useful information would assist and advise in evaluating law office activities, operations, and quality. The full and effective participation of consumer groups with lawyers in the evaluation process is essential for credibility. Yet this simple approach is being fought with tenacity by the ABA and state bars.[24] Why does the ABA go out of its way to fight such pro-consumer programs while citing the consumer as reason for specialization, certification, and CLE? If the bar truly wants to arrive at the elusive goals of competent, accessible, and inexpensive legal service, these three programs are more problem than solution. Voluntary, unregulated specialization, spurred by competition from general practitioners and others, with fully informed consumers, is a far preferable route.

III

Access to the Legal System: "Thou Shalt Not Ration Justice"

Representative John R. Conyers, Jr.[*]

Undermining Poverty Lawyers

THE OFFICES ARE, for the most part, nondescript—aging brown-stones, red brick affairs, perched at the top of a few flights of stairs. Inside, there is a warrenlike maze of small rooms, each with a desk piled high with a clutter of papers. Behind each desk sits a lawyer; seated in front, a client.

The cases discussed in each of these rooms would seem repetitive, even mundane, to most people. They would be of little interest to a public so preoccupied with national or global events, or even to the occupants of the large law offices downtown. But the citizens involved in these cases have little knowledge of lengthy precedents and abstract principles. To them, a landlord, a policeman, or a judge wielding a gavel are all symbols of the same mystifying and often menacing authority—the law. For the clients, then, these cases hold quite enough interest—they represent the day-to-day crises that punctuate their lives.

"You see, it's like this. I couldn't pay the rent last month. And now he's going to throw us out. He says he sent an eviction notice, but I know I never got one. . . ."

"He's supposed to send money for the children, you know, but now he's disappeared, and all his friends say they don't know where he is. And school's starting next week, and they need so many things. . . ."

"I've got to go to court next week. They're going to take away the refrigerator. They say they're going to take the money out of my pay. But it broke down last week, that's why I didn't pay them. It's supposed to be guaranteed. . . ."

Outside, in the small reception area, others sit in straight-backed chairs, waiting. Some are filling out forms, others talking idly to friends. Those who have come for the first time to the office look around at the many

* JOHN CONYERS IS A DEMOCRATIC CONGRESSMAN FROM MICHIGAN AND A MEMBER OF THE HOUSE JUDICIARY COMMITTEE.

signs and posters, signs like the one above the receptionist's desk. "Justice," it reads, "it's what we're all about."

The debate on the floor of the House the night of June 21, 1973, stretched on until midnight, and, as the hours dwindled slowly away, so too, it often seemed, did the logic of some of the House members. Under debate was House Resolution 7824, a bill designed to establish a Legal Services Corporation which would preserve legal aid to the poor and protect it from political influence. Some of the congressmen, however, saw the proposal in quite a different light.

What we're talking about here is legislation specifically designed to divide the American people into warring classes. Legal services financed by the Federal Government are to be provided to the have-nots that they may engage in battle with the haves. . . . a Federal legal services program is not the answer. The poor go on suffering while slick young activist lawyers go about fomenting rebellion and revolution at the taxpayers' expense. . . . It is another milestone in the road to social destruction.—Rep. Earl F. Langrebe, R.-Ind.[1]

All they [legal services lawyers] do is sit there and dream up something to draft legislation so that they can go out and harass elected officials in the cities and ending up with these crazy ridiculous things called "class action writs."—Rep. John E. Hunt, R.-N.J.[2]

. . . I believe it is the purpose and the practical effect of this proposal to conscript the dollars of tax-paying American citizens and to use these dollars to effect a redistribution of wealth and political power in this country in favor of the legal services attorneys and the militant pressure groups which have already grown rich and powerful as a result of the program. The entire concept strikes at the heart of American democracy. . . . —Rep. John H. Rousselot, R.-Calif.[3]

From its first appearance as a federally funded program under the auspices of the Office of Economic Opportunity (OEO), the legal services program has reaped a whirlwind of bitter controversy, rancorous debate, and overt manipulation. Controversy over the program often obscured the fact that the idea of equal access to the law for the poor did not spring full-grown from the ill-fated War on Poverty, but has always been a cornerstone of American democracy.

Unfortunately, however, that cornerstone has only recently begun to be constructed of the practical brick and mortar of lawsuits and courtroom battles; for the most part, it has rested only on the airiest of epigrams and wishful thinking. For even though politicians and history books have constantly prattled about the democratic system as one which has made equal justice a staple of every citizen's legal fare, millions of citizens, too poor to afford the cost of the courtroom, have found that full access to the law can prove to be more caviar than bread. The vast majority of poor people have been unable to afford the kind of comprehensive legal assistance their wealthier neighbors take for granted.

Given the distance between rhetoric and reality, then, the words "Equal Justice Under Law," engraved in marble on the front of the U.S. Supreme Court building, ring with hollow irony. The program that tried to fulfill the meaning of that stone inscription often found its purpose submerged in a welter of charges and countercharges. At the base of the controversy, however, has been a simple question—whether or not those unable to afford a lawyer are as entitled to a full, vigorous, and wide-ranging program of legal services as those with the money to pay for it.

The answer to such a question is, of course, an unqualified yes. And yet the history of legal services for the poor in this country is a testimony not only to the dedication of those who have fought for it, but to the formidable strength of those who have opposed it.

Long before politics and poverty lawyers began their inevitable tango under OEO, Reginald Heber Smith—the acknowledged champion of legal aid for the poor—provided an unequivocal analysis of the effect of denying indigents their legal rights. In his book, *Justice and the Poor*, first published in 1919, Smith noted that without equal access to the law, "the system not only robs the poor of their only protection, but it places in the hands of their oppressors the most powerful and ruthless weapon ever invented. The law itself becomes the means of extortion." [4]

Through Smith's leadership and prodding, the American Bar Association began early in the century to establish legal aid societies in cities throughout the country and to arrange funding for their support. But this private network of legal services projects, however well-intentioned, was skeletal at best. The local offices were woefully understaffed; community support was marginal. Cases were handled for the most part by private attorneys who could easily find themselves in court defending an indigent client one day and one of the powerful local interests inimical to the poor's well-being the next. Eligibility standards were stringent, to the point of excluding most potential clients.

As late as 1965, legal aid societies and the infant public defender system, which defended indigents accused of criminal acts, served less than 5 percent of the poor.[5] These fledgling programs, however, established the urgent need for extensive legal services for the indigent. In 1965, the legacy of these early efforts culminated in a federally funded legal services program established in what was then the field headquarters of the War on Poverty, the OEO.

The new program included 169 locally organized and controlled legal services projects, funded through OEO. By 1970, when the Office of Legal Services was elevated to independent status within OEO, the number of field projects had increased to 268, in ninety-nine locations around the country. Two thousand lawyers and 500 nonprofessional staff workers were handling over 900,000 cases. Two years later, the projects processed over 1.3 million cases on a relatively shoestring budget of $65.8 million.[6]

The lawyers who came to these projects were, for the most part, young, bright, and hardworking. Many had turned down more lucrative positions with established private law firms to lawyer at the storefronts and century-old office buildings. Like E. Clinton Bamberger, Jr., the program's first director, many of the attorneys saw their jobs as involving something more than a routine processing of divorce cases and other civil proceedings. To Bamberger, there was more to the legal services program than "just to see that someone who was unrepresented had a lawyer. We saw it as more—maybe removing some of the effects of poverty, maybe, in our wildest dreams, doing something about the causes of poverty." [7]

Although conservative opponents to the legal services program came to see these ambitions as more nightmares than dreams, the small army of poverty lawyers from the beginning deployed the full range of weapons in their legal armory to bring to their clients more of society's rights and benefits. The quality of the lawyers' work varied, of course, from project to project. Cases of incompetent lawyers and unwise tactics made their appearance as they do in private law firms; together with the perennial problems of overwork and underfunding, many lawyers felt that a lack of specific guidelines from Washington only increased the possibility of occasional mistakes and failures. Given these limitations, however, the program compiled a record of successes that any private law firm would have been proud to claim.

Much of this achievement centered around preventive law, as attorneys advised clients of their legal rights and explained to them the power and the limits of the law. Preventive efforts were accomplished not merely on behalf of the poor, but in conjunction with them. As their lawyers quickly discovered, the clients who came to their offices often had a firm knowledge of what they expected from poverty lawyers. In organizing meetings held to devise strategy and tactics, the lawyers usually provided the expertise, but the initiative and direction often came from the clients themselves. Patrons of legal services, then, were not, as some critics claimed, mere pawns in a lawyer's scheme to achieve his own version of utopia, but active participants in their legal problems, at least as much as private clients.

Beyond preventive law, most of the lawyers' work took place in the courtroom. The vast majority of their litigation was nuts and bolts, always an integral part of representing the poor—housing cases, domestic relations, creditor claims, employment cases. Yearly they won approximately 80 percent of these cases. But the poverty lawyers did not limit themselves merely to these cases. They did not hesitate to employ legal strategies and tactics to harness the law's power to their clients' needs. These lawyers, like the attorneys for the wealthy and for the corporations, filed class action suits on behalf of large groups of clients; they sued federal, state, and local governmental agencies; they attempted, in a variety of ways, to reform the law when they saw it harming poor people.

Law reform became an essential weapon in the poverty attorney's arsenal. There are currently about 380,000 lawyers in the United States, or approximately one for every 600 people. But there are only about 5,000 available to serve the needs of America's 35 million poor—one lawyer, in other words, for every 7,000 persons.[8] Law reform efforts, then, through class action and test litigation, quickly became the most economical way of bringing the law's benefits to large numbers of poor people.

While only 2 percent of the cases litigated by legal services lawyers can be classified under law reform, their impact on the poor's legal situation was disproportionately greater. In New York, Illinois, and California, legal services lawyers successfully prevented cutbacks in Medicaid programs. In Mississippi, they brought a case which ordered communities to provide the same public works and services to black neighborhoods as to white ones. They stopped the exclusion of handicapped children from public schools. They prevented cities from continuing urban renewal projects unless they provided adequate replacement housing.

Suits brought by legal services lawyers have challenged welfare laws in sixteen states and increased the poor's income by millions of dollars. They have won eight of the eleven cases they have brought before the Supreme Court, resulting in decisions that have banned midnight raids on the homes of welfare recipients,[9] abolished the "man in the house" rule which cut off aid to families with an able-bodied man in the home,[10] struck down state residency requirements concerning welfare eligibility,[11] and upheld a welfare recipient's right to a fair hearing before aid could be terminated.[12]

Throughout this torrent of legal activity, these lawyers were doing little more than giving life to Bamberger's initial directive to "do no less for their clients than does the corporation lawyer checking the Federal Trade Commission for sloppy rulemaking, the union lawyer asking Congress for repeal of 14(b), or the civil rights lawyer seeking an end to segregation in bus stations." [13] But as the legal services attorneys were soon to find out, representing the indigent involved all the legal complexities of representing General Motors or AT&T, with yet an added dimension—the crushing social and psychological weight of poverty on those who live under its dominion. While a corporation president's legal problems may be of labyrinthine proportions, he at least begins with a basic knowledge of the rules and premises upon which his problems are based and will be solved. For many of the poor, however, the legal world often seems more a part of the problem than its resolution. In helping a client with an eviction notice, for example, the poverty lawyer often found that that particular case was but one thread in a Gordian knot of personal, social, and bureaucratic difficulties which merely finding the rent money would not begin to solve. Poverty, it became clear to the lawyers, had to be attacked at its roots, whether those roots led to the police station or the welfare agency, the state legislature or the Supreme Court.

In taking such a comprehensive view of their clients' welfare, the legal services lawyers were not, as their critics often maintained, adhering to any specific ideological stand, or individual vision of social upheaval. Instead their actions stemmed from a relatively simple credo, not to be found in pamphlet or manifesto, but in a much more conservative source: the ABA's *Canons of Ethics* and *Code of Professional Responsibility*. There the lawyers were told to represent their clients' interests "fully and zealously within the bounds of the law."

Critics lost little time in making their opposition to the legal services program known. One of the first to take direct counter action was the Republican senator from California, George Murphy. He already had first-hand evidence of legal services attorneys' clout in the courtroom. When his friend, Governor Ronald Reagan, had tried to effect regulations that would have drastically cut Medicaid payments to California's poor, the local legal services project, California Rural Legal Assistance, filed a class action suit which eventually resulted in a permanent injunction against the governor's proposed cutbacks.

In 1967, Murphy introduced an amendment to the Equal Opportunity Act to prohibit legal services attorneys from bringing any legal action against local, state, and federal agencies. The amendment's inherent danger to a vigorous legal services program was self-evident—how could lawyers effectively represent poor people if they could not bring suits against the very institutions which often caused their problems?

The amendment was defeated in the Senate by a vote of 52 to 36. But program lawyers and organized bar lawyers sounded the alarm and amassed support to prevent a similar amendment from passing the House. Congressional offices were deluged with letters and visits by representatives from the entire spectrum of lawyers concerned with legal services, from the leaders of most of the national bar associations to the legal services attorneys themselves. Consequently, the amendment did not even reach the House floor. In 1969, however, an undaunted Murphy returned with an amendment which would permit state governors to veto OEO grants to specific projects in their states and which would strip the director of OEO of the authority to override such vetoes. This time the amendment slipped past the Senate, and it was only through an intense effort of crusade proportions on the part of legal services advocates around the country that its House counterpart failed to pass.[14]

Legal services attorneys were to face major squalls over direction and funding on the local level as well. Throughout the brief history of the legal services program, institutional resistance has flared up in more than fourteen states, from New York to California. A suit against a local housing authority in Oklahoma City, a class action against a governmental agency in St. Louis, a threat to prosecute police misconduct in Albuquerque—all led to the withdrawal of financial support in these cities, which, like all local communities, were required by OEO funding regulations to put up 20 percent of the cost of the local legal services projects in their area.

But direct threats to the program's effectiveness did not long remain the sole province of senators and city councils. In 1970, OEO director Donald Rumsfeld himself twice initiated a proposal to "regionalize" or "decentralize" the legal services program. Rumsfeld's idea was to transfer grant-making powers and other administrative responsibilities for legal services to the OEO regional directors. Although Rumsfeld blandly explained away the shift as a simple administrative technique which would bring some needed first aid to the tangled OEO bureaucracy, the proposal more closely resembled major surgery. OEO regional directorships were political appointments, filled for the most part by non-lawyers; the directors themselves were responsible for the survival of the OEO community action programs. Thus they were obliged to work closely with the state and local officials on whom the continuation and success of the individual programs depended. These same officials, however, were the very people with whom the legal services attorneys, on behalf of their clients, so often clashed. The Rumsfeld reorganization plan would indirectly have given local government officials the very influence that Congress, through the defeat of the Murphy amendments, had declined to bestow.

Subjected to the intense glare of public scrutiny by bar leaders, the press, and congressional committees, the Rumsfeld proposals were quietly buried. The battle, however, had not been without its casualties. Shortly after the proposal's defeat, Rumsfeld fired Legal Services director Terry Lenzner and deputy director Frank Jones, both strong advocates of the program's independence and its commitment to its clients. The firings signaled yet another turn away from controversial and innovative policies on the part of the national office.

The problems of the legal services program soon escalated. Early in 1973, President Nixon announced his intention to dismantle OEO and to transfer its various programs to other federal departments and agencies. Although initially described as merely another administrative measure designed to grease the wheels of the attendant bureaucracy, OEO supporters justifiably feared that the new policy would result in a wholesale gutting of federal poverty programs.

Presiding over the department's impending annihilation was acting OEO director Howard J. Phillips, former member of the Young Americans for Freedom and longtime admirer of then vice president Spiro Agnew. During his brief tenure as director, Phillips seemed to savor his assignment with all the glee of a necrophiliac surveying a freshly laid out corpse. "I personally believe in what I'm going to be doing," Phillips avowed stoutly shortly after his appointment, "so it's going to be a very easy job for me to do from that standpoint. I'm not going to have any mental hangups or reservations, and I'm just going to hope that I have the judgment and the skill to do it well." [15]

Phillips was quick to single out the legal services program as one of the primary targets of his amputative surgery. He did not hesitate to invest his mission with all the righteousness and honor he felt it deserved: "Every country needs its Cato," he said. "Well, I'm going to be this country's Cato. Cato destroyed Carthage because it was rotten. I think legal services is rotten and it will be destroyed." [16]

With Phillips in this self-described role, the first seven years of the legal services program began to look like the Golden Age of Greece to the prospective Carthaginians. Within weeks of his appointment, Phillips fired the program's director and other legal services administrators who had worked consistently for the use of test-case litigation and other law-reform techniques. In their places, he appointed both lawyers and non-lawyers known to be hostile to the existing legal services program. Phillips also issued an order limiting grant renewals to thirty-day extensions, thus making long-term litigation impossible. He sent out battalions of temporary employees to "inspect" the individual projects through auditing books, monitoring phone calls, and watching for such "internal problems" as friction between staff members, improper use of project funds, and failure to obey OEO regulations. Auditors were also instructed to take into account the reactions of local governmental institutions affected by the projects in assessing a grant recipient's impact on the community.

Phillips' tenure at OEO and the philosophy he tried to implement were destined to be short-lived. Congress renewed OEO's funding despite President Nixon's decision not to request any further appropriations, and Phillips himself resigned after U.S. district judge William B. Jones ruled that he had served illegally since his appointment had never been subjected to Senate confirmation.

To appreciate how people like Murphy, Reagan, and Phillips could scuttle these programs, legal service advocates had only to point to the history of Governor Reagan's clash with California Rural Legal Assistance (CRLA).

CRLA maintained local offices in nine rural California communities and specialized in the representation of farm workers. The project's central office in Sacramento monitored legislative and administrative activities affecting the rights of its clients. Concentrating on cases involving employment rights, education, housing, civil rights, and consumer problems, CRLA was considered one of the most effective legal services projects in the nation. In 1968, CRLA was designated "the outstanding legal services program of the year" by OEO.

CRLA was successful in a number of important law reform cases. In *Rivera* v. *Division of Industrial Welfare*, the program won a decision which raised the state's minimum wage, an order affecting 50,000 California workers. In *Hernandez* v. *Hardin*, the Department of Agriculture was ordered to establish food programs in nineteen California counties, yielding benefits of approximately $20 million for 85,000 people. In *Ybarra* v. *Fielder*, the court required the state director of agriculture to provide farm workers with information regarding the use of harmful pesticides. In one year, June 1968 through July 1969, CRLA represented a total of 2,433,000 people in both individual and class action suits and obtained a total of $48 million in benefits for the poor.

Such a string of successes, however, invited a political backlash. "Not surprisingly," veteran legal services advocate Jerome Shestack observed of CRLA, "legal services lawyers engaged in law reform activities have stepped on some powerful toes, from grape growers to governors. Legal services programs often challenge sacred cows. Public officials do not like to have to defend their actions; entrenched forces resent having their fairness challenged." [17]

Some of the toes CRLA apparently stepped on belonged to Governor Reagan. In 1971, he vetoed OEO's grant to CRLA, announcing that he had based his decision on a study of CRLA compiled by a former member of the John Birch Society, Lewis Uhler, the director of California's State Office of Economic Opportunity. Uhler had nothing good to say about CRLA. "Why should we pay the salaries of a lot of guys to run around and look up rules so that they can sue the state?" he asked. "The most a poor person is going to need a lawyer for is some divorce problems, some bankruptcy problems, some garnishment problems. What we've created in CRLA is an economic leverage equal to that existing in a large corporation. Clearly, that should not be." [18] Uhler's 238-page report threw the book at CRLA, accusing the program of disrupting the prison system and the public schools, violating various grant conditions, soliciting clients, inciting litigation, and bringing "frivolous" legal actions.

In response to Reagan's action, the then OEO director, Frank

Carlucci, who was empowered to override the governor's veto, decided instead to appoint a commission composed of three state supreme court justices to investigate the Uhler accusations. After two months of intensive hearings, at which state OEO representatives refused to appear in support of their claims, the commission found that the Uhler charges were "totally irresponsible and without foundation." The commission then went on to state that "CRLA has been discharging its duty to provide legal assistance to the poor . . . in a highly competent, efficient, and exemplary manner," [19] and recommended that the program be refunded. Carlucci took the commission's advice, but only after strapping the funds to a set of twenty-two "special conditions" designed to mollify state officials. Carlucci also gave Reagan $2.5 million with which to develop his own Judicare program—a precedent which would hardly deter other state executives from acting in a similar manner.

Reagan could take further comfort in his vendetta against CRLA early the next year, when then vice-president Spiro Agnew turned his rhetorical guns on the legal services program. Agnew made his debut in the legal assistance controversy in Camden, New Jersey, where he urged legal services lawyers to back off from a suit they had filed against two urban renewal projects. Then, in the *ABA Journal*,[20] Agnew proceeded to further delineate the conservative position against the legal services program. Throughout, the article reflected a tentative but clear concern over the effects that the poor's eventual inheritance of full access to the law might have on the existing American power structure.

Legal services lawyers, declared Agnew in the *Journal*, were nothing more than "ideological vigilantes, who owe their allegiance not to a locality, and not to the elected representatives of the people, but only to a concept of social reform." He painted a garish picture of poverty lawyers scrambling madly after every faddish cause that came down the pike while "a destitute mother of five cannot get help with an eviction notice." He warned the bar that attorneys who acted as "social engineers . . . will continue to exacerbate community tension and undermine the very purpose they were hired to accomplish," an indictment upon which Reagan could easily have looked with favor. Finally he suggested that the bar take "a harder look at how the *Code of Professional Responsibility* applies to legal services attorneys," a rather ironic suggestion in light of his own subsequent career.

Although Agnew had somehow omitted the citation of hard statistics to support his argument, so ringing an indictment from the nation's second-ranking official could not be ignored. Defenders of the program responded by showering the pages of the *Journal* with statistics and case studies effectively proving the success of the program and the emptiness of Agnew's rhetoric. It was becoming increasingly clear, however, that the program had to be removed completely from the political arena and placed within a context that would insure its freedom from threat and intimidation.

Throughout the program's history under OEO, a number of proposals had been advanced to secure its independence. Two of the plans, Judicare and the voucher system, would similarly permit indigent clients to choose their own lawyers. Under Judicare, private attorneys would be reimbursed by the federal government for legal assistance rendered to eligible clients. Under the voucher program, poor clients would "purchase" legal services with coupons that could be redeemed by private attorneys for cash from federal coffers.

Because both systems make use of private attorneys, however, they would be considerably more expensive than the staff attorney approach. Studies of the average cost of divorce and bankruptcy cases in rural legal services projects compared with the cost under existing Judicare experiments reveal that Judicare is three to six times as expensive as the staff attorney arrangement.[21] Both of the proposals leave the poor client dependent on local private attorneys, who will not only have less time to spend on their indigent clients but may be more responsive to the needs of local economic and political interests than to the needs of the poor.

Another alternative to OEO legal services would combine the voucher system with a type of prepaid legal insurance. Under this proposal, clients would join prepaid group legal services programs to hire attorneys under a closed panel system—the members of the program would be represented by the group's hired staff attorneys and could not choose their own private attorneys. Vouchers would be given to indigent clients so that they could join such a prepaid legal insurance plan and choose a plan they preferred. This type of program, however, would include private clients as well as poor. It would severely limit staff attorneys' ability to specialize in the legal needs peculiar to the poor, particularly when the interests of indigent clients conflicted with those of middle-class members of the group.

Of all the ideas promoted to free legal services from political strangleholds, the concept of a private, nonprofit legal services corporation appears to be the most viable. Advocates and critics alike of OEO legal services applauded the initial idea of placing legal services for the poor within the framework of an independent corporation. It was the only proposal for an independent legal assistance program to receive the endorsement of the organized bar as well as of Congress, with politicians on both sides of the aisle lending their support to the idea. Liberals liked it as a way to expand and enhance legal services for the poor, while conservatives hoped to use the independent corporation to restructure the program in order to control its lawyers.

The key issue in 1971 concerned precisely how the corporation's board of directors would be chosen. The philosophy of and the attitudes displayed by the majority of the directors would of course necessarily shape the law reform and funding policies of the individual projects. The Mondale bill—which called for a corporation governed by directors taken from the organized bar, legal services project attorneys, and the clients themselves—was altered in conference in deference to President Nixon, who demanded the right to appoint all of the corporation's board members. The conference committee insisted, however, that eleven of the seventeen board members be appointed from lists submitted by the organized bar, the Judicare Conference, the client community, and former legal services attorneys. President Nixon still vetoed it, objecting to his lack of full discretionary power to appoint all board members. "It would be better to have no legal services corporation than one so irresponsibly structured," [22] he observed in announcing his veto, assuming, evidently, that anything short of vesting complete authority in himself was *ipso facto* irresponsible. (A similar 1972 version died in conference following the threat of another presidential veto.)

The 1973 White House threats to dismantle OEO made the corporation issue an increasingly urgent one, providing the Administration with decisive leverage to affect the ultimate shape of the corporation bill. Accordingly, Nixon submitted a legislative proposal to Congress giving himself full discretion in the selection of the entire eleven-member board of directors. The bill also contained strong restrictions on the outside political activities of staff attorneys, prohibiting lawyers who received more than half their income from corporation-supported activities from engaging in political activity of any kind. In addition, legal services attorneys were precluded from lobbying before legislative bodies except when formally requested to do so by a member of the body itself—an unlikely possibility at best. The bill also gave the governors of each state the power to appoint an advisory council to maintain continuous review of all legal services activities within their respective states, with an eye toward reporting abuses to the national board of directors.

The restrictions and limitations contained in the Administration bill alarmed legal services advocates around the country. But as bad as it was, the House floor debate on a modified version of the proposal proved to be the stuff of which legislative nightmares are made. Twenty-two crippling amendments were added to the bill in eleven hours of floor debate; when the rhetorical dust had finally settled, the result was a bill which surpassed even the Administration's attempts to fetter poverty attorneys. Among other restrictions, the amended bill excluded staff attorneys from any political or lobbying activities, eliminated legal research back-up centers, prohibited corporation support of public interest law firms, and banned staff attorneys from bringing suits involving school desegregation or non-therapeutic abortions. By the time the bill passed the House with a vote of 276 to 95, exhausted House liberals could only hope that the Senate would pass a more recognizable form of the bill which might prevail in conference.

The Senate version was slightly better, but only slightly. It provided for a corporation run by an eleven-member board of directors appointed by the president with the advice and consent of the Senate. It barred legal services attorneys from most forms of lobbying, from bringing public interest lawsuits unrelated to the poverty problems of specific clients, and from representing clients involved in criminal cases. And finally, under threat of a presidential veto, Senate sponsors of the corporation agreed to delete back-up centers from the legal services program, centers which had provided much of the resources and research for seminal law reform cases. With this concession, a consensus quickly formed around the Senate draft, which was signed into law by President Richard Nixon in July 1974. The resulting Legal Services Corporation appeared insulated from the kind of state politics that had previously bedeviled the program, but presidential control over all board appointments made legal services advocates understandably anxious. Funding of $100 million for 1976 was a step up from the $70 million of earlier years, but still far short of the $600 million legal services supporters say is necessary to insure a full and effective program. And the back-up centers were gone.

Thus, for the present, the poor still cannot help but see the concept of full and equal access to the law as a privilege granted only to those Americans who can afford it, not as a basic right of all citizens. And yet, without effective representation, the poor person sees the law only as his enemy, forcing his acquiescence to its demands without providing him with a voice to protest them. As long as access to the courts is conditioned, in Justice William O. Douglas' words, "upon the length of a person's purse," [23] the law will remain, for the people upon whom its penalties most harshly fall, yet another arm of a monolithic and mystifying bureaucracy, which seems to care little enough for their rights and needs as it is. Fortunately, the last decade has seen the first glimmer of hope that the most basic premise of the American legal system, equal justice under law, might begin to have some meaning for the country's legions of poor people. Conscientious and dedicated efforts on the part of legislators, lawyers, law enforcement officials, and the public could make that hope, in the next decade, a reality. For now, at least, a start has been made.

*Jim Lorenz**

State of Siege:
Group Legal Services for the
Middle Class

SUPPOSE you have a limited income, several pressing legal problems, and you want to find a competent and inexpensive lawyer. What do you do if you don't know a lawyer you can trust? You can play Russian roulette with the Yellow Pages. You can call several attorneys whose names you've heard and ask them what they will charge for a contested divorce—but when you do so, three out of four say that they don't quote fees over the phone. You call the local Lawyers Referral Panel, which gives you the names of three attorneys but adds that it has no information about the fees the attorneys charge. You go to one of the attorneys, who quotes you a fee of $500. When you question him about this figure, he says he is only charging you the minimum fee schedule. After the second attorney on the list quotes you a fee of $450, you become discouraged, especially since there is a $15 charge each time you consult with an attorney on the referral panel.

In frustration, you call the local legal aid society, which says that your annual income is $1,000 over its eligibility requirements. Because of the special conditions established by federal rules for the legal aid society, the society is required to refer all "over-income" applicants to the local Lawyers Referral Panel, putting you right back where you started from. So you call a nonprofit corporation which, for $100 per case, has been advising people how to file their own divorce case, only to find that the

* JIM LORENZ BECAME THE DIRECTOR OF THE CALIFORNIA EMPLOYMENT DEVELOPMENT DEPARTMENT IN 1975. HE WAS PREVIOUSLY A PARTNER IN THE LAW FIRM OF LORENZ, BLICKER, MACKEY AND WEBB, A STATEWIDE PARTNERSHIP REPRESENTING MIDDLE-INCOME PEOPLE IN FIVE CALIFORNIA CITIES, AND THE FOUNDER AND DIRECTOR OF CALIFORNIA RURAL LEGAL ASSISTANCE, A LEGAL SERVICES PROGRAM FOR CALIFORNIA FARM WORKERS.

operation has just been enjoined from operating by the local bar association for alleged "unauthorized practice of the law." Lacking further alternatives, you return to the office of the second lawyer you spoke with and secure a divorce for $450—and then subsequently discover that the fee you paid was $200 more than that charged by other competent attorneys in your city.

Kafkaesque? Yes, this story is surely that, but it is also standard operating procedure for the legal services industry now operating in the United States. Present bar association regulations forbid any lawyer from advertising fees or services to the general public. Bar association Lawyers Referral Panels provide absolutely no fee information to the public, even though these referral panels collect a good deal of other, noneconomic information about the lawyers participating in their program. For years, bar association minimum fee schedules have either required attorneys to set fees at inflated levels or, in states where the schedules were not mandatory, have allowed attorneys to adopt parallel pricing policies, thereby leading to much the same result. Bar association regulations against "unauthorized practice" of the law have greatly inhibited attempts by non-attorneys to give less expensive legal advice, even though they may be fully competent to do so. OEO restrictions on referrals, negotiated with the American Bar Association in order to gain bar support for the OEO services program, have meant that over-income OEO applicants must go to the bar-controlled attorney pools.

This obstacle course has discouraged the pursuit of lawyers by middle-income Americans; and by reducing competition and hence increasing the cost of lawyers (as Mark Green has earlier described), it has discouraged middle-income citizens yet again. But lacking lawyers, Americans are unable to enforce their legal rights—in consumer cases, over 95 percent of which end up in default judgments; in instances of employment discrimination; in domestic relations disputes; and in countless other matters. Price fixing in some sectors of the economy may only result in economic inflation; price fixing in the legal profession results in a denial of justice as well.

One way of reducing the cost of legal representation is to foster the development of group legal services. The term "group legal services" normally refers to programs by which organizations such as labor unions, churches, or fraternal associations can provide legal assistance as a benefit of membership.

Group legal services arrangements can vary considerably. Groups may secure representation on a fee-for-services basis, whereby the group member pays only for legal services at the time he secures them; or groups may obtain services on a prepayment or insurance basis, whereby in return for an initial payment (which is made whether or not he uses any services), the member is guaranteed certain types of legal representation for no additional charge. The organizations may enter into arrangements with "closed panels" of attorneys, which are normally restricted to one or two law firms, or they may be represented by "open panels" of attorneys, which usually can be joined by any local attorney who pays the panel's registration fee.

Whatever its exact form, group legal services can lead to a substantial reduction of legal fees. Since an organization may have a considerable amount of legal business it can provide lawyers, it has substantial power to bargain for a reduction in fees. A group is also more likely than an individual to have the time and expertise to shop around for a "good deal." Because of the large volume of clients a group can refer to a particular law firm or legal panel, economies of scale and further reductions in fees may be possible. It can generate sufficient retainer or prepayment fees to justify investment in cost-saving equipment and in larger, cost-reducing non-attorney staffs.

It does not require elaborate analysis to realize that group legal services could also provide tremendous economic advantages for lawyers (consider doctors and Medicare, for example), particularly development of the middle-income market of some 140 million Americans previously priced out of the market for legal services. At the same time certain of these programs—particularly closed panel programs—could pose economic risks for the legal profession as a whole. If groups made exclusive referral arrangements with particular law firms, then other lawyers might find themselves substantially excluded from those group markets. And if groups bargained with panels of lawyers over the fees being charged, a broad pressure for the reduction of fees might develop throughout the entire profession.

Because of the threat to the legal profession posed by certain forms of group legal services, most state bar associations initially sought to prohibit them altogether. This was true from the mid-1950s, when group legal services were first being discussed, to the late 1960s, when selected unions began to institute group legal arrangements. In 1956, for example, the Virginia Supreme Court of Appeals, acting at the request of the Virginia

State Bar, prohibited the National Association for the Advancement of Colored People from hiring lawyers to assist members in the enforcement of their legal rights. The court contended that the NAACP was "fomenting and soliciting legal business in which they are not parties and have no pecuniary right or liability." Subsequently, the Virginia State Bar succeeded in restraining the Brotherhood of Railroad Trainmen from referring its injured members to particular attorneys. Similarly, the Illinois State Bar Association enjoined the United Mine Workers from employing a licensed attorney to prosecute workmen's compensation claims on behalf of its members. Finally, in the late 1960s, the Michigan State Bar Association sought to enjoin the United Transportation Union from adopting a plan whereby the union would select attorneys for injured members and their families in return for a commitment by each of the attorneys that his maximum fee would not exceed 25 percent of the recovery.

Fortunately, in all these cases the Supreme Court ruled that the bar associations could not frustrate access to lawyers by the group involved. (See the Freedman and Lieberman chapters for greater elaboration.)

The Court's decisions forced the organized bar to reevaluate its position on group legal services. In 1970, the American Bar Association adopted disciplinary rules which approved the principle of group legal services while limiting its implementation. Pursuant to Rule 2-103(d)(5) of the ABA's Disciplinary Rules, a lawyer could cooperate with a nonprofit group legal services operation so long as:

(a) The primary purposes of such organizations do not include the rendition of legal services.

(b) The recommending, furnishing, or paying for legal services to its members is incidental and reasonably related to the primary purposes of such organization.

(c) Such organization does not derive a financial benefit from the rendition of legal services by the lawyer.

(d) The member or beneficiary for whom the legal services are rendered, and not such organization, is recognized as the client of the lawyer in that matter.

Adopted by more than twenty-five state bar associations by 1973, Disciplinary Rule 2-103 contains a major limitation in subsection (b): Lawyers can work with group legal services arrangements *only if* their services directly relate "to the primary purposes" of the organization.

Thus, a group legal services plan with a union could provide representation for employer-related matters, but could not allow for representation for other general problems, such as domestic relations, probate, real estate, or consumer disputes.

Narrowly drafted to concede only the specific holdings of the *Button, Brotherhood of Railroad Trainmen*, and *United Mine Worker* cases, Disciplinary Rule 2-103 continues to prohibit the development of general-purpose group legal services programs for group members, thereby substantially reducing the market for such programs. There is one significant exception to this restriction, however: If the group legal services plan is promoted by a bar association representing the "general bar of the geographical area in which the association exists," then the plan can provide general services for any conceivable legal problem. (One possible reason why bar-sponsored programs are so favored by the American Bar Association is that, by including all the lawyers in a geographical area in one program, they are less likely to engage in price-cutting practices than are smaller "closed panel" programs.)

The ABA's "primary purpose" restriction was not the only bar strategy to limit the development of group legal programs. In California, where approximately 20 percent of the nation's group legal services programs developed during the early 1970s, the state bar association attempted to limit the extent to which closed panel plans could publicize themselves. Pursuant to Rule 20 of the California Rules of Professional Conduct, group legal services arrangements are barred from initiating any contract with prospective group members, from releasing any information about their plans unless requested to do so, and even from indicating the names of the lawyers providing the services after the groups sign up. But if group legal services attorneys cannot initiate contracts, then many groups will never know of their lost opportunity. They can then only find out about inexpensive prepaid group plans through some other agency, such as the state bar—and the state bar has persistently refused to publicize the existence of Rule 20 plans. And if group legal attorneys are prevented from identifying themselves by name or indicating their qualifications after groups sign up with them, then many group members will feel less than fully confident in seeking representation from lawyers who must remain anonymous.

These observations are borne out by statistics on group legal services programs in California. Of the 58,000 voluntary membership organizations operating in the state in 1974, only one percent had signed up for these services. At least 40 percent of these arrangements provided for no reductions in fees. Member utilization for most of the plans was running less than 5 percent per year. At least 70 percent of the 500-odd organizations involved in group legal services by 1974 had relationships with their group legal services attorneys before Rule 20 was passed. What Rule 20 meant, then, was more a memorialization of preexisting relationships than an extension of new services to previously underrepresented organizations.

Rule 20 was not the only action the California Bar took against group legal services. It acknowledged the lucrative middle-income market to be developed and exploited by the legal profession—and then set out to monopolize it. The California Bar decided to empower itself and county bar associations to establish open-panel group legal services programs financed on a prepaid basis by consumers. As set forth in Rule 23 of the California Rules of Professional Conduct, adopted in June 1973, the bar's group legal services plan seeks to enroll all the lawyers practicing in any given geographical area. All of the participants in the bar's program are required to charge fees according to the same fee schedules. In order to encourage the development of only one such plan in each geographical area, the state bar waives the traditional prohibitions against solicitation and advertising for any program which enrolls a substantial portion of the local bar.

It is little wonder that bar associations throughout the country have characterized this approach as the wave of the future, for the California Bar creates cartels of attorneys who comprise a pervasive network of price fixing and who will be required to function according to the same procedures for the provision of group legal services. Finally, by allowing bar-sponsored open panel plans to solicit and advertise while continuing to prohibit closed panel plans from doing so, the bar creates an enormous competitive advantage for bar-sponsored programs.

The next step was up to the American Bar Association. At its February 1974 meeting in Houston, the ABA's House of Delegates approved a series of actions to promote bar-sponsored open panel plans while at the same time discouraging, if not prohibiting, the establishment of closed panel arrangements. The House of Delegates urged state and local bar associations to design prepaid legal services programs which would be conducted on an open panel basis. Simultaneously, the House of Delegates amended Disciplinary Rule 2-103 to provide that bar-sponsored open panel plans can freely advertise while closed panel plans cannot. And it prohibited non-bar-sponsored programs from operating for profit and from being organized with the primary purpose of recommending or rendering group legal services—thereby *prohibiting* profit-making closed panel entities from being organized by groups of lawyers. Finally, the House of Delegates forbid closed panel programs to restrict their clients only to those lawyers enrolled in the panel. Hence, a closed panel would be required to allow group members to seek representation from lawyers not enrolled in the closed panel and would be required to reimburse them according to the same rate as would be paid to closed panel members—thus requiring closed panel programs to operate in an open panel manner. This provision could completely discourage reduced fee arrangements: Because attorneys enrolled in a closed panel can no longer be assured of receiving a given volume of business from the panel, they may have substantially less incentive to reduce their fees for group legal services arrangements.

As if these limitations on closed panels were not enough, the ABA's House of Delegates passed an additional Ethical Consideration stating that even those closed panel plans able to comply with the Association's previous restrictions might still violate the basic ethical requirement that lawyers operate in an "independent" manner. "An attorney . . . should carefully consider the risks involved before accepting employment by groups under plans which do not provide their members with a free choice of counsel," the Ethical Consideration concluded. As a further interpretation of this position, the ABA made references to an informal ethics opinion, passed by the ABA's Ethics Committee in 1972, which prohibits lawyers involved in a closed panel arrangement from making any promises to the groups regarding reductions in fees.

These rules involved nothing more than the exploitation of a new market at high rates unilaterally set by lawyer trade associations. ABA lawyers may have been pleased with their Houston slight-of-hand, but labor unions, consumer organizations, and the Justice Department were not. Labor and consumer groups balked at the restrictions imposed on closed panel plans. In late 1974, the federal pension reform law included a section preempting state laws and agencies from regulating legal service plans. Senator Jacob Javits, a legislative sponsor of the measure, declared, "The State, directly or indirectly through the bar, is preempted from regulating the form and content of a legal services plan, for example, open versus closed panels, in the guise of disciplinary or ethical rules or proceedings." Thomas Kauper, head of the Justice Department's Antitrust Division, warned that because the so-called Houston Amendments "raise very serious questions of competitive disadvantage for differing kinds of legal service delivery systems . . . they could be held to violate federal antitrust laws." Indeed, in January 1975 a consumer group sued the Tennessee Bar Association on antitrust grounds for adopting the ABA's rules on prepaid plans.

The bar finally saw the light because it felt the heat. The Association hired a Chicago law firm in 1974 to study its legal liability under the antitrust laws. And after some furious bargaining between advocates and opponents of closed panel plans at the ABA's February 1975 winter meeting in Chicago, the Association substantially eased its restrictions on prepaid legal service plans. No longer would there be any discrimination between open and closed panel plans, except that closed panel groups must provide for fair grievance procedures if a subscriber wants to opt out of the plan because he or she claims the law service would be "unethical, improper, or inadequate." Two other restrictions still disturbed labor and consumer forces: Insurance companies were barred from running closed panel programs; and although the new rules allow "dignified commercial publicity" for group plans, advertisements cannot include the prices charged or names of lawyers providing the service. Still, closed panel advocates considered the revisions a seminal breakthrough. "That was the last stumbling block," exalted Sandy Dement of the National Consumer Center for Legal Services, a group busily midwifing closed panel plans around the country.

It remains to be seen what organized consumer groups can do to counter the price-fixing efforts of the organized bar. Certainly, there have been stirrings of consumer interest. In August 1972 more than two hundred unions, fraternal benefit associations, and other consumer groups established the National Consumer Center for Legal Services, in part to counter bar association attempts to frustrate the inexpensive prepaid group legal services market. By the summer of 1973, the Center succeeded in persuading Congress to amend the Labor-Management Relations Act (LMRA) in order to authorize employer contributions to trust funds which would finance prepaid legal services for union members. (As a critical part of this lobbying effort, the Center helped defeat eleventh-hour attempts to limit LMRA trust funds to open panel programs.) These groups also proved instrumental in pressuring the ABA into its February 1975 revisions.

To ensure that local bar associations do not now constitute a new obstacle course for the creation of legal insurance programs, consumer and labor groups are going to have to continue their vigilance. One weapon in their arsenal is antitrust litigation against organized bar associations which discourage group legal services by local rules. According to Louis Bernstein, chief of the Special Litigation Section of the Antitrust Division of the Department of Justice, bar rules which favor bar-sponsored group legal services programs while discouraging non-bar-sponsored programs may well constitute a violation of antitrust laws. As Mr. Bernstein noted in a December 1973 speech to the American Bar Association:

> The monopoly problem would not appear to exist in cases of plans developed, promoted and administered by insurance companies, consumer groups, or small groups of private practitioners. The existence of a number of such plans would mitigate the risk of any one of them developing the power to control lawyers' fees or to exclude competition in the rendering of legal services. However, the opportunity for monopoly does arise when a bar association promotes, develops and administers a plan in those situations where the state's code of ethics permits only that plan to advertise. Clearly, if this result is intended, it is prohibited by the antitrust laws. If this goal is not intended, the plan might still be illegal if such effect would necessarily result from the plan.

Antitrust litigation could pose a particularly serious threat to the operations of the organized bar—for the simple reason that in antitrust cases successful litigants can recover treble damages for injuries resulting from the monopolistic arrangement. If, as has been estimated, legal fees in the United States are inflated by at least 25 percent, then the treble damage liability of the bar could amount to millions of dollars. Consumer litigants would not necessarily have to win a court judgment in order to force the bar to modify its regulatory policies; given the massive amount of money damages involved, even the mere prospect of such a recovery might be enough to bring about reforms. Were state bar associations to find themselves as the defendants in antitrust litigation, for example, they might be very wary about implementing restrictive rules against closed panel programs, such as those contained in amended Disciplinary Rule 2-103. And if the organized bar could be deterred from implementing its rules against closed panel programs, then there might be an opportunity for reduced-fee closed panel programs to develop on their own initiative —and for consumer groups to begin analyzing and disseminating information about these programs. This consumer involvement is crucial. It is the consumer groups, after all, which have the primary interest in the development of low-cost group legal services programs.

What might consumer groups do at the grass-roots level to foster the development of these programs? They could form a nonprofit corporation, composed completely of non-lawyers, which would survey all the group legal services programs in a particular state, analyze the data collected, and distribute the information to labor unions, fraternal benefit associations, churches, credit unions, and other potential utilizers of such services. Not only would such a survey apprise consumer groups of the availability of group legal services, it would also enable such groups to judge which are the lower-cost plans and which lawyers have the most experience in providing services. If, on the basis of more informed evaluations, a large number of consumer groups gravitated to the lower-fee programs, some pressure might be generally exerted for a reduction of fees throughout the legal profession.

Since the consumer organization would not be composed of lawyers, it would not be subject to direct regulation by bar associations. And because the nonprofit corporation would be collecting information about all lawyers providing group legal services, it could not be said to be operating as an advertising or solicitation agent for just a few; consequently, the lawyers providing information to the nonprofit corporation could not be accused of using it as their solicitation or advertising agent. Indeed, the nonprofit corporation would be doing nothing more than providing information about everything that was available.

What I describe here is not merely theoretical. For the past three years, various consumer groups in California have been working on such a project. In 1972, representatives of unions, churches, senior citizens, and other groups organized a not-for-profit task force, the Group Legal Institute of California, to conduct a survey of group legal services in California. During the summer of 1973, its staff personally interviewed firms providing group legal services. Somewhat surprisingly, 125 of the 144 group legal service firms in the state consented to be interviewed. On the basis of the data obtained, the Group Legal Institute prepared a survey chart, briefly describing seventeen different aspects of each firm's group legal services plan. In late 1973, the Institute held follow-up interviews with lawyers in order to obtain more fee information. By June 1974, the survey had been mailed to more than 58,000 voluntary membership organizations operating in the state.

The Institute's greatest difficulty during the survey was in comparing the fees charged by different firms. Some surveyed said they reduced their fees a certain percentage below "prevailing rates," without being able to say what those "prevailing rates" were. Other firms supplied printed fee schedules which described their services in widely different ways, making comparisons difficult. Other attorneys indicated that their fees were informally determined, on a case-by-case basis, making fee comparison impossible. Even where the firms surveyed quoted their fees in terms of a county minimum fee schedule, comparisons among attorneys in different counties proved difficult because minimum fee schedules varied from county to county.

To resolve this problem, the Group Legal Institute staff decided to collect and study local minimum fee schedules from all over the state. The types of services most commonly described in the minimum fee schedules were then listed on a single, new "California Standardized Fee Schedule," which in turn was sent to each group legal services firm in the state. After the firms returned this California Standardized Fee Schedule, the Group Legal Institute staff made an accurate comparison of the fees charged.

Once the Institute obtained comparable fee data, a major question remained—the extent, if at all, each firm was reducing its fees below statewide averages. In order to answer this question, the Group Legal Institute staff reviewed the county minimum fee schedules from all over the state, computed statewide average fees for certain types of services, and compared these statewide averages for certain services with the fees quoted by various attorneys for the same type of services. Thus, if the statewide average for a default divorce was determined to be $300, and law firm A said it was charging $250, while law firm B quoted a fee of $200, the Group Legal Institute staff could say that law firm A. was charging a divorce fee 16 percent below the statewide average and law firm B was charging a divorce fee $33\frac{1}{3}$ percent below the statewide average.

Having calculated fee reductions, the most difficult part of the survey, the Group Legal Institute staff then progressed to a more comprehensive description of the firm's practices on a comparison chart. For each firm, the chart indicated:

- The number of lawyers in the firm

- The percentage of minority and women lawyers in the firm

- The number of groups and total numbers of group members enrolled in the firm's group legal services plan

- The percentage of firm staff time spent on group legal services

- The fee which the firm charges for a default divorce

- The firm's fee for a will and trust

- The firm's fee for settlement of a personal injury case after pretrial

- The firm's fee for an individual bankruptcy

- The firm's hourly rate

- Whether the firm provides groups with a written fee schedule

- Whether the firm has filled out the California Standardized Fee Schedule

- Whether the firm has reduced its fees below certain statewide averages

- Whether the firm offers preliminary services to members without extra charge

- Whether the firm provides emergency services

- Whether certain types of services are excluded from the firm's plan

- Whether the firm's plan provides for evaluation and dispute-resolution procedures

- Whether the firm is willing to provide groups with financial information about the firm's profits from group legal services

On the left side of the descriptive chart, the name and address of each group legal services firm was indicated. Across the top of the chart, the seventeen different categories were indicated. In this way, a consumer group could compare each of the law firms in its geographical area according to the seventeen categories.

Accompanying the chart was a paper entitled "How to Evaluate Lawyers." The paper attempted to explain the seventeen categories: that is, how a firm's size can affect the quality of service which it offers; why it is important for firms to hire minority and women lawyers; why it is important for fees to be quoted on a printed fee schedule; what kinds of preliminary services should be offered without additional charge; and what kinds of emergency services groups may be able to obtain.

It is still too early, as of this writing, to measure adequately the success of the survey in developing consumer interest in group legal services or in bringing about a reduction of legal fees. Yet the initial experience of the survey—the willingness of lawyers to give the information and the ability of the Group Legal Institute to compare fees—is sufficiently encouraging to suggest that similar efforts in other parts of the country might succeed.

Ultimately, the expenses of surveying the legal profession should be borne not by consumer groups but by the organized bar. Bar associations collect substantial amounts of monies, in the form of members' dues, which could be used to finance such efforts. In addition, the *Code of Professional Responsibility* affirmatively obligates the bar to do justice: Canon 2 says, for example, that "a lawyer should assist the legal profession in fulfilling its duty to make legal counsel available," and Canon 8 reads, "A lawyer should assist in improving the legal system." If the bar is actually going to fulfill its professional responsibilities, it should itself undertake the preparation and dissemination of the type of survey conducted by the Group Legal Institute. While it may be expecting too much of bar associations to initially design consumer-type surveys, there is no reason why bar associations could not administer such surveys on an ongoing basis, once the surveys are developed and tested by consumers.

In addition, there is no reason why lawyers seeking the referral of cases from a lawyers referral panel cannot be required to fill out standardized fee schedules much like the fee schedule prepared by the Group Legal Institute. The fee schedules could be kept on file for consumers to examine and could be cross-indexed so that, for particular kinds of services, consumers could determine what various lawyers are charging— and opt for the less expensive lawyer if they so chose.

Are these suggestions viable? No less of an authority on the legal professional than James D. Fellers, the 1974–75 president of the American Bar Association, has posed the question: "Will consumers soon bargain with lawyers?" According to Mr. Fellers:

. . . [W]e have in Washington (1) a Congressional subcommittee whose jurisdiction specifically involves the delivery of legal services and . . . (2) a powerful consumer lobby promoting legislation to expand and improve the delivery of legal services to an estimated 140 million Americans . . . , combined further with (3) a reform-oriented group of lawyer activists who have great skill in mobilizing public, press, and Congressional interest in their news and projects.

These three ingredients provide the kind of mix that will have a major impact on the shaping of public policy as to the delivery of legal services and ultimately on the way we practice law.

Thus, there is now some admitted concern by the bar about the problem, to be sure, but there is also widespread apathy. Much of the legal process in the legal profession, as David Riley writes elsewhere in this volume, has been viewed by the public as a mysterious science understood only by lawyers. In the last analysis, this sense of mystery will have to be dispelled if the public is to effectively participate. The law is too important to be left solely to the control of lawyers.

Charles R. Halpern[*]

The Public Interest Bar:
An Audit

I N THE SPRING OF 1971, sixty lawyers and non-lawyers met for a
two-day working seminar, "The Bar and the Public Interest," at
Airlie House in the rolling Virginia hills south of Washington, D.C.
In contrast to the pastoral setting, the conferees were largely an urban
group. While they shared a common belief that the legal profession had
failed to provide legal services equitably to all groups in the society, a high
level of tension soon appeared among them. There were some suspicions
and even distrust between the Black and Chicano lawyers involved in
civil rights battles, the civil liberties veterans, and the poverty lawyers, on
the one hand, and the newer breed of "public interest lawyers"—the
environmental lawyers and consumer lawyers—on the other. George
Wiley of the National Welfare Rights Organization, for example, made it
vehemently clear that he viewed the environmentalists more as enemies
than as allies. The conference had been scheduled to develop plans for
financing needed for legal services, but it never got the chance. The only
thing peaceful about the meeting was the landscape.

Three years later, in April 1974, the Ford Foundation convened a
conference in San Diego, this time more narrowly limited to the new
public interest lawyers. While the sessions were more harmonious, the
same problem continued to plague the discussions: how to pay for public
interest law practice that cannot sustain itself financially. There was much
bonhomie and talk, but no solutions.

Advocates affected by this problem are familiar—civil rights lawyers,
ACLU lawyers, poverty lawyers, and the NAACP Legal Defense Fund,
for examples. In the past six years, however, a new species of activist

[*] CHARLES HALPERN WAS A FOUNDER AND THE FIRST DIRECTOR OF THE CENTER FOR LAW AND SOCIAL
POLICY IN WASHINGTON, D.C. HE IS PRESENTLY HEAD OF THE COUNCIL FOR PUBLIC INTEREST LAW, A
BAR-AND-FOUNDATION-SUPPORTED GROUP PURSUING ALTERNATIVES FOR PUBLIC INTEREST LAW
FUNDING.

lawyer has joined these ranks—the so-called public interest lawyer. While his territory is not precisely defined, this type of lawyer frequently deals with problems which arise at the intersection of corporate power and governmental responsibility, in those administrative and executive agencies where decisions affecting large numbers of private citizens used to be often quietly if not casually made. It has long been recognized that the decisions of the federal agencies are significantly influenced by Washington law firms which have for years represented corporations and other private clients with a large financial stake in the actions of such agencies. In contrast, the Senate Commerce Committee report on the Consumer Protection Agency bill blames the failure of government programs to consider consumer interests adequately on "the present lack of effective representation of consumer interests before federal agencies." Nicholas Johnson, a dedicated member of the Federal Communications Commission until his departure in 1973, summarized the situation at the FCC:

> Private citizens who seek to present their cases before the Federal Communications Commission . . . are positively discouraged in their efforts by the agency. Citizen participation in the FCC's decision-making process has therefore come to be virtually nonexistent—in large part due to the complex rules and procedures and the ordinary citizens' inability to hire competent counsel to lead them through the maze. One can, of course, always find exceptions to this bleak characterization, but most observers would agree that involvement in FCC decisions by persons who have no direct financial stake in the outcome is seriously and chronically deficient.

Believers in the adversary process, public interest lawyers aimed to develop legal counterweights to the corporate bar. Since a real adversary process had not been tried before many government agencies, they felt it should at least be given a fair trial. This approach drew inspiration from the successes of Ralph Nader and shared his perceptions of corporate irresponsibility, regulatory failures, and default by the legal profession. For example, public interest lawyers have recently been involved in these issues:

- Should the license of a racist television station in Mississippi be renewed? While this decision vitally affects the interests of many black Mississippians, traditionally it would have been made by the station and the Federal Communications Commission without participation of interested listeners.

- Should defective truck wheels, subject to sudden and catastrophic failure, installed on General Motors pick-up trucks, be recalled? This question, which potentially affects all highway users, would have been worked out between GM and the National Highway Traffic and Safety Administration without citizen representation.

- Should ineffective drugs be removed from the market and after what procedures? This issue historically had been negotiated between the FDA and the drug industry, but what of the millions of citizens who buy those useless drugs?

The public interest lawyers defined their role more broadly than the poverty lawyers of a decade ago. First, they believed that the poor were not the only people excluded from the decision-making process on issues of vital importance to them. All people concerned with environmental degradation, with product safety, with consumer protection, whatever their class, were largely uninvolved in key policy judgments. Second, public interest lawyers began to work an area that had only been tangentially touched by poverty or political lawyers—that domain where corporate power shaped governmental power. Here the legal system was not merely a neutral observer. By underrepresenting citizen interests and overrepresenting corporate interests, the legal profession exacerbated the problems inherent in governmental attempts to assert public control over corporate authority.

Armed with this critique of the judicial and administrative processes, some of these lawyers established tax-exempt institutes like the Center for Law and Social Policy (CLASP) and sought foundation support for their activity. Others, like Ed Berlin, Tony Roisman, and Gladys Kessler, organized conventionally structured partnerships in order to represent underrepresented groups. Suspicious of the long-term reliability of foundations, they sought to serve citizen groups, including conservation and consumer groups, who could pay modest fees.

The first years were lean for both groups. Fee-paying clients were slow coming and slow paying. The foundations were skeptical about underwriting litigation projects of this unconventional character, particularly at a time when foundations themselves were under fire from congressional committees, supposedly for their excessive activism. For its first six months, to take one example, CLASP was housed in a row-house rented by one of the attorneys; the Xerox machine sat on his kitchen table. At several points during this period, it seemed that the venture would have to be abandoned and the four lawyers return to traditional practice. Slowly, however, the elements of a successful project began to coalesce. With the support of Arthur Goldberg, then recently returned to private life, CLASP was able to recruit highly respected and concerned trustees. Some of the smaller and more venturesome foundations contributed start-up grants. CLASP began a clinical training program in cooperation with the Stanford, UCLA, Michigan, Pennsylvania, and Yale law schools. In the spring of 1970, major litigation successes in the Alaska Pipeline case and the DDT case helped establish the credibility and impact of the program. A year after its founding, CLASP received an eighteen-month grant of $375,000 from the Ford Foundation, and its immediate future seemed secure.

In 1970, though, the public interest lawyers were still only a small clutch of colleagues. Speaking about that time, Senator Edward Kennedy later said, "We were able to fit almost the entire public interest bar of Washington around a single table." [1] In the intervening years the public interest bar has grown, with several new groups established in Washington, New York, Chicago, San Francisco, and Los Angeles. Each of these law groups developed a different emphasis and structure. Some focused on particular subjects, like the Citizens Communication Center on federal communications policy and the Natural Resources Defense Council on environmental issues. Some emphasized clinical legal education and law-school ties (Institute for Public Interest Representation). Others focused on local (Stern Community Law Firm) or state (Center for Law in the Public Interest) matters. Some built memberships and filed suits in their own name (Environmental Defense Fund), while others were aligned with existing membership organizations (Sierra Club Legal Defense Fund and Consumers Union Law Firm).

Despite its growth during the past five years, the public interest bar is still a very small group, particularly when compared to the private bar. For example, there are more than 700 specialized communications lawyers who represent the industry and only six who represent viewers and citizen groups. Of the 18,000 lawyers who are members of the District of Columbia Bar, less than a hundred specialize in representation of consumer and environmental interests.* The total budget of Ralph

---

* Using the broadest definition of public interest law and conducting a survey in mid-1974, Mark Green has estimated that there are 190 public interest lawyers in 50 organizations in Washington, D.C.

Nader's Public Citizen Litigation Group, for example, is considerably less than the annual compensation of the top two partners in any of the city's big law firms.

Thus, the public interest bar by no means represents a massive mobilization of powerful citizen advocacy groups. The tangle of alphabetically abbreviated institutions resembles the New Deal agencies only in their confusing interrelationships and bewildering acronyms, not in size, scope, or power. In fact, the public interest bar is still so small that there are many areas of citizen concern that are untouched. There are still agencies, like the Civil Aeronautics Board or the Interstate Commerce Commission, in which industry is represented by hundreds of specialized practitioners but citizen interests are represented by only one or two part-time lawyers. The most impressive names—Centers, Funds, Councils, and Institutes—often have behind them only two or three relatively inexperienced lawyers.

Victories came relatively easily in the early years. Government agencies and the industries they regulated, unaccustomed to having their actions challenged, had grown careless about the ways they did business. The agencies did not take the trouble to make a record that would withstand even cursory judicial review, because in most cases there was nobody to appeal from pro-industry decisions. With the development of the public interest bar, however, the highway builders, the nuclear power promoters, the offshore oil explorers, and the automobile industry had to accommodate to a new kind of legal system—one in which their arguments did not invariably go unopposed. Public interest lawyers altered the equation. Two examples will suggest some of the impact—and the problems—of public interest litigation:

The Alaska Pipeline case: In April 1970, environmental groups obtained a preliminary injunction against the issuance of permits by the Department of the Interior for construction of a trans-Alaska pipeline. The permits were a matter of dollar urgency to the oil firms involved, their investment in the pipeline totaling more than a billion dollars. According to their estimates, each day of construction delay cost them $3.5 million.[2] The environmentalists considered the matter crucially important since Alaska contained unique wilderness areas, the pipeline was built across one of the most active earthquake zones in the world, and the case posed a critical test for the newly passed National Environmental Policy Act (NEPA).

Prior to this suit, the Department of the Interior had barely gone through the motions of complying with NEPA; and it had ignored the language of the Mineral Leasing Act which limited the width of pipeline rights-of-way over public lands. Yet legal challenges by environmentalists and other interested citizen groups were then a novelty. The grant of a preliminary injunction threw the Department of the Interior back into a process of reevaluation of the environmental consequences of the Alaska pipeline that lasted almost two years. After Interior had considered alternatives to the pipeline and satisfied itself that the pipeline plan was environmentally acceptable, the Court of Appeals for the District of Columbia nonetheless held that the issuance of the pipeline permit violated the Mineral Leasing Act width restrictions.[3] Ultimately, the decision whether to build the pipeline was made by Congress, which in November 1973 passed new legislation authorizing construction. While the oil companies lobbied heavily for the bill, environmentalists were handcuffed by the prohibition on lobbying by tax-exempt organizations. A tie-vote in the Senate was broken by Vice President Spiro Agnew's vote favoring pipeline construction—which was a harsh lesson on how to lose politically what you win legally.

The DDT litigation: In 1969, public interest lawyers filed a petition in the Department of Agriculture to institute cancellation proceedings for DDT. The petition relied on scientific evidence showing the long-term environmental harm caused by DDT and indicating that the pesticide caused cancer in experimental animals. At that time, the department did not even have a procedure for entertaining citizen petitions, and the petition was simply left on the desk of the Secretary's secretary. The Secretary assured the petitioning environmentalists that he had the matter under scrutiny and that their inputs were welcome but unnecessary. Reviewing this decision, the District of Columbia Court of Appeals held that the environmentalists had "standing" to petition the Department of Agriculture and to seek judicial review of the rejection of their petition. As a result, the Environmental Protection Agency (to which the pesticide-regulation responsibility had been shifted from Agriculture), began an administrative hearing that lasted seven months. Finally, the EPA concluded that DDT registrations should be canceled. In December 1973, four years after the initial petition had been filed by environmentalists, the Court of Appeals sustained this decision. The impact of the decision has been substantial: From 12 million pounds of sales in 1971, sales of DDT dropped to 325,000 pounds by 1974.

In both cases—the Alaska Pipeline and DDT—litigation was successful only in a limited sense. The Alaska Pipeline case was eventually lost in Congress, while the DDT litigation cost the public interest law firms involved a substantial percentage of their small and strained manpower and resources.

Furthermore, the litigation process itself is often a clumsy method for affecting policy decisions. Litigation is time-consuming and costly, and chance factors, such as the values and temperament of the judge assigned a case, are inordinately important. Indeed, as the Washington corporate lawyer knows, litigation against government agencies usually represents a failure of negotiation and informal lobbying efforts. While the problems of obtaining access to informal decisional processes are greater for representatives of citizen groups than for representatives of ITT or the milk industry, public interest lawyers have successfully used a variety of non-litigative methods to serve the interests of their clients. Consider just three examples:

- The Natural Resources Defense Council (NRDC) has established projects to monitor performance by EPA and state agencies under federal clean air and clean water legislation. NRDC lawyers have developed expertise in this matter, contacts with technical consultants, and relationships with personnel within EPA in order to help assert the environmentalists' interest in strict enforcement. Without resorting to court proceedings, except in unusual cases, NRDC has had substantial impact on EPA activities.

- One important technique that public interest lawyers have developed, particularly Ralph Nader, is the in-depth investigation of an agency's performance and publication of comprehensive reports on the successes and failures of the agency. To date, he has published some thirty critiques of what the government does and doesn't do. The pioneering report on the Federal Trade Commission, for example, revealed cronyism, lethargy, and a total failure by the agency to serve the public interest. This Nader report triggered a subsequent ABA investigation and led to the revitalization of the agency under the leadership of chairman Miles Kirkpatrick.

- The Project on Corporate Responsibility, focusing on corporations themselves, has developed innovative ways to attack socially irresponsible corporate behavior. The empty rituals of corporate democracy were made into a significant method to raise issues of corporate responsibility. Through Campaign GM, the Project spotlighted General Motors' policies which adversely affected minorities, environmentalists, and consumers—and even stung the auto dinosaur into some action. It also helped awaken institutional investors, such as universities, foundations, and church groups, to their social responsibilities as investors and led directly to the reformulation of investment policies in such institutions as Yale University and the National Council of Churches.

An appraisal of the first six years of public interest advocacy—1969 to 1975—reveals mixed results:

First, public interest lawyers have won important litigation victories. Case-law development has substantially expanded the notion of legal "standing" and has improved the enforcement of some consumer—and environmental—protection statutes. But winning lawsuits, as any lawyer knows, does not invariably mean that the client's objectives are attained. Particularly when a public interest lawsuit touches important corporate interests, corporations can often end-run the legal process by going to Congress and rewriting the rules. They can manipulate markets to generate scarcity and manipulate the media to create crises. These techniques, which are beyond the reach of the public interest lawyer or his clients, will always put outer limits on the value of litigation as a technique for citizen action.

Second, the public interest lawyers have begun to expand consciousness within the bar. For example, former ABA president Chesterfield Smith, noting that "all American lawyers . . . live and die as professionals" by the adversary system, has strongly endorsed public interest law and suggested that lawyers tax themselves to support public interest efforts. Yet the influential Administrative Conference of the United States, a public body, overwhelmingly represents the corporate bar, government attorneys, and academics. There are only two public interest lawyers among its membership of ninety-one; a recent suggestion that the membership of the conference should include additional public interest lawyers was rejected.

Third, during the past six years, representation by public interest lawyers has helped create a new administrative atmosphere that at times is more receptive to citizen advocacy and more sensitive to the agencies' public responsibilities. This is particularly true of those agencies in which public interest lawyers have been active, like the Environmental Protection Agency, the Federal Trade Commission, and the Food and Drug Administration.

Again, however, the success is a limited one. Some agencies still have never dealt with any public interest lawyers. While private law firms have groups of specialists who regularly monitor the agencies, much public interest practice has been more ad hoc than systematic, and few public interest lawyers have been involved in a single agency's decisions on a regular basis. Thus, administrative agencies have some reason to doubt the staying power of public interest lawyers and their clients. The Food and Drug Administration knows that Covington & Burling, and its clients like the Institute of Shortening and Edible Oils, will be back next year. They do not know whether the American Public Health Association, represented by foundation-funded public interest lawyers, will be back.

A public interest lawyer may bring a case before the Civil Aeronautics Board one day and the Federal Trade Commission the next, and in the FDA on the third day. Even if all these cases are won, the impact on agency decision-making is problematical. A core group of lawyers dealing with similar problems on a continuing basis in the same agency would appear to be a minimum requirement for effective citizen representation —a condition not now fulfilled.

Moreover, especially in agencies dealing with complex technological problems, lawyers need access to experts. The public interest bar has yet to solve this problem. Corporate lawyers have the benefit of the expertise lodged in the corporate clients; and they have vast resources to retain "independent" experts to buttress the opinions of their clients. Public interest lawyers have neither.

Fourth, citizen groups represented by public interest lawyers have been educated through their participation in litigation. They have learned about the power of litigation as a tool; some groups, like the National Wildlife Federation and Consumers Union, have funded in-house public interest lawyers. They have also come to understand more clearly the complex interrelationships between litigation, lobbying, and public education—all of which are necessary for realizing their program objectives. For instance, environmental groups have begun to develop more coherent strategies in seeking environmental objectives, rather than fighting brushfires through efforts to stop a highway here or a power-line crossing there. Still, few citizen groups have the financing, expertise, and stability to develop coherent strategies. Where interests are more diffuse and less urgently felt than in the environmental lobby, or where there are inadequate financial resources, effective citizen organization is even more difficult. Where is the group to develop an effective strategy for vigorous regulation of the pharmaceutical industry or increases in housing subsidies for the poor?

Fifth, any evaluation of the first years of public interest law must take into account the severe restrictions imposed by the tax laws and the Internal Revenue Service on lawyers associated with tax-exempt public interest law firms. One major problem is the tax code's prohibition of lobbying by tax-exempt groups. Since public interest advocates are precluded from lobbying, one-sided presentation of issues in Congress can lead to skewed legislative results.

Even worse than legislative restrictions is bureaucratic arbitrariness. In the fall of 1970, the IRS unexpectedly issued a ruling effectively suspending the tax exemption of public interest law groups. Under this ruling, no donor could safely make contributions even to programs which had already received an exemption ruling. Congressional criticism of the IRS spanned the political spectrum—from Senator Gaylord Nelson to (then) Representative Gerald Ford. A group of seventeen bar leaders with extensive governmental experience, including seven former chairmen of administrative agencies and two former cabinet members, protested to the secretary of the treasury. There was an avalanche of critical editorials. After six weeks of debate in the press and in Congress, the IRS suddenly relented and acknowledged that public interest law was properly viewed as a tax-exempt activity.

That, however, did not signal the end of IRS interference. The Center for Corporate Responsibility was virtually destroyed by the IRS's failure for thirty-eight months to act on its tax-exemption application. Finally, after a suit was filed by the Center in May 1973, the District Court for the District of Columbia ordered, on December 11, 1973, that the IRS grant the Center an exemption.[4] The Center eventually received its exemption notice from the IRS in February 1974, but by then was moribund.

After six years of steady development, public interest law is now entering a new phase. During the first phase, the public interest lawyers tested a hypothesis—that public interest representation could improve the quality of decision-making on important issues of public policy. This experiment was hardly carried on under ideal conditions. There were too few public interest lawyers; their services were offered to groups ill-prepared to take advantage of them; they were underfinanced, and insufficiently backed up with technical advice; and threatened by the IRS, they could not, as business groups could, carry their case to the legislatures. In recruiting lawyers the public interest firms were unable to offer competitive salaries, job security, or the prospect of conventional career advancement.

Yet public interest law took root and grew, so that by today these institutions must plan for continuity, which will in no way be an easy task. During the past year, several lawyers have left public interest practice and returned to the security afforded by conventional careers, either in private practice or government. The foundations, which have played a major role in the early development of public interest law, are also reassessing their commitments in the field.

Any abandonment of public interest law would be—there is no other way to say it—disastrous. Government agencies would be deprived of an important input which has increased their responsiveness and the quality of their output. The legal profession would be abandoning even the pretense that an adversary process is a sine qua non for justice and that the ability to pay legal fees is not the key to the courthouse door. The concerned citizen would be losing an important tool for affecting major government and corporate decisions that strongly influence his or her life.

As public interest enters its Phase II, a new and continuing subsidy of public interest practice will be necessary. Citizen groups cannot draw on their own resources to support public interest litigation at an adequate level. For example, the later phases of the Alaska Pipeline litigation involved more than 4,000 hours of lawyer time. Even environmental groups representing well-heeled constituencies can ill afford such litigation. The private firms doing public interest practice, like Bruce Terris, William Dobrovir, and Berlin, Roisman & Kessler, have not identified a sufficient pool of public interest client groups to support a substantial number of lawyers conducting this kind of practice.

The San Diego conference sponsored by the Ford Foundation in April 1974 focused on the dilemma of the financial future of the public interest bar. The conference urged the establishment of a Council for Public Interest Law which would explore alternative funding mechanisms and initiate activities to develop long-term financial resources. Established formally in January 1975, the Council is considering a Fund for Public Interest Law supported by the public, foundations, and the organized bar. Rather than a few foundations making grants to several public interest firms for a year or two at a time, the Fund could be established under the direction of leaders of the public interest bar and other elements of the legal profession. The Fund would explore new approaches—such as funding particular projects by individual lawyers or organizations or making loans available to carry the substantial pretrial costs of big litigation where there was significant promise of an important public benefit and the likelihood of an attorney's fee recovery. Its goal is to be large enough to expend between one and three million dollars a year.

The Council will also evaluate the future potential of *pro bono* programs of the type developed in some corporate law firms in recent years. Several firms, like Hogan & Hartson in Washington, D.C., have identified full-time *pro bono* partners and associates to coordinate the firm's public interest work. Others, like Arnold & Porter, have established policies of permitting attorneys to spend up to 15 percent of their time doing uncompensated public interest work. Big-firm corporate lawyers have appeared on behalf of Ralph Nader, the National Welfare Rights Organization, the Black Panther party, and the Sierra Club. A few years ago it appeared that these programs might provide a significant supplement to the efforts of full-time poverty lawyers and public interest lawyers. Skeptics, however, maintained that the programs were largely a public relations device at a time when it was difficult to recruit young attorneys for conventional commercial practice. There was also the conflict-of-interest problem inherent when a corporate lawyer represented a citizens' group in a matter which threatened his regular corporate clientele.

It now appears that the skeptics may have been right. The concept of major *pro bono* commitments by large firms has not been widely accepted. Indeed, the steam ran out in many firms' *pro bono* programs as the partners who set up the programs returned to their regular corporate clients. With the job market tightening for young lawyers, law school graduates are more willing to accept full-time corporate practice as the least unpalatable career alternative, and their pressure for *pro bono* programs has waned. Covington & Burling is even having trouble finding young associates to volunteer for its program of sending two lawyers for six-month stints to the Neighborhood Legal Services Program.

Another potential source of support involves the government itself. There are numerous ways individual administrative agencies could facilitate citizen participation—e.g., by simplifying procedures, by making information more accessible, and by waiving costly multiple-filing requirements. Moreover, agencies could pay the costs of citizen-group participants in agency proceedings in appropriate circumstances. The comptroller general advised the Federal Trade Commission in 1972 that it had such authority, but the FTC has been reluctant to use it. In 1975, however, under the Magnuson-Moss Warranty Improvement Act, Congress appropriated $500,000 to the FTC to pay for the legal expenses of citizens whose viewpoints would not otherwise be adequately represented and who can't afford representation.* Agencies could also require regulated corporations to pay the costs of citizen participation in agency proceedings, although specific legislative authority would probably be required.[5]

There have been significant developments in Congress toward awarding fees to public interest litigants in court.** Although prevailing parties in litigation do not usually get attorneys' fees from the losers, the award of attorneys' fees in order to encourage public interest litigation has at times received explicit congressional recognition. Title VII of the Civil Rights Act of 1964 provides for the award of attorneys' fees to successful plaintiffs in employment-discrimination cases, and a similar approach has been followed in recent environmental legislation. A 1974 revision to the Freedom of Information Act authorizes the award of attorneys' fees to successful plaintiffs who were forced to undertake the expense of going to court in order to obtain information from the government to which they are entitled. Paradoxically, the award of fees against the government is still generally barred by statute, except for such specific statutory exceptions.[7]

The award of attorneys' fees, however, is no panacea, for where would firms get "front money" to finance complex and lengthy litigation prior to its resolution? A firm which relied wholly on fees would necessarily tend to take on more conventional cases in which the likelihood of a fee was greater and a lengthy and expensive proceeding less likely. Furthermore, past experience suggests that fee awards to public interest lawyers are likely to be inadequate.

* The ICC, under congressional direction, has experimented with techniques for broadening citizen participation in its program to reorganize the railroads in the Northeast. The Commission has established an office of public counsel with the responsibility of assuring effective citizen involvement.

** During the past several years, several federal courts have awarded attorneys' fees in public interest cases to plaintiffs who have served as "private attorneys general." The Supreme Court reversed this trend in mid-1975 when it held that the federal courts lacked the power to award such attorneys' fees in the absence of explicit statutory authorization.[6]

Hopefully, some combination of these funding alternatives will be able to sustain public interest lawyers. "In recent years," said the Court of Appeals for the District of Columbia, approvingly, "the concept that public participation in decisions which involve the public interest is not only valuable but indispensable has gained increasing support." [8] Whether this generalized support can find sufficient funding will largely determine whether the new public interest lawyers become a fondly remembered relic or a permanent legal institution.

Beverly C. Moore, Jr.
*& Fred R. Harris**

Class Actions: Let the People In

THE PURPOSES of the American legal system seem clear enough. At its most elemental level, it gives the aggrieved citizen his "day in court." This may be called the "pacification function" of the civil justice system, with the objective to channel the hostility of injured parties into socially acceptable avenues of conflict resolution. Lawsuits can also compensate victims for their losses and guarantee that the perpetrator of the injury does not profit from his wrongdoing. Most important, however, is a third function, deterrence—i.e., discouraging the injurious conduct that gives rise to litigation by threat of court-awarded damages. As a matter of justice and economy, prevention of harm is preferable to its compensation after the injury has been inflicted.[1]

That is the theory. In practice, a series of hurdles has frustrated citizen access to the courts—with the result that victims are not compensated and illegality is not deterred. Some of these hurdles are discussed elsewhere in this volume: the high cost of lawyers; Canons of Ethics which discourage lawyers from telling citizens what their rights are; large corporate defendants able and often eager to hire platoons of lawyers specializing in the exhaustion of opponents. A legal system that is little more than theoretically available to prevent the powerful few from enriching themselves at the expense of the defenseless many would be intolerable enough. But when modern technology facilitates the corporate application of mass production and marketing techniques to the art of theft, the problem increases exponentially. "It is better to take one dime from each of 10 million people at the point of a corporation than $100,000 from each

* BEVERLY MOORE, A PUBLIC INTEREST LAWYER IN WASHINGTON, D.C., IS A COAUTHOR OF *The Closed Enterprise System* (1972) AND THE EDITOR OF *Class Action Reports*. FRED HARRIS IS THE FORMER SENATOR FROM OKLAHOMA, FORMER CHAIRMAN OF THE DEMOCRATIC NATIONAL COMMITTEE, AND AUTHOR OF *The New Populism* (1973).

of 10 banks at the point of a gun," said the eminent sociologist C. Wright Mills, adding, "It is also safer."

The greatest barrier to courtroom justice is the marketplace reality that most victims are not even aware that they have been injured. The supermarket shopper has no way of knowing, without the aid of extensive investigation or sophisticated scientific equipment, that the price of an item carries a 15 percent price-fixing surcharge, that meat sold as ground chuck is really hamburger, that the tampered scale which weighs the meat inflates the price by one percent, or that items placed in special "end display" bins, a device which increases the items' sales by over 600 percent,[2] are not necessarily reduced in price. In these and numerous other situations, the detection of harm requires an expert, which the consumer typically is not.[3] The invisible picking of millions of pockets for billions of dollars survives unnoticed. The chart on pages 174–176 roughly describes the total magnitude of the class harm being inflicted in the name of "free enterprise."[4] Adam Smith would turn over in his grave.

Enter now the class action lawsuit. This device allows one or a few individuals, whose damages may be only a few dollars, to prosecute in a single lawsuit the claims of perhaps millions of other similarly injured persons. By combining many small claims into one large claim to justify the cost of litigation, the economies of scale of the class action represent the legal system's response to the widespread injuries perpetrated by mass production and marketing technologies.

The class action, however, has more than a procedural rationale. It can transfer liability from victims to the corporations whose products and processes give rise to accidents, diseases, pollution, and congestion. Corporations are then—albeit involuntarily—given a profit incentive to reduce the magnitude of the harms they cause, since that is often cheaper than to compensate the victims. If the automobile industry were saddled with an annual damage liability of perhaps $100 billion for accidents, air pollution, noise, congestion, and highway and traffic-control costs, and were forced to raise its prices by that amount, it would have no choice but to redesign its vehicles to minimize these costs and their associated liabilities. Similarly, if the drug industry were held liable in class action damages for 60,000 to 100,000 deaths and 5 to 10 million serious illnesses each year from adverse reactions to prescription drugs, 70 to 80 percent of which are avoidable, it can be safely predicted that the industry would

Type of Injury	Magnitude of Annual Harm	Primary (Secondary) Potential Defendants	Present Legal Obstacles to Class Action Damage Suits
1. Economic concentration	$150 billion in lost consumer purchasing power	Oligopolistic industries	Antitrust laws require proof of explicit agreements (conspiracies) to restrain trade or the "intent" to monopolize and do not cover overcharges due to mere structural lack of competition
2. Price fixing and other violations of existing antitrust laws	$ billions to $ tens of billions	same	Court decisions on standing to sue (e.g., passing on, remoteness doctrines). Often only directly purchasing business middlemen can sue, and they are reluctant to do so. Also, many violations (mergers, tying arrangements, exclusive dealing contracts) injure business competitors who do not purchase at all.
3. Labor union featherbedding, wage inflation	$ billions	Unions	Unions exempt from antitrust laws
4. Employment discrimination	$ billions in lost productivity	Employers, especially large firms (unions)	Classes limited by courts to employees who were fired, hired but not promoted, or rejected after application for a specific job opening, leaving without a practical damage remedy persons not hired or promoted because of an employer's discriminatory policies.
5. Deceptive advertising, in-store sales promotion techniques, etc.	$ billions to $ tens of billions	Business enterprises generally	No federal cause of action. State causes of action, where they exist, may require individualized proof of consumer reliance on the misrepresentation or seller's intent to defraud.
6. Auto, appliance, home repair service frauds, professional malpractice	$ tens of billions	Repair industries, professions	Same
7. "Warranty of quality control" and other warranty breaches	$ billions	Manufacturers of consumer durables	No federal or state causes of action. Where state causes of action exist for blatant warranty breaches, individualized proof may be required.

		Business enterprises	
8. Occupational diseases	100,000 deaths, 390,000 disabilities	Business enterprises generally	No federal or state cause of action not requiring individualized proof
9. Adverse reactions to prescription drugs	60,000–100,000 hospital deaths, 5 million serious non-fatal illnesses	Drug industry (doctors, hospitals)	Same
10. Irrational over-prescription of antibiotics	Some fraction of 100,000 deaths from virulent disease organisms	Drug industry (medical profession)	No state or federal causes of action
11. Heart disease	Half of all American deaths	Producers of foods contributing excessive cholesterol, saturated fat, and sodium to the diet; cigarette industry all contribute significantly to injury.	Same
12. Lung cancer, emphysema, and chronic bronchitis	100,000 deaths	Cigarette industry, air polluters all contribute significantly to injury	Same
13. Colon cancer	50,000 deaths	Producers of fatty foods such as beef and fiber-deficient foods such as re-fined carbohydrates	Same
14. Cancers of the breast, prostate, pancreas, gall bladder, bile duct	75,000 deaths	Producers of fatty foods	Same
15. Tooth decay	$ billions	Sugar industry (food manufacturers)	Same
16. Maturity-onset diabetes	5 percent of U.S. population is or will be afflicted	Same	Same

Type of Injury	Magnitude of Annual Harm	Primary (Secondary) Potential Defendants	Present Legal Obstacles to Class Action Damage Suits
17. Diverticular disease, ulcerative colitis, hemorrhoids, appendicitis	Afflict tens of millions	Fiber-deficient food industry	Same
18. Cirrhosis of the liver, other alcohol-related health problems	Death rate among 5-10 million alcoholics is three times higher than general population	Alcoholic beverage industry	Same
19. Motor vehicle accidents	Until recently 57,000 deaths, roughly $60 billion	Auto industry	State causes of action require individualized proof of specific "defect" for recovery from manufacturer
20. Consumer product injuries, excluding firearms	30,000 deaths, millions of injuries, roughly $10 billion	Consumer products manufacturers	Same
21. Occupational accidents	15,000 deaths, millions of injuries, roughly $15–20 billion	Business enterprises generally	Workmen's compensation benefits not fully compensatory, state causes of action require proof of negligence or other individualized facts
22. Excessive use of X-rays	1,000 cancer deaths	X-ray equipment producers (doctors, dentists, hospitals)	No state or federal causes of action
23. Air, water, noise, other environmental pollution	Perhaps $50 billion in health, property, ecological, esthetic damage	Business enterprises generally	No federal cause of action clearly available, state causes of action (nuisance, trespass) often have defenses of "reasonableness," etc.
24. Urban congestion, overcrowding	Traffic congestion, increased crime, scenic decay, suburban sprawl to escape	Auto industry, developers	No state or federal causes of action

develop effective mechanisms to ensure that many or most such cases are in fact avoided.* In response to similar potential damage liabilities, food corporations would reduce the fat, sugar, salt, and cholesterol content of their products, and cigarette companies would reduce the tar and nicotine content of theirs. The idea is that if the profit motive helps reduce the costs of the beneficial products of our economy, it can be enlisted to reduce the harmful byproducts.

However compelling the *economic* rationale for this concept of absolute or "enterprise" liability, it remains alien to *legal* doctrines, which are largely wedded to considerations of "negligence" and "fault." After all, for a legal system concerned only with pacification, what matters is that the rules governing victory or defeat be considered fair or acceptable to angry litigants. Whether these rules when enforced would improve the welfare of society seems secondary. But even that explanation is unsatisfactory. For example, it is difficult to ascribe fault or negligence to corporate pollution or congestion victims, who can hardly avoid their injuries by "driving carefully" or "eating wisely." The law nevertheless provides them no remedy. And damage liability is curiously unavailable for most marketplace "overcharges" (items 1–7 of the chart).

This disdain of economic logic is not unrelated to the fact that certain special-interest groups have substantial influence in writing, enforcing, and interpreting the laws that grant or withhold the right to recover damages in private lawsuits. Whatever the motive, the result of these restrictions is clear: On the one hand, there are very few types of harmful business practices for which a class action remedy is available. On the other, the chief beneficiaries of this situation are the small propertied classes that are so influential in defining legal remedies.

Only a few states have either (1) allowed consumers to sue for deceptive advertising, defective merchandise, and other forms of consumer fraud, or have (2) enacted effective class action provisions through which such lawsuits can be prosecuted, and even fewer states have provided both. The Supreme Court has ruled that citizens may not bring class actions in federal courts for violations of state laws unless each member of the class claims damages of $10,000 or more. The historical fact is that class actions for damages can be filed in federal courts (with at least some chance of success) only for certain violations of the antitrust,[5]

---

* Of course, it might be advisable to phase in these new liabilities over a reasonable period of time to allow the industries involved to develop technological solutions which they have never before contemplated.

securities, and employment discrimination laws. This is surely a legal remedy on a short leash.

Given these severe limitations on class action lawsuits, the opposition of corporate interests to this remedy seems overwrought. Class actions have been called "Frankenstein monsters" and "engines of destruction," supposedly pursued by unscrupulous plaintiff attorneys using this device as a form of "legalized blackmail" in search of a "pot of gold." These adjectives invariably originate with corporate defense lawyers who protest the slightest insinuation of a conflict of interest in their own conclusions. Class actions have been condemned by panels of the American College of Trial Lawyers and by the American Bar Association sections on Antitrust Law and on Corporation, Banking and Business Law, which issued proposals aimed at curing the "widespread disrepute" into which consumer class actions have fallen. The suggested cure is the virtual elimination of such lawsuits, which are often filed against the corporate clients of the bar association authors of these reports.

Defendant corporations and their lawyers have been largely successful in persuading a receptive judiciary that class actions threaten to engulf the meager resources of the courts and that these are frivolous suits to which corporations nevertheless must capitulate to avoid any prospect of "staggering" liability. "Only the attorneys [for the successful class] benefit" from very substantial contingent fees, they allege, which, together with other costs of this complex and protracted type of litigation, consume most of the damage recoveries and leave little to be distributed to the class members who have been injured.

How accurate are these contentions?

The argument that class actions are overburdening the federal courts begins with the statistics compiled by the Administrative Office of the U.S. Courts. By the end of 1974 there were 4,760 class actions pending in the federal court system, or 4.2 percent of all cases pending. But a substantial majority of these "class action" cases seek injunctive relief or damages for the named class representatives only, not for thousands of others similarly situated. The controversy surrounding class actions applies not to these types of cases but to those seeking damages for an entire class of victims.

As an illustration of the statistics' distortion, one study found that of 408 class actions filed in the U.S. District Court for the District of Columbia between 1966 and 1972, only 170 sought recovery of damages;

in many of these cases, damages were ultimately pursued only on behalf of the named plaintiffs.[6] Upon closer examination, this court was "burdened" during this six-and-a-half-year period with only fourteen cases in which damages were awarded to an entire class, usually by out-of-court settlement. Studies in other districts covering roughly the same period and using the same elimination criteria have confirmed this pattern: 144 antitrust class actions filed in the Northern District of Illinois reduced to 44 and 280 class actions filed in the District of Minnesota dropped to 70.[7] But assume, for the sake of argument, that class actions are overburdening the federal court system and that the number of courts and judges cannot be expanded. The most logical remedy for this predicament would be to restrict, not class actions, but frivolous individual actions, which are less efficient instruments for producing justice. A bus can carry forty passengers more efficiently than forty cars can carry one passenger each. So too with class actions versus individual cases.

The allegation that plaintiff attorneys file frivolous class actions to "blackmail" corporations into out-of-court settlements is not even a theoretically plausible contention. First, all settlements of class actions, including awards of attorneys' fees, must be approved by the court. The considerable time and expense that a plaintiff attorney must invest in class action litigation—usually out of his own pocket until and unless there is a damage recovery—should adequately deter the filing of frivolous cases as long as there is any significant chance that the defense attorneys will call his bluff. And they do, consistently. In the study of District of Columbia class actions, defendants not only won 58 percent of the cases, but forty-four of their forty-seven victories were achieved at preliminary stages of the litigation, long before reaching the trial stages at which the expense of defending might induce some corporations to settle. Furthermore, in personal interviews, most defense counsel stated unequivocally that they would challenge rather than capitulate to any class actions they thought lacked merit.[8]

When class action plaintiffs are successful, the damages awarded hardly approach the "astronomical sums" that would confer "blackmail" leverage. In the nine (out of fourteen) District of Columbia cases for which final class damage award data were available, one recovery involving a pension-rights dispute within the United Mine Workers union was for $30 million, and another labor pension case was settled for $500,000. The remaining seven recoveries averaged slightly more than a mere $100,000 each, which is comparable to recoveries in individual lawsuits involving serious automobile accidents. On a nationwide basis, there have been perhaps up to two dozen class actions in which damages in excess of $5 million have been recovered, and even in those cases the recoveries usually represent a small fraction of the actual injuries to the class. "So far as we are aware," noted a federal court of appeals, "not a single one of these class actions including millions of indiscriminate and unidentifiable members have [sic] ever been brought to trial and decided on the merits." [9]

Defense attorneys have been unwilling or unable to identify specific cases which they deem "frivolous" or "blackmail" attempts. A Senate Commerce Committee inquiry addressed to opposing lawyers in over 400 class actions, including 127 defense counsel or firms, did not elicit reference to a single "frivolous" class action. About the strongest response to this type of inquiry was given by anti–class action lawyer Irving Scher, from the ABA Section on Corporation, Banking and Business Law, who said that "it is not necessary to prove the existence of class action abuses: it is a matter of common knowledge."

Whatever abuses may be attributed to class action plaintiff lawyers, defense counsel surely cannot claim moral purity. At least as prevalent as the "strike suit"—parlance for the "blackmail" class action coined during the earlier days of stockholder suits against corporate mismanagement—are the "strike settlement" and the "strike defense." The "strike settlement" refers to the practice of defense attorneys seeking to "buy off" the named class representatives or their attorney in order to leave the class unrepresented, thus mooting the case. The "strike" or "harassment" defense consists of exhausting the potential of legal technicalities to protract and inflate the cost of the litigation to a degree that the plaintiff is forced to drop or settle the case.

Defense counsel have demanded separate jury trials for each class member's damage claim and have threatened unnamed class members with interrogatories and counterclaims. Hoping to uncover violations of the Canons of Ethics, defense counsel have initiated inquiries into whether the plaintiff attorney "solicited" class representatives as his clients or whether he is "maintaining" their case with his own money. Defendants can delay by initially resisting discovery and then by sending boxcars of documents instead of the specific materials requested. Direct economic sanctions have also been used. When a railroad decided to join in a class action against Bethlehem Steel, Bethlehem threatened to find another railroad for its steel shipments if the plaintiff railroad didn't drop its case. It did.

Business defense attorneys often oppose the "contingent fee," which compensates the plaintiff attorney with a percentage of the damages recovered on behalf of the class—just as, for example, salesmen are often compensated on a commission basis. The contingent fee is critical to the economic feasibility of class action lawsuits. Plaintiff attorneys must be compensated in excess of ordinary hourly rates in cases they win to make up for the time and expense they devote to cases they lose—for which they usually receive no compensation at all.[10] Certainly defense counsel would be unwilling to bill their corporate clients only for cases they won.

Class actions also face difficulty due to the approach many judges bring to them. The exercise of judicial power is in many respects unaccountable. Judges need not fear "going out of business" if their rulings are wrong or slow, and this applies especially to *abdications* of the judicial function. Like other institutions vested with monopoly power, judges can opt for the "easy life." Or, in this context, they can prefer simple individual actions to difficult and complex class actions, without being forced to consider the impact of their preference upon the quantity of justice that they render.

The genesis for this view goes beyond mere laziness. For judges, too, are drawn primarily from the propertied classes. And as former lawyers they have been imbued with the business maxim that "litigation is always to be avoided." This class bias is most familiarly illustrated by the judicial hostility to New Deal economic regulation that prompted President Roosevelt's "court packing" proposal. Since then, even the "liberal" rulings of new but still upper middle class judges primarily have concerned issues of civil rights and civil liberties. The courts remain essentially conservative on economic issues. Consider, most recently, Chief Justice Burger's jurisprudential nihilism that the federal courts exist for a "limited purpose"; also, the trend of recent Supreme Court decisions has been to loosen constraints on private economic power.[11]

In this setting, it is not surprising that judges have resorted to a wide variety of legal sophistries to rid themselves of bothersome class action litigation. Some courts have ruled that the ultimate consumers lack "standing to sue" in price-fixing class actions and that only the middlemen purchasing directly from the price fixers can recover.* One

---

* This occurred in a class action filed by homeowners and apartment dwellers against plumbing-fixtures manufacturers whose price-fixing had been carried on intermittently since the

judge dismissed a case on the ground that the class action device itself is an "unethical" means of soliciting business because members of the class other than the named representatives automatically become clients of the plaintiff attorney.[14] A number of cases have also been thrown out because the attorney, not allowed to solicit a client, named himself as the representative of an injured class of which he was in fact a member. Then there was the case where homeowners with mortgages sought payment of interest from savings and loan associations on escrow accounts used to pay property taxes and insurance on their homes. The judge reasoned that "the interest of the community" could suffer from "a large class action recovery [that] might well have a deleterious effect upon the area lending market at a time [of tight money] when the community can least afford it." [15] Never mind whether the injured class could "afford it."

Judges unable to rationalize or manipulate the substantive law to dismiss class actions can always resort to the various procedural requirements applicable to class suits set forth in Rule 23 of the Federal Rules of Civil Procedure. One of these requirements, that "questions of law or fact common to members of the class predominate over any questions affecting only individual members," has filled the lawbooks with conflicting rulings in similar cases. Another requirement is that the plaintiff, at his own expense, notify class members "who can be identified with reasonable effort" that an action is pending. This notice is mandatory, the Supreme Court recently ruled, even when the defendant conveniently produces computer tapes containing the names and addresses of 2 million class members whom it would cost the plaintiff hundreds of thousands of dollars to notify individually.[16]

As a practical matter, however, the threat of prohibitive notice costs seldom arises. When the class is large enough for the notice costs to be high, the names and addresses of individual class members are often *not* readily available. The computerized billing records of the coming checkless society may change that, but cases involving large classes can in any event be thrown out on another Rule 23 ground—that the action is "unmanageable." This term is really shorthand for abdicating the judicial

---

1920s and at its height involved more than a billion dollars of commerce annually. The middlemen plumbing wholesalers and contractors, to whom the consumers' right to sue was transferred, settled for $3 million.[12] In another case, a federal district court judge allowed some class actions on behalf of air pollution victims charging an auto industry antitrust conspiracy to delay the introduction of emission control devices; but the appeals court ruled that the victims of pollution, here aggravated by lack of competition, did not have "standing to sue" under antitrust laws. Only inventors and manufacturers of pollution-control devices that could have been sold to the auto industry could sue.[13]

function on the ground that the case is just "too big." Thus, a consumer class of 1.5 million bread purchasers charging price fixing was ruled "unmanageable." [17] In the auto smog conspiracy case, the district judge who decided to permit classes of government entities and farmers whose crops had been damaged tersely dismissed the class of all individual auto pollution victims. Another judge ruled that consumers individually had "standing to sue" General Motors for antitrust violations, but denied class action status to GM's 30 to 40 million consumer victims.[18] While corporations are in the twentieth century, courts insist upon remaining in the nineteenth.

Indeed, it is clear that the courts are not treating these cases as *class* actions at all, but rather as umbrella devices for the assertion of claims by individual class members. When class actions involving small overcharges of millions of consumers are dismissed on "manageability" grounds, the judge is effectively saying that the defendant corporations have no damage liability to the class, independent of claims asserted and proven by identifiable class members. This premise destroys class actions, since most class members can never be identified at reasonable expense, and since, even if they could be, their damage claims would be so small that few would bother to assert them.

For class actions to become effective instruments of justice, a "class" should be treated as an independent entity with a status not unlike that of a corporation in relation to its stockholders. Using scientifically valid statistical projections, damages then could be computed on an *aggregate* injury basis and could be awarded in a lump sum to the class as a whole. For example, if the entire class purchased one million units of a product whose price was illegally rigged at an average of $5 above competitive levels, the "aggregate class damage fund" would amount to $5 million.

Suppose that individual class members step forward to claim only $1 million of the total damages awarded. What is to be done with the $4 million remainder? If the product involved is one, such as bread or gasoline, which many of the previously overcharged class members are likely to purchase again, they can be compensated for their past losses by applying the $4 million to reduce the prices charged for the product in the future. This is called the "fluid recovery." Because some of the injured class members will not make repeat purchases, not all will be compensated—and some persons who did not purchase in the past will receive windfall price reductions. But some compensation is better than none, and, as a last resort, any leftover funds can be donated to the public treasury. Under no circumstances should a losing defendant retain illegal gains because of the fortuitous circumstance that not all of the actual victims can be compensated. Otherwise, the goal of deterrence would be lost.

At the moment, this point is largely academic. Although most courts have not yet clearly rejected the fluid recovery and other "aggregate class damage" concepts, the prospects are far from bright. Prior to 1966, Rule 23 explicitly rejected the "class as a whole" concept by limiting the defendant's liability to the claims of class members who affirmatively "opted in" to the lawsuit. In 1966, however, Rule 23 was changed to provide that all class members were automatically to be included in the class except those individuals who affirmatively "opted out." This change, however, has not significantly altered the manner in which courts award damages in class actions. Opting in is still required.

When an individual consumer attempts to recover damages in behalf of others who do not step forward to claim them, the class action device is accused of being Big Brother in disguise. But if GM were successfully to sue ITT, the full damage award would be paid directly to GM, to be then applied to the benefit of the "class" of stockholders GM represents. ITT would hardly be allowed to retain that part of the damage liability which individual GM stockholders did not "opt in" to claim. And it would be unthinkable for GM to require each of its stockholders to affirmatively claim any dividend increases or stock market appreciation afforded by the damage recovery, with all sums not claimed by the stockholder class used to increase the salaries of GM executives. The interests of the 5 percent of the population who own 86 percent of all corporate stock[19] are thus treated more seriously than the interests of the consumers that corporations purportedly exist to serve. And until legislation corrects the legal defects which plague class actions, many companies will continue to appreciate and apply C. Wright Mills's observation about taking dimes from millions.

IV

The Business Lawyer: The Limits of Representation

*Joseph A. Califano, Jr.**

The Washington Lawyer:
When to Say No

A PATRON of the legal profession, Saint Ives, was a thirteenth-century poverty lawyer and a saint, a dual role which prompted a contemporary to comment: "He was a lawyer, yet not a rascal, and the people were astonished."

The average American would probably be even more astonished to find a saint among present-day attorneys. In Washington, the portrait of lawyers as unprincipled rascals has been painted in the stark colors of their involvement in the Watergate scandals, with hues likely to deepen as the investigations, trials, and books further expose the dirty tricks and shady financing of political campaigns. The conduct of the Washington Watergate lawyers should at least serve to focus attention on the standards lawyers set for themselves: Do those standards need reformulation; are they being ignored by a significant number of attorneys; are the Watergate lawyers aberrations, or representatives of their profession?

Two different conceptions of the lawyer's role face off against each other in ethical duel. The traditional view, imbued with the neatly trimmed whitening hair of experience, perceives the lawyer as an instrument of his clients, a purchased pistol with his hand raised in intentionally uncritical pursuit of his client's interests. Considerations of broad social responsibility and obligations to impose moral judgments on a client's activities fade against the background of the lawyer-advocate's role in the adversary system.

The other, less orthodox view sees the lawyer in a larger social context, imposing upon him or her the moral responsibility to temper representa-

* JOSEPH A. CALIFANO, JR., A WASHINGTON LAWYER, WAS PRESIDENT JOHNSON'S SPECIAL ASSISTANT FOR DOMESTIC AFFAIRS. HE IS THE AUTHOR OF TWO BOOKS, *The Student Revolution: A Global Confrontation* (1969), AND *A Presidential Nation* (1975), AND IS A FREQUENT CONTRIBUTOR TO THE *Washington Post*'s EDITORIAL PAGE.

tion of the client's interests with an overriding concern for societal morality and objective justice. At its blandest, this view calls upon the lawyer to render moral judgments in many situations where the traditional view would require such judgments to be put in limbo. At its sharpest, this view calls into question the entire advocacy system of Anglo-American jurisprudence.

The traditional view is vividly illustrated by a passage from Boswell's *The Life of Johnson*:

> BOSWELL: But what do you think of supporting a cause which you know to be bad?
>
> JOHNSON: Sir, you do not know it to be good or bad till the Judge determines it. I have said that you are to state facts thoroughly; so that your thinking, or what you call knowing, a cause to be bad, must be from reasoning, must be from your supposing your arguments to be weak and inconclusive. But sir, that is not enough. An argument which does not convince yourself, may convince the Judge to whom you urge it: and if it does convince him, why then, sir, you are wrong and he is right. It is his business to judge; and you are not to be confident in your own opinion that a cause is bad, but to say all you can for your client, and then hear the Judge's opinion.[1]

Professor Charles Reich reflects the less orthodox view:

> It is important to recognize explicitly that whether he is engaged publicly or privately, the lawyer will no longer be serving merely as the spokesman for others. As the law becomes more and more a determinative force in public and private affairs, the lawyer must carry the responsibility of his specialized knowledge, and formulate ideas as well as advocate them. In a society where law is a primary force, the lawyer must be a primary, not a secondary, being.[2]

Different as these views are, they do not present an ethical Hobson's choice between morally uninhibited advocacy of a client's interest and sublimation of that interest to some personal, ethical standard. Most who espouse the rhetoric of the traditional view recognize certain fundamental limitations on the role of the lawyer as representative of a particular client. For example, no responsible Washington lawyer would attempt to mislead the Food and Drug Administration into approving a thalidomide today. At the same time, the most avid public interest environmental lawyers would not deny an oil company the right to legal representation on the ground that they believe the position of that company to be morally bankrupt. Even the traditional American Bar Association straddles the ethical picket fence:

. . . a lawyer should always act in a manner consistent with the best interest of his client. However, when an action in the best interest of his client seems to him to be unjust, he may ask his client for permission to forego such action. . . . The duty of a lawyer to represent his client with zeal does not militate against his concurrent obligation to treat with consideration all persons involved in the legal process and to avoid the infliction of needless harm.[3]

General ethical principles, pronounced by self-interested corporate law associations and self-righteous public interest law firms, are easily formulated in the abstract by articulate attorneys, but they are difficult to apply in realistic recognition of man's human nature. This is particularly true for the Washington lawyer, who has special ethical problems.[4] He often represents not merely an individual client, but an entire industry or combination of clients: the sugar growers, the environmentalists, the oil industry, the Federal Housing Administration. The Washington lawyer rarely litigates cases; rather, he tries to appoint judges. Instead of writing to his congressman, he seeks to deliver a majority on the committee. He doesn't complain that his household goods were damaged in transit; he is after a certificate of permanent authority to move your household goods. The Washington lawyer is both counselor and lobbyist; he spends much more time and energy on Capitol Hill and in the halls of the Federal Trade Commission than in any courtroom.

The Washington lawyer is not drafting wills, straightening out a bad-conduct discharge, or trying to get the United States attorney to drop a marijuana charge against a teen-ager. Rather, he is involved in drafting estate tax laws, molding military procurement policies and regulations, and trying to change the drug laws. Unlike his "brother at the bar" in other cities across the nation, his private practice steps on the brass rail of public policy every time he has an expense-account luncheon. Whether he represents private, public, or governmental interests, this attorney in a very real sense operates at the interface between public and private interest and is an active participant in the exercise of government power.[5]

Washington lawyers are not unaware of the special ethical problems inherent in their practice. But it is extremely difficult to find a usable set of commandments. For the ethical terrain is treacherously jagged and unmarked, a moral minefield of gray. The ethical problems are as situational as any professor of behavioral philosophy could devise. While all Washington lawyers must face the question of "when to say no," the context may require different answers, depending upon the client, the forum, and the facts of each case.

The threshold question is relatively easy: whom to represent. For all, that question is highly personal and should be left to the sole discretion of the individual attorney. It is his choice, and his alone, to whom he will devote his time, energy, and talents. He makes a basic and broad decision when he chooses to enter private, government, or public interest practice. But whatever general practice an attorney chooses at any given point in life, he must repeatedly make judgments about which interests to represent, and how far to go in representing them. If, on occasion, he is asked to work on a case he finds personally repugnant, then he should be free to say no. This recognition of personal moral codes is important not simply as the moral analogy in the practice of law to the conscientious refusal of a young man to fight in a particular war or of an Amish parent to send his children to public school. There is also the practical consideration that a lawyer's personal repugnance may inhibit his professional obligation to represent a client adequately. Whether the decision to say no in private practice carries with it nonparticipation in the profits from the particular client or case involved is something for the conscience of the individual attorney and the attitude of his law firm.

The second question, once an attorney has agreed to represent a client, is how to represent him. In considering the private practitioner's obligation, a distinction can often be drawn between defending the client for past acts which he has already committed and advising the client on his future course of conduct. In the former situation, when a client at the outset discloses all material facts to his attorney, he is entitled to the fullest possible representation, and the option to say no should be exercised at the start.

In the latter situation, where the lawyer is an adviser on future conduct, there are more options open to determine how the client will conduct himself, and the lawyer's responsibility to exercise moral judgments may consequently be greater. If a substantial public interest will be affected by his client's conduct, the lawyer's advice should not be limited to the technical validity of the proposed action, without regard to its social or economic consequences. Just as many corporations are increasingly coming to recognize their broader social responsibilities, so must their attorneys. Here the lawyer may have an opportunity, even an obligation, to enlarge the perspective of his client, to persuade as well as advise. He certainly has the right to say no.

The problem for the Washington attorney is that the defense of past conduct and advice concerning future conduct tend to merge when a law firm represents a corporate client on a continuing basis. Here, it is unrealistic for lawyers to argue that they are simply guns-for-hire utterly irresponsible for the actions of their clients. The situation is readily distinguishable from attorneys who, for example, represent a defendant in a single lawsuit. Corporate law firms that have been representing a particular bank or large corporation for five, ten, or twenty years, are no more completely free of responsibility for corporate actions in Washington than are its top corporate officers. Attorneys in this situation must recognize that, on the whole, they should assume moral responsibility-by-association just as they share in material affluence-by-association.

Often overlooked in this context is the extent to which a lawyer is an advocate for his clients' interests not only in relation to the outside world but in relation to the clients themselves. The attempt to formulate boundaries to the lawyer's advocacy of his client's case is perceived by traditional counsel as pitting the lawyer against his client. If a lawyer is not one hundred percent for his client, the conventional wisdom goes, he is then something of an adversary of his client, as divided loyalty interferes with the lawyer's duty of devotion to his client's interest.

But this simplistic view ignores the fact that an inherent part of the lawyer's function in being "for" his clients is helping determine what exactly *is* their interest in a particular set of circumstances. Certainly, when a corporate client comes to a Washington lawyer with a problem, the lawyer is charged with furthering his client's "interest." But often a client knows only in a general sense what that interest is, and seeks the lawyer's skills and knowledge in defining as well as implementing that interest. A client's perception of its interest may be unfocused, or subject to change as more is learned about the problem, the law, and public policy. The definition of this interest is not forged in a vacuum, divorced from considerations of public policy. Here the Washington lawyer in particular has an obligation to present to his client constructive alternatives for harmonizing corporate and public goals. So his job is at least in part that of a mediator, seeking a congruence between the public interest and the client's interest.

As a result, Washington counsel can act as information gatherers and objective evaluators of corporate practices. They may bring to the attention of corporate management certain policies of which they were unaware, or the social significance of which had been misconstrued or overlooked. More often than most people realize, merely pointing out socially objectionable practices to the client will modify or eliminate them.

When a lawyer does not give his client a down-to-earth appraisal because of an inordinately narrow conception of the client's interest, he does an enormous disservice to his client and to his profession. Too often a lawyer's pocketbook pang—his fear of alienating the client—results in pandering reinforcement of the client's unjustified expectations. But a lawyer may inadvertently mislead a client by being subservient to the client's perceptions of the problem and tailoring advice to what he thinks the client wants to hear. A lawyer has an obligation to argue with his client when not to do so would jeopardize the client's interest or put the client in significant conflict with the public interest. He may not end up saying no, but he should not shirk his obligation to expose his client to important public interest considerations.

For example, when the Traffic Safety Act of 1966 was being drafted, any decent Washington lawyer knew that strong legislation would sail through the Congress. Instead of recognizing that their interest lay in acceding to the public clamor for legislation, the auto industry resisted vociferously to the bitter end. Those lawyers who advised a fight to the death merely contributed to serving up the auto industry as one of Washington's favorite whipping boys for at least a decade—a course of events that could hardly be thought of as furthering the client's interest.

Many lawyers balk at this analysis, arguing they are merely advocates for one side in legal battle, and not the referee of all interests. Yet there is a sharp difference between legislative lobbying and informal agency relationships, on the one hand, and representation in the courtroom, on the other. In the courtroom, it all hangs out on the public record. *Ex parte* communications between judge and lawyer-advocate are generally not permitted. The public and its representatives in the press have a full view of the proceedings. A host of procedural rules protects the interests of both sides and governs the entrance of additional interested parties into the case.

Lobbying on Capitol Hill is quite different, as Senate Commerce Committee chief counsel Michael Pertschuk fully explains in the next essay. Most contacts are not on any public record and the public does not have access to most discussions. *Ex parte* communications are the accepted rule, not the disparaged exception. True, there are often situations in which testimony is presented in open hearing in support of or opposition to a particular bill. But anyone sophisticated in the legislative process realizes that, except for the most publicized situations, effective representation of a client's interest resides in private face-to-face conversations with a senator or congressman, or their aides, not in public testimony. This situation, of course, works both ways: The "public interest" advocate and government attorney have their own private contacts and telephone conversations with senators, congressmen, and legislative aides. It seems fair to impose standards of factual full disclosure on all attorneys in their *ex parte* lobbying activities, whether private practitioner, public interest lawyer, or government attorney; most easily, members of Congress or their staff could log all such contacts. In addition to their client's hat, lobbying lawyers wear one as "officer of the Congress," much like the "officer of the court" hat that obliges litigators to cite and discuss judicial precedents adverse to their client's interest.[6]

Informal contacts with administrative agencies and executive department officials require the same high standards. Thus, if a commission is hearing a specific case involving a client, and the client requests his attorney to engage in private discussions with a member of that commission, the attorney should refuse. Many commissions now have rules prohibiting such contracts, but they are too often honored in the breach.

Other situations can impose high ethical standards on the corporate Washington bar. When a client has market control in some particular industry, its actions can be imputed with "state action" because society has given the client control over a significant segment of the economy. It might be reasonable to impose a duty of public interest comparable to the duty imposed on the government prosecutor who, theoretically at least, is an officer of the court seeking justice as much as he is an attorney trying to win a conviction in a particular case. The same standard might be imposed when an attorney represents an entire industry, like the automobile, steel, or food industry. Similarly, when the client corporation is essentially an extension of the government (the most notable example being large defense contractors), the private attorney's obligations might take on the broader ethical obligations and restraints imposed on a government attorney.

In general, the model of the adversary system is not easily engrafted upon the different forums in which the Washington lawyer operates. The adversary system serves us best when all participating sides are supported by vigorous advocacy in open confrontation. In Washington, the lack of formal confrontation and the imbalance of forces often results in a pale ghost of protest where a healthy clash of public and private interests should have been. Until all sides—and especially the public interest—are adequately represented, it is incumbent upon those representing privileged dominant interests to assume a special measure of responsibility. When the lawyer representing large corporate interests is pitted against an overworked, understaffed public interest group or underequipped government body, the responsibility for integrity should be greater.

A recent plea by the Securities and Exchange Commission for just such an exercise of responsibility by the securities bar appears to be equally applicable to Washington lawyers:

> Members of this commission have pointed out time and time again that the task of enforcing the securities laws rests in overwhelming measure on the bar's shoulders. These were statements of what all who are versed in the practicalities of securities law know to be a truism, i.e., that this commission with its small staff, limited resources, and onerous tasks, is peculiarly dependent on the probity and the diligence of the professionals who practice before it. . . . Very little of a securities lawyer's work is adversary in character. He doesn't work in courtrooms where the pressure of vigilant adversaries and alert judges checks him. . . . Hence, we are under a duty to hold our bar to approximately rigorous standards of professional honor.[7]

The SEC has demonstrated its determination to enforce its expectations by holding lawyers legally responsible for the truthfulness of registration statements and other material contained in communications to investors. And the Federal Trade Commission in the seventies began to name advertising agencies in false-advertising suits. If Madison Avenue is held to that standard of probity, it is inconceivable that we hold lawyers to a lower standard.

The corporate Washington attorney also has serious obligations within the legal profession itself. If he is an antitrust lawyer, he may sit on government commissions or an American Bar Association committee writing reports on various aspects of our trade-regulation statutes (see the first chapter). If he is a tax lawyer, he may be involved in helping candidates formulate tax programs, or in helping committees of the Congress write legislation. If he is a communications lawyer, he may have clients with profound concerns about who sits on the Federal Communications Commission.

Practitioners before government commissions, such as the Civil

Aeronautics Board, the Federal Communications Commission, and the Interstate Commerce Commission, are deeply interested in the membership of those bodies. Their clients are even more interested. In my judgment, it is improper for Washington attorneys to press for the appointment of a particular person to one of these commissions on behalf of an individual client without revealing that they represent a particular client. Indeed, when an attorney is asked his view of a proposed appointee to a particular agency, as many Washington attorneys are, he should promptly disclose any client interest he is representing before that agency at the time he gives his view.

Personally, I believe that the obligations of Washington attorneys extend beyond that. They should make it their business to press for the most competent lawyers in all the adjudicatory positions in the federal government: from administrative law judges to commission members. Yet, only on rare occasions does the private bar become broadly involved even in the appointment of federal judges. That the bar can act effectively is clear from the defeat of the Supreme Court nominations of Haynsworth and Carswell, but equal efforts do not seem to be expended before those regulatory bodies that on a daily basis affect their clients' interests.

Difficult as these ethical problems are, they must be faced. As one attorney noted, in an article urging higher ethical and professional standards:

> The rise of big business has produced an inevitable specialization of the Bar. The successful lawyer of our day more often than not is the proprietor or general manager of a new type of factory, whose legal product is increasingly the result of mass production methods. More and more the amount of his income is the measure of professional success [rather than] . . . the intangible and indubitably more durable satisfactions which are to be found in a professional service more consciously directed toward the advancement of the public interest. Steadily the best skill and capacity of the profession has been drawn into the exacting and highly specialized service of business and finance. At its best the changed system has brought to the command of the business world loyalty and a superb proficiency and technical skill. At its worst it has made the learned profession of an earlier day the obsequious servant of business, and tainted it with the morals and manners of the market place in its more antisocial manifestations. . . .
>
> . . . Before [the Bar] can function at all as the guardian of public interests committed to its care, there must be appraisal and comprehension of the new

conditions and changed relationships of the lawyer to his clients, to his professional brethren and to the public. That appraisal must pass beyond the petty details of form and manners which have been so largely the subject of our codes of ethics, to more fundamental consideration of the way in which our professional activities affect the welfare of society as a whole. . . . We must not permit our attention to the relatively inconsequential to divert us from preparing to set appropriate standards for those who design the legal patterns for business practices of far more consequence to society than any with which our grievance committees have been preoccupied.[8]

Those words were not written by Ralph Nader or Mark Green in the *New Republic* or *The Nation* in 1975.[9] They were written by Justice Harlan F. Stone in the *Harvard Law Review* in 1934. The professional tragedy of the American bar, and the Washington lawyers in particular, is perhaps symbolized by the fact that only a few have seen these words, and few of those have paid any attention to them. At best, the ethical and professional concerns reflected in the committees and House of Delegates of the American Bar Association demonstrate that most of its members have not read these words. At worst, they reveal a cold-blooded rejection of them.

While lawyers, particularly articulate Washington lawyers, will argue interminably over such ethical questions because the problems are complex and because the terrain is uncharted, history does provide one clear lesson about saying no: It can be a very expensive proposition, calling for the best in any of us confronted with the problem. The two most outstanding examples of lawyers who said no as a matter of personal conscience and professional standards are Thomas More and Thomas à Becket. When Thomas à Becket said no to King Henry II's request to lawyer a state takeover of the Church, the king had him murdered in Canterbury Cathedral. When Thomas More refused to renounce his Catholic faith, declare the king to be the head of the Church in England, and legally rationalize the sovereign's divorce, King Henry VIII had him beheaded. It is interesting that Thomas More and Thomas à Becket are remembered as saints, not as lawyers.

Michael Pertschuk

The Lawyer-Lobbyist

HEN I CAME to the staff of the Senate Commerce Committee, green and overwhelmed, my first major assignment was the Cigarette Advertising and Labeling Act of 1965. After eight days of hearings, I was to prepare for executive session a summary of the medical evidence linking cigarette smoking and disease. I spent two days with Public Health Service doctors attempting to summarize the evidence for, and against, the medical claims against cigarettes.

Having heard about my activities, a representative of the tobacco industry demanded that its lawyers have an equal opportunity to review my memorandum. So one Sunday morning I found myself in the *fin de siècle* townhouse offices of Arnold & Porter, in the intimidating presence of perhaps a dozen giants of the bar—from Covington & Burling, Arnold & Porter, and Wall Street firms whose names have long set the heads of ambitious law students spinning.

One of the lawyers present was Robert Wald, then representing P. Lorillard. At several crucial points, when I began to sink under a barrage of quibbles, he intervened in my behalf. But Wald proved to be the exception. For hours, the others chewed and picked at every word in my memorandum, insisting that no assertion or statement of evidence could appear which had not been adduced in hearing records. I later realized that this was nonsense—never within memory has Congress been bound by evidence produced at its own hearings. They haggled and wheedled and gradually wore me down. Smoking victims were not present to argue the contrary position. The net result was a document that vastly understated the evidence against smoking.

Despite my first brush with lobbying—I have, by now, fully recovered

* MICHAEL PERTSCHUK IS THE CHIEF COUNSEL OF THE SENATE COMMERCE COMMITTEE. HE COLLABORATED IN PREPARING *The Dark Side of the Marketplace* BY SENATOR WARREN MAGNUSON (1968) AND SERVED AS A MEMBER OF THE NATIONAL COMMISSION ON PRODUCT SAFETY FROM 1968 TO 1970.

—it is important to emphasize that, contrary to popular opinion, lobbying is not a social disease. Indeed, lobbying is so favored a form of human expression that it merits a constitutional safeguard. In the 1954 *Harriss* decision, Chief Justice Earl Warren observed that no less than three of the freedoms guaranteed by the First Amendment establish the right to lobby: "Freedom to speak, publish and petition the government." [1] And Justice Robert Jackson warned: "We may not forget that our constitutional system is to allow the greatest freedom of access to Congress, so that the people may press for their selfish interests, the Congress acting as arbiter of their demands and conflicts." Thus, let us by all means give praise to the constitutional role of lawyer-lobbyists, who at their finest scrupulously convey to the bureaucracy and the legislature the needs, wants, and fears of their clients in order to conform remedial action to basic public purposes.

But the mischief lies with the lawyer-lobbyist who parks his conscience and personal moral accountability on Delaware Avenue outside the Russell Senate Office Building. Far too many lawyers have conveniently lost sight of the origins of that peculiar societal role which permits the lawyer to suspend his own moral judgments. It is the *courtroom* not the *legislature* that frames the adversary system. When the state seeks to deprive a citizen of his liberty, it is proper that the lawyers undertake the defense of the accused without regard to their own judgments or morality. None of us would deny that the glory of the common law resides in the refinement of precedent and gloss through the combat of lawyers in open court, on the record, rigorously circumscribed by due process and the rules of evidence and conducted under the close supervision of a judge.

But imagine, if you can, a *lawsuit* which followed this bizarre scenario: Instead of a courtroom, the relevant events take place in a floating forum. To be sure, there are several minor scenes played out in a congressional hearing room, which displays the familiar props of a court-like tribunal, such as witnesses testifying publicly upon a record. But the scene, and the forum, shifts abruptly:

- Now to the cramped enclave of a beleaguered junior staff counsel;

- Next to the sixth hole at Burning Tree Country Club;

- Back to the spare, obscure committee room, packed with a curious amalgam of Administration bureaucrats and corporate lawyers and sprinkled with a handful of sympathetic congressional staff;

- Next a circuit of quiet, *ex parte* sessions in senatorial offices;

- On to Redskin stadium, intermission of the Dallas game;

- And final argument over the diet special at the Federal City Club.

If this forum seems elusive, so do the parties. At least one party may be identified with certainty: a corporate entity with a heartfelt economic stake in the status quo. But the adversary party or parties appear in several guises, including "competition," "labor," "the consumer," "the environment," and "the public interest." These adversaries are as fairly matched as the Oakland Athletics and the Bushwick Little League irregulars. On the bench for the corporate interests sit a rich assortment of power hitters—administrative law specialists, litigation specialists, FDA specialists, FTC specialists, home state local "counsels" nurtured by the warmth of key congressional friendships—a half-dozen house counsels steeped in industrial know-how, and of course Washington counsel steeped in congressional know-who, a sprinkling of legal academicians with impressive credentials (a deanery or two), and a handful of eager gleaming rookies from the editorial boards of Harvard, Yale, and Columbia law reviews.

Representing the opposing interests is, quite often, no one. Occasionally, the corporate interests are challenged by a government lawyer whose agency's power-lust pits him temporarily in opposition to an industry he may later either accommodate or join. At times a handful of in-house, congressional aides—committed, but suffering from sharply circumscribed time and resources—may rise up to advocate what they regard as the public interest. But what of the vaunted, "public interest" bar, those scarlet pimpernels of the law, whose very existence strikes fear and loathing in the corporate heart? In a city of an estimated 5,000 lobbyists (or approximately 10 per member of Congress), there are perhaps 190 full-time public interest advocates. They lack the WATS lines and hot copy transcripts, the ranks of seasoned clerks and typists; they take not limousines but buses, are forced to exist on handouts from foundations, and can suffocate in the tax code. The reality is somewhat less than advertised.

The problem, however, is not merely that the process begins with a stacked deck. Through a series of typical, but by no means exhaustive, vignettes, consider the elevating functions typically performed by corporate counsel:

1. A former senator, whose once formidable legal skills have long since eroded, calls his good friend and neighbor, an old colleague now chairman of a key Senate committee, and offers to drive him to work the next morning. While stopped at a red light, on the corner of Ninth Street and Constitution Avenue, he delivers his complete brief in support of the House version of a consumer bill: "I've never asked you for much, friend; but this one is really important to my people."

2. Attorney B, the old, hometown law partner and current campaign treasurer of a critically placed House member, drops into the member's office while "passing through" Washington: "I wonder if you would have a few minutes to meet with the board chairman of X Corporation. He's a reasonable man and he is having a hard time getting through to your staff on the practical difficulties of this so-called tax reform amendment—I'd appreciate it."

3. Lawyer D, the name partner in a prominent Washington law firm, invites a young committee counsel to lunch at the Metropolitan Club. "What are your plans?" he inquires with fatherly concern. "You know you ought not to stick around on the Hill too long; you've served your apprenticeship; you owe it to yourself and your family to move on before you get stale. And, when you are ready, come see us."

4. Lawyer E is a legend in Washington; law Professor F, a legendary member of the faculty of a legendary law school. These legends converge to convey to a junior staff member, whose luck it is to bear the principal responsibility for a major environment bill, the bill's "unconscionable neglect of the rudiments of due process." It is out of expensive lessons in administrative law, such as these, that flow administrative proceedings stretching into decades.

5. Finally, we come to lawyer G, a former cabinet officer and confidential adviser to half a dozen presidents, not the least of which is the present incumbent. He calls the ranking committee member of his own party and he says: "George, *we* don't like this one." He leaves to his colleague the task of fleshing out the content of the collective pronoun.

I know of no apologist for the profession so morally myopic that he would defend such cases of cronyism and manipulation—contemptible tactics when employed by lawyer and non-lawyer alike. But short of such behavior, some would say, why should a lawyer not be as free to advocate his client's cause in the legislative forum as vigorously as in any other appropriate forum? Again, the answer becomes clearer when the legislative process is viewed not in the abstract but in context. Here a lengthy (not-so) hypothetical might be helpful.

Assume that the Office of Arcane Hazards of the Consumer Product Safety Commission has unearthed epidemiological evidence that the excessive emission of noxious gases generated by the interaction of decaying garbage in the metal or plastic walls of standard garbage cans is contributing to premature cardiac arrest among middle-aged Americans at the rate of 25,000 to 30,000 cases a year. Assume further that the Senate Commerce Committee has pending legislation authorizing the Product Safety Commission to set standards for the maximum permissible emissions of such gases, it having been demonstrated that application of an inexpensive coating to the inner surface of the garbage can will reduce such gaseous emissions to safe levels. Also imagine that the GCMA (Garbage Can Manufacturers Association) is resisting the legislation for fear that the added costs of coating garbage cans could result in a substantial shift to home compost heaps and hence stagnating sales.

Despite a thick smoke screen of delaying tactics, the GCMA finds itself facing a strong bill pending before the Commerce Committee, hearings completed, and a markup of the bill in executive session barely a week away. Representatives of the five major garbage can manufacturers which make up the GCMA convene in extraordinary session. "What we need here," warns the Washington representative of the GRC (General Refuse Disposal) company, who had been diligently reading Jack Anderson, "is a lawyer like Newbold Skinner. They say he's got a mind like a steel trap, that he can weave a dozen alternative provisos without blinking an eye, each one equally capable of serving his clients' objectives. In short, we need a legislative craftsman. If we're prepared to face the reality that there's going to be a law, then we had best defang it."

So they hire Newbold Skinner, weaned on the Food, Drug, and Cosmetic Act Amendments of 1938, bloodied before the Federal Trade Commission, and a veteran of the cigarette, automobile, gas pipeline, textile, and toy industries' last stands. In parsing the nooks and crannies of the Administrative Procedures Act, he is nonpareil. He can visualize prophetically how the flesh of actual regulation would fit the bones of legislation. Whatever one might say about his affinity for undeserving causes, Skinner perceives his role not as a policy maker but rather a lawyer-advocate prepared to dazzle the policy makers (senators and staffs) with the skill and symmetry of his arguments. In this he is aided by Macqwait, the general counsel of GCMA, and the production managers of GWD (General Waste Disposal) and Amalgamated Refuse—men who understand at precisely which points in the manufacturing process a federal presence can prove most disruptive, and who can chart the precise relationships between federally mandated design changes and production costs. Skinner also can draw upon the encyclopedic knowledge of Phil Coates, the seasoned garbage can personal injury defense lawyer from Omaha.

After meeting in intensive day and night session, drafting and redrafting amendments, memoranda, and briefs, Skinner calls the committee staff counsel assigned to the bill: "We'd like to sit down with you, if we can, to iron out as many 'technical problems' as possible before the committee meets in executive session, so that we won't have to impose upon the time of the committee members." The committee's young attorney, despite his determination to remain cool and independent, finds himself intimidated by the fame and the eloquence of the great advocate. When they meet, Skinner speaks coolly, with exquisite logic, without notes:

"As you know, the garbage can industry believes that no legislation is necessary, but if there is to be legislation, they want to make certain that it is workable, that while it achieves the purposes of its sponsors, it does not impose needless economic burdens on the industry—burdens which will only be passed on to the consumers of garbage cans—and that it does not violate the elementary dictates of democratic due process to which, under our system, rich and poor are alike entitled *[so long as each can afford $150 an hour for the services of the likes of Skinner].*

"God knows, the Consumer Product Safety Commission has no expert knowledge of the manufacture and distribution of garbage cans. The Department of Commerce has, however, worked with this industry and is familiar with its practices. In our judgment, Commerce would be a far more appropriate agency for implementing this legislation. *[Yes, Commerce is familiar with business practices; it ought to be, as business's prime apologist within the federal establishment and a tepid regulator at best.]*

"Whatever the agency, in elemental fairness the industry should be entitled to a hearing on any proposed standard, or amendment to a standard, with *full* opportunity to present testimony and to examine and cross-examine witnesses *[thereby delaying the promulgation date of standards by months and, with skill, years].*

"On the other hand, the government should not be burdened by the intervention in hearings of persons (i.e., Nader) with no legally recognizable interest in proposed standards. *[What of the indivisible interest of the public in not being gassed to death?]*

"In the setting of standards the government should be guided by express criteria such as the 'reasonableness' of the costs which would be generated by compliance with the standard and the 'technical feasibility' of the standard in relation to 'the state of industrial art.' *[If this language ended up in the bill, Skinner would later argue before the regulatory agency that the cost entailed by any standard more stringent than the present voluntary standard was manifestly 'unreasonable' and vastly beyond 'the state of the art.']*

"The industry certainly shares the desire of the bill's sponsors to make certain that standards reflect the most advanced and sophisticated technology available to the nation. Unfortunately, this knowledge does not exist now in the government nor is it likely that at government pay scales the agency can attract the most qualified engineers. We would propose, therefore, that the bill provide that all standards should be submitted for approval to a technical standards committee, to be composed of nationally recognized experts in gas-emission technology *[virtually all of whom are either employed directly by the industry or serve from time to time as handsomely compensated consultants to it]*.

"The legislation must allow the industry adequate lead-time to make production adjustments after a standard has been promulgated. Three years would permit orderly retooling and would not break the industry's model-year cycle *[although any foreseeable standard could be met at modest retooling costs in less than six weeks]*.

"I'm sure it was an oversight, but the sponsors of the bill have omitted the customary 'grandfather clause' which would permit the companies to market any cans which they had made or were in the process of making on the date any standard takes effect. And in the spirit of federal-state cooperation, any state which adopts a standard similar to *[but not necessarily equal to]* the federal standard should be left free to regulate those garbage cans within its own confines *[thereby leaving the industry's operations within that state subject only to chronically understaffed and 'sympathetic' state enforcement authorities]*.

"I see no evidence that this industry has been shown to be other than a responsible citizen of the business community. There can be no doubt that the industry will conform with the utmost scrupulousness to whatever standards the federal government sets. So there seems little reason other than bureaucratic imperatives to burden the industry with elaborate record-keeping and reporting requirements or to authorize federal inspectors to roam freely about the plants exposing trade secrets. The government is certainly free to buy garbage cans in the marketplace and to test them for compliance with standards. *[It may be years before such "after market" inspection systems uncover ineffective garbage cans; the threat of a thorough on-site inspection can be far more effective in inhibiting corner-cutting on the assembly line. It is difficult to imagine the Senate and House Appropriations Committees approving hundreds of thousands of dollars for the purchase of garbage cans for enforcement testing. And, last, the trade-secret umbrella has become a notorious rubric for shielding corporate activities widely known in "the trade" from the prying eyes of the public's servants. Most trade-secret provisions offered by industry lobbyists are designed to ensure that—like the cuckold—the public is the last to know.]*

"As for the penalty provisions of this bill, we see no reason to provide that any official who knowingly authorizes the shipment of garbage cans which violate a standard may be subject to criminal fines and jail sentences. This industry is no Mafia. To treat the leadership of this industry as common criminals is to stain the name of an honorable American enterprise *[although the plant manager who discovers his production lines are producing substandard cans might well choose to let them go rather than fail to meet the strenuous product quotas set by his superiors—unless he personally faces the risk of spending six months in jail for making the wrong decision].*

"I will leave you with a brief listing of similar regulatory laws which carry no criminal penalties. *[These five recent laws bear the imprint of Skinner's own legislative handiwork. The list, however, is not complete. The brief excludes an equally impressive list of regulatory laws which do carry criminal penalties.]*

"Finally, once a standard is in effect, elemental fairness requires that any manufacturer sued in a private or class action lawsuit for damages caused by gas emissions should expressly be authorized by the statute to cite compliance with a federal standard as a shield against liability *[despite the fact that political and economic pressures on the regulatory agency or simple incompetence may have resulted in a woefully inadequate or antiquated standard]*."

Each argument is buttressed by a document, and each document is characterized by superb craftsmanship, subtle persuasiveness, exhaustive research, and the finest quality bond paper. Under this avalanche of argument, citations, memos, briefs, and choruses of indignation, staff counsel begins to give way. A word modified here, a phrase amended there, a deletion, even a change in punctuation—all "technical amendments" which will be later ratified by the Commerce Committee without close scrutiny and be destined to stand in the future like so many boulders in the path of effective regulation.

The "great garbage can lobby" is, of course, fictional, but not sheer caricature. There are few veteran committee counsels who have not heard these worn but seductive pleas from learned counsel, on behalf of automobile manufacturers, interstate gas pipelines, cigarette makers, giant and not-so-giant retailers, supermarket chains, TV set assemblers, oil giants, "ethical" drug companies, grocery manufacturers, makers of children's sleepwear—almost every major American consumer industry (with the possible exception of used-car dealers). And the lawyers who make these arguments carry a very special aura of status and power and wisdom, as books by Joseph Goulden and Mark Green on Washington lawyers make clear.[2] Writing in the *New Republic* in 1963, for one example, Murray Kempton skewed the sugar-lawyer lobby.[3]

The sugar lobby sells a product one can weigh—the kindness and the exhaustion of the Congress of the United States. The members of this lobby, possibly by lot, represent nations which are bitter rivals for shares of the U.S. Sugar quota; but the tie among them is stronger than any flag any one of them flies. They meet because they have liberal tastes in all matters except in the case of such bar necessities as the choice of clients.

Their tone is set in a recollection of the sugar hearings of 1956 when Oscar Chapman, former Secretary of the Interior, was arguing the case of his client, Mexico, before the Senate Finance Committee. At one point, Senator Robert Kerr leaned forward to ask Chapman to tell him about the Dominican Republic and the state of its people, the nature of its liberties, the character of its rulers. Now Chapman represented a country, Mexico, which had every personal, political, and commercial reason to be hostile to Trujillo. Instead Chapman gave the Dominican Republic a description that would have seemed a little fulsome for Athens, which deeply gratified some Dominicans because they knew what a lie it was and were perhaps confident that Chapman did too. But one doubts that Chapman even knew Trujillo, except as a client of old friend Walter Surrey (ECA, NATO). All clients are gray; there is only the bond of fraternity whose rule is that you stand up for the damned scoundrel who pays your brother and he'll stand up for the damned scoundrel who pays you.

What is the proper role for a conscientious lawyer in the legislative process—not only in Washington but in state and local legislative bodies around the country?

The eighth canon of the *Code of Professional Responsibility* is entitled "A Lawyer Should Assist in Improving the Legal System." With respect to the representation of clients in the legislative process, the canon states simply: "A lawyer may advocate changes on behalf of a client even though he does not agree with them." If he views his role in the legislative process with a critical eye, however, the ethical lawyer-lobbyist comes to realize that he cannot escape moral accountability for the public impact of his advocacy. He knows that he shares the responsibility for assuring that the legislative process serves the public weal. These realizations lead to refined standards for the ethical lawyer-lobbyist beyond the precise letter of the law and the *Code of Professional Responsibility*.

For a prospective client whose very existence is at variance with the public good (e.g., dictatorships and cigarettes), the ethical lawyer-lobbyist may well simply decline to make available his skills and resources. Or he may choose to advocate internally only such courses of conduct and pleading as may be consistent with the public interest (e.g., support of legislation designed to stimulate the development and sale of safer cigarettes). At the least, he will remain acutely sensitive to the vulnerability of the forum. If active public interest lobbies participate in an open hearing, the legislature approaches the adversary system of a court; then he may prepare for his clients a brief which develops only those facts and arguments most favorable to the client's cause. But if he is making his presentation to a congressman or a staff person, without the other side represented, as an expert drawing upon his own experience in government, the ethical lawyer-lobbyist will share his knowledge fully rather than ration it in one-sided advocacy. He will take pains to predict accurately the likely impact of his proposed course of action and will refrain from laying down a smoke screen of shrouded objectives and implications. When he proposes legislative language, he will disclose latent complexities and ambiguities, pitfalls to efficient administration.

The ethical lobbyist will avoid trading on his own political leverage for the benefit of his client. If his personal relationship with legislative decision-makers affords him unique access, steps ought to be taken to ensure that a knowledgeable staff person or public interest advocate is present to help filter his own advocacy through a counter-advocate's intelligence. This lawyer will not accept uncritically the bald representation of his clients as to the workability or burdens of proposed public interest legislation. He will seek to ascertain for himself the truth of assertions that proposed consumer, health, or environment standards cannot be practicably met within a given period of time or that their costs will be overbearing or that competitive conditions require a blanket of secrecy over information which can be useful to the consuming public. He will make efforts to ascertain their truthfulness before becoming the vehicle of their advocacy.

Nor will the ethical lawyer-lobbyist be content merely to inflict no deliberate harm on the process by which the laws are shaped. As Ralph Nader says, "Lawyers derive their influence from their status in society, they are accorded status because they are alleged to have certain responsibilities that transcend their responsibilities to their clients. A lawyer's first client is the public." If all lawyers share a positive duty to improve the law in the public interest, as even the *Code of Professional Responsibility* insists,[4] then it is not enough for the lawyer-lobbyist to satisfy his *pro bono* urgings by serving as treasurer to a building fund for an orthopedic hospital. He earns his living and status because of his skills as a lobbyist, and it is these skills that he has an obligation to apply to the public good.

The larger the firm and the greater the stable of corporate clients, the more squeamish the lawyer-lobbyist becomes in taking up a public interest cause before the legislature, fearing to antagonize at least one of his accounts. But there is nothing in the *Code of Professional Responsibility* which suggests that a client owns the soul of his attorney. And there is no reason why an attorney who has discharged his contractual obligation to represent Ford in a case before the Department of Transportation cannot advocate the strengthening of auto safety laws before the House or Senate. Louis Brandeis said it best in 1905:

> . . . The leaders of the bar have, with a few exceptions, not only failed to take part in constructive legislation designed to solve in the public interest our great social, economic and industrial problems; but they have failed likewise to oppose legislation prompted by selfish interests. They have often gone further in disregard of the commonweal. They have often advocated, as lawyers, legislative measures which as citizens they could not approve. They have erroneously assumed that the rule of ethics to be applied to a lawyer's advocacy is the same where he acts for private interests against the public, as it is in litigation between private individuals.[5]

Jay M. Smyser

In-House Corporate Counsel: The Erosion of Independence

FOR THE PAST DECADE corporate law department practice has increased at a faster rate than any other field of law practice. A little over twenty years ago a survey found a mere 5,428 lawyers on company payrolls.[1] In 1973 *Fortune* reported corporate law departments to be a "growth industry"—employing some 40,000 lawyers at a cost to American business in the neighborhood of $2 billion a year.[2]

Aside from their own self-serving descriptions of their work delivered at frequent and well-attended conventions, there is surprisingly little data available on exactly what they are *supposed* to do. As Professor John D. Donnell, author of a pioneering study on this slice of the legal profession, put it, "It is probably clear to all that their principal function and reason for being on the corporate payroll is to assist in keeping the corporation out of legal difficulty and to gain the protection of law for its actions."[3]

Current management theory tells us that job performance is to be judged by results. There seem to be two levels on which to gauge the results obtained by corporate counsel in keeping the corporation out of legal difficulty and gaining the protection of law for its actions. The first involves the extent to which corporate counsel successfully influences business policy in such a manner that the corporation finesses legal problems. According to the general counsel for one of our corporate giants, competent corporate counsel must

> know how to deploy corporate forces so that on most occasions battle lines will never be formed. He must rise above the cautious role of the lawyer who simply advises that a proposed course of action is legal or illegal and leaves to others the wisdom of corporate policy. The corporate counsel's voice should be

* JAY SMYSER, WHOSE CAREER INCLUDED A PERIOD ON THE GENERAL COUNSEL STAFF OF GENERAL MOTORS, IS A VISITING PROFESSOR AT THE UNIVERSITY OF MIAMI LAW SCHOOL. HE WOULD LIKE TO THANK MS. DOROTHY BERNDT FOR HER ASSISTANCE IN THE PREPARATION OF THIS ARTICLE.

insistent in favor of going beyond bare legal minimal when to do so will build his company a reservoir of public good will, or minimize or eliminate what would otherwise be a widespread feeling of injury or injustice.[4]

The success of corporate counsel on this level is comparable to the Edsel's in its invasion of the medium-price car market. New evidence accumulates daily that the unremitting pursuit of traditional corporate goals continues to produce massive collisions between these businesses and what Professor A. A. Berle called the inchoate law, which, in my view, calls for an end to the deterioration in the quality of our environment, reasonable safety on the job and in the products we use and consume, and a healthy regard for the problems inherent in the finite nature of the physical resources on this increasingly crowded planet.

If corporate counsel have failed as "keeper of the corporate conscience," however, it does not necessarily follow that they lack the needed influence in corporate councils. The failure more likely owes to an almost universal refusal among house counsel even to attempt to perform this function. In his study of the breed, Professor Donnell found that "almost all of the corporate counsel interviewed commented that they believed that the top management of their company sought to conduct the company's business on a very high level of commercial morality, and therefore, there was no need for them to perform the conscience function." [5]

Another gauge of the results obtained by corporate counsel is the modern corporate client's expectation that its legal business will be handled without resort to court action.[6] Yet according to *Fortune*, over the past six years there has been almost a 100 percent increase in lawsuits brought before the federal courts in six major corporate areas.[7]

In short, judged on the basis of results, corporate counsel, despite their swelling ranks and salaries, may be short-changing their customers.

As to why corporate counsel are not fulfilling their prescribed role—keeping their clients attuned to the inchoate law and out of court—I have a hypothesis to offer: The success of any lawyer employed as corporate counsel bears an inverse relationship to the degree of his identification with corporate management and its short-term goals. In other words, I believe corporate counsel must fail when they permit themselves to labor under conditions which destroy the independence necessary to professional judgment.

The independence of a lawyer's professional judgment is traditionally regarded as the hallmark of the legal profession. Canon 5 of the ABA *Code of Professional Responsibility*—"A lawyer should exercise independent professional judgment on behalf of a client"—continues the lip service we pay it. But, in practice, a variety of professionally sanctioned practices, from the contingent fee to ownership of a client's stock, necessarily undermine this principle. Obviously, the profit motive plays an important role in the life of our society, but its appropriateness as a conditioning influence on the lawyer is subject to profound question. When the terms of a lawyer's employment make the profit motive an inevitable influence on his judgment, the "independent professional judgment" to which the client is entitled becomes little more than a fond notion. The profit motive's obliteration of the distinction in the lawyer's mind between his personal interests and his client's cause has had a particularly disastrous impact on the ethical standards of the legal profession in this country. The ruthless partisanship that results is not offset, under our system, by any definable, enforceable countervailing duty to the courts and other institutions of law-government through whom the lawyer may work. "Organized legal ethics never in this country worked out solutions for the conflict of duty to the court and to the client," said Karl Llewellyn. "Duty to client reads in terms of taking advantage of each technicality the law may show, however senseless. . . . Duty to self resolved the conflict, as canons of ethics did not. The resolution was in favor of the client." [8] So, while considering the extent to which corporate counsel's employment deprives him of independence, we should not ignore that the entire spectrum of today's practice of law is riddled with analogous practices having the same effect, both on the lawyer's independence and the quality of service he is able to render his client.

It wasn't always so. In the nineteenth century the lawyer's independence of his client was understood in terms of its value *to the client.* The advice a client received from a truly independent lawyer could be assumed to be based on a dispassionate, objective appraisal of the situation. The leaders of the bar in that earlier day, observed Charles P. Curtis,

> knew that they could not give their clients the full measure of their devotion unless they kept themselves detached. Thereby they were able to offer their clients what they had come to get—advice and counsel from someone above the turmoil of their troubles or at least far enough away from them to look at them. By not putting themselves as well as their minds up for hire, they saved, for the clients as well as for themselves, the waste of spirit which some lawyers confuse with devotion.[9]

Mr. Justice Frankfurter, trained in this older tradition, saw this quality as of the essence:

> If lawyers are true to their function, then they are what I venture to call experts in relevance. And an expert in relevance is a person who has intellectual disinterestedness, who penetrates a problem as far as the human mind dealing with affairs is capable of penetrating, who is free, who is not entangled with making a fair judgment and is not thwarted by personal, partial or parochial interests.[10]

Events in the latter part of the nineteenth century, however, conspired to undermine many of the circumstances supportive of the lawyer's independence. The emergence of corporate industrialism and finance capitalism made possible the rapid exploitation of our natural resources and brought the day of "the organizer, the man who prospered by inventing new ways of drawing small units into more profitable combinations. In the sprawling nation," says Daniel Boorstin, "the lawyer was apt to know how it could (and couldn't) be done." [11] Thus, by 1870 the focal point in the practice of law in America shifted from courtroom advocacy to office counseling. From that point on, noted Wall Street lawyer Robert T. Swaine, we find

> many of the former great advocates were not only devoting most of their own time to the new corporate practice but had drawn around themselves other lawyers whose abilities lay rather in negotiation in the conference room and in drafting documents than in persuasiveness before the courts. The corporation lawyer had developed, with functions and working habits quite different from those of the advocate.[12]

Historian Richard Hofstadter saw the same development.

> With the rise of corporate industrialism and finance capitalism, the law, particularly in the urban centers where the most enviable prizes were to be had, was becoming a captive profession. . . . Metropolitan law firms, as they grew larger and more profitable, moved into closer relationships with and became "house counsel" of large investment houses, banks, or industrial firms that provided them with most of their business. But the relation that was the source of profit brought with it a loss of independence to the great practitioners. The smaller independent practitioner was affected in another, more serious way: much of his work was taken from him by real-estate, trust and insurance companies, collection agencies and banks, which took upon themselves larger and larger amounts of what had once been entirely legal business.[13]

Thus the economic impetus for lawyers to cultivate corporate clientele came not just from the promise of financial rewards but also from the threat posed by corporate usurpation of what had been considered lawyers' jobs.

Many of the bar's best minds, most of its inevitable leaders, moved, in the words of Karl Llewellyn, "massively out of court work, out of a general practice akin to that of a family doctor, into highly paid specialization in the service of large corporations." [14] Such continuing relationships with corporate clients brought increasing identification of these lawyers with the interests they represented. As Llewellyn explained, the resulting effect on their vision was understandable enough in human terms:

> Now, any man's interests, any man's outlook, are shaped in greatest part by what he *does*. His perspective is in terms of what he knows. His sympathies and ethical judgments are determined essentially by the things and people he works on and for and with. Individual exceptions there are; rarely indeed do they work deflection of the mass movement. Hence the practice of corporation law not only works for business men toward business ends, but develops within itself a business point of view—toward the work to be done, toward the value of the work to the community, indeed toward the way in which to do the work. [15]

There were, of course, some protests at the appearance of the "corporation lawyer" and the effects of such specialization on the legal profession. But apparently they had little contemporaneous impact. For instance, it is only in recent years that a 1905 statement by Louis Brandeis has achieved wide currency:

> Instead of holding a position of independence between the wealthy and the people, prepared to curb the excesses of either, able lawyers have, to a large extent, allowed themselves to become adjuncts of great corporations and have neglected their obligation to use their powers for the protection of the people. We hear much of the "corporation lawyer," and far too little of the "people's lawyer." [16]

And there was little recorded reaction when Woodrow Wilson exhorted the American Bar Association in 1910

> to recall you to the service of the nation as a whole, from which you have been drifting away; to remind you that, no matter what the exactions of modern business, no matter what or how great the necessity for specialization in your practice of law, you are not the servants of special interests, the mere expert

counsellors of this, that, or the other group of business men; but guardians of the general peace, the guides of those who seek to realize by some best accommodation the rights of men.[17]

Although the nature of their work may have produced an inevitable bias, that first generation of corporation lawyers sought to preserve their professional independence by refusing to go on corporate payrolls and rejecting financial interests in and positions on the boards of the clients they advised. Largely forgotten now, Samuel C. T. Dodd was the lawyer whose imagination turned that familiar device of English equity, the trust, into Rockefeller's instrument of business combination. When trusts later came under attack, Dodd devised the holding company. But, according to Daniel Boorstin, Dodd—in order to give Rockefeller the most detached and reliable device—refused to accept his client's stock.[18] Frederick P. Fish, who left a position as leader of the patent bar to head the Bell Telephone system around the turn of the century, would never accept stock in a client.[19] Robert T. Swaine, in his history of the firm that became synonymous with representation of large business interests, wrote that Paul D. Cravath

> early came to believe that in most cases the client is best advised by a lawyer who maintains an objective point of view and that such objectivity may be impeded by any financial interest in the client's business or participation in its management. Accordingly, he made it the policy of the firm that neither its partners nor its associates should hold securities of any client, or serve as a director of a corporate client, or have a financial interest, direct or indirect, in any transaction in which the firm was acting as counsel.[20]

At this time the infrequent lawyer who took a salaried position with a corporation was regarded as little more than a scrivener and notary public, contemptuously dismissed by his brothers at the bar as "kept counsel." William Howard Taft probably spoke for most lawyers when, in 1914, he wrote off such lawyers as "unprofessional": "Such employment leads to a lawyer becoming nothing more than an officer of a corporation as closely identified with it as if he were the president, the secretary or the treasurer." [21] Mr. Justice Brandeis cut to the heart of the matter. "Long ago," he wrote, "it was recognized that 'a man who is his own lawyer has a fool for a client.' The essential reason for this is that soundness of judgment is easily obscured by self-interest." [22]

It was only a matter of time, however, before the distinction between outside corporate lawyers and those on the company payroll began to blur; corporate clients sought and obtained exceptions from law firm policies forbidding their members from becoming directors or officers or stockholders in client companies.[23] Pressures of competition created further exceptions. A partner in a large Wall Street law firm explained:

> Our experience has been that the corporations are better off if the partner who attends their meetings is not a member of the board. It reduces problems, avoids conflicts of interest, facilitates decision-making, and gives the participating lawyer more independence . . . [b]ut competition prevents any individual firm from establishing such a policy. The fear of turning around some day and finding a lawyer from a competing firm on the board leads you to keep one of your partners there.[24]

Shortly before his death, Swaine surveyed the exponential growth in exceptions to Cravath's policy and sighed, "I believe that most of us would be greatly relieved if a canon of ethics were adopted forbidding a lawyer in substance to become his own client through acting as a director or officer of a client. But the practice is too widespread to permit any such expectations." [25]

Ironically, the law firms that permitted exceptions to swallow the earlier policy not only diluted the quality of service they were able to offer their clients but, simultaneously, greased the skids on which their most lucrative business began to slip away. With their loss of independence they erased the primary reason a corporation might have for preferring their counsel to that of the more convenient, economical house counsel. As *The New York Times* reported in 1973, "Many corporations, in an attempt to reduce their legal bills, have buttressed their legal staffs and are relying less on outside counsel." [26] Alcoa's former general counsel corroborated this conclusion. "Since World War II, house counsel has emerged as the 'corporate counsel.' The head lawyer has commonly become the general counsel, usually an officer of the company, not infrequently a member of the board, and, if circumstances are right, a party to the corporation's innermost councils and planning. . . ." [27]

The transformation of salaried corporate counsel from little more than glorified clerks to full participants in the corporation's inner councils reflects one of the least noticed but more significant power shifts in the legal-corporate community. The quantum leap in their numbers is only a reflection of their enhanced potential to influence corporate policy. The growing power of in-house counsel correlates with the growing legal problems facing corporations in an increasingly aware consumer economy. Given these problems, management has shown an understandable tendency to defer to corporate counsel the judgment of whether a problem should be handled in-house or by outside counsel and, if outside counsel is to be used, which law firm gets the business. Corporate counsel's decisions on such matters seem to be heavily influenced by one of C. Northcoate Parkinson's axioms, the one that says an official wants to multiply subordinates, not rivals. More troubling, as Blaustein and Porter pointed out in their famous study of the American lawyer, is that house counsel's "closeness to detail and his intimacy with his employer may blind the lawyer to the ultimate implications of local decision. It may give rise to a temptation to consider problems in their business aspects rather than from their legal ramifications." [28]

This historical progression raises the general question whether the terms and conditions of the corporate counsel's employment present more than a temptation, indeed make it inevitable, that he or she will consider problems in their business aspects rather than from the point of view that independent professional judgment would bring to bear on their legal ramifications. More specific questions emerge:

Whom does corporate counsel represent? That monument to the profession's imagined self-interest, the *Code of Professional Responsibility*, says the business lawyer is lawyer to the "corporation," not the officers, directors, or stockholders.[29] What guidance does this provide in those inevitable conflicts between and among the various constituencies of the modern corporation? To what extent can it insulate the lawyer seeking to serve the "corporate interest" (whatever that abstraction means to him) from the ineluctable influence exercised on his judgment by the self-serving opinions of members of the corporate hierarchy who can fire him, raise his salary, and control any bonuses?

How is he paid? Many large corporations, such as General Motors, include members of the legal staff in the annual bonus cut from this year's profits, a system shrewdly designed by Alfred P. Sloan to give management employees ample incentive to make decisions maximizing short-term profits. Isn't it apparent that decisions so influenced may be at odds with long-term corporate interests? Can a lawyer so compensated pretend to be uninfluenced by such considerations as he purports to exercise "independent professional judgment" on questions that may determine if there is to be any profit from which to award a bonus?

How does corporate counsel conceive his role? As mentioned earlier,

Professor Donnell's study found virtually all corporate counsel he interviewed loath to perform the conscience function. My limited experience on the legal staff of a large corporation confirms Donnell's impression. The able, hard-working man who for twelve years supervised day-to-day operations of the legal staff of General Motors, Louis H. Bridenstine, frequently reiterated his conception of the role of the staff lawyer: fireman. Needless to say, the man concerned with dousing the fire ordinarily had not been consulted about the architecture of the structure before it went up.

These questions deserve a consideration they have not received. For it now appears that the American corporation, as it relies more and more on the advice of house counsel, isn't getting its money's worth, and the entire society suffers from the lack of vision such legal counsel now offers. Perhaps the bar—pressed by consumer critics or disappointed investors—can be persuaded to lay down terms under which he can work which will have the effect of restoring his independent professional judgment. If so, the bar will not only be doing corporate counsel a favor but, more importantly, his client and the society which his client inevitably affects.

V

The Government Lawyer: Who Is the Client?

Ramsey Clark*

Crisis at Justice

THE BEGINNING was modest. The Judiciary Act of 1789 establishing the federal system of courts created the Office of Attorney General and provided it should be filled by the president with ". . . a meet person, learned in the law." The first attorney general, Edmund Randolph, as most of his successors, filled that prescription. Like his father before him, he had served as attorney general of his state. He was at General Washington's right hand through the Revolution and an important delegate to the Constitutional Convention in Philadelphia, though he did not sign the final draft because he wanted the greater protection for individuals later afforded by the Bill of Rights. The salary was $1,500 per year with no funds for office rent, clerks, secretaries, or supplies. While the salary doubled in the first decade to $3,000, it was thirty years, 1819, before the attorney general of the United States was authorized a single clerk. William Wirt, who became attorney general November 13, 1817, wrote by hand the first record of the office, which began: "Finding on my appointment, this week no book document or papers of any kind to inform me of what has been done by any of my predecessors. . . ." This merely reflects the nature of the office in that epoch. It provided no precedent for an L. Patrick Gray to destroy records.

In 1853 Caleb Cushing became the first attorney general to abandon the simultaneous private practice of law. Most of his predecessors had engaged extensively in major cases and legal matters of the day for powerful private interests while serving as attorney general. All had practiced some law on the side. While this ethic, in light of current wisdom, is of course troubling, there at the same time existed an ethic, which would by and large endure, of what an attorney general was to do.

* RAMSEY CLARK WAS ATTORNEY GENERAL OF THE UNITED STATES (1967–1969) AND WROTE *Crime in America* (1971). HE IS NOW A NEW YORK CITY ATTORNEY ACTIVELY ENGAGED IN CIVIL RIGHTS AND CIVIL LIBERTIES LITIGATION.

"The office I hold is not properly *political,* but strictly *legal,*" said Abraham Lincoln's attorney general, Edward Bates, "and it is my duty, above all other ministers of state, to uphold the law and resist all encroachments from whatever quarter."

Still, in the mid-nineteenth century, the attorney general was an individual, not an institution. President Andrew Jackson first proposed the creation of a law department for the government. His proposal was defeated, largely through the efforts of Daniel Webster, who said it would make the attorney general "a half accountant, a half lawyer, a half clerk, a half everything and not much of anything." The Department of Justice, however, was finally established July 1, 1870, with a total budget of $67,000 and a single assistant attorney general. A century later department employment approaches 40,000 people and its budget is near $2 billion.

Historically there have been times of tragedy, politics, and lawlessness in the Department of Justice. Attorney General Mitchell Palmer led the department in open violation of the Bill of Rights in the 1920s. Attorney General Harry Daugherty was indicted, but not convicted, for his role in Teapot Dome. In the main, however, it has been a House of Law, above politics, devoted to the pursuit of justice. It has endeavored impartially to fulfill rights and enforce laws, conceiving the law as an instrument of the people's compact seeking social change. Its duty to the rule of law has tended to make its function quasi-judicial. As I wrote in the introduction to the last annual report of my tenure there:

> The Department of Justice is not an office of flinty-eyed prosecutors. Its mission is justice. It is moving steadily toward the role of Ministry of Justice. In days of turbulence filled with frustration, anger and hatred, the Department of Justice with steady purpose must move effectively toward equal justice for all, unperturbed by the emotion surrounding it. . . .

For the years 1961–1969, in the Department of Justice, excellence in law and government service were the highest personnel standards. As was usually the case in the preceding decades, no presidential appointee, no attorney general, no deputy attorney general, no solicitor general, or assistant attorney general had ever been a political candidate for statewide office. Among those who held one of the dozen key presidential appointments in the department, Byron White, Warren Christopher, Louis Oberdorfer, John Douglas, Norbert Schlei, Don Turner, Edwin

Zimmerman, and Frank Wozencraft had all clerked for justices of the U.S. Supreme Court. Nicholas deB. Katzenbach, Archibald Cox, Erwin Griswold, Don Turner, Edwin Zimmerman, and Clyde Martz had been professors of law. Thurgood Marshall and Lee Loevinger had served in the judiciary. John Doar, Sal Andretta, Walter Yeagley, Leo Pellerzi, and Mitchell Rogovin had distinguished careers in government service. A majority of all the presidential appointees had been editors of their law reviews in law school. Only Robert F. Kennedy and Byron White had been significantly involved in a presidential political campaign.

A radical change, unprecedented in its history, began in the Department of Justice in 1969. President Richard Nixon staffed the Department of Justice with politicians: Mitchell, Kleindienst, Richardson, Saxbe, Wilson, Gray, Leonard, Ruckelshaus, Frizell, Mardian, Rehnquist, Kashiwa. These men, all presidential appointees, had substantial direct political involvement in personal candidacies or presidential campaigns. Eight were candidates for or had previously held statewide political offices. Politicians can make extraordinary contributions to law and government even in the management of the bureaucracy. But when professional legal discipline becomes shaded by political consideration, we become a government of men, not laws. When politicians are placed in key legal positions, the appearance of political infection is immediate and its probability high.

Political people brought political postures and political judgments to the Department of Justice under Richard Nixon. In crime control, civil rights enforcement, pardons and parole, antitrust and civil litigation, and First Amendment areas, among others, the department took political positions and actions. A brief documentation can illuminate this disastrous pattern and what must be done.

President Nixon espoused wiretapping. He caused conversations in his office to be bugged for several years, with few others than himself aware of it. For the first time in history an attorney general, John Mitchell, contended there was an inherent power in the president to tap without congressional or judicial approval in domestic security cases. This view was later rejected by the Supreme Court, but we do not know how many lost their constitutional rights in the interim.

The first Nixon assistant attorney general for the Criminal Division, Will Wilson, a candidate on many occasions for statewide office in Texas, took a hard political line on law enforcement. Later, he was forced to resign under a cloud. He was the private attorney for a man under federal investigation for fraud, from whom Wilson borrowed tens of thousands of dollars after becoming chief prosecutor of the United States. Mr. Wilson signed a check payable to a private investigator indicted for wiretapping. Who was tapped? A federal bank examiner, assigned to investigate Mr. Wilson's client.

Attorney General Mitchell met in his office in the Department of Justice with political campaign officials, listened to suggestions for wiretapping the Democratic National Committee, a federal crime, and never admonished them of the law or threatened prosecution. Subsequently, of course, he was found guilty of obstruction of justice for his role in the Watergate scandal—thereby joining his successor, Richard Kleindienst, earlier convicted of failing to testify truthfully before Congress, as the only attorneys general in our history to be convicted of a crime.

To demonstrate their strong commitment to tough law enforcement, President Nixon's first chief marshal of the United States was recruited from the military. The chief marshal is the highest civilian law enforcement officer in the federal establishment, just as the attorney general is the highest lawyer and the director of the FBI heads the major investigative office. When John Caulfield, a man with civilian police experience, expressed an interest in becoming chief U.S. marshal, Attorney General Mitchell told him that the Administration was looking for a military man. A paramilitary concept of civilian police is foreign to the spirit of a free, democratic society. Yet General Carl Turner, the provost marshal general of the United States (and as such the commander of the U.S. Military Police), was appointed chief marshal. He became the first departmental official in twenty years to be indicted and convicted for crime. His offense was stealing and converting guns forfeited by persons possessing them when arrested by U.S. marshals and local police. General Turner appropriated the guns for his personal collection, and bank account, perversely paralleling the Administration's view of gun control —to take them from bad people and give them to good people.

For the courts, President Nixon proudly proclaimed his intention to appoint people devoted not to the rule of law but to his values. The Justice Department recommended such men as G. Harrold Carswell for the United States Supreme Court. William H. Rehnquist, as assistant attorney general in the Department of Justice, participated in developing a policy of subpoenaing newspaper reporters before grand juries.

Sometimes the philosophy claimed was "strict construction," but neither acts nor words could meet this test. A more sweeping and unfounded claim of executive privilege has never been pronounced than that espoused by Attorney General Kleindienst (who cavalierly and, in retrospect, ironically added that if Congress didn't like it, they "could impeach him [Nixon]").

After invoking the symbolism of the death penalty, preventive detention, and the no-knock law while attacking Supreme Court rulings enforcing rights essential to freedom and dignity, the Department of Justice slowly abandoned enforcement of the equal-protection clause of the Fourteenth Amendment. By June of 1969, the Department of Justice stood with the state of Mississippi in opposing the right of black children to an equal education. In October 1969, when young attorneys in the Civil Rights Division began the first employee protest in the department's history over the failure to enforce the law, some resigning, Attorney General John Mitchell said, "I couldn't care less." In a major case involving school desegregation in Mississippi in 1970, the U.S. Court of Appeals for the Fifth Circuit, using unprecedented language, referred to the obtuse, patronizing failure of the department to "do its duty." And when the department failed to enforce a court order it had obtained requiring removal of the Vietnam Veterans Against the War from the Capitol grounds in Washington, D.C., Judge George L. Hart in open court told Assistant Attorney General L. Patrick Gray that he had "degraded the court."

Nor was the problem only a wayward Justice Department. The president himself politicized the Calley trial, telling the world and the military courts he would be the final judge. A brave young Army prosecutor, Captain Aubrey Daniel, stood up for the rule of law and criticized his commander-in-chief for demeaning it. And the Administration authorized the largest, most lawless sweep arrests in our history, 7,000 persons protesting the war in Vietnam in May 1971. H. R. Haldeman, former president Nixon's chief of staff, wrote in internal memoranda that such demonstrations were "good" and "great" for his Administration's political interests.

The Department of Justice protected the violence and deadly force of the National Guard for those years by refusing to convene a federal grand jury to investigate the deaths of students at Kent State, and to this date at Jackson State and elsewhere. Following a police raid in Chicago in 1969, the Department of Justice first assured a private Commission of Inquiry that indictments would be returned, itself an improper act, then released a grand jury report which Senator John L. McClellan criticized as without authority in law. The report blamed everyone but indicted no one in the death of Fred Hampton and Mark Clark and the wounding of four Black Panthers in a police raid in Chicago. FBI ballistics found one shot at most fired by Panthers and at least 83 fired by police.

U.S. Attorney Harry Stewart, in San Diego, interfered with a grand jury investigating a major Nixon contributor who supported Stewart for a judgeship. Deputy Attorney General Kleindienst sat in his office and listened to the administrative assistant to a Republican senator plead for a constituent and suggest a large political contribution in return. He did nothing. Later he said he did not recognize the conduct as an attempt to bribe, yet the person was convicted subsequently of attempting to bribe Mr. Kleindienst in that very meeting. (Presumably Mr. Kleindienst's inability to recognize a bribe when he was offered one should have had a bearing on his qualification to become attorney general—but the Senate Judiciary Committee never asked him about this incident in its initial review of his nomination.)

James R. Hoffa was granted parole by Administration pandering to the Teamsters and not pretending to give equal consideration for other applications. (One might ask what lesson tens of thousands of offenders take from this single act.) L. Patrick Gray became the second head of a federal bureau that never had an agent charged with corruption in office. Yet, as acting director of the FBI, he accepted and destroyed files that might have contained evidence of federal crime. Agents in a new federal drug agency—created for political visibility, thus destroying morale among career professionals—smashed into private homes in Illinois, without search warrants required by the Fourth Amendment or facts supporting their action. They terrorized the families, threatened death, used force, destroyed property—and found nothing.

Finally, although Republicans are quick to remind us how much they favor the free enterprise system and the antitrust laws which underwrite it, the Nixon Administration permitted politics to corrupt the antitrust enforcement process. In the ITT debacle, that company literally lobbied the government into exhaustion. Richard Nixon's *post facto* explanation that he personally intervened in the case because he was opposed to cases attacking bigness per se doesn't wash. If so, why did he do nothing for the two years the Justice Department's anti-conglomerate lawsuits were being brought and argued in court; why did he do nothing until about the time ITT pledged a large contribution to the Republican National Convention? ITT may be the most notorious example, but not the only one. In cases involving milk co-ops, the Warner Lambert–Parke Davis merger, the Alaskan oil pipeline, Las Vegas casinos of Howard Hughes, and the giant National Steel–Granite City Steel merger, groups which made large political contributions to Richard Nixon's reelection campaign won antitrust concessions from a Justice Department overruling its own expert Antitrust Division.

Five years after Richard Nixon vowed to attack crime, he left as his legacy the most criminal administration in our political history. As one result, an enormous tragedy has befallen an essential and great department of government. We can leave it to the new and future officials in the department, to the courts, the Congress, and history to tell us how close we came to tyranny and irremediable corruption. For now, we can detect the value patterns that guided the misadventure. They were lawless, truthless, and violent values that sought power regardless of the law. A young lawyer, ashamed of having served in the Department of Justice during these years, was reported by the *Wall Street Journal* to have said on resigning, "There was a time when a career with the Justice Department was all I wanted in life."

We must make that time come again. Lawyers, particularly, have an obligation to make this department of lawyers a place of justice. The first need will always be the selection of "meet person[s], learned in the law." A man who believes it is more important that a president be reelected than that the Constitution be followed and the law obeyed is not a meet person. Lawyers who have made the law their "political religion," in Lincoln's phrase, who have manifested their clear commitment to the rule of law, to the Constitution, to the Bill of Rights and the Fourteenth Amendment are meet persons. There are thousands of lawyers who would rather serve the public than bend the power of their intellects to "petty causes" and private interest; who will not abuse their power or the rights of any person however feared or despised; who will be the first to divulge to a person accused of crime any evidence relevant to his defense; who will not radicalize the country by political symbolism, with phrases full of fear and hate like "soft on crime," or "Communist conspiracy," which signify nothing; people who do what they say and need not caution others to watch what is done, not what is said. Most career lawyers in the Department of Justice have these qualities. Their leadership should have no less.

The Department of Justice is not part of a political administration. It is a place of law, enforcing the laws in accordance with the purpose of Congress even as it endeavors to reform laws it deems undesirable. It must faithfully enforce the laws as finally interpreted by the courts, however it may disagree with those decisions. It can only participate in the policy views of a president when action is consistent with law, for it ultimately represents the public, not the president.

To help restore institutionally this approach to the Department of Justice, the following measures should be considered in a new Declaration of Independence for the Department of Justice:

• *The President, the White House staff, or others acting for the President, should be prohibited from interfering in cases or matters in the Department of Justice.* If there is to be equal justice, discussions about pending cases or matters between the president or his staff and officials of the department are improper.

It is impossible for the president to oversee all cases. The few he selects will inevitably cause discrimination. The president is often not a lawyer, but even when he is, he is not the attorney general. Former president Nixon said on several occasions that he would personally decide matters in the Department of Justice. This necessarily politicized those matters, making the presidency the focal point for powerful interests that aim to influence cases. The president has burdens enough without this, a point President James Monroe understood well. At the end of his presidency, he asked everyone in his cabinet to resign except the attorney general, who could remain because his ". . . duties are different. The President has less connection with them, and less responsibility for them." President Johnson understood my belief that it was improper to discuss pending cases with him. A president can enunciate general policy guidelines and appoint an attorney general who shares his philosophic views. If there is dissatisfaction with the performance of the attorney general, the president can remove him, but should not supersede his administration of the law. Congress should enact a law prohibiting the president and his staff from intervening in any case or matter in the Department of Justice, and prohibiting officials in the department from following such directions when they are contrary to law as determined by the attorney general.

- *To discourage political direction or influence in cases or matters before the Department of Justice, the existence of every communication referring to any matter in the department from the White House, the Congress, or the private sector should be made a public record.* The concealment of such communications should be a crime. The Department of Justice ought to regularly record the fact of each such communication in a place open to the public so that the president, the Congress, and the public may have the fullest knowledge of that conduct subject only to the rights of privacy to persons under investigation.

- *The Senate, in acting on the confirmation of appointees, should insist that the Judiciary Act of 1789 be enforced and that not only the attorney general but all other presidential appointees to the department be "meet person[s] learned in the law."* A person whose experience and interest is largely political is not meet to serve as lawyer for the people.

It would be wise to prohibit by law the appointment of any person to such positions who has participated significantly in the presidential campaign of the incumbent president. The law could also prohibit appointment of anyone who held a high political party position, or managed a campaign or himself sought high political office within two years of his appointment.

- *Presidential appointees and their personal assistants in the Department of Justice should be prohibited from giving, receiving, or soliciting political contributions; from managing or advising a political party or campaign while in office and for two years thereafter; from attending political meetings, public or private, and from political speeches and endorsements.* Robert F. Kennedy asked this of his assistants when he became attorney general. It is a small price to pay for needed insulation from political influence and for public confidence in the integrity of law.

- *Presidential appointees and their personal assistants should be prohibited from meeting with principals, attorneys, or other representatives of interests with cases or matters in the Department of Justice without public notice of such meeting and the presence of staff attorneys chiefly responsible for handling the case or matter.* The publicity rationale behind the Federal Advisory Committee Act of 1973 has obvious relevance here. A glaring violation of this principle which illustrates the need are the numerous off-the-record meetings by various department officials with representatives of ITT.

- *The law should require that of the attorney general, the deputy attorney general, and the assistant attorneys general, a minimum number, perhaps three, be of the opposite party from the administration in power or be politically independent.* Herbert J. Miller, Jr., who served as assistant attorney general of the Criminal Division from 1961 to 1965, a brilliant and effective lawyer who participated in all criminal cases and most significant department matters during those Democratic years, was a staunch Republican by philosophy. During this period, department officials like Erwin Griswold, Walter Yeagley, and Sal Andretta all served in administrations of the opposite party. Similarly, tradition should encourage that the law might require a minimum number, perhaps three, of the presidential appointees to be drawn from the federal career legal service or held over from prior administrations.

- *The Congress should remove the United States attorney from Senate confirmation.* As has been true with all such offices limited to a single state, Senate confirmation has placed the effective appointing power in the senators from the state or local politicians of the party in power. It has politicized this critically important law enforcement agency to a dangerous level. Legislation to accomplish this recommendation was proposed by the Department of Justice in 1968. The positions of U.S. attorneys should usually be staffed by federal career lawyers and should be insulated from political influence.

- *Congress should vest in the Judicial Conference of each United States Court of Appeals power to appoint a special prosecutor on application by any member of the public, or on its own motion, when it finds the interest of justice requires grand jury review of allegations that should be presented by an independent prosecutor.* Failure to promptly convene a grand jury following the Kent State and Jackson State killings and the handling of the grand jury in the Fred Hampton case illustrate the need.

- *The directors of the FBI, the Bureau of Narcotics and Dangerous Drugs, and other investigative agencies should be subject to Senate confirmation and serve for terms of four years to begin at the end of the second year of each presidential term.* Total service as director should be limited to eight years, and he or she should be removable only for malfeasance.

- *The FBI and all other federal investigative and enforcement agencies should be required to publish a current list of all investigative and enforcement techniques, the legal justification for each, and the controls and limitations on their use.* This would include such practices as wiretapping, electronic surveillance, and other eavesdropping, use of informers, mail covers, phone call checks, phone dial registers, polygraphs, use of false identification or false pretense, agent infiltration, physical observation not related to specific criminal conduct, stop and frisk, and entering without knocking. Regular reporting on the times, places, persons, and purposes for each utilization should be required in a manner similar to the reporting required for wiretaps and bugs under court order pursuant to Title III of the Omnibus Crime Control Act of 1968.

- *The FBI and other federal investigative agencies should be prohibited from accumulating information or intelligence other than in connection with a specific criminal investigation except from public sources.* Information gathered from public sources for purposes of general law enforcement knowledge should be made available to the public in the form accumulated.

- *Dossiers on individuals or organizations should be prohibited and every individual should be entitled to all information about him in the possession of a federal agency that is not exclusively part of an ongoing criminal investigation, and in any event within two years after its receipt by the agency unless the release of the information in the judgment of a court might endanger life.*

- *It should be a crime for any agent to engage in any unauthorized investigation or enforcement act.* Aggrieved persons and the public should be empowered to compel full disclosure of the existence of such conduct, to enjoin its continuation, and to recover damages.

- *A Federal Investigative and Enforcement Review Board should be established, composed of broad-based citizens' groups, to hear and act on complaints of abuse* and review and recommend reforms of all federal investigative and enforcement agencies to the Congress, the president, the attorney general, and the public.

- *Responsibility for crime statistics should be removed from the FBI to the Bureau of the Census, and made as scientific as possible to assure their objectivity and prevent misrepresentations for political purposes.*

- *Personnel throughout the Law Enforcement Assistance Administration should be under the same limitations on political activity as other presidential appointees in the Department of Justice.* The state block-grant provisions necessarily place the federal funds in political channels and should be repealed. Political influence should be prohibited in the allocation of funds. The office should be required to publish and record all decisions and grants in detail and all communications concerning them.

• *Guidelines for the release of departmental information to the press that involves the privacy of individuals or organizations whether in relation to a trial or otherwise should be established in law to prevent abuse of such information and the coercion of, or injury to, individuals.* Penalties for violation should be established.

While rules cannot eliminate corruption, they can render it less likely by making it more costly. And rules such as those suggested above can inspire a tradition that could become self-generating: that the department should be not a political hatchetman of the White House, but truly a ministry of justice.

Victor Rabinowitz

The Prosecutor: The Duty to Seek Justice

T HE LEGAL PROFESSION, like most human institutions, stands firmly based on a multitude of clichés and platitudes that have, at the very best, only a peripheral relationship to reality. They are honored almost exclusively in the breach, and are repeated either sanctimoniously by those who seek to clothe their self-interest in an outward show of liberalism or by those who would hope to make them come true. One of the noblest of the clichés has been written in stone on a facade of the Department of Justice, so that archaeologists from some distant planet 10,000 years from now will be able to reconstruct a false image of our society. It reads: "The United States wins its point whenever justice is done its citizens in the courts." The late judge Simon Sobeloff, who was one of our better solicitor generals and judges, once said, "The Solicitor General is not a neutral; he is an advocate, but an advocate for a client whose business is not merely to prevail in the instant case. My client's chief business is not to achieve victory but to establish justice."

It is perhaps a reflection of the nature of our society that such fine sentiments should be phrased in terms of "winning points" and the "business" of the United States. But we ought not to quibble over minutiae. The goals stated are unexceptionable. The problem is to move our legal system even a small distance in the direction of achieving such goals.

One of these goals, of course, is that prosecutors should seek justice, not merely convictions. I am extremely skeptical as to whether this object is often achieved, perhaps because of my sympathies as a lawyer who has never represented the United States and whose entire career has been

* VICTOR RABINOWITZ IS A PARTNER IN THE FIRM OF RABINOWITZ, BOUDIN & STANDARD, DEFENSE COUNSELS IN THE SPOCK, BERRIGAN, AND ELLSBERG TRIALS. HE IS A PAST PRESIDENT OF THE NATIONAL LAWYERS GUILD AND HAS BEEN ACTIVELY ENGAGED IN CIVIL LIBERTIES CASES FOR FORTY YEARS.

spent on the other side in both criminal and civil litigation. Having confessed proudly my bias, I can now freely observe that, based on my experience, most prosecuting officials appear arrogant, aggressive, over-zealous, and unscrupulous. Of course, there are exceptions, which occur either on the very highest administrative levels, where the individual concerned may be above the battle, or on the most junior levels, where the prosecuting lawyers are, in a sense, "passing through" the prosecutor's office on their way to other and perhaps better things. In between is a vast sea of hostility and indifference to human rights.

This prosecutorial arrogance has understandable origins. The prosecutor has at his disposal the vast resources of the state, which, if not limitless, at least seem so to the average impecunious defendant. I concern myself here with poor and/or political defendants; there are, of course, corporate defendants, but, often commanding preferential treatment, they have not won my sympathy. The prosecutor can call upon the police in all of its many manifestations, upon the power of the grand jury, upon scientists and economists to act as experts, and in doing all of this he hardly need concern himself with expense. His opponent, a good deal of the time, perhaps most of the time, is less experienced, and almost all of the time lacks the funds to secure the facilities which come naturally to the prosecutor.

There are other aspects of the office of the prosecutor which can convert arrogance into an occupational trademark. Since he is located normally in the courthouse, cases are tried on his "turf." He is likely to be on terms of personal friendship with most of the courthouse personnel and, far more easily than most defense counsel, can secure cooperation from stenographers, bailiffs, clerks, and the entire courthouse crowd. He practices before judges whom he knows well and who were often themselves once prosecutors. By and large he controls the court calendar and can call cases up for trial in order to suit his convenience. He can invariably obtain extensions of time for late briefs, and default judgments are just not enforced against the government. And above all, he has the power to decide whether and when to prosecute. So the naked power over the liberty of human beings quite literally reposes in his hands. Not many persons could retain their humanity in such circumstances and not many prosecutors do. On this personal level the duty to "do justice" can rarely survive the corrupting effect of power.[1]

On a substantive level, the duty to seek justice doesn't fare far better.

Consider, for an example, the *Brady* rule and its operation in the courts.

In 1963 the United States Supreme Court in the case of *Brady* v. *Maryland* said: "The suppression by the prosecution of evidence favorable to an accused who has requested it, violates due process irrespective . . . of the good faith, or bad faith, of the prosecution." [2] Such a rule, of course, would be quite unnecessary if the prosecutor were genuinely interested in justice. But the *Brady* rule has become a sine qua non of our criminal justice system. As in the case of all general rules, courts have differed significantly on what it means. What does not vary is the response of almost all prosecuting attorneys, who devote an extraordinary amount of energy and thought to an effort to construe the language of *Brady* as narrowly as possible in order to disclose as little evidence as possible. Such conduct is, of course, quite consistent with standard gamesmanship and the desire to win cases, but it is totally inconsistent with the desire to do justice.

The *Brady* rule, for a specific instance, was applied in the prosecution of Daniel Ellsberg and Anthony Russo for violation of the espionage law. The statute under which Ellsberg and Russo were prosecuted referred to documents "relating to the national defense, or information relating to the national defense which information the possessor has reason to believe could be used to the injury of the United States or to the advantage of any foreign nation." [3] The issue of whether the disclosure of the Pentagon Papers could be harmful to the United States was therefore central to the prosecution.

Very early in the prosecution, on April 11, 1972, the District Court in Los Angeles ordered: "The government will provide reports that were prepared, if any, by the Department of Defense and the Department of State, which reports indicate either very slight or no damage as a result of the release or dissemination of the documents set forth in the indictment." At the same time the court issued a general *Brady* order requiring the government to turn over to the defendants "all material that it believes and finds to be exculpatory or may be exculpatory. The government is under a continuing duty to turn over evidence of this nature to the defendants. The government has an obligation to make good faith effort to make itself aware of any exculpatory evidence."

Actually, four months before this order, in December 1971, the Justice Department had asked the Defense Department to make exactly such an investigation; Justice had asked Defense "precisely how do the contents of each volume or document [of the Pentagon Papers] relate to the national defense" and "how could the release of the contents or part of the contents of each volume or document have injured the national defense in 1969?" The request in due course came to J. Fred Buzhardt, then general counsel to the Defense Department, who assigned William Gearhart to make such an inquiry.

Such studies were in fact made and sent to the prosecution, led by David Nissen, a prosecutor with many years of experience. Indeed he had, for a time, worked as an assistant to Judge Matthew Byrne, who presided at the Ellsberg trial, when the latter was serving as United States attorney in Los Angeles. He had the reports in his files within a month after the April 1972 court order. The result reached by the studies was later summarized by Lieutenant Colonel Edward A. Miller of the Defense Department: "Except for a few items that State might be willing to certify are sensitive, we held that the volumes do not contain classified information and that the contents could have been cleared for publication had they been submitted for review." Other surveys by other representatives of the Defense Department came to a similar conclusion. It is hard to conceive of clearer examples of exculpatory material, material required to be turned over by the court order and by the *Brady* doctrine, and certainly material that should have been turned over voluntarily by any prosecutor really interested in treating defendants fairly.

But prosecutor Nissen did not turn over the results of the studies. On the contrary, he repeatedly denied to the court that any exculpatory reports even existed. The defendants' discovery of the "no damage" surveys came about purely by luck. The story is too long to detail here, but a series of fortuitous circumstances alerted defendants' counsel to the fact that the Defense Department had made some surveys and that they might be helpful to the defense. When the matter was called to the attention of the court, the trial was halted for several days and the jury excused while the court held extensive hearings into the existence of the reports, in the face of Nissen's continued denial that he had any exculpatory material.

At the suggestion of the defense, the court called a number of witnesses, including Buzhardt and Gearhart. They both testified, albeit reluctantly, that such reports had in fact been prepared and given to Nissen. It was only at that point, almost a year after the court order directing production of the material, after a jury had been chosen and the trial actually started, that Nissen submitted the surveys at the explicit direction of the judge. The court, upon receiving the documents, said, "I don't understand how you can possibly feel that you were not required to produce these documents ten months ago."

While the late production of the documents was better than no production at all, the government hardly deserves applause for its actions. Had the documents been in the possession of the defense from the beginning, the defendants' opening to the jury might have been different, the cross-examination of witnesses might have been different, and the entire tactics of the defense might have taken a different tack. Furthermore, days of testimony establishing the existence of these documents proved to be a very expensive waste of time.

This is not to say that Nissen did not submit some material to the court pursuant to the *Brady* order. The principal witness for the government was General William Depuy, whose testimony received widespread newspaper publicity. On February 7, 1973, the prosecution filed with the court a document entitled "Notice of Information Which the Court May Consider Brady Material." The document stated that, in compliance with the court's order and under the *Brady* rule, the government was advising the defendants that "a Mr. Samuel A. Adams, Route 4, Box 240, Leesburg, Virginia, has expressed the view that he has information which would rebut statements of government witness William Depuy as reported in a newspaper." The notice went on to state that the government had also received information from "a Mr. Chester Cooper" and "a David A. Monroe" to the effect that in the opinion of those persons the testimony of another government witness was untrue and that the prosecution itself was "a criminal conspiracy." The notice also referred to an anonymous letter from somebody who had expressed his unfavorable opinion of the prosecution. The court, after looking at the document, understandably said: "It is not what I consider Brady material and it falls into the category of whether one of the jurors went to high school with [assistant prosecutor] Reese."

But Nissen failed to advise the court or the defendants that the communication from "a Mr. Samuel A. Adams" was hardly a crank letter, to be equated with an anonymous protest against the trial. Mr. Adams was an employee of the CIA and he had been assigned, in the course of his duties, to carry out extensive research into United States operations in Vietnam. When he read of Depuy's testimony in the press, he filed a memorandum with the Justice Department advising it of his personal knowledge of the situation, which contradicted much of the testimony by General Depuy. For a week the Justice Department and

CIA sought to persuade Adams not to contact the defendants directly, falsely telling him that his memorandum had been submitted to the court and that the court had adjudged it irrelevant. Adams agreed not to press the matter in view of his understanding that the court did not want to hear him. It was only when defense counsel, again accidentally, heard that Adams was not merely an interested citizen, but a CIA agent, that they communicated with him and eventually called him as a defense witness.

All of these facts, together with a host of similar material, were summarized by the defense in support of a motion asking, alternatively, for a mistrial, a dismissal of the indictment, the citation of government counsel for contempt and/or the removal of government counsel from the case. The defense charged that the prosecution had repeatedly and deliberately lied both to the court and to the defense; action by the court was therefore necessary to preserve the integrity of the trial. The motion was denied in all respects. Yet, any defense attorney who disregarded court orders and concealed evidence in like manner would without hesitation, I think, have been found guilty of contempt. The prosecution in *Ellsberg* was not punished at all, not even by reprimand. As a matter of fact, the whole story was kept from the jury, which was sequestered during weeks of hearings devoted to obtaining evidence the defense should have received as a matter of course.

Of course, the concealment of evidence was not a phenomenon invented by the prosecution in *Ellsberg*. In the Berrigan prosecutions in Harrisburg, Boyd Douglas, the principal witness for the government, wrote a letter to the prosecuting officials shortly before the trial began, demanding $50,000 as the price of his testimony. One would have thought that attempted extortion had some bearing on the witness's credibility and that a conscientious United States attorney, interested in doing justice, would have disclosed this fact. It was not disclosed. Again, it was discovered by accident.

For another example, in the *Mesarosh*[4] case, Solicitor General J. Lee Rankin confessed error before the Supreme Court because the prosecution had secured a conviction for violation of the Smith Act principally on the testimony of a witness who had committed perjury on many occasions. Despite this fact, he had been presented to the jury as a reliable witness. The reversal of the government's position may be attributed to the fact that Mr. Rankin, unlike the trial prosecutors, found this conviction impossible to swallow.

Widespread violation of the *Brady* rule is, of course, only a small part of the story. Present rules require United States attorneys to disclose to defendants full information concerning wiretapping. Resistance to such disclosure is at least as strong as resistance to the *Brady* rule. Indeed, it was the belated disclosure that Ellsberg's telephone conversations had been "intercepted" (another fact withheld by the prosecution until the end of the trial despite a broad court order) that ultimately led to the dismissal of the indictment in that case. As an interesting footnote, it might be added that the government denied having possession of the logs of the Ellsberg conversations; the case was then dismissed and twenty-four hours later the logs turned up in the safe of a man named Ehrlichman.

Wiretapping is an intolerable invasion of privacy, whether authorized or not. Unauthorized wiretapping is illegal and a crime. That the practice is widespread has been conceded by the Justice Department on many occasions—indeed, until the decision in *United States* v. *United States District Court* [5] in June 1972 the attorney general claimed the legal right to tap wires and to "intercept" conversations without a court order when in his opinion national security interests so required. Since attorney generals' interpretations of national security can be notoriously loose, this authority, if constitutionally upheld, would have virtually eliminated judicial control over wiretaps in any case that had a political flavor.

Volumes could be written on the subject of wiretapping, and, indeed, many volumes have been,[6] so this treatment will necessarily be brief. In 1971 more than 1,000 wiretap orders were issued in the United States;[7] how many unauthorized taps there were is, of course, not susceptible to computation, but that there were very many cannot be doubted. In *People* v. *Ellis*, a sedition case pending in Queens County, New York, the police had installed unauthorized taps on the telephone wires of two of the defendants, which had resulted in more than 400 hours of recording. The taps were admittedly illegal. It would take defense counsel ten or twelve weeks of uninterrupted listening, at forty hours a week, merely to hear the tapes. I did listen to about four hours of those tapes. They consisted almost entirely of conversations between the defendant's teen-age daughter and her teen-age friends and of extended conversations between the defendant's wife and her mother discussing the state of her relations with her husband and children.

At the time of the submission of briefs in *United States* v. *United States District Court*, the plaintiffs submitted to the Supreme Court a list of sixteen important criminal prosecutions in which there had been extensive wiretapping. This included proceedings against the Black Panthers, against the Weathermen, against the defendants in the Berrigan case, and in the conspiracy trial against the Chicago Seven. All of the wiretaps were illegal, yet all had been approved by government lawyers.

Actually, the widespread use of electronic surveillance has begun to backfire for the prosecutors. It has become standard procedure for lawyers involved in felony cases to make a routine motion for full disclosure of any taps. To an increasing extent district courts have been ordering disclosure of such surveillance; where it has been found to exist, they have required the government to submit logs and/or transcripts of its recordings either to the court *in camera* or to the defendant. In many cases, the federal government has discontinued prosecution rather than disclose the taps.[8]

One odious aspect of widespread electronic surveillance has been the overhearing of conversations between attorneys and clients. At the risk of seeming guilty of special pleading, I suggest that such surveillance poses an even greater threat to our liberties and constitutes an even greater abuse by the prosecutorial arm of our government. Such interceptions go to the very heart of the attorney-client privilege and to the protection of the Sixth Amendment right to counsel. Almost fifteen years ago a conviction in *Coplon* v. *United States*[9] was set aside because, among other things, the defense charged that the government had tapped conversations between the defendant and her counsel; the court directed that if such conversations did exist they had to be disclosed or, alternatively, the prosecution had to be dropped. Ultimately, the prosecution was dropped. Disclosures in the *Ellsberg* case and in the Weathermen prosecutions in Detroit *(United States* v. *Ayers)* have further confirmed that conversations between many lawyers and their clients have been overheard because of government intercepts. And, in a recent proceeding by Arthur Kinoy in the Southern District of New York, the government disclosed that many conversations between Kinoy and his clients in many parts of the country had in fact been overheard.

Another major area where the prosecutor's desire for a conviction conflicts with elemental fairness involves the widespread use of informers. The problem of criminal law enforcement based on informer testimony is obvious. To justify their continued employment, informers must produce evidence, and often that evidence can be most easily produced by perjury or by the provocation of crime. This is probably just as true whether the prosecution relates to the narcotics laws or the sedition laws, but in the latter case the government is not only violating the defendant's right to a fair trial but also his or her free exercise of First Amendment rights. The history of the utilization of informers and *agents provocateurs* in political cases is an ancient one. When we hear stories of the use of informers and provocateurs by the kings of France and the czars of Russia, we recognize such conduct as characteristic of a police state; when precisely the same policy is followed in this country, many are not quite so quick to recognize the evil.

The Smith Act prosecutions of the 1940s and 1950s, for example, were based almost exclusively on informer testimony. Much of it, we now know, was perjurious. Currently, we more or less take for granted that every active leftwing political organization has in its ranks one or two informers who will step forward to testify when needed by the prosecution. For one especially glaring incident, it was disclosed in February 1974 that William O'Neal, Panther "security chief" in Chicago at the time of the Fred Hampton killing, had been a paid FBI informer. His duties included making sure that all members were properly armed and their weapons working.[10]

One of the most encouraging aspects of the present political scene is the increasing reluctance of juries to accept such informer testimony at face value; in many cases the jury reaction has been either acquittal or a mistrial. The Berrigan prosecution in Harrisburg resulted in a hung jury and the prosecution was dropped. The trial of the Vietnam Veterans Against the War in Gainesville, Florida, resulted in an acquittal. In the Camden trial, where defendants were indicted for the destruction of draft records, the testimony showed that much of the alleged criminal activity was planned and carried out by an FBI informer, and his role in those activities became perhaps the principal issue in the case. The judge charged the jury that they should acquit if they felt that government agents had provoked the illegal activity, and the jury did acquit all of the defendants. Indeed, the jury system in the past few years has proven itself the bulwark against government oppression, which has been its justification over the centuries. These experiences contrast sharply with the role of the jury during the sedition trials of a quarter of a century ago when convictions were almost automatic.

Juries can refuse to convict, but overzealous government prosecutors can still misuse the indictment and grand jury process. The widespread use of conspiracy indictments, as in the *Spock* case, the case of the Chicago Seven, and the prosecution of the Berrigans, has placed an enormous burden on defendants who have done little more than engage in normal protected activity. The use of conspiracy indictments, of course, has a long history, but its great expansion in recent years has posed a very real and serious threat to the pursuit of any kind of radical political activity.*

Prosecutorial abuse can also result from inaction rather than action. The prosecution of police who break the law is almost unknown. Although wiretapping in many circumstances is a crime, it almost invariably goes unpunished. For example, many persons were killed in the Attica prison riots not by the prisoners but by troops who recklessly shot into the prison yard. Although sixty of the "rioters" have been indicted, as of mid-1975 not one of the prison guards has been indicted. The perpetrators of the murders on the campus of Kent State University several years ago still go unpunished.

Still, as noted above, the struggle has not been without its victories. The mistrial in *Ellsberg*, the acquittals at Camden and Gainesville, and the hung juries at Harrisburg and Chicago all indicate that there still remain in our legal system opportunities for combatting government lawyers who seem to have forgotten, or never learned, their oaths of office. But such victories are hardly evidence that "our system works." In each of these cases and scores of others the defense was required to spend hundreds of thousands of dollars in legal fees and expenses, while long and difficult legal proceedings slowly worked their way through the courts. In every one of those cases, a net political advantage probably accrued to the government even though the prosecution failed to obtain convictions. Political activity was discouraged; an atmosphere of terror was created in which thousands of persons, both defendants and their friends, were diverted from political activity to legal defense. These are indeed cases in which the government may have lost battles but won wars.

One final caveat. I have discussed only the most prominent political prosecutions, which is somewhat misleading. For every year thousands of people whose names are not Spock, Ellsberg, Russo, Berrigan, or Seale are unfairly prosecuted—their names are John Doe and Mary Doe, and they are charged not with big political crimes but with relatively petty offenses. They don't have millions of dollars to mount enormous defense

---

* So has the extensive use of the grand jury as a technique to chill or terrorize radicals, a prominent aspect of the political scene for some years. Armed with broad subpoena powers and the associated power to grant immunity to witnesses, grand juries held extensive hearings all over the country into the activities of political radicals.

efforts and their lawyers are frequently either overworked attorneys assigned by Legal Aid or underpaid and marginally competent retained counsel. But they are subject to the same prosecutorial abuse as are the big names. The *Brady* rule is ignored, informers are used on a broad scale, wiretapping prevails. And John Doe and Mary Doe, unable to cope with an aggressive and brutal governmental machinery, suffer unjust convictions, spurred by energetic prosecutors who never read the writing on the facade of the Justice Department offices.

*Alan B. Morrison**

Defending the Government:
How Vigorous Is Too Vigorous?

WHEN THE PUBLIC thinks of a government trial attorney, it is generally of a prosecutor. But government attorneys at the federal, state, and local levels increasingly spend their time defending public officials sued in civil court proceedings against charges that their actions are illegal. It turns out, perhaps not too surprisingly, that governments prefer to sue than be sued. Citizen suits often provoke an impulsive governmental retaliation, as defense counsel are instructed, to paraphrase the closing command in *Casablanca*, to "round up all the usual defenses." These defenses in many instances aim not so much to do justice as to chase away pesky citizens, especially when the government's case is of dubious validity. But, notwithstanding Canon 7 of the American Bar Association's *Code of Professional Responsibility*, which permits a lawyer to "represent a client zealously within the bounds of the law," is a government lawyer to be judged by the same ethical criteria as a private lawyer or by other criteria?

There are, in my opinion, limits on the behavior of a government attorney defending federal officials in a civil lawsuit. Here a lawyer is not merely a client instrument but a public servant, a status which differentiates the government lawyer from other lawyers. When the government attorney raises a defense which in effect tells the citizen, "the agency may be breaking the law, but the court can't do anything about it," it is difficult to understand how the oath to "uphold and defend the Constitution and laws of the United States" is being fulfilled.

Recent years have seen a significant increase in the number of civil

* ALAN B. MORRISON IS THE DIRECTOR OF THE PUBLIC CITIZEN LITIGATION GROUP IN WASHINGTON, D.C. PREVIOUSLY HE REPRESENTED THE GOVERNMENT FOR NEARLY FOUR YEARS IN CIVIL CASES AS AN ASSISTANT UNITED STATES ATTORNEY IN THE SOUTHERN DISTRICT OF NEW YORK, THE LAST TWO OF WHICH HE SERVED AS ASSISTANT CHIEF OF THE OFFICE'S CIVIL DIVISION.

lawsuits brought against government officials due to greater citizen awareness and an increased willingness by the courts to adjudicate matters formerly considered "political." When the challenged action or policy is an important one to the government, its attorney may be instructed to prevail by any means whatsoever. A favorite opening tactic is to claim the party bringing the lawsuit "lacks standing." Theoretically, the concept of standing meets the constitutional requirement that there be an actual "case or controversy" between the parties.[1] In practice, it is deployed to avoid deciding troubling cases, and becomes the defense of "go mind your own business."

Although the concept of standing has significantly broadened in recent years, the government continues to read the applicable decisions in the most narrow way possible—a tack it can take to ridiculous lengths. For instance, four members of the United States Senate, all of whom were on the committee with oversight responsibility for the Office of Economic Opportunity, brought a lawsuit in 1973 to prevent Howard Phillips from continuing as acting director of OEO because he had not been confirmed by the Senate as required by the Constitution and the applicable statute. Government counsel actually argued that the plaintiffs—*four United States Senators*—had no legitimate interest in the resolution of the controversy or the removal of Mr. Phillips from office, an argument the court promptly rejected.[2] In a March 1975 case brought by drivers, passengers, and pedestrians against the secretary of transportation to require him to enforce federal safety standards for drivers and highways, the government claimed that the plaintiffs had no standing because none of their legal rights had been violated—a claim the court again overruled.[3] Finally, the government has even gone so far as to have first raised a defense of absence of standing *after* an unfavorable adjudication on the merits, even though the issue was specifically discussed between counsel for the government and plaintiffs, but not included in the government's opposing papers.[4]

In June 1974, however, the Supreme Court, in two narrowly divided decisions, ruled against the standing of citizens who sought to enforce two specific provisions in the Constitution: one forbidding members of Congress from holding positions in the executive branch and the other requiring the publication of the budgets of all federal agencies.[5] Because these plaintiffs lacked standing, the government acknowledges, no citizen can litigate these issues; consequently, asserted violations of the Constitution will go uncorrected.

A second string on the bow of government defense counsel is the claim that the federal courts lack the power to decide a plaintiff's claim even if he or she has standing to raise it. The legal rubric is lack of "subject matter jurisdiction," with its English translation of "go someplace else."

The principle of subject matter jurisdiction limits the power of the federal courts to hear only those cases assigned to them by the Congress. Under this defense, the government contends that Congress has not given the federal courts the power to hear the particular claim raised by the plaintiff. Since the state courts will generally refuse to pass upon alleged violations of the Constitution or other federal laws by federal officials,[6] a successful defense of no subject matter jurisdiction means that plaintiffs may be left without a state *or* federal forum to vindicate their rights.

One federal statute appears broad enough to permit most cases in which this defense is made,[7] but government attorneys again often give it the narrowest construction. The statute specifically authorizes federal courts to decide cases arising under the Constitution and laws of the United States when "the matter in controversy exceeds the sum or value of $10,000. . . ." When money damages are sought, the $10,000 test presents little difficulty; but many cases involve alleged violations of fundamental rights by governmental agencies and thus do not carry a convenient price tag.

In *Fifth Avenue Peace Parade* v. *Hoover*,[8] for example, the plaintiffs sought to enjoin the FBI from operating a program of surveillance which allegedly violated their First Amendment rights and the rights of others active in the peace movement. The government claimed that the rights at issue were not worth $10,000, but Judge Harold Tyler (now deputy attorney general of the United States) rejected that contention, noting that plaintiffs' rights may be "difficult of evaluation, but 'priceless' does not necessarily mean 'worthless.'" In the Howard Phillips case, government counsel similarly contended that the Senate's right to "advise and consent" on the Phillips nomination was not worth $10,000, and hence the court had no jurisdiction. Without passing on that valuation question, the court held that since Mr. Phillips administered a multimillion-dollar program and since he would lose more than $10,000 in salary if removed, the requisite jurisdictional amount had been met.[9] As that case indicates, the defense of no subject matter jurisdiction, like that of standing, can be generally avoided by agile plaintiffs when federal rights are involved. This result should please former chief judge Edward Lumbard of the United

States Court of Appeals for the Second Circuit, a jurist never accused of being a radical, who once wrote:

Few more unseemly sights for a democratic country operating under the system of limited governmental power can be imagined than the specter of its courts standing powerless to prevent a clear transgression by the government of a constitutional right of a person with standing to assert it.[10]

Even when a statute can be found which confers jurisdiction on the federal courts, the government still contends in many cases that the suit must be dismissed under the doctrine of "sovereign immunity"—a doctrine derived from the quaint medieval notion that "the king can do no wrong." In its modern incarnation, it is a claim that the sovereign (here the government) cannot be sued without its consent and that Congress has not permitted the particular lawsuit to be brought. The government asserts this defense usually in actions which seek to compel an official to spend funds he does not want to spend. This tack does not impress district court judge Gerhard Gesell:

. . . any affirmative order of this Court would be premised on a determination that official action by the defendants in refusing to spend is beyond their statutory or constitutional powers. This would go no further than to require the spending of funds already appropriated by Congress to achieve the declared purposes of the Act. Accordingly, there can be no effective assertion of sovereign immunity and the defendants' actions are reviewable by the courts.[11]

Government attorneys nonetheless continue to raise the defense of sovereign immunity, ignoring the counsel of Henry Friendly, another former chief judge of the second circuit, that "law officers of the Government ought not to take the time of busy judges or of opposing parties by advancing an argument so plainly foreclosed by Supreme Court decisions." [12]

Yet another tactic employed by government counsel—unfounded in any legal doctrine though virtually foolproof—is the defense of delay, delay, and more delay. Unlike the normal civil litigant, who has only twenty days in which to reply to a complaint, the federal rules permit the government sixty days, or three times the usual amount. This liberality is dubious at best, but there is no justification for the practice under which answering within sixty days is the exception not the rule. As attorneys who regularly litigate against the government can attest, either on the sixtieth day or, in some cases, thereafter, government counsel will submit a *pro forma* request that the needed information has not been furnished and that a delay of thirty or, in some cases, sixty additional days is necessary.

These requests are routinely granted, regardless of the inconvenience to opposing counsel or the resulting delay in the proceedings. In *Petkas v. Staats*,[13] to take only one instance, a court of appeals ordered government counsel to file a brief by a certain date, the court adding that no extensions would be granted "except for extraordinary circumstances." When that deadline expired and the brief had not been filed, undaunted governmental counsel requested another extension without any showing of extraordinary circumstances—and obtained one. But even that concession proved inadequate, as government counsel missed the final deadline by three days; their perfunctory application to file the brief late was granted. The solicitor general's office has even taken the view that it will not "bother" the Supreme Court for extensions of time when it will be only a few days late.

The courts are extremely reluctant to do anything about these tactics. One obstacle is the limitation in the Federal Rules of Civil Procedure that a default judgment in the district court may not be entered against the government unless the petitioner clearly shows the court that he is entitled to relief. Furthermore, as a practical matter, few courts will deny government counsel the opportunity to submit even tardy papers arguing that the responsible official has acted within the law. The problem is further complicated when the government has prevailed in the lower court, and denial of permission to file might leave one side of the question only partially presented. In addition, there are often private, as well as governmental, interests that might suffer unjustly if a default by government counsel resulted in a decision for the private party opposing it (e.g., setting aside a CAB order affects the airlines much more than it does the CAB).

Unfortunately, there is very little that counsel for the non-government party can do in such situations. But even if courts are reluctant to impose sanctions on the client agency, sanctions ought to be imposed against the offending attorneys. Perhaps then, the notion that the government has an affirmative obligation to see that important questions are litigated in a timely fashion will begin to impress government counsel.

The use of these and other similar tactics seems wrong, both practically and philosophically. Raising indefensible defenses surely cannot have made Judge Gesell sympathetic to the government's position after he characterized those defenses as "standard objections so typical in these cases and many other categories of current Government litigation" and dismissed them with an admonition that "it is time this litany was displaced by a modicum of common sense." [14] Furthermore, these defenses, so obviously intended to prevent a court from deciding the basic legal dispute, cannot help but give the impression that the defendant has something to hide. Moreover, persistent claims of no standing and no jurisdiction become like the little boy crying "wolf" and are not heard on those rare occasions when they do have some merit.

In reply, government officials argue that these defenses prevent the opening of "floodgates of litigation" which could inundate the federal courts. This position seems founded on unsupported speculation, for even today there are few plaintiffs discouraged to any significant degree by the doctrines of standing, no subject matter jurisdiction, and the like. On the other hand, there is an enormous amount of time and money spent by both counsel and the courts in adjudicating these defenses, both in the district and appellate courts. It is an obstructionist government rather than citizen-litigants which is burdening our courts.

But there is a more compelling reason for the government to stop raising these procedural defenses—their use runs counter to a basic assumption of our society that not even government officials are immune from the judgments of the law. As Judge Gesell noted,

> To say that persons immediately and seriously affected by failure to commit funds authorized by the Legislature cannot go to court is to ignore the democratic base of our society. Indeed, it is only when the three equal and coordinate branches of government function that a stable government can be assured. *Cf. Marbury* v. *Madison.* . . . We are a government of law, not men, and the law must be determined and upheld. This is the never-ending process by which the Constitution is molded to the exigencies of the times and will be made rational in this and succeeding centuries. These cases should move to higher courts for prompt, definitive determination shorn of the confusing inconsequential defenses so typical of government legalese these days.[15]

This expectation of "prompt, definitive determination" is not fulfilled when fundamental statutory and constitutional questions are left unanswered because of government reliance on procedural shields. One would suppose that federal officials, believing their conduct lawful, would avoid evasiveness and instead seek judicial confirmation of the correctness of their position. Surely, it enhances the moral force of a policy when its legality has been upheld by a court of law far more than when its validity is left unresolved as a result of evasive defense tactics.

Apparently, this rationale does not persuade many government lawyers. They assume they have little to lose by asserting any defense which might conceivably produce a victory. Since legal services are provided by the Justice Department and not out of the defendant agency's own budget, the client is not concerned with paying the bills. There is no alternative source of defense counsel, and hence there is no possibility that the Department of Justice may be "fired" for doing an incompetent or overly time-consuming job. Nor are government counsel unduly worried by the bad precedent of a loss on a procedural issue, as they continually construe decisions as narrowly and begrudgingly as possible; in fact, even decisions on the merits often are not honored except to the precise extent of the court-ordered relief.*

This misplaced sense of loyalty to the policies of the agency or the current administration characterizes a revealing 1970 speech given by former attorney general Richard G. Kleindienst. In discussing the inadvisability of giving complete civil service status to federal attorneys, he noted that government lawyers had a responsibility to the judiciary, as well as to their superiors:

> Attorneys must be responsive to the law and to their understanding of the Canons of Ethics. On occasion, serious conflicts may arise in the minds of government attorneys as a result of having these several masters. If, after discussion, these conflicts persist, an attorney's continued presence in the government may be unworkable.[16]

Unless I am badly misreading the inference of this statement, it appears that Mr. Kleindienst advocates that even when deference to the judiciary conflicts with deference to one's superiors, a government attorney should not always insist upon upholding the law and maintaining his job. It is this

---

* A journalist, Malvin Schechter, sought copies of fifteen nursing home reports under the Freedom of Information Act. When the court decided the case in his favor, the government chose not to appeal. Thereafter, he sought identical reports for other nursing homes, but his request was denied. He then brought another suit but lost before another judge, and had to take the case to the court of appeals, where he finally prevailed two years later. Similarly, the General Services Administration was enjoined in early 1974 from enforcing certain regulations dealing with the disposal of government-owned patents which were to be binding on all federal agencies; yet other agencies with almost identical regulations, issued prior to those of GSA, continued to operate under them since the court order was directed only against GSA.

kind of attitude which undoubtedly led President Nixon to believe he could direct Acting Attorney General Kleindienst not to appeal the ITT case to the Supreme Court with the now-memorable language "You son of a bitch! Don't you understand the English language?" (Perhaps the only surprising aspect of that exchange is that Kleindienst did not back down and that the president eventually abandoned his effort to withdraw the appeal.)

Mr. Kleindienst's insensitivity to the obligations of a government lawyer simply demonstrates the prevailing view that suits against a federal agency are no different from suits between private parties. But this view ignores obvious differences. For one, the salaries of the agency official and his counsel are paid by the taxpayers, including the one who is the plaintiff. The difference exists, it seems to me, because the government is not a separate entity, but is an amalgam of all the interests of all the citizens, including the one who is the plaintiff in a particular lawsuit. As Justice William O. Douglas observed in 1974, "we tend to overlook the basic political and legal reality that the people, not the bureaucracy, are the sovereign." [17] The result is, or rather ought to be, that government counsel have special obligations to insure that they treat fairly citizen-plaintiffs and that they serve the interests of the public by their conduct in the lawsuit; thus, even if they lose a particular case, their true client, the public, may win because justice is done.

There are a number of reasons why government attorneys have historically been so insensitive to responsibilities beyond those of an advocate for a federal defendant. The problem begins at the inception of a government attorney's service, when the oath of office simply requires him to uphold and defend the Constitution of the United States. At the time of the swearing-in, assistant United States attorneys are typically loaded down with forms and a pamphlet explaining their political rights (or, more properly, non-rights) under the Hatch Act. But there is no attempt to instruct the new attorneys about the meaning of their role or the scope of their responsibilities under law. The *U.S. Attorney's Manual* is of no help, and other training aids focus primarily on the how-to-do-it kinds of questions.

Nor does the American Bar Association's *Code of Professional Responsibility* offer much guidance to the government attorney. Canon 7, with private attorneys in mind, specifically directs him to represent a client "zealously within the bounds of the law." The defense tactics of, for example, intentional delay probably do not violate that canon, yet plainly ought to cease. The Ethical Considerations of the code, which are "aspirational in character and represent the objectives toward which every member of the profession shall strive," [18] contain the only code reference to the duty of a government lawyer in a civil case: EC 7-14 provides that in such cases the attorney has "the responsibility to seek justice and to develop a full and fair record, and he should not use his position or the economic power of the government to harass parties or to bring about unjust settlements or results." That standard seems correct as far as it goes, but it does not, with sufficient specificity, exhort government lawyers to take a broader view of their professional roles in civil cases. And the Disciplinary Rules, which are the only part of the code in which a violation can give rise to a sanction against an attorney, discuss the conduct of government attorneys only with regard to criminal cases. The Federal Bar Association, a voluntary agency of present and former federal attorneys, adopted Federal Ethical Considerations in 1974 which supplement those of the ABA. While this action seems to appreciate the special status of the government attorney, the actual considerations adopted are little more than a bland restatement of the obvious.[19]

There is little help elsewhere even for a government attorney who desires it. The Winter 1973 issue of the *Federal Bar Journal* contained a symposium on "The Lawyer in Government," yet the only reference to ethical considerations concerned the "Lawyer's Recognition Award," in which it was suggested that lawyers should attend a minimum of five hours of classes on the *Code of Professional Responsibility* and *Canons of Judicial Ethics*. A search of the index to the *Guide to Legal Periodicals* under the topics of "Legal Ethics," "Attorneys General," "Public Officials and Employees," "United States (Department of Justice)," "Attorneys," and "Public Legal Services" for the period from August 1970 through July 1973 produced not a single article dealing with any of these questions.[20] In 1974, however, the *Federal Bar Journal* reprinted a valuable speech given in 1950 by circuit judge Charles Fahy. A veteran of many years of federal service, including several as the solicitor general, representing the United States in the Supreme Court, Judge Fahy showed his understanding of the special duties of government counsel, supporting his views with quotations from two former presidents (Taft and Wilson), a former attorney general and Supreme Court justice (Robert Jackson), and many others who have taken a broader view than is now prevalent of the primary obligation of the government employee, and particularly the government lawyer.[21] It is not, of course, required reading for government attorneys, but it ought to be.

In addition, government attorneys should begin to ask themselves a question, a question which Egil "Bud" Krogh suggested in a statement he made upon his sentencing after pleading guilty to conspiracy: "When contemplating a course of action, I hope they [government-employees] will never fail to ask, Is this right?" [22] A responsible government attorney must do more than simply carry out the requests of an agency to defend it on any conceivable grounds. There ought to be more to litigating on behalf of the government than simply a drive for victory whatever its costs. Government counsel have an obligation to attempt to persuade their client and their superiors that it is wrong, both tactically and morally, to assert defenses that preclude or delay important questions from being decided on the merits. This is not to say that government counsel should act as a judge rather than an advocate, but there is a significant difference between an unquestioning acceptance of any direction, on the one hand, and an assumption of the function of the judge or opposing counsel, on the other. Government lawyers must prefer the legal process to their immediate superiors.

A corollary obligation—though widely unrecognized—exists when government lawyers are convinced that their position is the correct one. That obligation is the obligation to stay on in difficult times and to resist directions to undertake improper actions. The resignations of Elliot Richardson and William Ruckelshaus during the so-called "October massacre" were seen by many as statesmanlike and bold, yet resignation may have been the easy way out. Given the president's breach of his promise to Attorney General Richardson, and the regulations entitling the special prosecutor to continue in office provided he committed no "extraordinary improprieties," the obligation of the highest law enforcement official in the country was to stay in his job and to insist that the president withdraw the direction to fire Archibald Cox, or if the direction was not withdrawn, discharge the attorney general for failing to carry out that illegal order. The obligation of an attorney not to quit when he believes that he is right is an obligation which government counsel simply ignore or fail to assert. I do not suggest that attorneys should subject themselves to firing over differences of opinion as to strategy or tactics in a given case, but on matters of fundamental importance, fundamental lines must be drawn.

It is essential to the operation of our democratic, tripartite form of government that disputes of law be decided in the courts and not in the streets. Every government attorney has an obligation to insist that important questions of law be decided and not avoided, and that they be decided sooner rather than later. Victory as counsel for the government agency being defended is more than a dismissal of the complaint. Victory requires a decision on the merits, and if the government official has acted correctly, the approval by our courts is worth far more than an avoidance of the issues on technical grounds. It is time that such considerations be brought to the attention of government attorneys and that they start to give proper consideration to their responsibilities to all of the people, who are, after all, the real "clients."

VI

Judges: Sketches from Detroit, New York City, Chicago

Judge Justin C. Ravitz[*]

Reflections of a Radical Judge: Beyond the Courtroom

T IS FRIDAY, SEPTEMBER 14, 1973, and I am attending a judicial conference being held at a luxury resort in northern Michigan. After a morning conference of three hours, Michigan judges are frolicking during the 2:30 to 7:00 P.M. "free time" period prior to tonight's "informal luau." Several Detroit attorneys, vacationing for the weekend, are speaking to a judge at the swimming pool located directly outside my open window. A lawyer has just asked the judge if one of my colleagues, who happens to be black, is at the conference. The judge tells the attorney that his fellow judge left this afternoon. The attorney smiles as he says, "Oh, you must have had the barbecue last night." All laugh loudly.

I contribute to this volume because the smug attitudes of these men outside my window are typical of those which dominate and control the American legal system. I also contribute because it is vitally important that the American people begin to render a genuine verdict on lawyers and judges—a verdict which ultimately depends upon our answer to this question:

Do members of the legal profession objectively advance or retard the realization of the deserved and just rights, needs, interests, and aspirations of the vast majority of the people who populate this country and this earth?

My focus is on that species of lawyer called judges. Here, as in most other situations, the analysis of how one group of people affects others begins and ends with an analysis of the use of power. For judges exercise enormous power. "It is the sentence of this court that you be confined to the custody of the Department of Corrections for a period of not less than

* JUDGE JUSTIN C. RAVITZ SITS AS A CRIMINAL COURT JUDGE IN DETROIT'S RECORDER'S COURT. ON NOVEMBER 12, 1972, *The New York Times* CALLED HIM "AMERICA'S FIRST RADICAL JUDGE"—A DESCRIPTION HE WILLINGLY ACCEPTS.

fifteen years nor more than. . . ." Persons empowered to determine whether one resides in the "free world" or one of those Department of Corrections cages, which in reality do more to breed than correct crime, do indeed sit on high. These high personages almost invariably are over-fifty, white males who are fairly prosperous and have never toured a jail or prison, let alone ever thought of being incarcerated. The judge wears a black robe, people rise when he enters the courtroom, folks repeatedly refer to him as "Your Honor," and he speaks in "legalese"— that intimidating Latinate parlance best understood by lexicographers.* He is a living example of that mystical propaganda which says ours is "a government of laws, not men."

Before examining the role of a judge in the criminal justice system, we should first glance at the realities and myths of the legal system itself. A "government of laws, not men" or "liberty and justice for all" or "equal protection under the law" are not the only propaganda slogans unconnected to reality. Consider the famous line of the elder Supreme Court justice John Harlan, who wrote in 1896 that "our constitution is color blind and neither knows nor tolerates classes among citizens." The difficulty with Harlan's language, written in a dissenting opinion, is that it was not true in 1896 nor is it true today.

Few today could believe that this situation was resolved fifty-eight years later when the liberal Earl Warren Court broke away from *Dred Scott* and *Plessy* v. *Ferguson* by ordering school desegregation "with all deliberate speed." The past and present reaction to the 1954 decision in *Brown* v. *Board of Education* is well known. However, we should briefly focus on the legal and political reality of that case.

It was not until the early 1960s that the federal government saw that there had been little or no compliance with the landmark decision in the southern United States. To enforce the law and to achieve integration before the next century, the federal government sought to enforce the Court's ruling. It met local resistance and the spectacle of Governor George Wallace standing defiantly in the schoolhouse door. He, Bull Connor, and Byron de la Beckwith represented the same vicious bigotry that had led to a Civil War more than a century earlier. But what has happened since the early sixties?

---

* Judges are so obsessed with maintaining an imposing image that the Michigan Supreme Court, which includes some outstanding liberal jurists, bothered itself recently to pass, unanimously, a new Michigan General Court Rule which requires every judge to wear a robe and conspicuously display the American flag. Because I was the only judge in the state who did not wear a robe and display the flag, many people jokingly refer to this as the "Ravitz Rule."

The cast of characters remains the same. De la Beckwith is still in the news, fighting for fascism; the image of Bull Connor invades our homes in the form of slick television ads; and George Wallace has changed not his politics but his image. He is accepted now, though this acceptance should not be viewed as sympathy engendered by his near assassination during the 1972 presidential primary. If John Schmitz, the American Independent Party's candidate for the presidency in 1972, had been gunned down by bullets, Senator Edward Kennedy would not have hurried to his bedside. What happened is that George Wallace had ventured to the northland, "up south," and millions of the same Americans who were shocked by his conduct less than ten years earlier greeted him warmly. On August 8, 1972, he ran first in the Michigan Democratic presidential primary, receiving a vote total of 808,943, nearly doubling the tally of the second-place finisher, George McGovern. Governor Wallace hadn't changed, but *Brown v. Board of Education*, eighteen years later, had, "with all deliberate speed," reached Michigan's Wayne, Oakland, and Macomb Counties in the form of a court finding of near-total segregation and an apparent order for tri-county busing. What had happened in the North was more insidious than the open defiance of the South. For nearly twenty years the law and the courts—with the support of the media, the liberals, and other social architects—had managed to camouflage the reality of racial segregation.

The point is not that *Brown v. Board of Education* or forced cross-district busing offer a real solution, but that the law is a means of social control. While "equality" has been the law's promise, the law makes certain that the promise is never realized. For example, if blacks get on juries after years of lawlessly being kept off them, then: Rescind the need for unanimous jury verdicts (Louisiana);[1] or move to gerrymander and adopt a county or metropolitan court system to dilute the black input (Detroit); or call into question the wisdom and need for juries in this complex, industrialized, crowded-docket "democracy" (Chief Justice Warren Burger).[2]

Such legal moves and countermoves have come to be the expected concomitants of the push for social justice, for one constant theme has remained at the very heart of the American legal system. Today, as in 1896, the law is not only not "color blind," but it is *designed* to tolerate and perpetuate class divisions.

• When there is a wildcat strike at a Chrysler plant, corporate attorneys rouse a friendly judge from bed in the middle of a weekend night, get an *ex parte* injunction,[3] and pass the injunction to the local police, who eagerly bust, in one fell swoop, picketers, picketers' heads, and most importantly, the strike.[4]

• When police or National Guardsmen kill and murder, courts and law-enforcement in general strain to cover up or otherwise protect the guilty.[5]

• In 1972, 402 individuals in the United States earned more than $100,000 and paid not one penny in income taxes; in 1971, the five largest oil companies (Gulf, Texaco, Mobil, Standard of California, and Standard of New Jersey) received oil-depletion deductions totaling $2,585,000,000.[6]

Thus the law—supposedly the neutral, impartial, peaceful, just, and orderly arbiter of societal disputes—tolerates and promotes class and racial bias, and imperialistic wars as well. For months on end a majority of Americans bitterly took issue with the Vietnam War. Millions protested while more than 50,000 Americans were killed, another 300,000 were wounded, and millions of innocent Vietnamese were murdered, maimed, or made refugees. All the while, Their Honors refused even to hear the obvious constitutional issue pertaining to the exclusive right of the Congress, not the president, to declare war. Though the courts said they had "no jurisdiction," these two words *were* the exercise of power.

And what of the "war" back home? Daily headlines remind us of the escalating homicide rate in America; in 1972 alone, there were 18,520 homicides.[7] Law enforcement, which typically reacts only after crimes are committed, offers the same stale non-solutions: more police, more laws, more prisons. While hysteria is whipped up on these issues, we are trained to ignore the most profound and daily threats to life and limb. The criminal law has hardly focused on other systems of violence which sacrifice people for profits. For example, why is it not a crime for 56,000 people a year to die in motor-vehicle accidents and another 2 million people to be injured, annually, by such accidents?[8] How is concern for human life given real expression if 30,000 people are killed in one year and another 110,000 people permanently disabled through unsafe manufactured products used outside the home?[9] In this same vein, it has been estimated "that from 70 to 90 percent of all work injuries could be prevented by proper safety devices," [10] yet workers are told how lucky they are that workmen's compensation laws exist and we are trained not to wonder why corporate crime goes unprosecuted and unpunished. These and other vital questions are being asked and answered with greater frequency. As the contradictions between the interests of profit and the interests of people become clearer, the opportunity and the necessity for building a socialist alternative can and does exist.

Detroit is a city of over one and a half million people. With more than 700 homicides a year, it is known, not without justification, as the "murder capital of the world." In one way or another every Detroiter feels and is victimized by crime, by the criminogenic conditions surrounding us.

A judge who hears 5 percent of the crimes prosecuted in Detroit occupies an important and visible position. Thousands of people a year pass through my single Detroit courtroom, leaving with many and varied impressions. At the very least, I expect to leave them with the impression and understanding that serious socialists do not have horns, do care about people, and do address the many problems that shape the lives of nearly all Americans.

Consider the following illustration. Each year 10,000 misdemeanor cases are heard by a single Detroit Recorder's Court judge assigned on a rotating monthly basis. In August 1973 I was that judge—laboring on what has been properly called "America's only working railroad." [11] More formally, the misdemeanor courtroom is called Early Sessions. Perhaps its name is derived from the fact that judges have characteristically finished court early—early enough to get to the track, golf course, or related relaxations. It was not unusual for judges to arrive at 10:00 A.M. and leave by 1:00 P.M., after having "heard" approximately fifty cases. During our month in Early Sessions, my staff worked six days a week from 9:00 A.M. until anywhere from 7:00 to 9:00 P.M.

On Friday, August 28, 1973, we were all physically weary and mentally exhausted. It is very hard to see, day after day, lines of victims who are charged with shoplifting or being drunk, or to observe the overt psychotics brought in as "disorderly persons," or to hear the complaints of women brutalized and assaulted by their "men." Still, at midday, my clerk and comrade, Suzette Salisbury, smiled and handed me File Number 73-55433:

"People of the State of Michigan, Plaintiff,

vs.

Arthur DeClerk and Wrigleys Supermarket, Inc., Defendants."

The defendants were charged with violation of the Michigan Weights and Measures Act; specifically, they were charged with gouging customers by misrepresenting the weight of thirty-three of forty packaged meats tested, at random, by a state meat inspector.

After the case was called, a Wrigleys district manager appeared alongside Mr. DeClerk and with an aura of great confidence offered to plead the corporation guilty and pay a fine on their behalf. In return, I was to dismiss charges against the individual defendant, Mr. DeClerk. The prosecutor assured me that "the People" had no objection to this offer and that this was the "usual" method for disposing of such cases. Nevertheless, I informed the district manager that he had better call the corporation's lawyer and advise him that at least one judge regarded the cozy agreement between the prosecution and the corporation to be unacceptable. The case was adjourned for a later trial date.

On the adjourned date the corporation again offered to plead guilty. I accepted the plea and fined it the maximum amount permitted by law. Mr. DeClerk then went to trial and was found guilty; at great length I explained the situation to him at sentencing, saying that:

1. On a daily basis persons are herded through courts charged with stealing from stores, often from supermarkets such as Wrigleys;

2. Even when such persons steal out of necessity they are too often sentenced to serve time—as if prison will somehow cure the crime of poverty;

3. Corporate crime is much more serious than individual crime; it is in no way deterred when the state provides only twenty meat inspectors to police such violations through the five largest counties in Michigan and when the corporation, the prosecution, and the courts conspire to impose minimal fines and to hold no individual accountable for crimes against the public.

I concluded, saying:

[T]here is one way in which I can make it clear to all of the stores in the area and to all persons who work in the stores that the criminal courts are to protect the public, and that is to make an example of you, Mr. DeClerk, and that's what I am prepared to and will do now. And, you should understand that it is not done with any . . . malice toward you, as an individual, . . . but to promote the principles of deterrence, it is my sentence that you serve, sir, one day [in the Detroit House of Corrections].

During post-conviction proceedings, the corporation lawyer repeatedly asserted that Mr. DeClerk was less blameworthy than the corporation itself and that DeClerk should not have to bear the burden of a jail sentence. I agreed that Mr. DeClerk was a mere functionary, and in a written opinion, denying the motion for a new trial, I stated that the corporation could feel free to designate any corporate officer to serve Mr. DeClerk's sentence for him. This offer was met with silence, and Mr. DeClerk is presently free on bond while the case is before the Michigan Court of Appeals.[12]

Finding an individual who could be held accountable for corporate crime was more difficult in the cases of *People* v. *Kelsey-Hayes*, File Numbers 73-54562 and 73-54563. In these cases, the corporation-defendant was charged with violating Michigan anti-pollution statutes on two consecutive days. It seems the air-control equipment had broken down and corporate officials decided to maintain production while seeking to cure the problem. As a consequence of this "public be damned" attitude, residents of southwest Detroit lived under the pall of a steady stream of excessive pollution for forty-eight consecutive hours. Only the corporation, but no corporate official, was charged with a criminal offense. Realizing that a corporation cannot be imprisoned, the Kelsey-Hayes lawyer offered an Agnewesque *nolo contendere* plea, which I accepted. I then, however, fined the corporation and placed it on probation for two years (an apparently unprecedented move), requiring, as conditions of probation, that: the corporation designate an officer to be held accountable for compliance with the terms of probation; the corporation seek to ascertain the identity of persons injured by its crime and pay restitution for such injuries; and the corporation not commit any like offense during the probationary period. I further stated that if the corporation failed to designate an officer to comply with the terms of probation, that officer would be the corporate president who would be in contempt of court in the event of a violation of probation. This case, too, is on appeal.

These illustrations, because they are exceptional, illuminate how corporate criminals are, as a rule, not prosecuted; and how, in those rare instances when a case is commenced, judges and prosecutors work together to keep members of the privileged class from getting their hands cuffed or white collars replaced by prison blues.

While individual cases are of obvious importance, what is more important is the ongoing effort to bring about institutional changes that will help to make the system less oppressive and more responsive to the needs and rights of the community. Several such changes began almost immediately, in January of 1973, after seven of us newly elected judges became a part of the twenty-member bench. During our first month in office, Judge Samuel C. Gardner was assigned to Sunday Arraignments. After arraigning numerous persons on felony charges, he was informed that there were no more prisoners to be arraigned. Judge Gardner asked where persons being held on misdemeanors were, and was told that those who posted station-house bonds* were released, while others, since there were no arraignments on Sunday, had to wait until Monday. Judge Gardner dispensed with the "never on Sunday" rule and ordered the Detroit Police Department to bring all misdemeanor prisoners before him. He promptly released all the misdemeanor defendants still in custody on their own recognizance. At the monthly bench meeting in February, a majority of the judges passed a new rule requiring that all misdemeanants not arraigned and not able to post a station-house bond be released on recognizance within six hours and ordered to appear on the next court date.

Judge Gardner led the way to a significant institutional reform by simply doing what others before him had, for years, failed to do. He followed the law. Michigan, like most states, has a statute that requires all arrestees to be brought before a magistrate "without unnecessary delay." To apply this law to "all arrestees," including misdemeanants, simply required that prisoners be brought before a judge speedily or released. In this situation, the majority of the judges voted for a "release" of misdemeanants within six hours. This accomplishment was relatively simple and uncontroversial.

When the price of following the law is additional judicial work, however, the situation becomes extremely complex and controversial. The ongoing quest for nighttime arraignments illustrates this point.

In 1972 there were 102,928 people arrested in Detroit, the nation's fifth largest city. Arraignments were held at 11:00 A.M. and 2:00 P.M., Monday through Friday, and once a day on Saturdays, Sundays, and all holidays

---

* Michigan law enables all persons arrested on misdemeanors to post a cash bond at the station house so as to secure immediate release. The bonds vary, depending upon the offense charged, from $27.50 to $87.50. Persons posting the bonds appear the next day, voluntarily, at court; however, many thousands of people a year are unable to post even these nominal bonds.

except for Christmas.* Judges never involved themselves in the matter of "unnecessary delays," although it was commonplace for many, many people who were charged with crimes to be held for up to thirty-six hours before being arraigned.

Of equal, if not greater, importance is the fact that of the 102,928 citizens arrested, 23,070—or 22 percent—were never taken to court and charged with a crime. Most of these thousands of citizens were illegally arrested, falsely imprisoned for varying periods of time up to seventy-two hours, and then told that they would be given a break and released. Judges never even saw these arrestees, few of whom ever formally complained because few people have ever understood how to go through legal channels to seek redress in individual cases of false arrest and false imprisonment. Nonetheless, judges should have been aware of the thousands of people systematically victimized by the law, because: every day judges look at police records, or rap sheets, and see documentary evidence of the multitude of people whose records reflect arrests without prosecutions; every day jurors, when questioned during jury selection as to whether or not they have ever been arrested, indicate arrests without prosecution; and the statistics that I cite are taken directly from the December 1972 *Detroit Police Department Statistical Report,* a document readily available to judges.

During the judicial campaign of 1972, I, along with others, spoke out on the need for nighttime arraignments. After taking office, the real struggle began. In February 1973 I was assigned to handle preliminary examinations and to conduct weekday arraignments. One night during the first week in February, I ordered the Detroit Police Department to bring before me all prisoners who had been in custody for ten or more hours and not brought to court. I then released some of these prisoners and set bond on others. The next morning I received a telephone call from our late presiding judge, John R. Murphy, who informed me that he had received telephone calls from the police commissioner's office and the Wayne County prosecutor's office expressing concern over what I intended to do for the balance of the month. As a result and with my consent, Judge Murphy issued a court order requiring the police department to provide me with police write-ups so I could review, at the

---

* On Christmas Day, 1973, the bench rejected my request to conduct arraignments. However, the presiding judge arranged with the Detroit police commissioner to allow me to go to police headquarters and review police write-ups and then conduct writ-of-habeas-corpus hearings at the station house.

close of each day, every case in which prisoners were detained for more than twelve hours and not taken to court. I then wrote the other judges that I would comply with the February court order if the court would, in turn, institutionalize the process whereby arraigning judges would conduct similar reviews at the end of each workday. At the same time, I indicated that if this minimal position was not adopted, I would, for the balance of the month of February when I was the arraigning judge, order the police to bring before me all prisoners in custody and not confine myself to those held for twelve hours. The motion passed.

The effort continued, and at the September 1973 bench meeting I moved for initiating arraignment sessions in Detroit every night at 6:00 P.M. and 1:00 A.M. Mindful of judicial laziness, the motion allowed the judge assigned to night arraignments the prerogative of not working his or her regular docket the next day. Also aware of the utterance of an incumbent judge during his judicial campaign—"I wouldn't come down to court at night, that's a high crime area"—a clause was written in to allow a police escort to and from court. The motion, supported by a memorandum, emphasized that it was the responsibility of highly paid judges to follow the law and require police to take arrestees directly to court. If police in Detroit had to immediately justify their purpose for holding an arrestee, many of the more than 20,000 people a year illegally arrested would not be arrested in the first place. In addition, thousands of police hours would be freed to apprehend real criminals rather than illegally arrest innocent citizens; and law enforcement could function more effectively by lessening the objective basis for wholesale distrust between large sectors of the community and the police.

Discussion on the question of nighttime arraignments began with two of the more reactionary judges, who in other situations emphasized strict "law and order"; they asserted that they would not participate in any program requiring their working at night, regardless of how the bench voted. Others suggested that our crowded docket prohibited making a judge available at night; and others worried about what the economic consequences of an added court shift would be. The vote was taken and we lost, 11–8.

Other institutional problems persist, not the least of which is the problem presented by counselors-at-law. I routinely hold irresponsible attorneys in contempt and fine them for their habitual failure to appear on time in court. One needs to combat not only the institutional inefficiency that keeps litigants, witnesses, and jurors waiting, but also the incompetence of a criminal bar that compels thousands of defendants a year to "waive" their "constitutional rights." Lawyers are integral to maintaining the pace of the assembly line. In fact, 90 percent of all guilty convictions in Recorder's Court—and throughout urban America—have traditionally been by way of guilty pleas, thus making a whole range of constitutional rights no more than paper promises to the vast majority of persons accused of crime. Objectively, the only right that exists for most persons accused of crime is the right to "cop a plea" to a lesser offense.

To some it may appear a contradiction for a radical to be a judge. But not to me. When the decision was made in June of 1972 to organize an electoral campaign to win a seat on the Recorder's Court bench, it was but another example of the integration of the work of radicals with the daily struggles of large numbers of people. Like it or not, we are in this system, and we must struggle with every weapon at our command to overcome endless crises: the energy shortage, wars, inflation/depression, and political corruption from the top down—crises we did not create but which we daily suffer.

Having decided the race worthwhile, my campaign emphasized the differences between myself and other politicians. One campaign slogan was "Radical problems require radical solutions." Another was "Justin Ravitz is a lousy politician and that's good." Campaign literature pointed out that while the politicians were talking about problems, I was, along with others, doing something about them; we had, for example:

- Challenged, exposed and, in part, changed the barbaric conditions in the Wayne County Jail and, in the process, reduced the population in the jail by more than 500 persons;

- Successfully defended a worker charged with murdering two foremen and another worker at Chrysler's Eldon Avenue plant and proved, in the process, that working conditions and Chrysler and American racism were responsible for these deaths, not James Johnson;

- Successfully defended members of the Republic of New Africa, who defended themselves when attacked by police and, in the process, exposed and altered the previously discriminatory jury selection process;

- Successfully challenged the constitutionality of Michigan anti-marijuana laws and, in the process, freed 130 persons from prison.

Though we had little experience in electoral politics, we learned. Our campaign was both conventional and unconventional. Like others, we sought after and received major endorsements, such as those of the Democratic Party districts, the United Auto Workers, and the *Detroit Free Press*. Some endorsed enthusiastically; others did so in order to lessen the gap between themselves and masses of people.

Bumper stickers, posters, and brochures were widely circulated. We raised less money than nearly all the other serious contenders for the seven newly created Recorder's Court judgeships; but we raised enough —approximately $10,000—to run our campaign and project our positions. Although our supporters were economically poor, they dug deep for dollar bills and change, and more importantly, offered themselves to the campaign. On primary and general election days (it rained both days) more than 400 workers were out at the polls or preparing and distributing food to our poll workers. Our campaign staff, led by a brilliant and young Sheila Murphy, put together the best-organized electoral apparatus in town. In the August 8, 1972, primary we ran first among forty-two candidates vying for fourteen ballot posts in the general election.

The *Detroit News*'s reaction to our success was characteristically myopic and reactionary. It believed we won only because I had the same last name as the city's then president of the Common Council. So as to distinguish, clearly, Justin and Mel Ravitz, it featured our victory on page one of the August 9 edition, picturing myself and my well-known, long-time comrade Kenneth V. Cockrel at our election headquarters reviewing the returns. The *News* continued to give us helpful identification. Between August 8 and November 7, it paid major attention to the Recorder's Court race. My positions at speaking engagements were headlined "J. Ravitz Calls for 24-hour Arraignments," and stories were accompanied by pictures of myself. The paper ran, for free, the advertisements that we could not afford. Presumably it thought that exposure of my views would repel the electorate—which is not exactly what happened.

In the general election we received 130,154 votes, placing us second among the seven newly elected judges. On December 19, 1972, we attended the official swearing-in ceremonies at the City-County Building. My ten-year term was to begin January 1, 1973. Even before that date, certain opponents tried to impeach me for failing to stand for the Pledge of Allegiance at the swearing-in ceremony, a failure based on the renewed and intensified bombing of Indochina and the stark absence of "liberty and justice for all."

Our electoral victory, and modest court reforms since then, do not prove the system works. Indeed, on November 9, 1972, the day after the election, Ivan Barris, the Detroit Bar Association president, called a press conference. He spoke on the compelling need for appointing rather than electing judges. He was asked if a person like Justin Ravitz could ever, under the plan he advocated, be appointed a judge. He answered, saying: "I think he'd have, in all candor, a very poor chance." [13]

Mr. Barris is no doubt correct, and his is but one commentary on the history of electoral politics in this country. To me, it is clear that those who own and control this country will not peaceably relinquish power; and if electoral results threaten their privileged status, they can still maintain power so long as they control the military. The overthrow of democratic socialism in Chile in 1973 is but one recent example of this reality.

Nonetheless, it is still true that a successful electoral incursion is of value. There are a number of things, for example, that a judge who is part of a people's movement can and must do:

- Struggle internally for institutionalized changes to promote the fulfillment of constitutional guarantees and equal justice under law.

- Openly and candidly expose those judges who resist such efforts and demands.

- Meticulously and humanely apply their law and demonstrate that the "radical judge" knows more about the law and how it can and should be used than do judges differently inclined.

- Conduct the type of courtroom that will offer at least a glimpse of how people ought to comprehend what is going on and feel comfortable in courts of law.*

- Make sure that losing litigants understand the realities of both their case and the law.**

* The only people my courtroom stands for are, not the judge, but the jury, which represents a cross-section of the community and is one of the rare and best examples of working democracy. Moreover, the entire court staff tries to make the atmosphere less intimidating, and we try, as much as possible, to make the proceedings comprehensible.

** Legal education should be a conscious and built-in part of all trial-court proceedings and it should benefit litigants, attorneys, jurors, police, lay witnesses, and spectators. Persons sentenced to prison should know and understand why there is no "alternative to prison" in their individual

- And finally, and fundamentally, such a judge will understand the limits of the law's present capacity to promote change and will realize that we cannot litigate nor elect our way to liberation but we can help build and organize a mass, multinational, radical people's party which is committed to fundamentally altering the basis upon which this society is presently arranged.

So long as these purposes can be served, I shall continue the ten-year term, recognizing that this is only one small part of an overridingly important struggle which will, ultimately, be won by and for millions of people who may be best described poetically:

GENTLE PEOPLE

I know
we were
a gentle people
                    once.

but
the rulers
have made us
fighters. fighters
better than they.
and
we will fight
so
we can become
gentle people
                    again.[14]

---

situation and should be honestly told that they cannot rely on the Department of Corrections for rehabilitation; police should be instructed why an arrest or a warrantless search was illegal; and citizens victimized by police brutality should be helped to make their grievances heard.

*Jack Newfield**

The Ten Worst Judges

EACH MONTH more and more evidence seems to support the observation by the learned justice James Leff of the New York state supreme court that some of his fellow judges are "outright thieves, fakers, failures, and misfits." Although four judges in New York in late 1974 were awaiting criminal trials for corruption, venality is only part of the problem. And the part almost impossible for journalists to document without undercover informants, subpoena power, manufactured cases, wiretaps, and grants of immunity. The greater and more accessible concern is the dull, methodical absence of justice that seems to be the personal experience of so many defendants, litigants, cops, lawyers, assistant DA's, and crime victims. It is not the dramatic, well-publicized murder trials in the state supreme court that prove the decay of the judicial system. It is what happens in anonymity, every day, in the landlord-tenant parts, in the arraignment parts, in family court, criminal court, where justice resembles more a rampant meatgrinder than any Holmsian visions.

Just spend a month inside the chaotic courtrooms and you will see judges with unstable temperaments, judges with unmistakable biases, judges who are insulting and sarcastic, judges who open court at 11:00 A.M., take long lunches, and quit at 3:00 P.M., judges who are not intelligent enough to understand complex or subtle legal argument, judges who are incoherent from too many martinis at lunch, judges who bend the law to favor the clients of lawyers who are clubhouse cronies. You will see judges rule time after time against tenants, and then go out and have lunch with the landlord's lawyer. You will see defendants awaiting trial who have been locked in jail for six months on $250 bail because their

* JACK NEWFIELD IS AN INVESTIGATIVE REPORTER WITH, AND SENIOR EDITOR OF, THE *Village Voice* IN NEW YORK CITY. HE IS THE AUTHOR OF, AMONG OTHERS, *A Prophetic Minority* (1966), *Robert Kennedy: A Memoir* (1969), AND COAUTHOR OF *A Populist Manifesto* (1973).

files have been lost. You will see law secretaries, who are also district leaders, spending all their time on politics, and no time on the law. You will see judges coerce guilty pleas, improperly force settlements, malinger, manipulate the calendar, do anything to escape the mental labor of conducting a jury trial.

Such procedural inequities invariably lead to substantive injustice:

- In September 1974, the State Select Committee on Crime released a report that showed that more than sixty illegal sen ences were given by Manhattan judges to defendants convicted of narcotics felonies between 1969 and 1972. An illegal sentence under the state's penal law is a conditional or unconditional discharge to anyone convicted of a narcotics felony. Some of those illegally freed by Manhattan judges were large-scale narcotics wholesalers. A similar study by the same committee the previous year revealed twenty-four illegal sentences by Queens judges over the same period.

- A *New York Times* editorial on August 24, 1974, acknowledged that despite an exhausting effort, "no dent has been made in the discouragingly large backlog of serious felony cases awaiting trial here."

- In July 1974, New York City's special prosecutor, Maurice Nadjari, filed motion papers in the Judge Rao case, which stated that "a virtual cesspool of corruption" was found within the Brooklyn court system.

- On April 8, 1974, the State Commission of Investigation released a report that concluded that the judiciary of New York City "has failed to fulfill its obligation to properly discipline judges. . . . The present practice of allowing the judiciary to police itself has not worked." The report added, "In certain cases where serious allegations were made involving corruption, potential corruption, ulterior motives for decisions, and the failure to accord litigants basic rights, the responsible persons in the judicial system either took little action . . . or at best, investigated them in a most cursory and unprofessional manner."

- On April 8, 1974, the *Daily News* disclosed the existence of a secret bar association study that accused five state supreme court justices of misconduct ranging from having "improper" connections to lawyers, to laziness, to "screaming at lawyers and witnesses from the bench" and imposing "unduly harsh" sentences.

- In October 1972, the New York State Joint Legislative Committee on Crime published an analysis of 1,762 organized-crime cases in state courts in New York City between 1960 and 1970. It concluded that while 44.7 percent of the indictments against mobsters were dismissed by state supreme court judges, only 11.5 percent of indictments against all defendants were dismissed.

To a large extent, justice has broken down in the courts for a variety of institutional reasons: the overwhelming volume of cases, dilatory defense counsel, the political way judges are selected, the lack of monitoring and accountability. But while it has become fashionable to stress institutional failings in our society, it cannot be ignored that there are clear *individual* differences between judges. To be simple yet accurate: There are good judges and bad judges; the good ones approximate justice, in spite of the system's inhibitions, while the bad ones care about little more than their own sense of self-importance.

This critique is not widely written about. The *Canons of Ethics* discourage lawyers from criticizing judges by name, except to official bodies. Assistant DA's are fearful of reprisal if they go public with their suspicions and unhappy experiences. Police officers usually have no access to the media. Criminal defendants have no credibility with the general public. Judges themselves, except for a few like the legendary Leff, are often a close-knit group which closes ranks for self-protection.

Until the state develops an effective disciplinary process which earns the public's confidence—especially since the report of the State Commission of Investigation acknowledged that judges won't, and can't, discipline themselves—the press may be the only institution that can possibly hold judges accountable. Armed with this presumption, I began an investigation into "the ten worst judges" in local New York City courts. This format is admittedly a journalistic device that simplifies and personalizes. But the device can usefully educate the public about what is going on in their courtrooms, can perhaps to a small degree help deter similar or repeated malfeasance, and can give constructive remedies a better chance of implementation.

As research for this article, I read more than one hundred court transcripts and interviewed more than fifty trial lawyers. I also interviewed judges, court officers and stenographers, prosecutors, cops, members of judicial screening committees, and other journalists who cover the courts. I studied several private reports on the court system and analyzed public documents compiled by the State Commission of

Investigation, the State Select Committee on Crime, and various bar associations.

Twenty-two judges were "recommended" by five or more people interviewed as standing for cruelty, stupidity, bias against the poor, short tempers, or total insensitivity to civil liberties. From this list of twenty-two, ten emerged as the worst of the worst—a judgment sufficiently subjective that, to the extent possible, I refer to court transcripts in which my ten judges indict themselves.

Allen Moss, criminal court: When Allen Moss was elevated to the bench in February 1970, most people expected him to make a good judge. He was appointed by Mayor John Lindsay on the recommendation of Liberal Party leader Alex Rose. (Moss's law partner was Rose's son, Herbert.) Moss was approved by a screening panel and he seemed to have an amiable disposition. But after four years as a judge, the sixty-six-year-old Moss is condemned by lawyers for unstable temperament, for a lack of impartiality, for impatience, and for being indifferent to the quality of justice.

In March 1974, Harold Harrison, a lawyer, wrote a letter to the Appellate Division describing Judge Moss's conduct as that of "an uncivilized, uninformed, unknowledgeable, despicable individual." Lawyer Harrison said that Judge Moss ordered his son, a complainant who was ill and wished to go home before a late-night arraignment, into a detention cell with a man his son had accused of robbing him with a gun. A *Daily News* story on the incident indicates that Judge Moss apparently falsely reported the facts to the reporter, who then quoted the court transcript to expose the judge's misleading comments.[1]

Judge Moss's lack of fairness is also demonstrated in *People* v. *Stevens et al.,* in which the judge admonished the defendant *before any trial:* "Well, you shouldn't commit crimes, lady." [2]

Two recent official court transcripts document Judge Moss's extreme hostility to civil liberties. The first outburst took place on July 10, 1974, in *People* v. *Shields.*[3]

JUDGE MOSS: Are you willing to waive the presence of the defendant during the rest of your cross-examination until he's produced by Correction?

MISS HABER (the Legal Aid attorney): No, Your Honor, I feel that it's necessary.

JUDGE MOSS: You'll save the time of the court.

MISS HABER: I feel that my client would be deprived of his right to confront witnesses.

JUDGE MOSS: Oh, nuts, stop that crap, please. You can put this on the record. . . .

The next day, in *People* v. *Artis*, Judge Moss fixed cash bail for a defendant, who could not pay it, *after* the defense lawyer requested a jury trial against the wishes of the judge.[4] When the lawyer objected to the length of time his client would remain in jail, pending receipt of the grand jury minutes, the following colloquy took place:

MR. RUSKIN (the Legal Aid attorney): Your Honor, defense counsel is entitled to grand jury minutes.

JUDGE MOSS: Talk to your client before you keep on talking about this routine crap you are giving the court. Give him a chance. Have a fair trial [presumably referring to the non-jury trial Judge Moss preferred].

MR. RUSKIN: Your Honor, the defendant will not have a fair trial without possession of the grand jury minutes.

JUDGE MOSS: Six weeks from today.

MR. RUSKIN: Your Honor, I object to the six weeks.

JUDGE MOSS: Objection is noted and overruled. . . . Put the defendant in.

MR. RUSKIN: Your Honor, I request the district attorney be requested to get the grand jury minutes within a week.

JUDGE MOSS: August 22. . . .

MR. RUSKIN: Your Honor, I am requesting that the district attorney—

JUDGE MOSS: Stop it. Stop these games now. . . .

MR. RUSKIN: Your Honor, I am not playing games with the Court. I am requesting my man be given all his rights, constitutional rights. He is entitled to have those minutes.

JUDGE MOSS: Both attorneys will keep quiet please, or I will charge both with contempt of court. . . .

MR. RUSKIN: Your Honor, the defendant wants to make a statement. He wants to place that statement on the record.

JUDGE MOSS: Denied. I ordered him back into the pen, and I want no statement from the defendant. . . .

Morgan Lane, Brooklyn Civil Court: Judge Lane's courtroom character can be seen from reading the transcripts of an occasion in 1974 when he ordered a Legal Aid attorney held in contempt of court.

On March 4, 1974, in *People* v. *Holstein*, Judge Lane, sitting on the criminal side, ordered the experienced and respectful Legal Aid lawyer Robert Levy held in contempt.[5] Judge Lane was interrupting and harassing the lawyer all afternoon during a *voir dire* of jurors. Then came this colloquy:

MR. LEVY: Do you understand that if she [the defendant] fails to take the stand, that that is no evidence at all?

JUDGE LANE: Mr. Levy, I am going to stop you. I already gave him what the law is, and don't ask him any more questions. They're taking the law from me, . . . Go to something else.

MR. LEVY: I object under *People* v. *Preston Williams.*

JUDGE LANE: Don't give me no citations.

A few minutes later, the following:

MR. LEVY: Let the record reflect that while the defendant [is] making the responses previously placed on the record, Judge Lane was looking at the jury with a broad smile on his face.

JUDGE LANE: You're asking for a mistrial? . . . Motion for mistrial is granted. . . . Put this on the record. I have just declared a mistrial, and Mr. Levy, I am directing my attention toward you. Don't you ever appear before me under any circumstances to try a case, because I won't permit you to try any case in front of me because of your conduct. Your total disregard of court and order.

MR. LEVY: Is it on the record?

JUDGE LANE: Yes. And I am directing you now, and I am telling you, don't you ever come before me to try any case because I won't permit you.

MR. LEVY: Yes, and I'd like to place on the record that I have appeared as an attorney for fourteen years, in courtrooms—

JUDGE LANE: Well, you won't appear before me. . . .

MR. LEVY: Let me say this, on the record. You're obviously not permitting me to say this. I have been in courtrooms for fourteen years, from the criminal courts, to the Court of Appeals, and into the Second Circuit. And I have hardly, if ever, been pleasured to see such a gross abuse of judicial authority. And I regard the judge's action in this case as thoroughly injudicious. Thank you, Your Honor.

JUDGE LANE: Get everything on the record. Get everything on the record. Mr. Levy, appear here tomorrow morning on a citation for contempt. . . .

MR. LEVY: I am sure that the Legal Aid Society will find an attorney to defend me. . . . I'd like it placed on the record that—

JUDGE LANE: Just a minute. Nothing—

MR. LEVY: I can't go on the record when you're holding me in contempt?

JUDGE LANE: There is nothing further on the record as of now. Appear here tomorrow morning. The proceedings today are over.

Judge Lane was born with the name Moe Levy. He was a prosecutor in the Brooklyn DA's office before being picked for a judgeship in 1964 by the Brooklyn political machine. According to the oral history of Brooklyn politics, Moe Levy picked the name Morgan Lane after watching Errol Flynn play a swashbuckling character named Morgan Lane in a movie, *Montana*, released by Warner Brothers in 1950.

Milton Shalleck, criminal court: Judge Shalleck has the judicial temperament of Leo Durocher. He uses insults and sarcasm against lawyers, defendants, and prosecutors alike. During one arraignment he once called the defendant a "liar," and then ridiculed the defendant's lawyer for objecting to the characterization, as the following transcript reveals:[6]

DEFENDANT: I'm on a methadone program and I'm on bail, and I showed up for the cases each time . . . I'm on the Bronx State Methadone Program, Your Honor. . . ."

JUDGE SHALLECK: Let me see the evidence he is on that program.

DEFENDANT: I don't have it.

JUDGE SHALLECK: One thousand dollars bail. Mr. Ambrosini [the Legal Aid defense counsel], you know he's a liar.

DEFENSE COUNSEL: Excuse me, Your Honor?

JUDGE SHALLECK: He's a liar.

DEFENSE COUNSEL: Is that on the record, Your Honor?

JUDGE SHALLECK: Mr. Ambrosini, would you do me a favor? Stop trying to be contemptuous, because you won't succeed. You've got to be knowledgeable to be contemptuous, and not just a young, unsophisticated individual. . . .

Another court transcript reveals Judge Shalleck's contempt for the constitutional guarantee of a speedy trial. The Bronx DA's office was not prepared for a hearing because the police laboratory report on seized drugs was not available. The defense lawyer made a reference to defendant's right to a prompt trial, to which Judge Shalleck replied, "It sounds so lovely what you say, counsel, so lovely in the record and on paper, and they make a good talking point. But let's not be so theoretical. . . ."

Next, Judge Shalleck directed his sarcasm at the assistant district attorney:

JUDGE SHALLECK: I thought you were the prosecutor here. You mean you represent defendants now?

ASSISTANT DISTRICT ATTORNEY: We all live in a . . . real world, where 180.80 has good cause to—

JUDGE SHALLECK: How do you spell that, R-E-E-L?

ASSISTANT DISTRICT ATTORNEY: That applies to the cinema.

JUDGE SHALLECK: This almost sounds like a show, believe me, to get mouthings of things that mean nothing. . . .

A few moments later Judge Shalleck cruelly mocked the defendant.

DEFENSE COUNSEL: . . . [defendant] is now a retired merchant seaman living in this city.

JUDGE SHALLECK: He's retarded, did you say?

Canon 10 of the *Canons of Judicial Ethics* says: "A judge should be courteous to counsel, especially those who are young and inexperienced. . . . Canon 15 says: "In addressing counsel, litigants, or witnesses, he [the judge] should avoid a controversial manner or tone. He should avoid interruptions of counsel. . . .

Morris Schwalb, criminal court: Morris Schwalb, in a reasonable world, should never have become a judge in the first place. When he was first appointed to the bench, on December 20, 1968, by John Lindsay, the bar association refused to approve him. The association said Schwalb had "very little criminal experience . . . the Criminal Court bench is not a place for on-the-job training."

Although he had minuscule legal background, Schwalb did have heavy political credentials. Morris Schwalb was the chairman of the Bronx Republican Law Committee for seven years. He had run for the state senate and lost. He had twice run for judgeships and lost.

But within three years of ascending to the bench, Judge Schwalb became a celebrity of sorts, even getting on the front page of *The New York Times.* He had ordered two women charged with prostitution held without bail—an act so repressive and vindictive that it was without known legal precedent in the history of the city. Judge Schwalb, according to lawyers, was not known to have ever denied bail to a pimp or a prostitute's client. (Normally prostitutes plead guilty to lesser offenses and are fined $50; prostitution is a misdemeanor.) Incredibly, in a "chamber of commerce" speech from the bench, Judge Schwalb justified his unconstitutional ruling by confusing constitutionalism with boosterism. "They [the prostitutes] have created a hazard to the business . . . and hotel interests."

Judge Schwalb also cited the Sam Melville bombing case, and said: "While we do not have preventive detention, nevertheless there is authority for police action when the welfare of the public is in serious jeopardy." A short time later, the two prostitutes were released from jail by other judges. One was allowed to plead guilty to a lesser charge after it was discovered that two alleged bail jumps on her record were "administrative errors." The second prostitute was paroled in her own recognizance by state supreme court justice Xavier Ricobono.

This was not a unique performance by the judge. "Schwalb is the meanest man I ever saw in my whole life," said one Bronx Legal Aid lawyer. "He likes to hurt people. I once saw a poor black guy with no previous record come before him on a charge of driving without a license. He ordered the guy held on $500 bail. The arresting officer was mortified. The DA was shocked. This is never done. The guy went off to the Bronx House of Detention for months. He could never raise $500. And he had no record at all."

Aaron Koota, Brooklyn Supreme Court: Nearly all the lawyers and judges I spoke with had a low regard for Judge Koota's knowledge of the law, several noting his bias in favor of the prosecution—Koota being a former district attorney of Kings County. For example, on March 25, 1974, the Appellate Division reversed a conviction in a narcotics case (*People* v. *Baker*) because Koota had denied the defendant "a fair and impartial trial." The decision, reversing a jury conviction and ordering a new trial, said Koota had engaged in "over-active participation," and was guilty of "verbatim repetition" of a phrase used by the prosecutor in his summation. The majority opinion said: "That repetition in the very language used by the prosecution could only have led the jury to believe that the court was in accord with the prosecution's view of the defendant's guilt." In unusually blunt language, the reversal concluded: "The defendant did not have what he was entitled to—a fair trial."

Koota suffers from numerous reversals, reversals which flow not from creative or innovative decisions but from an ignorance of the law. One involved a major heroin dealer, Ira Karl Issacs. Two weeks before the hearing, Koota told prosecutor Martin Hershey that he was going to throw out the indictment against Issacs on the basis of technical error in the drafting of the search warrant. On March 2, 1972, Issacs' lawyer (who was a former assistant to Koota in the DA's office) made a motion to suppress evidence on the basis of an insufficient search warrant. According to the court transcript, the prosecution pointed out that under the law there must be a hearing with witnesses before Justice Koota could make such a ruling. At that point, Koota admitted his legal error and acknowledged there must be a formal hearing, that he could not legally dismiss the indictment on the basis of the written briefs. Prosecutor Hershey then made a motion for Koota to disqualify himself from the case, pointing out that the judge had already made up his mind, since he had said two weeks earlier that he was going to throw the case out of court.

Koota lost his temper; he denied the motion to disqualify himself and then reversed his earlier ruling, saying he was now dismissing the indictment, even without a formal hearing. To his credit, Brooklyn DA Eugene Gold appealed Koota's decision. In November 1972, the Appellate Division ruled unanimously that Koota was in error and reinstated the original indictment against Issacs. The five appellate judges found the evidence supporting the search warrant to be "more than sufficient to justify the issuance of the warrant."

George Starke, Manhattan Supreme Court: Justice Starke has made a practice of raising the amount of bail set by other judges. In *People* v. *Ashby*, Justice Arnold Fein set bail of $100. Justice Starke raised it to $500, and said Justice Fein's judgment was "utterly ridiculous" and "stupid." [7] In *People* v. *Crowell*, the defendant had been in jail for five months in lieu of $20,000 bail.[8] When bail was reduced to $5,000 by Justice Samuel Silverman, the defendant was able to raise it. For the next two months, Crowell made all his scheduled appearances in court. He was married, with two children, and had a job. The defense counsel was ready for trial, but the district attorney was not. But Justice Starke raised the bail to $10,000 and remanded Crowell to jail.

Judge Starke has shown similar disrespect to juries. In *People* v. *Callah*, the jury was deadlocked at 11 to 1 in favor of acquittal. Justice Starke told the jurors: "This is a disgrace." He twice called the defendant's testimony a "cock and bull story." He called it "B. S.," and asked, "How can anybody in his right mind fall for this baloney? . . . It is a pity that people can be fooled. . . . At any rate, I'm walking out." The defense counsel said he "would like to be heard." Justice Starke said simply, "No." [9] The Standing Committee on Professional Ethics of the American Bar Association has said it is a violation of judicial ethics for a judge "to berate a jury for errors the judge thinks the jury has made in reaching its verdict."

In another case, the five appellate judges of the First Department reprimanded Justice Starke in a unanimous May 1974 opinion for his failure to give a burglary defendant "a fair and impartial trial." The five-member court reversed the conviction of William Harris, who had been sentenced to a five-to-fifteen-year prison term, and ordered a new trial before another judge. The reversal said of Justice Starke:

> Throughout the trial, the court unduly interjected itself into the proceedings, examining witnesses, including the defendant, with prosecutorial zeal; making personal comments upon the testimony . . . and generally conveying to the jury the court's attitude . . . both in respect to the merits of the case and to the credibility of witnesses.

Justice Starke is a sixty-eight-year-old former city marshal. He is a close friend of both Liberal Party leader Alex Rose and Manhattan Republican leader Vincent Albano. He has been elected several times with the endorsement of those two parties.

William Suglia, criminal court: On the evening of February 22, 1971, Judge Suglia met with Mrs. Vivian Becks in his chambers at 100 Centre Street. The woman went to Judge Suglia because her son was to be arraigned that evening on a charge of possession of marijuana. According to Mrs. Becks, Judge Suglia made sexual advances to her in the privacy of his chambers that night. She later told the city's commissioner of investigation that Suglia made her feel "like a slave on a plantation." (Mrs. Becks is black.)

She submitted a sworn statement to then investigations commissioner Robert Ruskin alleging that the judge lunged at her and attempted to remove her panties.[10] The Appellate Division consequently investigated Judge Suglia's conduct, and on April 22, 1971, unanimously censured the judge for admitting Mrs. Becks to his chambers, which provided "the opportunity from which an implication of impropriety could be drawn." The charge based upon sexual advance did not reach the Appellate Division, but the fact of the physical contact was not disputed. One of the five appellate judges—James McNally—issued a separate concurring but much stronger opinion, in which he called Judge Suglia's behavior "extremely reprehensible" and "inexcusable." He concluded that Judge Suglia's actions "tend to bring the administration of justice into disrepute."*

The April 1974 report of the State Commission of Investigation dealt

* Despite his alleged sexual advances to Mrs. Becks, Judge Suglia has a reputation for judicial puritanism. He has signed several warrants for the arrest of theater operators for obscenity. Judge Suglia signed these dubious warrants after viewing the films and deciding himself they are obscene.

with the Mrs. Becks case and suggested that Judge Suglia deserved a more severe punishment than a wrist-slapping censure. The report revealed that the Judiciary Relations Committee had found that Judge Suglia

> violated important provisions of the Canons of Judicial Ethics. . . . The judge appeared to have exercised his discretion for either the sexual favors, or potential sexual favors, from the mother of a defendant appearing in his court. . . . In spite of a finding by the committee of a serious violation of the Canons of Ethics, the Appellate Division did not remove this judge, but censured him.[11]

If the degrading episode of Mrs. Becks stood alone, I might not have included Judge Suglia in this pantheon of robed misfits. But there is a general pattern to his behavior that indicates a pleasure in being punitive, and a lack of sound temperament and judgment. In *People* v. *Quinn*, for example, the judge ridiculed a recommendation for release by the probation department, and instead held the defendant in $1,000 bail.[12] (The defendant had no prior convictions.) Said Judge Suglia:

> I am not going to follow Probation's recommendations on Quinn . . . I will doubt whether their evaluation is correct; that applies to all defendants. They tell us they verify three factors. I would be willing right now to wager, if I were a wagering man, which I am not, that they never verified his employment .   . $1,000 cash or bond.

Judge Suglia did not himself independently check the facts. He chose to presume that the professional judgment of the Probation Department was wrong and the defendant's family was lying.

Judge Suglia is a protégé of Manhattan Republican leader Vincent Albano. In 1966, at Albano's urging, Mayor Lindsay appointed Suglia to be the chairman of the Bureau of Assessors. In December 1968, again at Albano's suggestion, Lindsay appointed Suglia to the criminal court for a ten-year-term. Despite his censure in 1971, Judge Suglia was recently rewarded with a promotion: For some time he was serving as supervising judge of the Brooklyn Criminal Court.

Howard Goldfluss, criminal court: The Honorable Howard Goldfluss likes to compare himself to Supreme Court justices Louis Brandeis and Benjamin Cardozo. But the transcripts of his court unmask him as far more akin to a star chamber judge, as he repeatedly ignores the rights protected by the Constitution.

In *People* v. *Roman and Garcia*, Judge Goldfluss ruled two men accused of selling $10 worth of marijuana must be held in $500 bail for a grand jury.[13] The Legal Aid attorney made an appeal for parole: "A recent report by the President's study commission on the subject points out that 25 to 26 million people in this country at some time utilize this substance. . . . I don't see how the judicial system can benefit from the incarceration of these defendants." Judge Goldfluss ignored the plea and remanded the two men to the dungeon known as the Bronx House of Detention.

People v. Guzman[14] came before Judge Goldfluss in Bronx Criminal Court on March 1, 1974. In this case the judge ordered the Legal Aid Society not to provide remedial social work counseling to the accused while awaiting trial.

DEFENSE COUNSEL: . . . the defendant is employed and has been steadily for the past two months.

JUDGE GOLDFLUSS: This defendant will have no program. . . . This defendant will face trial. . . . No programs for this defendant. Legal Aid Diversionary Program will not be involved in this at all.

DEFENSE COUNSEL: I do not request that he be paroled in their custody.

JUDGE GOLDFLUSS: I am directing that Legal Aid Diversionary Program have no longer to do with this defendant. That is the direction of this court.

DEFENSE COUNSEL: I think it is grossly unfair.

JUDGE GOLDFLUSS: . . . I am the one who decides what is unfair.

DEFENSE COUNSEL: Your Honor, you may direct that the defendant will not be paroled to the Legal Aid Diversionary Program. However, they have for a long time, and I hope will continue to provide social work.

JUDGE GOLDFLUSS: I am directing that they have nothing further to do with this defendant. Now that is the order of this court.

In *People v. Acosta*, Judge Goldfluss, unconstitutionally, used bail coercively against a defendant.

JUDGE GOLDFLUSS: . . . the defendant is remanded. You may bring a writ. One thousand dollars bail. If that's the only way I can get a trial.

DEFENSE COUNSEL: I don't see any purpose in remanding this man. He already spent eight days in jail when the People were not ready.

JUDGE GOLDFLUSS: Ready and passed. Remanded.

DEFENSE COUNSEL: Why?

JUDGE GOLDFLUSS: Because it appears that is the only way we can get a trial in this case.

The defendant was paroled later in the day by the supervising judge of the Bronx Criminal Court.

Abraham Margulies, Queens Civil Court: Talk to any lawyer or civil litigant who has appeared in Judge Margulies' courtroom, and after a while, inevitably, one word is heard: "nut."

Year after year individual lawyers filed complaints against him. Finally, in 1971, the cautious, establishment Queens Bar Association reached its limit. It filed a formal complaint against Margulies covering the years 1963 to 1971. Judge Margulies was then officially censured for his misconduct by the Appellate Division.

The Queens Bar Association submitted a second well-documented petition against Margulies in 1973. Nine lawyers filed sworn statements detailing their humiliations before Margulies. One affidavit said the judge "acts like a maniac." Another attorney swore he witnessed Judge Margulies enter his courtroom at 9:20 A.M. and direct a court officer to move the hands of the clock forward to 9:30 A.M. Then Margulies called the daily calendar, and those lawyers not present had their cases dismissed! And, in February 1974, the Appellate Division censured Margulies—with no public announcement—for the second time. An investigation is still continuing to consider if more serious action—including removal—should be taken.

Like most of the worst judges, Margulies acquired his black robes as the result of political influence. His wife was a district leader in the Rockaways. In 1965, when he was nominated for the civil court, Margulies was found "unqualified" by the Queens Bar Association. He was elected anyway. His term expires in 1975.

Frank Blangiardo, Manhattan Civil Court: In interviews, anti-poverty lawyers say Judge Blangiardo is biased in favor of landlords. Prosecutors say Blangiardo knows less law than a bright law school freshman. Defense lawyers say he is rude and authoritarian. Judges say he is their most political colleague.

In 1972, Blangiardo was given a brief assignment as an acting state supreme court justice in a case involving alleged Mafia leader Jimmy Napoli. With both defense and prosecution objecting, Blangiardo declared a mistrial, after maneuvering the court calendar so he would have jurisdiction over the trial. During the pretrial hearings, Blangiardo infuriated the Manhattan DA's office with his suspiciously aggressive efforts to bargain a misdemeanor plea for Napoli, which would have meant no jail sentence. (Napoli had been indicted on felony perjury charges.) At one point, Blangiardo paid an off-the-record visit to the chief assistant district attorney, Al Scotti, and urged him to agree to a misdemeanor. Scotti refused and was outraged that the judge had gone over the head of the assistant trying the case. Scotti insisted the judge's visit be placed on the record. Other assistants in the office considered Blangiardo's approach to Scotti highly improper, and a sign that he had a special interest in the disposition.

Napoli waived a jury trial and agreed to a trial before Blangiardo. One week into the trial, Blangiardo declared a mistrial on the most flimsy legal grounds.

Judge Blangiardo's whole career is based on political connections. His father was a power in Tammany, and reportedly a partner with Assemblyman Louis De Salvio in a liquor store. Blangiardo himself was a protégé of former Tammany boss Carmine De Sapio. In the mid-1950s, Blangiardo applied for a job in New York County DA Frank Hogan's office. He was interviewed and rejected. According to sources in the office, Blangiardo had flunked his bar exam twice, and his grades had been in the bottom third of his Brooklyn Law School class.

But De Sapio and several judges pressured Hogan, and Blangiardo was finally hired for a minor job in the Complaint Bureau. Lawyers have subsequently heard Blangiardo claim to have been chief of the Complaint Bureau. Just after Blangiardo's thirty-sixth birthday, in 1959, Carmine De Sapio arranged for him to become a municipal court judge. The law has suffered ever since.

Of course there are many good judges—like Milton Mollen, James Leff, and Ernest Rosenberger—in New York courts. But as one sits in these courts and reads their transcripts, there is also evidence of gross incompetence, of venality, of racial and class discrimination. Many of these problems occur so often they arouse in some not outrage but boredom. A middle-class white kid shows up wearing a new suit for sentencing with his parents, a clergyman, a letter from a psychiatrist, and a letter from his congressman. He is accompanied by a high-priced lawyer who makes a moving speech. This defendant is likely to get a suspended sentence.

A ghetto kid, convicted of the same crime, shows up only with an overworked Legal Aid lawyer. He comes from a broken, scattered family. He has no political connections. He can't afford a psychiatrist or a private lawyer. He is wearing sneakers and torn dungarees. He is not the kind of kid a clubhouse judge knew growing up, and the judge has little time to place this defendant beyond his prejudices. So this defendant is likely to receive a jail sentence.

We have had inept and prejudiced judges for so long that it may seem impossible to reduce their frequency. But steps can be taken. For one thing, political bosses like Pat Cunningham and Vincent Albano have no business selecting judges. Every judge that has been chosen in the Bronx during the last decade has been associated with the regular clubhouses. Law school professors or gifted lawyers are not considered. Knowledge of the law and integrity seem irrelevant. Cunningham would ask a modern Brandeis to get a letter from his district leader.

An appointment system based on merit, with independent screening panels that include street-smart community representation, should be used to select judges. Too often reformers devise screening panels dominated by an Ivy League, white shoe mind-set. We need consumer and community activists, tenants, trade unionists, and Legal Aid lawyers on these panels.

Second, there must be a mechanism within the judiciary for investigation and removal of unqualified or corrupt judges. There should be a permanent commission, with a full-time staff, to continually monitor the performance of judges who feel superior to scrutiny. (A temporary commission of this kind began to function in New York State in December 1974. By September 1975 it had received more than a hundred complaints against judges.)

And third, we must continue to have New York City's version of a special prosecutor, independent of the political system. Special Prosecutor Nadjari was appointed by Governor Rockefeller in the fall of 1972 as a result of a crisis of corruption within the criminal justice system of New York City. Nadjari superseded the five elected borough district attorneys. He recruited a staff independent of the political clubhouses. Though Nadjari personally has gotten mixed reviews, for his indifference to civil liberties and his penchant for leaking grand jury proceedings, the very presence of a permanent special prosecutor can help make some judges think twice before violating their office.

These measures will not guarantee perfect justice in our courts, but they will help disinfect the judicial disease of incompetence and insensitivity to law. And they at least contribute toward fulfillment of the two transcendent goals of our judicial system: the separation of law and justice from politics and patronage, and the achievement of equal justice regardless of class, color, or connections.

*John R. Schmidt**

Lawyers on Judges: Competence and Selection

LAWYERS KNOW a great deal about judges. Any active trial lawyer in Chicago, for example, is likely to have had significant experience before most of the thirteen full-time sitting judges on the federal district court. And to compound that experience, attorneys continually hear their colleagues recount *their* courtroom experiences.

While lawyers know a lot about judges, however, they never tell. They never convey to the public at large, and certainly not to the judges themselves, what they think about them. Supreme Court justices are something of an exception to this rule. Their judicial opinions are often the subject of professional scrutiny, and sometimes harsh criticism, in law reviews and elsewhere.[1] Appellate court opinions are also analyzed in the law reviews and an occasional federal court of appeals judge may develop a reputation for exceptional distinction—Judge Learned Hand, for one prominent example. Yet even at the appellate level, there is little public discussion or awareness of the qualities of less competent judges. Few people knew anything about G. Harrold Carswell, for example, when he was simply a judge on the fifth circuit. At the district court level, where an assessment of a judge necessarily involves much more than simply an analysis of published opinions, public appraisal of the performance of judges is almost nonexistent.

Why this lack of scrutiny? Surely not because the quality of trial-court judges is unimportant. The notion that any errors at the trial level can be reversed by competent appellate judges is simply wrong. A trial judge—with his power to make all kinds of day-to-day, nonreviewable decisions directly affecting the rights of litigants—may have even more

* JOHN R. SCHMIDT, A PRACTICING LAWYER IN CHICAGO, IS THE PRESIDENT OF THE CHICAGO COUNCIL OF LAWYERS.

power to do good, or harm, to the legal system than an appellate-court judge. When it was announced in late 1974 that Philip Tone, an extremely able new federal district judge in Chicago, was being nominated for the Seventh Circuit Court of Appeals, the view was widespread among Chicago lawyers that the promotion, although well-merited personally, represented a net loss to the overall effective functioning of the federal judiciary. Conversely, it is often suggested that one way to deal with the problem of an incompetent district court judge is to "promote" him to the court of appeals, where he can "do less damage"—in part because court of appeals judges always sit in panels, on which, presumably, the "bad judge" can be restrained (and, if necessary, outvoted) by his colleagues.

In 1971, the Chicago Council of Lawyers—founded in 1969 by young lawyers dismayed by the inadequate response of the established Chicago bar to events like the "Chicago Seven" trial and the Chicago "police riot" at the 1968 Democratic Convention—surveyed practicing lawyers in Chicago for their evaluations of sitting federal district court judges.[2] To our knowledge this poll represented the first time any bar association had attempted systematically to evaluate sitting federal court judges. The questionnaire was sent to all lawyers who had filed appearances in the district court in the preceding three years (approximately 2,400), plus the full membership of the council. At the time of the poll, thirteen judges were on the bench and lawyers were asked a variety of questions about the judges' qualities and judicial performance. A total of 529 lawyers responded. Analysis by a social scientist who provided methodological advice indicated that the aggregate responses which were unfavorable were not the results of "skewing" from indiscriminate or malicious responses.[3] While certainly not infallible, the results of the poll present a valuable—and, to date, unique—picture of the federal trial bench as viewed by lawyers in one major city.

Three sitting judges received overwhelmingly negative responses from lawyers responding to the poll. One was Judge Julius J. Hoffman, who had previously achieved a degree of national notoriety as a result of his conduct in the Chicago Seven trial. A substantial majority (about 70 percent) of those who expressed an opinion on Judge Hoffman responded negatively to the question: "Viewed overall, do you favor his continued service in his present post?" Judge Hoffman received generally high ratings for his legal ability in civil cases, but what bothered lawyers most were the judge's temperamental characteristics. Only 12 percent and 13 percent of the lawyers, respectively, responded affirmatively when asked whether Judge Hoffman "demonstrates patience and a willingness to listen to all sides" and whether he is "impartially courteous toward lawyers and litigants." (To give some perspective on these figures, none of the other sitting judges received less than a 57 percent favorable rating as to patience or courtesy.) A majority of lawyers who expressed an opinion responded negatively when asked whether Judge Hoffman's decisions were uninfluenced by the identity of the parties before him or free of political, religious, racial, or other bias.

This critical view was subsequently corroborated by the Seventh Circuit Court of Appeals in reversing the Chicago Seven convictions. Judges rarely express open criticism of their judicial brethren; by the standards of judicial discourse, the Court of Appeals' comments about Judge Hoffman are extremely harsh. He is said to have displayed a "deprecating and often antagonistic attitude toward the defense," and, it is stated, his comments "were often touched with sarcasm, implying rather than saying outright that defense counsel was inept, bumptious or untrustworthy, or that his case lacked merit." Various specific instances are cited by the Court of Appeals:

> After a ruling on hearsay grounds, Mr. Kunstler [one of the lawyers for the defense] said in an attempt at argument, "I just don't understand it." The judge replied: "You will have to see a lawyer, Mr. Kunstler, if you don't understand it." . . . On occasion the judge resorted to ridicule. When Mr. Weinglass [another defense lawyer], on cross-examination, suggested the witness and he "explore" areas of disagreement, there was an objection and the judge said: "No. We are not at the North Pole. We are not going exploring, Mr. Weinglass." [4]

A second judge who received overwhelmingly negative responses in the council's poll was James B. Parsons. Over two-thirds of the lawyers responding said that he lacked the ability to fully appreciate and properly rule upon legal issues prior to or in the trial of civil or criminal cases. Over 80 percent said he lacked the legal ability to appreciate and properly rule upon complex or highly technical matters—which make up a substantial portion of the federal-court workload. Overwhelming percentages of lawyers responded negatively to questions dealing with such basics as whether he convened court with reasonable punctuality, devoted a reasonable portion of the working day to court proceedings, or acted on legal matters with reasonable promptness.

Descriptions of Judge Parsons' extraordinary judicial behavior—long a staple in conversations among Chicago trial lawyers—have recently begun to appear publicly. For example, according to Joseph Goulden's *The Benchwarmers*, the following transpired one evening in a case involving railroads:

> On and on he [Judge Parsons] talked, for a full half-hour, oblivious to the incredulous expressions, half-hidden yawns, and gradually glazing eyes of the listeners. The economics of railroads. The social significance of railroads. Parsons seemed prepared to talk all night—"in pure gibberish," in the words of one of the lawyers there.
>
> Then in mid-sentence he paused and stifled a burp. He sipped from a glass of water, and looked down at the lawyers. "Well, gentlemen, since most of our business seems to be at an end, why don't we adjourn and go home?" With a great gathering and flapping of his black robes, Parsons vanished into his chambers.
>
> The Honorable James B. Parsons, the lawyers judged when he was gone, had appeared to preside over court while stone-eyed drunk.[5]

Judge William J. Lynch also received overwhelmingly negative responses. About 65 percent of the lawyers expressed the view that he should not continue in office. A majority found him lacking in legal ability and a very substantial majority believed that he could not appreciate and rule correctly on complex or highly technical issues. Large majorities also said his decisions were not free of bias or uninfluenced by the identity of the parties before him, and about 80 percent responded negatively to the question "Do you believe that his decisions are not susceptible to influence by direct or indirect solicitation or approach of any nature?" The "influence" to which respondents are probably referring is that of the Chicago Democratic machine. Judge Lynch is the former law partner of Chicago mayor Richard J. Daley and his ties to the mayor and the machine continue to be extremely close. The Chicago press reported in 1974 that the judge's personal fortune, estimated at $2.5 million and derived to a large extent from profits on race track stock, will be left to the mayor's wife and children pursuant to "a gentlemen's agreement between the mayor and the judge." According to one prominent independent political activist in Chicago, Judge Lynch "makes automatic rulings in favor of the political establishment."[6]

The results of this survey might understandably lead a layman to ask, "Why are these judges allowed to remain?" During the Chicago Seven trial, newspapermen, incredulous at Judge Hoffman's behavior, frequently asked Chicago lawyers this question. The answer is twofold.

First, it is of course very difficult to remove a sitting federal judge. Federal judges serve for life "during good behavior." Currently the only mechanism for removing them is by impeachment—which is only slightly less cumbersome for judges than for presidents. Yet even granting this difficulty, one must recognize that there is a second factor at work: the bar hasn't really tried. On the contrary, even in the seemingly most indefensible case, bar leaders nearly automatically defend judges against any criticism. At the time of the Chicago Seven trial, the president of the Illinois State Bar Association issued a public statement extensively criticizing the conduct of the defendants and their attorneys in the case—and saying nothing at all about the behavior of the judge.[7]

What accounts for this silence of lawyers? One reason sometimes given is simply belief in the long-standing tradition—in part imposed by the Canons of Ethics—of the bar defending the judiciary against public attack. Representatives of the Chicago Council of Lawyers and the Illinois State Bar Association once appeared together on a radio program on which the council representative talked bluntly about the inadequacies of certain judges. After the program the bar-association leader approached the council representative and said he agreed with much of what had been said, but, he added, "You shouldn't say such things on the radio."

The Ethical Considerations set forth in the ABA's *Code of Professional Responsibility* state that "adjudicatory officials, not being wholly free to defend themselves, are entitled to receive the support of the bar against unjust criticism." But, of course, the key word here is *unjust.* The code itself states that "a lawyer, as a citizen, has a right to criticize such officials publicly" and the United States Supreme Court has said that "courts are not, and should not be, immune to such criticism." [8] Indeed, the code imposes a general duty upon lawyers "to assist in improving the legal system," and in practical terms that may well mean that lawyers have an *obligation* in particular circumstances to criticize judges.

The real reason for lawyers' silence lies primarily where one might expect: in lawyers' own interests. This is not an interest in having incompetent judges on the bench. To be sure, some lawyers may benefit from "cronyism" with bad judges, but on the whole lawyers would like to have competent judges. The self-interest inhibiting lawyers is simply fear of the consequences of criticizing a bad judge. Lawyers who know the judge best are the ones who practice frequently before him—and are, therefore, precisely the same lawyers who have the most to fear in being critical. Even a lawyer who does not himself practice before a particular judge may have partners who do so or clients who may come before him.

Yet even this is not the entire answer. To some extent these individual fears could be alleviated by acting through bar associations so that there would be a degree of "safety in numbers." In the case of bar associations, however, one runs up against what might be described as the "political factor." Bar-association hierarchies tend to attract the kind of lawyers likely to have a variety of other political involvements. To be successful in a bar association, after all, requires basically political skills and temperament, and lawyers so inclined are unlikely to have limited their scope to a single organization. "Bar association types" are the kind of people likely to know powerful political figures of all parties; they are ultimately members of the "party of the establishment." In associations dominated by such men, the same political forces which put judges on the bench in the first place operate to protect them, whatever their faults, once they are there. To put the matter in more concrete terms: It is hard to imagine that the Chicago Bar Association will ever be in the forefront of efforts to remove a former law partner of Mayor Daley from the federal bench.

To the extent that there is pressure to remove "bad judges," it may come less from the organized bar than from other sitting judges. It should be remembered that only three of the thirteen Chicago judges in the council's poll received such overwhelmingly negative responses. The competent judges, on the whole, welcome public appraisal of their own and their colleagues' judicial performance. Several court of appeals judges have urged the council to conduct an updated survey.[9] There is said to be "reliable evidence" that at least two fellow judges have urged Judge Parsons to retire,[10] but the other judges have no power to compel such retirement.

The near-impossibility of removing a sitting federal judge from office makes especially crucial the character of the original appointment process.

As a practical matter, federal district judges are appointed by the senior senator of the president's party from the state involved. Thus, in Chicago we have what might be described as "Everett Dirksen judges" from the Eisenhower years (all but one of whom were on "senior" status at the time of the council's poll), "Paul Douglas judges" from the Kennedy-Johnson years, and "Charles Percy judges" under Nixon.

Only two "Percy judges" were on the bench at the time of the council's 1971 poll and both received over 90 percent favorable responses.

A Chicago writer recently attempted to "update" the council's poll by interviewing Chicago lawyers about the more recent Percy appointments. His conclusion was that of the six Percy appointments to the district court, all but one rank very high in the opinion of the bar.[11] Senator Percy has also made a number of appointments to the Seventh Circuit Court of Appeals of extremely high quality. Some credit for the quality of the "Percy appointments" goes to the American Bar Association's Committee on the Federal Judiciary, whose member from the seventh circuit during most of the Percy years was a lawyer of exceptional conscientiousness and independence. The Chicago Council of Lawyers also played a role in evaluating potential nominees for Senator Percy.

But Senator Percy, as others before him, could have ignored such organizations or, in the case of the ABA committee, found candidates who met its lowest rather than its highest standards (and its low standards are very low—namely, G. Harrold Carswell). He did not, for reasons which probably include both personal conviction and a desire to project a political image of competence and integrity. Senator Percy, a Republican, recently went so far as to appoint an exceptionally well qualified Democrat—Prentice Marshall, a professor at the University of Illinois Law School—to the federal district court in Chicago. It is testimony to the generally political character of federal judicial appointments that this action was attacked openly by some Illinois Republican leaders as an example of gross party disloyalty on the part of their senator.

The "Douglas judges," as measured by the council's poll, have a more mixed record. They include several who rank very highly but others (Judges Bernard M. Decker and Abraham L. Marovitz) who are more marginal and two (Judges Parsons and Lynch, discussed earlier) who rank at the very bottom. That may surprise those who know Paul Douglas as a distinguished Senate crusader for causes such as civil rights and consumer protection. The explanation lies in the fact that these are less "Douglas judges" than "Daley judges." For example, one (Judge Lynch) is a former Daley law partner and another (Judge Marovitz) a long-time Daley political associate who even after becoming a federal judge has continued his practice of always spending election night with the mayor. The "deal" Douglas made, at least tacitly, for continued Daley organization support had one basic element: no interference with local Democratic politics, and federal judicial appointments were regarded as local Democratic politics. As one local commentator has put it, Douglas "was content to abandon the matter to the machine and restrict his own good works to Washington." [12] Friends of Senator Douglas have also explained that he had a long-standing contempt for lawyers and the legal profession, and simply did not consider judicial appointments very important.

If a Democrat is elected president in 1976 or 1980, what will the "Adlai Stevenson judges" be like? No one really knows. Hopefully there will not simply be more "Daley judges," though that possibility may depend on Senator Stevenson's position at the time vis-á-vis the Chicago Democratic machine. It is on those kinds of considerations—and in part on accidents of senatorial personality—that the quality of the lower federal judiciary currently depends.

Is there a better way? The answer in part turns on the question of whether it is possible to identify, in advance, the qualities which will make a candidate a good federal judge. Particular political connections are neither a plus or minus in making such determinations. For example, two close Daley associates (Lynch and Marovitz) rank poorly in the council's poll, but two others who became federal judges largely because of Daley connections (Hubert L. Will and Richard B. Austin) rank very highly. The difference is that Will and Austin, in addition to their political connections, had—and I believe any reasonable person could see that they had—substantial additional qualifications for the bench which were lacking in Lynch and Marovitz. Mayor Daley could not be expected to see these differences, but independent outsiders could do so without much difficulty.

The problem is that there is no formal screening structure at the local level which requires such an independent evaluation; there is no tradition of local bar associations, which are in the best position to know about potential candidates, filling the formal gap with vigorous efforts of their own. Indeed, some of the same reasons which inhibit criticism of a judge once he is on the bench operate to deter a tough-minded evaluation even of a prospective nominee. He may, after all, be appointed anyway and lawyers will have to appear before him. He must be supported by strong political forces or his name would not be under consideration. Thus, it is extremely rare, almost unthinkable, for a local bar association to publicly oppose a proposed nominee for the federal bench.[13] Indeed, it is unusual for a local bar association even to express opposition privately, prior to a nomination. The ABA's Committee on the Federal Judiciary may be of some value in opposing a bad nominee, but it operates more as a "last ditch" defense against utter incompetence than as an active proponent of high-caliber nominees, as John MacKenzie has earlier explained. And the committee's structure of a single member from each judicial circuit, who consequently has enormous influence, makes it vulnerable to the vagaries of ABA internal politics and personalities as they affect the choice of its members.

In its consideration of prospective judicial nominees, the Chicago Council of Lawyers has sometimes found itself in the position of refusing to endorse a candidate supported by all other local bar groups and also acceptable to the ABA. In these circumstances it is not uncommon to begin to receive pressure from the potential nominee or his friends. Often the question they ask is: What makes him unqualified? But that question misstates, by implication, the true purpose of judicial selection. If one accepts any proposed nominee who is *not unqualified*—i.e., no real reason why he should *not* be appointed has been discovered—one will end up with a mediocre bench and indeed with some very bad judges. In every case where the Chicago Council has been "wrong"—i.e., where it has supported a nominee who has not turned out to be a very good judge—it was because we fell into applying the "not-unqualified" standard. But to be a federal judge requires an exceptional degree of legal ability, character, independence, and judicial temperament. The question to be asked is whether a potential nominee has demonstrated that he or she has this mix of exceptional qualities. If the prospective nominee does not, then the mere fact that he or she seems to be a decent person, about whom no one has anything really bad to say, is not enough.

Chicago has been lucky in recent years to have a senator generally prepared to adhere to high standards in judicial selection. But bar associations need not be dependent upon senatorial good will. Typically powerful and well-connected, bar-association leaders are not the kind of persons whom any politically astute and ambitious senator wants arrayed against him. Consequently, if they possessed the *will* to do so, bar associations could do much to insist that high-quality judges be appointed and that bad ones be removed when necessary.

It is unrealistic to expect that politicians will, as a general rule, not be political—that they will not want to reward old friends and make new ones, placate existing constituencies and appeal to emerging forces. Federal judicial appointments, as long as they are made by senators and presidents, will remain part of this political process. The question is whether other forces will insist that standards of intellectual ability, temperament, and independence must nevertheless be met. It is doubtful if there is any magic institutional framework for the assertion of such standards which would be likely to prevail in the absence of strong and sustained support from the local bar. One might, for example, set up some sort of federal screening commission to nominate federal judges, which would be independent of the current ABA apparatus. But in the end the local bar would be likely to have substantial influence in determining who would be on the screening commission and in determining what attitude its members would be likely to adopt when faced with the inevitable pressures of party politics, friendships, and vocal constituencies. It is doubtful if such institutional changes would be needed if the local bar were willing to commit itself to judicial excellence. In the end the legal profession probably gets the judges it deserves.

Senator John V. Tunney
*& Jane Lakes Frank**

Epilogue: A Congressional Role in Lawyer Reform?

ARE VULNERABLE citizens confronted by the compounding perils of bankruptcy, domestic disintegration, tax delinquency, fraud, or accident liability any less handicapped than victims of disease? Are they any less in need of crucial professional services at a reasonable cost which do not add to the tragedy? For want of a caring lawyer, the delicate fabric of mental health or family tranquility can be destroyed as ruthlessly as by cancer.

Without lawyers our institutions of justice are rudderless hulls, crucial processes of representation and of redress cannot occur, and the law fails to be the equal protector of citizens against predatory government and predatory corporations. Yet legal care, like medical care, is rationed through a crude marketing system primarily to the wealthy and privileged, which is a festering source of anger and injustice. Public disillusionment and cynicism about a system in which some are clearly more equal than others can only be accelerated when many of those trained and able to render needed services to citizens appear more interested in their own pocketbooks. So it is understandable that an aroused public is beginning to demand access to justice—at a minimum, a competent lawyer at a reasonable cost.

In May 1973 the Senate Subcommittee on Representation of Citizen Interests (now merged in the Senate Subcommittee on Constitutional Rights) was established to undertake the Congress's first comprehensive study of the adequacy of legal care. We have probed such soft spots as high legal fees and long-standing bar association practices that keep them

* SENATOR JOHN V. TUNNEY (D.-CALIF.) IS THE CHAIRMAN OF THE JUDICIARY COMMITTEE'S SUBCOMMITTEE ON CONSTITUTIONAL RIGHTS. JANE LAKES FRANK IS THE SUBCOMMITTEE'S CHIEF COUNSEL.

high, government programs which reap bonanzas for some lawyers at taxpayer expense, and bar association attempts to block progress in prepaid legal plans, the use of paralegals, legal clinics, and other new delivery systems—all ways to lower legal costs. Based on the subcommittee's findings, we will in this article assess the scope of federal jurisdiction to regulate lawyers, the failures of the current federal policy, and the options for a more significant federal presence in the future.

Although one state bar president repeatedly accused the subcommittee of encroaching upon a "free and fearless profession," he overlooked the fact that the federal government has long recognized its jurisdiction to regulate lawyers. Subcommittee witnesses alternately bemoaned or exalted the vast subject matter covered by ever-increasing numbers of federal laws, some of which contain "citizen suit" provisions granting rights to sue to enforce them. Such rights are meaningless unless lawyers are there to help, and in recognition of this fact, thirty laws provide that courts may award attorneys' fees to the prevailing plaintiff in a suit against the government.[1] Until precluded by the *Alyeska* decision,[2] courts were using their equity powers to award attorneys' fees when necessary to achieve congressional policy underlying certain federal laws. Some federal statutes, moreover, contain limits on attorneys' fees.

The complex network of federal courts, established under Article III of the Constitution, have authority to admit lawyers to practice before them, to discipline those lawyers, and to require lawyers to observe Federal Rules of Criminal and Civil Procedure. The Supreme Court has declared a constitutional right to counsel for suspected persons taken into custody.[3] While the Court has not gone this far in the civil area, an increasing number of cases have derived certain rights to legal services from First and Fourteenth Amendment guarantees. In four recent decisions, the Court has declared a First Amendment right of groups to provide legal services as an incident of membership.[4]

To effect congressional policy in the 1964 Economic Opportunity Act and to meet court-mandated rights, the federal government directly subsidized a small corps of attorneys who serve the poor. In addition, the Criminal Justice Act of 1964 funds public defenders and provides hourly stipends to members of the bar who represent indigents accused of crimes.

The president of the State Bar of Texas, a witness at our hearing on the organized bar, commented that the whole idea that the profession which is counsel and advocate on men's lives, liberties and properties is engaged in mere trade and commerce which should be controlled under the federal antitrust laws is an intellectually moth-bitten concept which should be scorned by lawyers and the courts.[5]

Fortunately, however, after years of looking the other way, the Antitrust Division of the Department of Justice has finally made clear that activities involving the economics of professional law practice are subject to regulation under the antitrust laws. This view was vindicated in June 1975 when a unanimous Supreme Court held that bar association minimum-fee schedules are "a classic illustration of price-fixing."[6]

Despite this overwhelming evidence of jurisdiction, actual federal regulation of lawyers has been limited and sporadic—usually only as an afterthought to granting new rights under federal law. The profession itself—to which more than two-thirds of the Senate, one-half of the House of Representatives, and 40,000 members of the executive branch belong—has resisted external scrutiny, contending that self-regulation is perfectly adequate. Beyond this, congressional committees have traditionally exercised primary jurisdiction over substantive areas (like housing or environment or civil rights) and only secondary, uncoordinated jurisdiction over the need for legal services to enforce these substantive guarantees. Until the Subcommittee on Representation of Citizen Interests was established, no federal agency or congressional committee had, as its primary mission, the regulation or oversight of the legal profession.[7]

The result has been a federal policy of "benign neglect." Virtually exclusive control over lawyers' conduct remains vested in the American Bar Association and a network of state and local bar associations that promulgate rules of professional conduct for lawyers as well as standards for accreditation of law schools, admission to practice, and disciplinary procedures. This situation would be tolerable (and, indeed, preferable to an increased federal role) if the profession could manage, by itself, to meet the public's needs for legal services. But experience has shown that it cannot.

While law school enrollments have increased 50 percent in the last five years and the number of lawyers is expected to perhaps double within ten years, more and more lawyers are concentrating in group practice in large city firms serving primarily business and corporate interests.[8] Too few lawyers provide legal services to the poor and the middle-income citizen; subcommittee hearings on legal fees provided substantial evidence that because of the high cost of lawyers, Americans are deterred from obtaining needed legal counsel.[9] Witnesses characterized the average home-buyer as feeling that "law and legal process work against him as often as for him, and that the costs of his legal remedies often exceed the benefits." [10]

Equally serious, witness after witness complained that lawyers are usually consulted only after trouble develops. Testimony indicated that because access to lawyers is difficult and fees are high, preventive counseling is seldom used by the average citizen, who often enters into major transactions, such as buying a house or signing a lease, unaware of the legal implications and complications of the arrangement. Having foresaken the ounce of prevention, consumers may often end up paying high sums for a legal cure.

Worse, studies and testimony show that citizens are often unaware of the procedural opportunities or remedies available to them. They may have rights to appear and be heard in public hearings preliminary to some federal rulemaking, but few understand the implications of these hearings or avail themselves of lawyers to aid them.[11] In areas of less immediate and more diffuse consequences to individuals—polluted air and water, inadequate treatment facilities in the county hospital, unsafe auto manufacturing standards—citizens feel unfairly burdened by legal expenses which a larger community should rightly share, and often are not adequately organized to pool resources to obtain representation.[12] Three days of legislative hearings on the Consumer Controversies Resolution Act[13] showed that even existing redress mechanisms not requiring the use of lawyers (for example, many small claims courts) are most frequently used by credit agencies and other businesses against citizens; indigent and even middle-income defendants often have little or no understanding of their procedural rights and the basic elements of their defense.

New federal programs should proceed on two fronts: first, to reduce the need for lawyers in routine transactions, and, second, to lower the costs and increase the availability of essential lawyer services.

Reducing the need for lawyers in routine transactions: A federal role here could have both positive (incentive) and negative (regulatory) aspects. On the positive side, we need far more intensive citizen education about the law, including such elementary issues as how to read a standard contract, when a lawyer is needed and how to find one, and how to secure redress without a lawyer. With this help, the average citizen should be able to avoid some pitfalls, to employ self-help in many situations, and also to recognize when a lawyer's advice is really needed. Some law-related education courses are now being offered in high schools and community colleges; the State Bar of California has received a Law Enforcement Assistance Administration (LEAA) grant to implement a program called Law in a Free Society which provides casebooks and curricula for secondary schools. In addition, publications like the Washington Urban League's *Small Claims Court: Make It Work for You* have been distributed to help the average citizen cope without a lawyer. Federal funding may prove necessary to give these projects their proper prominence.

Federal funds should also be used to stimulate states to develop and improve systems of consumer redress that are accessible, quick, inexpensive, and in most cases usable without the aid of lawyers. Such redress mechanisms include small claims courts which are located in neighborhoods and remain open at night and on weekends, informal business procedures such as money-back guarantees and consumer-complaint divisions, conciliation services, mediation, and arbitration. These procedures are especially useful when a small amount of money is at issue—as in the price of a defective product, a default on an installment contract, or a repair cost. The Consumer Controversies Resolution Act would provide $15 million over a two-year period in matching federal grants to states and local jurisdictions with satisfactory consumer-redress plans.[14] If consumer interests are to be represented in the grievance process, more and better mechanisms for redress have to be structured so that consumers can represent themselves.

The federal government should encourage the use of nonlegal and paralegal personnel to provide counsel in routine transactions where costly lawyers' help is unnecessary. The citizen interests subcommittee pinpointed workmen's compensation as an especially appropriate area. Our hearings revealed how ten Kentucky lawyers in 1973 were each awarded fees from $100,000 to $1,008,000 under the Black Lung Benefits Act of 1972 for securing black-lung benefits for miners—fees ultimately paid by the federal taxpayer. The work involved helping miners complete unnecessarily complex forms, scheduling medical check-ups, and attending hearings to gain approval of claims (and, sometimes, subsequent hearings to ensure the award of legal fees!). Miners needed only to prove that they were employed when they contracted black-lung disease in order to receive lifetime benefits according to a fixed schedule. Issues occasionally arose as to whether a miner was actually employed or over medical claims. Most of these problems, however, could have been solved by a knowledgeable paralegal familiar with the legislation. Lawyers' skills were rarely needed, and a far less expensive program can easily be undertaken to train and perhaps to fund paralegals or others to process miners' claims.

Standardization and simplification of ordinary transactions, as well, can reduce or eliminate the need for certain types of legal assistance. It is less costly to prevent a controversy than to resolve it; numerous controversies resulting from everyday transactions could be prevented if the documents on which they were based contained understandable, uniform provisions. A federal role is essential: to encourage private efforts to simplify and standardize; to prepare model contracts for retail installment payments, insurance policies, sales contracts, and finance charges; to provide federal funds as an incentive to states that adopt these uniform practices; and, if necessary, to require that transactions affecting interstate commerce or involving the use of federal funds (like FHA mortgages) utilize uniform contracts. Uniform provisions where justified have long been required by the Securities and Exchange Commission, and the approach can logically be extended to contracts to purchase cars and to borrow money.

One appropriate way to simplify the law and thus decrease the need for lawyers is to eliminate the fault concept when it serves to further neither justice nor efficiency in the allocation of responsibility. "No fault" automobile accident insurance has been adopted by many states, and minimum standards recently passed by the Senate should be enacted at the federal level. The same notion is being applied to divorce in some states such as California.

Lowering the cost of essential lawyer services: The federal government can, in this area, again have both positive and negative roles in lowering the cost of lawyer services. In hearings, studies, and reports, the subcommittee publicized recent developments in the low-cost delivery of legal services—including increased use of computers, standardized client interview forms, and nonlegal or paralegal personnel—and the obstacles to these developments. These practices reduce the time lawyers must spend on individual cases, and allow "wholesaling," in contrast to "retailing," of legal services. In a legal clinic, for example, a lawyer is able to review in a concentrated period of time a large number of standardized client forms for application to a particular subject area like bankruptcy. Research and expertise can be applied to all of these cases generally, and they can be handled far more quickly and more cheaply than individual cases.

Related to the wholesaling of legal services is the trend toward specialization of lawyers, a trend which merits support *if,* and only if, any cost savings are passed on to the consumer. The model of the lawyer-generalist equipped to handle any and all tasks has long been an anachronism. As laws and regulations become more complex, it becomes clearer that the legal jack-of-all-trades is increasingly the master of none. Since it takes certified lawyer-specialists far less time to handle cases in their field, some states and the American Bar Association claim that they can perform work with greater competence and at less expense. The California State Bar has recently begun certifying specialists in three fields—criminal law, workmen's compensation law, and tax law—and has also begun permitting these specialists to advertise their specialties in the Yellow Pages. Other states are developing their own specialization programs, as Jerome Hochberg earlier described.

New financing mechanisms have also decreased the amount that the individual citizen with a substantial legal problem must pay. Prepaid legal plans, given new impetus by Congress's recent amendment of the Taft-Hartley Act,[15] permit the burden of legal fees to be shared by all members of the labor union or group. The federal government could force down lawyers' fees more directly. As mentioned earlier, the federal government now reviews and limits lawyers' fees involved in securing benefits under thirty federal laws. Restrictions on fees should not be so severe as to deter lawyers from representing citizens, but they should control excessive fees charged for securing federal rights.

The delivery of lawyer services to needy citizens is already partially subsidized by the federal government, though new ways are now necessary. Partial subsidies might also be provided, as they are in England, directly to lawyers who represent middle- or lower-middle-income clients at less than market rates. Various forms of "Judicare" have been studied by the ABA, but Congress must now take its own look, as it must also evaluate indirect subsidies by means of tax incentives. Attorneys might be allowed a charitable deduction for the value of services they provide to the needy without cost or at less than a fair market rate. A taxpayer's donations of money or property can already be deducted, and it has been forcefully argued that donations of professional time and talent should be treated in the same fashion.[16] Abuses could be avoided by subjecting the services rendered to an objective federal evaluation before allowing the deduction and by requiring that recipients of the services be charitable organizations.

A more severe approach is to compel all attorneys, as a condition of practice before the federal courts, to render a certain amount of their services or a certain percentage of their income to *pro bono* activities. Legislation in this area is reasonably related to the purpose of admission to practice before the federal courts, and is likely to be upheld as constitutional. In our view, arguments that it would be hard to enforce and might dilute both the commitment and the competence of lawyers who represent the poor are not persuasive, although former ABA president Chesterfield Smith's alternative of an adequate program of *pro bono* service sponsored by bar associations seems preferable—if it works.[17]

The federal government may have to intervene to change restrictive bar association rules that limit advertising and solicitation by lawyers and legal services by non-lawyers. Several Justice Department antitrust officials have suggested that these restrictions raise antitrust problems, and that the entire system should be revised.[18] Instead of prohibiting advertising unless narrowly defined conditions are met, the Antitrust Division would permit it unless fraudulent or misleading—the standards applied now by the Federal Trade Commission to general advertising. In our view, more price information must become available if we are ever to lower artificially inflated fees, and revision of the advertising rules (preferably, by bar associations themselves) is essential.

Aside from the requirements of the antitrust laws, new federal legislation has been suggested to regulate directly the practices of the organized bar. Such legislation might preempt bar association restrictions on advertising, solicitation, unauthorized practice, and the use of voluntary minimum fee schedules. Already the pension reform legislation does preempt bar rules restricting the "form or substance" of labor union prepaid plans. New legislation also might establish standards for conflicts-of-interest, including, for example, a requirement that lawyers on bar association committees or acting in a formal or informal capacity before or as members of public interest groups disclose their clients who stand to benefit from such activities. Legislation might also specify disciplinary standards to be enforced against lawyers by the courts, the organized bar, or new agencies.

Subcommittee hearings underscored two disparate functions of the organized bar: One evolves from its responsibility to the public for setting standards for admission to practice and disciplining lawyers; the other evolves from its responsibility to its members as a private trade association. Federal regulation would affect primarily the first function and might suggest that the organized bar divide itself into two parts: a public part and a trade association part. This division would go a long way to eliminate the tension—the battle over no-fault auto insurance is a good example—between representing public interests and private interests simultaneously.

We have been focusing primarily on essential legal care to aid citizens in their daily transactions. But it is clear that all of the remedies we have discussed, taken together, would not assure adequate representation of the more generalized public interests. We acknowledge enormous definitional problems here: What public? What interest? Who can legitimately represent it? How?

Beyond these remedies and definitional problems, public interest law has become an essential ingredient for delivering justice. It is a branch of law with some common themes: 1. the issues involved are of extreme importance; 2. final judgment in the cases will affect not only the named plaintiffs but also a substantial element of the public; and 3. the litigation can be started only by private plaintiffs rather than the government.[19] But as Charles Halpern discussed earlier, the public interest bar faces a financial bind. Foundations are now warning that they will not subsidize public interest law indefinitely. Nor is the marketplace a likely source: There will always be important legal issues that have no fee potential because an individual's economic interest in the matter—hikers and canoeists who want to prevent construction of a dam which will destroy a wild river—is simply too small to justify retaining a lawyer.

One promising alternative is court awards of attorneys' fees to the prevailing party in public interest litigation, to be paid by the losing party—in many instances the government. Before the *Alyeska* decision restricted such awards, the courts increasingly used their equity powers to award fees in cases involving such diverse issues as school desegregation,[20] privacy,[21] union democracy,[22] highway relocation,[23] and buying a home.[24] The citizen interests subcommittee held two days of hearings in the fall of 1973 on this issue, learning that new legislation was needed to assure uniformity and consistency in fee awards for public interest advocacy. A woman attorney testified at our hearings that she was awarded a fee of $25 per hour by a federal district court judge, while a male attorney, who argued a less complex case after hers, received an award of about $80 per hour. Without guidelines, a judge is able to discriminate between attorneys not only on grounds of sex but also of ideology. In light of

Alyeska, such legislation has become essential, and numerous bills have been introduced. In designing the statute, a number of issues must be evaluated. Should all public interest cases in federal courts be covered? How should those cases be defined? What should be the precise criteria for awarding fees and determining their amount? Should fees ever be awarded to a defendant? Under what circumstances?

Many reforms could stimulate or compel the legal profession to devote more talent, time, and other resources to representing those in need. Some changes have occurred and more are expected from voluntary reform by bar associations and by individual lawyers themselves. ABA president James Fellers recognized the bar's obligations in this discussion of Canon 2 of the ABA *Code of Professional Responsibility:*

> Under Canon 2 . . . it is the obligation, not only of the American Bar Association and of state and local bar associations but also of every member of the bar to "assist the legal profession in fulfilling its duty to make legal counsel available." This language admonishes all lawyers to work together in fulfilling this obligation.[25]

But experience shows that these changes may well be insufficient to meet the needs. At the turn of the century the nation's meatpackers were pleading for an opportunity to excise the evils portrayed in Upton Sinclair's *The Jungle* through self-regulation. Similarly, in the throes of the economic and moral collapse of the stockmarket, the securities industry in 1933 begged for time to clean its own house, as did the automobile industry in 1966, responding finally to outrage at the carnage on the nation's highways. Each supplicant to Congress failed miserably to respond to its own challenge of self-regulation, and Congress relieved each in turn of the opportunity for continued failure. Congress is still heeding the legal profession's pleas for voluntarism. But time has about run out.

Notes

Notes

GREEN: The ABA as Trade Association

1. *2 Reports of the ABA* 69 (1878).
2. Jaworski, "The American Bar Association: A Quasi-Public Institution," *58 ABA J.* 917 (1972).
3. C. Rhyne, ABA president, "The Role of the Lawyer in Legislative Affairs," speech delivered Oct. 3, 1958, in Portland, Maine, before the Conference on National Legislation.
4. Brockman, "Laissez-Faire Theory in the Early American Bar Association," *39 Notre Dame L. Rev.* 270, 274 (1964).
5. 57 *ABA Reports* 397–400 (1932); 61 *ABA Reports* 864, 874 (1936); "ABA Trains Usual Barrage on New Deal, Then Covers Up with Own Court Reform Plan," *Newsweek*, Aug. 8, 1938, at 18; "Government of Lawyers," *Nation*, Oct. 9, 1937, at 366.
6. "The Lawyers' Loyalty Oath," *37 ABA J.* 128 (1951).
7. "Communism," *35 ABA J.* 574 (1949).
8. 78 *ABA Reports* 263–64 (1953); see more recently *Committee and Section Reports to the House of Delegates,* Paper No. 145, Aug. 14–17 (1972).
9. Berman, "Voice of the American Bar," *Nation*, March 21, 1959, at 247.
10. *Committee and Section Reports to the House of Delegates,* Report No. 12a (1972).
11. See generally Hirschberg, "Transportation Report/ Congress to Consider Radical Cures for Auto Insurance Ills," *National Journal*, July 4, 1970, at 1409, 1411; *Washington Post*, May 14, 1971, at 2; remarks of Senator Philip Hart, 117 *Congressional Record*, S 3741 (Feb. 24, 1971); Frank, "Washington Pressures/ Ponderous, Public Oriented American Bar Association Has an Image Crisis," *National Journal*, March 4, 1972, at 387.
12. For the specific arguments *pro*, see Bittker, "Genocide Revisited," *56 ABA J.* 71 (1970); Goldberg and Gardner, "Fine to Act on the Genocide Convention," *58 ABA J.* 141 (1972); and *contra*, Philips and Deutsch, "Pitfalls of the Genocide Convention," *56 ABA J.* 641 (1970).
13. Powell, "The President's Page," *51 ABA J.* 101 (1965).
14. See V. Countryman and T. Finman, *The Lawyer in Modern Society* (Boston: Little, Brown, 1966), at 514–15.

TUCKER: *Pro Bono ABA?*

1. G. Martin, *Causes and Conflicts: The Centennial History of the Association of the Bar of the City of New York, 1870–1970* (Boston: Houghton, Mifflin, 1970), at 37–38.
2. E. Johnson, *Justice and Reform: The Formative Years of the OEO Legal Services Program* (New York: Russell Sage Foundation, 1974), at 7.
3. R. H. Smith, *Justice and the Poor* (New York: Carnegie Foundation, 1919).
4. Johnson, *supra* note 2, at 9.
5. Cahn and Cahn, "The War on Poverty: A Civilian Perspective," *73 Yale L. J.* 1317 (1964).
6. These understandings included a promise by OEO that the ABA could participate on a permanent legal services advisory committee which would provide policy guidance to OEO.
7. Johnson, *supra* note 2, at 64.
8. Address to Bar Association of Baltimore City, Dec. 15, 1965.
9. Headed by former New Jersey governor Richard J. Hughes, the twenty-four-member commission was established in 1971 as an action-oriented body to study existing problems and develop programs to help solve them. It has received more than half a million dollars annually in funding from public and private sources to run seven national projects dealing with problems such as employment restrictions, model standards for correctional institutions, and providing research and information for lawyers working in the field.
10. Initiated in 1970 to educate the youth of the nation to the medical and legal aspects of drugs and their abuse, the committee has involved about 400,000 junior and senior high school students and is funded by a $160,000 grant from the Law Enforcement Assistance Administration of the Department of Justice.
11. In January 1973, the ABA Young Lawyers Section entered into a joint agreement with the White House Office of Emergency Preparedness to provide specially trained local lawyers in fifty states to dispense voluntary legal aid following a major disaster.

12. The committee, created in 1967, is designed to consider the need for revising laws and legal procedures as they relate to substandard housing in urban areas; to train minority lawyers in the complexities of federal, state, and local housing legislation; and to run nine pilot Lawyers for Housing programs which provide legal help to those seeking to utilize government housing programs. Each program has been funded for two years for more than $1,500,000 in public and private grants.

13. The $1 million special project of the Criminal Law Section was begun in 1964 to formulate minimum standards for the administration of criminal justice in both state and federal jurisdictions. It is responsible for developing seventeen sets of standards which have been adopted by the ABA. As of May 1973, two states had adopted most of the standards.

14. The Council on Legal Education Opportunity was launched in 1968 as a national program to increase the number of minority group lawyers in the legal profession. Thus far, CLEO has brought 500 minority lawyers into legal practice, with financial assistance totaling more than $2 million, exclusive of tuition and fees, which have been furnished by more than one hundred participating law schools.

15. The Consortium on Legal Services and the Public was created in 1972 to provide a continuing forum for the interchange of ideas between groups within the ABA, with the common goal of increasing legal representation for lower- and middle-income individuals. It is composed of the chairmen of six ABA committees and other members appointed by the ABA president. Committees represented include: Standing Committee on Lawyer Referral Service, Standing Committee on Legal Aid and Indigent Defendants, Standing Committee on Legal Assistance for Servicemen, Special Committee on Prepaid Legal Services, Special Committee to Survey Legal Needs, and Special Committee on *Pro Bono Publico* Activities.

16. Smith was no stranger to the Project. He was active on the Council of the Section on Individual Rights and Responsibilities at the Project's inception. He was largely responsible for its eventual acceptance by the ABA leadership.

17. *Code of Professional Responsibility*, Preamble and Preliminary Statement 1 (1970).

18. 18 U.S.C. 3006A.

19. Letter to Charles T. Duncan, Nov. 20, 1973.

20. Letter to Chief Judge Harold H. Greene, June 23, 1973.

21. *District of Columbia Bar* v. *Kirks*, Civil Action No. 449–74.

22. Statement of the District of Columbia Bar (Unified) as to the Public Service Obligations of Its Members, March 12, 1974.

23. R. F. Marks, K. Leswing, and B. Fortinsky, *The Lawyer, the Public and Professional Responsibility* (Chicago: American Bar Foundation, 1972), 291.

24. R. Pound, *The Lawyer from Antiquity to Modern Times* (St. Paul: West, 1953), at 5.

MACKENZIE: Of Judges and the ABA

1. "ABA" and the ABA's Standing Committee on the Federal Judiciary will be used interchangeably. The committee is virtually autonomous and is authorized to speak for the ABA.

2. A. L. Todd, *Justice on Trial: The Case of Louis D. Brandeis* (New York: Saturday Review Press, 1964), at 159 and chapter 7 generally.

3. Testimony of Bernard G. Segal, Feb. 15, 1966, before the Senate Subcommittee on Improvements in Judicial Machinery inquiring into "Judicial Fitness."

4. Letter to the Editor, *Washington Post*, June 22, 1973, at A-23.

5. The committee members for 1974–75 were John A. Sutro, San Francisco, chairman and member-at-large; Gael Mahony, Boston; Albert R. Connelly, New York; Robert M. Landis, Philadelphia; Norman P. Ramsey, Baltimore; Sherwood W. Wise, Jackson, Miss.; Joseph E. Stopher, Louisville; Don H. Reuben, Chicago; Richard E. Kyle, St. Paul; DeWitt Williams, Seattle; John R. Couch, Oklahoma City; and Charles A. Horsky, Washington, D.C.

6. *Washington Post*, Aug. 11, 1969, at 1.

7. Mr. Nixon's language is quoted nearly verbatim in the author's profile of Warren E. Burger in IV *Justices of the United States Supreme Court* 3114–3121 (1975).

8. The ABA reports usually are printed in the early pages of the Senate Judiciary Committee's printed confirmation hearings for each nominee.

9. Text of the speech is excerpted in *Hearings on the Nomination of George Harrold Carswell*, 91st Cong., 2d sess. (1970), at 21.

10. *Id.*, at 11–12.
11. *Id.*, at 13.
12. *Id.*, at 32.
13. *Id.*, at 68.
14. *Id.*, at 70.
15. *Washington Post*, Feb. 22, 1970, at 2.
16. IV *Justices of the United States Supreme Court* 3118 (1975).
17. Mitchell is said to have suggested at the White House meeting that the ABA would disapprove Senator Robert C. Byrd (D-W.Va.) if the president chose him. Mr. Nixon is reported to have replied, "Fuck the ABA." I resort to hearsay for this footnote. The best evidence may be on a White House tape recording.
18. *Washington Post*, Oct. 18, 1971, at 3.
19. For purposes of this discussion, a good summary of the Walsh ITT role is contained in P. Hoffman, *Lions in the Street* (New York: Saturday Review Press, 1973). It must be noted that the entire story has yet to be laid out in full. Kleindienst subsequently admitted that despite his testimony at his own Senate confirmation hearings, President Nixon and others in the White House did in fact interfere with the objective handling of the ITT antitrust case.
20. The memorandum, released by the Chamber of Commerce of the United States in 1972, was quoted extensively in the Jack Anderson column, *Washington Post*, Sept. 28, 1972, at B-11.

GARBUS & SELIGMAN: Sanctions and Disbarment: They Sit in Judgment

1. Marks and Cathcart, "Discipline Within the Legal Profession: Is It Self-Regulation?", Univ. of Ill. L.F. No. 2, 1974. See also "The Public Is Banging at the Door," *Juris Doctor*, Oct. 1973, at 21.
2. J. Carlin, *Lawyers' Ethics* (New York: Russell Sage, 1966).
3. Marks and Cathcart, *supra* note 1.
4. *American Bar Association Special Committee on Evaluation of Disciplinary Enforcement, Problems and Recommendations in Disciplinary Enforcement* (1970).
5. *Erwin M. Jennings Co.* v. *DiGenova* 107 Conn. 491, 499; 141 A. 866, 868 (1928).
6. For history, see Note, "Controlling Lawyers by Bar Associations and Courts," 5 *Harv. Civ. Rights–Civ. Liberties L. Rev.* 301, 303–308 (1970); and J. W. Hurst, *The Growth of American Law: The Law Makers* (Boston: Little, Brown, 1950).
7. Books and articles documenting the breakdown of disciplinary enforcement include *ABA Special Committee on Evaluation of Disciplinary Enforcement*, *supra* note 4; MacGregor, "Lawyers on Trial," *Wall Street Journal*, April 28, 1969, at 1; Marks and Cathcart, *supra*, note 3; Papke, "The Watergate Lawyers All Passed the Character and Fitness Committee," *Columbia Forum*, Seminar, 1973, at 15; *Report of the Grievance Committee of the Chicago Bar Association* (1965–1966); W. Seymour, *Why Justice Fails* (New York: William Morrow, 1973).
Books and articles specifically concerned with abuse of the disciplinary process against unpopular lawyers include "Civil Rights Lawyers Under Attack," *Southern Patriot*, Feb. 1969, at 8; Countrymen, "Loyalty Tests for Lawyers," 13 *Lawyers Guild Rev.* 149 (1953); N. Dorsen and L. Friedman, *Disorder in the Courts* (New York: Pantheon, 1973); "Controlling Lawyers by Bar Associations and Courts," *supra*, note 6; Lyman, "State Bar Discipline and the Activist Lawyer," 8 *Harv. Civ. Rights–Civ. Liberties L. Rev.* 235 (1973); Note, "Counsel for the Unpopular Cause: The Hazard of Being Undone," 43 *N.C.L.R.N.* 9 (1964). See also In Re *Hallinan*, 43 Cal. 2d 243, 272 P.2d 768 (1954); *Cincinnati Bar Association* v. *Bowman*, 15 Ohio St. 2d 220, 239 N.E. 2d 47 (1968); In Re *O'Connell*, 184 Cal. 584, 194 P. 1010 (1920); and In Re *Clifton*, 33 Idaho 614, 196 P. 670 (1921).
An article concerned with the Supreme Court's application of criminal trial standards to the disciplinary process is Note, "Self-Incrimination: Privilege, Immunity, and Consent in Bar Disciplinary Proceedings," 72 *Mich. L. Rev.* 84 (1973).
8. *Spevack* v. *Klein*, 385 U.S. 511 (1967).
9. Cary, "Professional Responsibility in the Practice of Corporate Law—the Ethics of Bar Associations," 29 *The Record of the Association of the Bar in the City of New York* 443 (1974).
10. *SEC* v. *Spectrum, Ltd., CCH Fed. Sec. L. Rep.* ¶ 94,300 (Dec. 4, 1973).
11. See Marks and Cathcart, *supra* note 1, at 212–214.

12. Witt, "The Bar Goes to Court," *Juris Doctor*, Feb. 1975, at 12.
13. See Dorsen and Friedman, *supra* note 7, at 161; and 5 *Harv. Civ. Rights–Civ. Liberties Rev.* 301, 302, n. 7 (1970).
14. Material on Hirschkop derived from interview Dec. 3, 1974, by J. Seligman and review of civil complaint filed by Hirschkop against the Virginia State Bar Association.
15. See generally *U.S. News and World Report*, March 25, 1974, at 23.
16. "A Grievance Committee at Work, the Michigan Story," *Juris Doctor*, Oct. 1973, at 22.
17. Material on Minnesota derived from telephone interviews with Allen Saeks, member, Minnesota State Board of Professional Responsibility, and review of Opinions 1–8 issued by the board.

GREEN: The Gross Legal Product: "How Much Justice Can You Afford?"

1. Testimony in *The Effect of Legal Fees on the Adequacy of Representation*, hearings before the Subcommittee on Representation of Citizen Interests of the Senate Judiciary Committee, 93rd Cong., 1st sess., Sept. 1973, at 40.
2. See Alburn, "Some Researches into the Matter of Minimum Fees for Lawyers," 21 *ABA J.* 556 (1935); G. Sawyer, *Law in Society* (New York: Oxford University Press, 1965), at 109.
3. J. W. Hurst, *The Growth of American Law: The Law Makers* (Boston: Little, Brown, 1950), at 311.
4. Swaine, "The Impact of Big Business on the Legal Profession," 35 *ABA J.* 89 (1949).
5. Internal Revenue Service, *Business Income Tax Returns* (1973), at 13, 25.
6. R. Weil, *The Census of Law Firms* 10 (1972).
7. "In Search of the Average Lawyer," 56 *ABA J.* A 1164 (1970).
8. Phone interview with Daniel J. Cantor, July 7, 1975.
9. Weil, *supra* note 6, at 10, 11.
10. Illinois Bar Association, *Economic Survey* (April 1969); Oklahoma Bar Association, *1970 Economic Survey* (1970); State Bar of Georgia, *Profile of a Profession* (1969).
11. "The Gilt-Edge Profession," *Forbes*, Sept. 15, 1971, at 30.
12. Illinois State Bar Association, *Economic Institute Handbook* 3 (1960).
13. Quoted in M. T. Bloom, *The Trouble with Lawyers* (New York: Simon & Schuster, 1969), at 199–200.
14. "The Fee Fracas," *Time*, June 3, 1974, at 48.
15. C. Warren, *A History of the American Bar* (Boston: Little, Brown, 1911).
16. Quoted in Arnould, "Fee Fixing in Professional Services," speech before the Industrial Organization Workshop, Iowa State University, April 25, 1974, at 2.
17. Haberman, "Wisconsin's Experience with a Minimum Fee Schedule Based on a Positive Approach to the Problem," *Journal of the Kansas Bar Association*, Spring 1965, at 10–11.
18. *Supra* note 16, at 10.
19. Arnould and Corley, "Fee Schedules Should Be Abolished," 57 *ABA J.* 655, 660 (1971).
20. See American Bar Association, *Minimum Fee Schedules* (1970), and *id.* at 657.
21. The 16 percent figure is based on three assumptions: minimum fee schedules (a) have been promulgated by half of all bar associations, (b) have been used substantially by half of all the lawyers in those bar associations, and (c) covered half of all possible legal services, the others commanding more than the minimum fee. Combining the three estimates ($\frac{1}{2} \times \frac{1}{2} \times \frac{1}{2}$) equals 12.5 percent of all legal income.
22. Testimony in *The Organized Bar: Self-Serving or Serving the Public?*, hearing before the Subcommittee on Representation of Citizen Interests of the Senate Judiciary Committee, 93rd Cong., 1st sess., Feb 3, 1974, at 50, 63.
23. *Supra* note 19, at 659.
24. Note, "A Critical Analysis of Bar Association Minimum Fee Schedules," 85 *Har. L. Rev.* 971, 989 (1972).
25. *Goldfarb* v. *Virginia State Bar*, 43 U.S.L.W. 4723 (U.S., June 16, 1975), (# 7470).

26. Department of Housing and Urban Development, *Mortgage Settlement Costs* iii (Jan. 1972).

27. See also "Kicking Back on Title Insurance," *Business Week*, April 13, 1974, at 97.

28. *Washington Post*, Jan. 10, 1972, at 1.

29. Quoted in *Money* magazine, Jan. 1973, at 33. For a study of the very high legal fees earned in municipal bond issues, where lawyers also earn fixed percentages of large transactions, see The Center for Analysis of Public Issues, *Local Attorney's Fees in Bond Issues* (Princeton, N.J., 1971).

30. *New York Times*, June 19, 1974, at 1, 16.

31. See D. Hapgood, *The Screwing of the Average Man* (New York: Doubleday, 1974).

32. J. Goulden, *The Superlawyers* (New York: Weybright & Talley, 1972), at 274–75.

33. L. Chester et al., *American Melodrama: The Presidential Campaign of 1968* (New York: Viking, 1969).

34. ABA Opinion 250 (1943).

35. W. Hudson, Jr., *Outside Counsel: Inside Director* (1973), summarized in "The High Cost of Corporate Law," *Business Week*, July 22, 1972, at 23.

36. *Washington Post*, Dec. 26, 1973, at A-1, A-6.

37. *Minneapolis Tribune*, April 4, 1974, at 1-A.

38. *New York Times*, Jan. 22, 1973, at 1.

39. *Id.*, Oct. 12, 1974, at 1.

40. *Supra* note 36.

41. *Eisen v. Carlisle & Jacquelin* 391 F. 2nd 555, 571 (Lumbard, dissenting) (2nd Cir. 1968).

42. Brief for Class Members–Appellants, *City of Detroit* v. *Grinnell Corp.*, Dkt. # 73-1211, 2nd Cir., o. 2.

43. Quoted in *id.*, at 32.

44. *Washington Post*, June 6, 1971, at 1.

45. Kohn, "Symposium on Class Actions: Panel Discussion," 41 *Antitrust L. J.* 321, 345 (1972).

46. Note, "Attorneys' Fees," 60 *California L. Rev.* 1656 (1972).

47. Hurst, *supra* note 3.

48. Carlin and Howard, "Legal Representation and Class Justice," 12 *UCLA L. Rev.* 381 (1964).

49. Curran and Spalding, *The Legal Needs of the Public*, preliminary report, American Bar Association (1974).

50. Bartosic and Bernstein, "Group Legal Services as a Fringe Benefit: Lawyers for Forgotten Clients Through Collective Bargaining," 29 *Virginia L. Rev.* 410, 430 (1973).

RILEY: The Mystique of Lawyers

1. On America's historic religious attitude toward the Constitution, see H. S. Commager, *The American Mind* (New Haven: Yale University Press, 1950), at 361; E. Goldman, *Rendezvous with Destiny* (New York: Alfred A. Knopf, 1952), at 68; and T. Arnold, *The Folklore of Capitalism* (New Haven: Yale University Press, 1937), at 79. In a statement almost identical to one in Goldman made a century earlier, ex-Senator Sam Ervin invoked the Constitution as "the greatest and most precious possession of the American people."—Naughton, "Constitutional Ervin," *New York Times Magazine*, May 13, 1973, at 85.

2. See W. Lippmann, *The Public Philosophy* (Boston: Little, Brown, 1955), at 83, 107.

3. According to *Webster's New Collegiate Dictionary* (1959), the word "shyster" comes from a notorious nineteenth-century New York attorney named Scheuster. On the unpopularity of lawyers, see K. Llewellyn, *The Bramble Bush* (Dobbs Ferry, N.Y.: Oceana, 1960), at 141, and M. Mayer, *The Lawyers* (New York: Harper & Row, 1967), at 19–20.

4. David Riesman describes the mystique of the law as a reason the social role of the law and lawyers has been so little studied. See his "Toward an Anthropological Science of Law and the Legal Profession," 57 *American Journal of Sociology* 121 (1951), reprinted in his *Individualism Reconsidered* (New York: Macmillan [Free Press], 1954), at 440. Striking exceptions to the lack of study of the mystique of law and lawyers are F. Rodell, *Woe Unto You, Lawyers!* (Brooklyn: Pageant-Poseidon, 2nd ed., 1939), Arnold, *The Folklore of Capitalism* (*supra* note 1), and J. Frank, *Courts on Trial* (Princeton, N.J.: Princeton University Press, 1939).

5. See O. Maru, *Research on the Legal Profession, A Review of Work Done* (Chicago: American Bar Foundation, 1972) at 45, on "the profession's propensity for self-praise."

6. R. Pound, *The Lawyer from Antiquity to Modern Times* (St. Paul: West, 1953), at 23.

7. *The Mind and Faith of Justice Holmes: His Speeches, Essays, Letters, and Judicial Opinions*, ed. M. Lerner (New York: Modern Library, 1943). Holmes also said later in life, when asked by a friend if he had any general philosophy to guide him as a judge: "Yes. Long ago I decided that I was not God."—Quoted in Goldman, *Rendezvous with Destiny (supra* note 1), at 105.

8. See C. Becker, *The Declaration of Independence, A Study in the History of Political Ideas* (New York: Alfred A. Knopf, 1942), at 38.

9. *Webster's New Collegiate Dictionary* (1959).

10. MacCrate, "Populist and Elitist Conceptions of the Bar," 5 *ALI-ABA CLE Review* 4 (March 1, 1974). On the history of the American bar, see generally Pound, *The Lawyer From Antiquity to Modern Times (supra* note 6), and J. W. Hurst, *The Growth of American Law: The Law Makers* (Boston: Little, Brown, 1950).

11. Stone, "The Public Influence of the Bar," 48 *Harv. L. Rev.* 1, 7 (1934); Brandeis, "The Opportunity in the Law," 39 *Am. L. Rev.* 559 (1905).

12. Riesman, "Law and Sociology," 9 *Stan. L. Rev.* 643 (1957), reprinted in D. Riesman, *Abundance for What? and Other Essays* (New York: Doubleday, 1964), at 433, 437, 440.

13. See M. Green, *The Other Government: The Unseen Power of Washington Lawyers* (New York: Grossman, 1975). Of the 380,000 lawyers then in the country, a 1966 conference on legal manpower needs in criminal law estimated that "there are between 2,500 and 5,000 lawyers who accept criminal representation more than occasionally."—The President's Commission on Law Enforcement and Administration of Justice, *Task Force Report: The Courts* (1967), at 57. The public trial lawyer is not always favorably viewed by the public, because the public doesn't fully understand the lawyer's role as an advocate in the adversary system, under which lawyers may appear to be obstructing justice on their clients' behalf rather than finding it.

14. A. de Tocqueville, *Democracy in America* 177. A hundred and thirty years later Justice Felix Frankfurter made an almost identical statement: "Our society, now more than ever, is a legal state in the sense that almost everything that takes place will sooner or later raise legal questions."—Quoted in Mayer, *The Lawyers (supra* note 3), at 24. Mayer also points out here that the United States has vastly more lawyers than any other country, either numerically or in proportion to population.

15. Lewis, "Sounding Loud and Clear," *New York Times*, March 7, 1974, sect. 4.

16. During the Senate's Watergate Committee hearings, commentators often mentioned the all-lawyer makeup of the committee. No one raised any noticeable objection, and the presence of lawyers seemed to reassure people that the matter would be handled wisely. The House of Representatives Judiciary Committee that handled the investigation of the impeachment charges is also made up entirely of lawyers.

17. H. Thoreau, *Walden; Or, Life in the Woods*, and *On the Duty of Civil Disobedience* 301–2 (1962).

18. Whether legal practice is a profession providing a service or a livelihood supplying a commodity is a long-standing debate that vitally affects the availability of legal service to the public. In 1975 the Supreme Court held that though legal practice is a profession, a standard fee for a title search is an antitrust violation. *Goldfarb* v. *Virginia State Bar*, 43 U.S.L.W. 4723 (U.S. June 16, 1975), # 7470. See also Mayer, *The Lawyers (supra* note 3, at 38), quoting Felix Stumpf: "A lawyer's fee is the price of a commodity just as much as the numbers stamped on a can of beans are the price of a commodity," and Harrison Tweed: "The law is a profession, but its clients are also customers."

19. See also Green, *The Other Government (supra* note 13).

20. Holmes, "The Path of the Law," 10 *Harv. L. Rev.* 39, 43 (1897). For similar views on law and government as the product of living men, not abstract principles, see K. Llewellyn, *The Bramble Bush (supra* note 3), at 13; C. Horsky, *The Washington Lawyer* (Boston: Little, Brown, 1952), at 68; and Bickel, *New Republic*, Oct. 10, 1964, at 9. As for the term "justice," Clarence Darrow spent a lifetime in search of it, but still kept an unsentimental view of it: "Whatever vision we may form of the word 'justice,' still it has never meant anything except adjusting human claims and human conduct to the established habits and customs and institutions of the world."—C. Darrow, *Verdicts Out of Court* (Chicago: Quadrangle, 1963), at 312.

21. *Webster's New Collegiate Dictionary* (1959).

22. Fortas, "Thurman Arnold and the Theater of the Law," 79 *Yale L. J.* 988, 996, 1002 (1970); Cutler, "Book Review," 83 *Harv. L. Rev.* 1746, 1750–1 (1970). See also my article on the GM case

dispute quoting the Cutler law firm press release: Riley, "The Challenge of the New Lawyers: Public Interest and Private Clients," 38 *Geo. Wash. L. Rev.* 547, 554 (1970).

23. "The social implications of the position to be taken on the client's behalf were submerged by the lawyer's dedication to the value of the legal and constitutional system as he saw it, to the duty of the advocate, and to the obligations of advocacy in an adversary system."—Fortas, *supra* note 22, at 996.

"The lawyers are a priesthood with a prestige to maintain. They must have a set of doctrines that do not threaten to melt away with the advances of psychological and social science. . . . They must, in order to feel socially secure, believe and convince the outside world that they have peculiar techniques requiring long study to master."—E. S. Robinson, *Law and the Lawyers* (Toronto: Macmillan, 1935), at 28.

24. Steinberg and Paulsen, "A Conversation with Defense Counsel on Problems of Criminal Defense," 7 *Proc. Law* 25, 26 (1961).

25. J. C. Esposito, *Vanishing Air: The Nader Report on Air Pollution* (New York: Grossman, 1970), at 82–83.

26. K. Lamott, *The Moneymakers: The Great Big New Rich in America* (Boston: Little, Brown, 1969). On the effect of economics on law, see also the excellent article by Hale, "Economics and Law," reprinted in M. R. and F. S. Cohen, *Readings in Jurisprudence and Legal Philosophy* (Boston: Little, Brown, 1951), at 853, 857.

27. Quoted in Mayer, *The Lawyers* (*supra* note 3), at 263.

28. J. H. Skolnick, *Justice Without Trial: Law Enforcement in Democratic Society* (New York: John Wiley, 1966), at 88.

29. *The Challenge of Crime in a Free Society, A Report by the President's Commission on Law Enforcement and Administration of Justice* 58 (1967).

30. "Discussion is . . . ended at a question-beginning phrase about 'competing social policies' at the very point where it should properly begin. . . . Those higher domains where the important truths are examined and revealed are outside the province of a mere legal technician. Thus law, which is the keystone of the arch of public policy, is robbed of vitality and significance . . . the consequence of pedagogic failure which for three years drowns imagination in technique."—David Reisman, quoted in Mayer, *The Lawyers* (*supra* note 3), at 9. On the hostility of lawyers to social sciences, see also W. O. Weyrauch, *The Personality of Lawyers* (New Haven: Yale University Press, 1964), and Riesman, *supra* note 12.

31. E. Warren, "Equal Justice Under Law," in *Law and Theology*, ed. A. J. Buehner (St. Louis: Concordia, 1965).

32. Quoted in Mayer, *The Lawyers* (*supra* note 3), at 15–16.

33. Jean and Edgar Cahn write of the positive effect of the spirit of law on children, enabling the child "to sort out real from fancied injuries, to honor obligations, and to hold both his peers and seniors to standards of conduct which are equitable and rooted in reasonable expectations."—Cahn and Cahn, "Power to the People or the Profession?—The Public Interest in Public Interest Law," 79 *Yale L. J.* 1005, 1021. The late Edmond Cahn listed some positive values of law, and the risk of their becoming negative ones in practice, in his *Moral Decision: Right and Wrong in the Light of American Law* (Bloomington: Indiana University Press, 1955).

34. T. Veblen, *The Theory of the Leisure Class* (New York: Modern Library, 1934).

35. Quoted in Mayer, *The Lawyers* (*supra* note 3), at 82.

36. H. Miller, *The Wisdom of the Heart* (New York: New Directions, 1941), at 37.

37. Quoted in Bazelon, "Clients Against Lawyers," *Harper's*, Sept. 1967, at 104. As J. P. Morgan said: "I have had many lawyers who have told me what I cannot do; Mr. Root is the only lawyer who tells me how to do what I want to do."—B. Levy, *Corporation Lawyer: Saint or Sinner?* (Philadelphia: Chilton, 1961), at 10–11.

38. The obvious exceptions are people like William Kunstler and a handful of other crusading lawyers who have personally gotten in trouble for their connection to a cause. While some crusading lawyers like the Cahns (*supra* note 33) insist that the lawyer's role in political causes should be secondary, others are bothered by that role: e.g., "I want to practice law less and less, and focus more and more on living the things that I believe."—"Comment, The New Public Interest Lawyers," 79 *Yale L. J.* 1069, 1144 (1970). See also Nader, "Law Schools and Law Firms," *New Republic*, Oct. 11, 1969, at 23, quoting Charles Reich: "In a society where law is a primary force, the lawyer must be a primary, not a secondary, being."

39. Weyrauch, *The Personality of Lawyers* (*supra* note 30), at 268–69. Weyrauch discusses his own study of lawyers and refers to others, including Llewellyn, *The Bramble Bush* (*supra* note 3), at 148.

40. M. K. Gandhi: *Selected Writings*, ed. D. Duncan (London: Fontana, 1972), at 74. On Confucius, see G. Sawyer, *Law in Society* (New York: Oxford University Press, 1965) at 57–58, and see also *Sources of Chinese Tradition*, ed. W. T. DeBary, Jr., et al. (New York: Columbia University Press, 1960), at 34, 138, 590 ff.

41. *The New English Bible with the Apocrypha* (1961), Luke 11:52.

42. Frank, Introduction in F. Rodell, *Woe Unto You, Lawyers!* (*supra* note 4).

FREEDMAN: Advertising and Soliciting: The Case for Ambulance Chasing

1. *Gunn* v. *Washek*, 405 Pa. 521, 176 A.2d 635 (1961); M. Freedman, *Contracts* (St. Paul: West, 1973), at 245.

2. DR7-101(A)(1): EC 7-1, 7-4, 7-8, of the ABA *Code of Professional Responsibility* (1969).

3. EC 6-9, 7-8.

4. EC 2-26; DR 2-109, 2-110(C)(1)(e).

5. *See also* DR 7-102(a)(1).

6. Jaffe, *Report to the Committee of Censors of the Philadelphia Bar Association of the Investigation into Unethical Solicitation by Philadelphia Lawyers* 41 (March 1, 1971). The report also mentioned the possibility of remedial legislation, but no effort appears to have been made by the bar association toward that end.

7. *Id.*, at 40.

8. DR 2-101-105.

9. *Jacksonville Bar Assn.* v. *Wilson*, 102 So.2d 292 (Fla. 1958). See also EC 2-9.

10. *Id.*, at 295.

11. Kaufman, "The Lawyers' New Code," 22 *Harv. L. Sch. Bulletin* 19 (1970).

12. Shuchman, "Ethics and Legal Ethics: The Propriety of the Canons as a Group Moral Code," 37 *Geo. Wash. L. Rev.* 244 (1968); Cohen, "Confronting Myth in the American Legal Profession," 22 *Ala. L. Rev.* 513 (1970).

13. EC 2-9.

14. Jaffe, *supra* note 6, at 5.

15. Campbell and Wilson, *Public Attitudes to the Legal Profession in Scotland* 69 (mimeograph, 1973).

16. *Id.*, at p. 68.

17. *In the Matter of Solomon Cohn*, New York Law Journal, Feb. 19, 1974, 1:6–7, 3:3. The opinion of the court notes that the attorney had an unblemished record and that before he undertook to represent people in court, he had worked as volunteer for, and then as a staff member of, the Legal Aid Society. The last paragraph of the opinion reads:

> We cannot, of course, condone respondent's unprofessional conduct. However, after giving due consideration to all the circumstances here involved, including respondent's expressions of self-reproach and the humiliation he has already suffered, we believe leniency to be warranted in this instance. Accordingly, the respondent should be censured. . . .

18. Radin, "Maintenance by Champerty," 24 *U. Cal. L. Rev.* 48, 72 (1935).

19. EC 2-2.

20. EC 2-3.

21. *Id.*

22. *NAACP* v. *Button*, 371, U.S. 415 (1963); *Brotherhood of Railroad Trainmen* v. *Virginia*, 377 U.S. 1 (1964); *United Mine Workers* v. *Illinois State Bar Assn.*, 389 U.S. 217 (1967); *United Transportation Union* v. *State Bar of Michigan*, 401 U.S. 576 (1971).

23. The Court recognized the critical importance of solicitation to public interest litigation in noting the proscription of solicitation in *Button* would have "seriously crippled" the efforts of the NAACP.—*United Mine Workers*, at 223.

24. *Button*, at 438–39.

25. *Brotherhood of Railroad Trainmen*, at 9.

26. *Supra* note 22, at 223.

27. *United Transportation Union*, at 597 (dissent).

LIEBERMAN: How to Avoid Lawyers

1. See M. Kammen, *People of Paradox* (New York: Alfred A. Knopf, 1972).

2. J. Schukers, *The Life and Public Services of Salmon Porter Chase* (1874), at 30; cited in L. Friedman, *A History of American Law* (New York: Simon & Schuster, 1973), at 277.

3. Quoted in J. Young, *The Medical Messiahs* (Princeton, N.J.: Princeton University Press, 1967), at 19.

4. See generally D. Boorstin, *The Mysterious Science of the Law* (Gloucester, Mass.: Peter Smith, 1941); *contra* F. Rodell, *Woe Unto You, Lawyers!* (Brooklyn: Pageant-Poseidon, 1937).

5. Quoted in Friedman, "Freedom of Contract and Occupational Licensing 1890–1910: A Legal and Social Study," 53 *Calif. L. Rev.* 487, 501 (1965).

6. See Doyle, "The Fence-Me-in-Laws," 205 *Harper's* 89 (1952).

7. Calif. Assem. Bill No. 1671 (Reg. Sess. 1955). See Hetherington, "State Economic Regulation and Substantive Due Process of Law II," 53 *Nw. U. L. Rev.* 226, 249 (1958).

8. J. W. Hurst, *The Growth of American Law: The Law Makers* (Boston: Little, Brown, 1950), at 319.

9. See *New Mexico* v. *Credit Bureau of Albuquerque, Inc.*, 42 *U.S.L.W.* 2176 (N.M. Sup. Ct. 1973).

10. *Supra* note 8, at 323.

11. Opinion of the Justices, 277 Mass. 607, 611, 180 N.E. 725, 727 (1932); expressly adopted by Connecticut in *State Bar Assn. of Connecticut* v. *Connecticut Bank and Trust Co.*, 145 Conn. 222, 140 A.2d 863 (1958).

12. *State Bar of Arizona* v. *Arizona Title & Trust Co.*, 90 Ariz. 76 366 P.2d 1 (1961). The story is told in M. Bloom, *The Trouble with Lawyers* (New York: Simon & Schuster, 1969).

13. J. Carlin, *Lawyers on Their Own* (Brunswick, N.J.: Rutgers University Press, 1962), at 270.

14. *Grievance Committee of Bar of Fairfield County* v. *Dacey*, 154 Conn. 129, 222 A.2d 399, rehearing den. 387 U.S. 938 (1966).

15. *New York County Lawyers' Assn.* V. *Dacey*, 28 A.D.2d 16, 17 (1967).

16. *New York County Lawyers' Assn.* v. *Dacey*, 21 N.Y.2d 694, 287 N.Y.S. 2d 422 (1968).

17. See J. K. Lieberman, *The Tyranny of the Experts* (New York: Walker & Co., 1970), chapter 6.

18. "Kicking Back on Title Insurance," *Business Week*, April 13, 1974, at 97.

19. For Williston, see Opinion No. 309, in *Opinions of the Committee on Professional Ethics* (ABA, 1956). For union attorney, see *United Mine Workers* v. *Illinois State Bar Assn.*, 35 Ill. 2d, 219 N.E. 2d 503 (1966).

20. *United Mine Workers* v. *Illinois State Bar Assn.*, *supra* note 19.

21. *United Mine Workers* v. *Illinois State Bar* 389 U.S. 217 (1967).

22. See generally D. Matthews, *Sue the B*st*rds!* (New York: Arbor House, 1973).

23. Matthews suggests a separate branch of small claims courts for automobile and large appliance claims, with specific higher limits for these claims only.

24. *New York Times*, Dec. 3, 1972, Section 4.

25. The table is compiled from Appendix A of Matthews, *supra* note 22.

26. See Matthews, *supra* note 22, at 137.

27. See Selinger, "Functional Division of the American Legal Profession: The Legal Paraprofessional," 21 *J. Legal Ed.* 523 (1969).

28. See Rothmyer, "The Emergence of the Paraprofessional," 1 *Juris Doctor* 14 (1971). See Larson, "Legal Paraprofessionals: Cultivation of a New Field," 59 *ABA J.* 631 (1973).

29. *ABA News*, Jan. 1974, at 5.

30. "Putting Law Libraries into the Computer," *Business Week*, Jan. 26, 1974, at 30.

31. "An Indexing System to Speed Lawsuits," *Business Week*, March 30, 1974, at 32.

32. "Computers May Cut Legal Costs," *New York Times*, Feb. 17, 1974, at 63.

33. See generally J. O'Connell, *Ending Insult to Injury* (Champaign: University of Illinois Press, 1975).

34. At least one vigorous proponent of antitrust enforcement demurs to the general view that this type of consumer legislation is beneficial. Victor Kramer, director of the Institute for Public Interest Representation of Georgetown University Law Center, told the New York State Bar Association such reforms "will have anti-competitive effects by making it more difficult for the smaller competitors to obtain financing for their credit sales. I would rather run the risk of being gypped in a

competitive market than being compelled to do business in a monopolistic market."—Address on Jan. 23, 1974, at 16.

HOCHBERG: The Drive to Specialization

1. Sonnett Lecture by Chief Justice Warren Burger at Fordham Law School, Nov. 26, 1973.
2. Kaufman, "Does the Judge Have a Right to Qualified Counsel?", 61 *ABA J.* 569 (1975).
3. Order of Supreme Court of Minnesota, *In Re Rules Relating to Continuing Professional Education*, April 3, 1975; Order of Supreme Court of Iowa, *In the Matter of Adoption of Rules Pertaining to Continuing Legal Education for Members of the Iowa Bar*, April 9, 1975.
4. *Supra* note 1.
5. *Supra* note 2.
6. *Id.*
7. Speech to Society of American Law Teachers, Dec. 1974.
8. Kurland, "Polishing the Bar," *New York Times*, April 24, 1975, at 35.
9. Remarks to ALI-ABA Mid-Atlantic Conference on CLE and Specialization, Philadelphia, May 9–10, 1975.
10. Address by Joe Sims, Deputy Assistant Attorney General to National Council on Occupational Licensing, Inc., Virginia Beach, Va., Aug. 4, 1975.
11. Rayack, "The Physicians' Service Industry," in W. Adams (ed.), *The Structure of American Industry*, 4th Edition (New York: Macmillan, 1971), at 419.
12. R. H. Zehnle, *Specialization in the Legal Profession* (American Bar Foundation, 1975).
13. *Supra* note 11.
14. *Id.* at 452.
15. *Id.* at 453.
16. American Bar Association Special Committee on Specialization, *Report of Conference on Minimum Standards for Trial Advocates and State Specialization Programs* (June 1974).
17. Remarks to ALI-ABA Mid-Atlantic Conference on CLE and Specialization, May 9–10, 1975.
18. Wolkin, "A Better Way to Keep Lawyers Competent," 61 *ABA J.* 574 (1975).
19. Remarks to ALI-ABA Mid-Atlantic Conference on CLE and Specialization, May 9–10, 1975.
20. *Faretta* v. *California*, 43 U.S.L.W. 5004 (S.Ct., June 1975).
21. Remarks to ALI-ABA Mid-Atlantic Conference on CLE and Specialization, May 9–10, 1975.
22. *Supra* note 11, at 423.
23. *Id.* at 424.
24. *Consumers Union, et al.* v. *American Bar Association, et al.*, Civil Action No. 75-0105-R, E.D. Va.

CONYERS: Undermining Poverty Lawyers

1. *Congressional Record*, H 5074 (June 21, 1973).
2. *Id.*, H 5101.
3. *Id.*, H 5087.
4. R. H. Smith, *Justice and the Poor* (reprint, Montclair, N.J.: Patterson Smith, 1972), at 8.
5. J. Shestack, "The Right to Legal Services," in *The Rights of Americans*, ed. N. Dorsen (New York: Pantheon, 1971).
6. Justification of FY 1972 Economic Opportunity Act Authorizations, Legal Services, Federal Budget, 1972, at 69–70.
7. E. C. Bamberger, Jr., *Hearings of OEO Commission on California Rural Legal Assistance, Inc.*, reporter's transcript (1971), at 55.
8. *Supra* note 6, at 118.
9. *Wyman* v. *James*, 404 U.S. 309 (1971).
10. *King* v. *Smith*, 392 U.S. 309 (1968).
11. *Shapiro* v. *Thompson*, 394 U.S. 618 (1969).

12. *Goldberg* v. *Kelly*, 397 U.S. 254 (1970).

13. Bamberger, "The Legal Services Program of OEO," 41 *Notre Dame L. Rev.* 84 (1966).

14. For a more detailed discussion of the bar's support of legal services see Pious, "Congress, the Organized Bar, and the Legal Services Program," *Wisc. L. Rev.* 418–46 (1972).

15. *Washington Post*, Feb. 4, 1973, at 1.

16. *Congressional Record*, H 5078 (June 21, 1973).

17. Shestack, *supra* note 5, at 121. CRLA and the program's clash with Reagan are also discussed in Hiestand, "The Politics of Poverty Law," in *With Justice for Some*, ed. B. Wasserstein and M. Green (Boston: Beacon, 1970), and in Falk and Pollak, "Political Interference with Publicly Funded Lawyers: The CRLA Controversy and the Future of Legal Services," 24 *Hastings L. J.* 599–646 (1973).

18. Quoted by Abrams, "Poverty Law," *New Republic*, April 22, 1972, at 32.

19. *Report of the Office of Economic Opportunity Commission on California Rural Legal Assistance, Inc.*, at 84, 88.

20. Agnew, "What's Wrong with the Legal Services Program," *ABA J.*, Sept. 1972, at 930–32. The article was responded to by the chairman of the ABA Standing Committee on Legal Aid and Indigent Defendants in Klaus, "Legal Services Program: Reply to Vice-President Agnew," *id.*, at 1178, and by Falk and Pollak, "What's Wrong with Attacks on the Legal Services Program," *id.*, at 1287.

21. Feuillan and Goodman, "The Trouble with Judicare," 58 *ABA J.* 476–81 (1972).

22. *New York Times*, Dec. 10, 1971, at 20.

23. *Williams* v. *Shaffer*, 385 U.S. 1037, 1039 (1967).

HALPERN: The Public Interest Bar: An Audit

1. Speech to ABA National Institute on Federal Agencies and the Public Interest, March 14, 1974.

2. *Wilderness Society* v. *Morton*, 479 F.2d 842 (D.C. Cir. 1973), *cert. den.*, 411 U.S. 917.

3. *Id.*

4. 368 F. Supp. 863 (D.C. D.C. 1973).

5. See *Office of Communications of the United Church of Christ* v. *F.C.C.* 465 F.2d 519 (D.C. Cir. 1972).

6. *Alyeska Pipeline Service Co.* v. *The Wilderness Society* 421 U.S. 240 (1975).

7. 28 U.S.C. 2412.

8. *Supra* note 5.

MOORE & HARRIS: Class Actions: Let the People In

1. See, e.g., Scott, "Two Models of the Civil Process," 27 *Stan. L. Rev.* 937 (1975).

2. Kress, "The Effect of End Displays on Selected Food Product Sales" (New York: Point of Purchase Advertising Institute), undated.

3. Even if the consumer were an expert, he or she would lack the time and resources for an expert assessment of each purchasing choice. Consumers' evaluative skills and shopping time are relatively finite, while the complexity of marketplace decision making continues to multiply.

4. For a discussion of the subjects and cost estimates contained in this chart, including references, see B. Moore, *A Modest Proposal for the Reform of the Capitalist System (Part A)* (Washington, D.C.: Center for the Study of Capitalist Institutions, 1974).

5. The effectiveness of the antitrust laws and the private treble damage suits they authorize in curbing monopoly is open to serious doubt. See W. Comanor and R. Smiley, *Monopoly and the Distribution of Wealth* (Stanford Grad. Sch. Bus. Res. Paper No. 156, May 1973), and M. Green, B. Moore, and B. Wasserstein, *The Closed Enterprise System* (New York: Grossman, 1972). According to the Comanor/Smiley study, the effect of monopoly profits on the distribution of wealth during the first seven decades following the enactment of the antitrust laws was to raise the share of total private wealth held by the richest one percent of Americans from 15 percent to 33 percent and to deposit 53 percent rather than 26 percent of the wealth in the hands of 5 percent of the population.

6. Note, "The Rule 23(b)(3) Class Action: An Empirical Study," 62 *Geo. L. J.* 1123 (1974).

7. Moore, "The ABA, the Congress and Class Actions," 3 *Class Action Rep.* 36 (1974).

8. Note, *supra* note 6, at 1137.

9. *Eisen v. Carlisle & Jacquelin*, 479 F.2d 1005 (2d Cir. 1973), *vacated and remanded*, 417 U.S. 156 (1974).

10. This is not to suggest that the contingent fee necessarily be based upon a strict percentage of the class recovery achieved through the plaintiff attorney's efforts. The preferable approach, now followed by most federal courts, is to apply a multiplier to what the attorney would reasonably charge for the hours he has expended on the litigation. *Lindy Bros. Builders, Inc., v. American Radiator & Standard Sanitary Corp.*, 1974-2 Trade Cases ¶ 75,361 (E.D. Pa.). See generally 3 *Class Action Rep.* 154–158, 168–170 (1974).

11. For a summary article see "The Court Turns Against Antitrust," *Business Week*, July 14, 1975, at 52.

12. See *Mangano v. American Radiator & Standard Sanitary Corp.*, 309 F. Supp. 1057 (E.D. Pa. 1970), 438 F.2d 1187 ¶ 73,609 (3d. Cir.); *In re Plumbing Fixtures Multidistrict Litigation*, 1970 Trade Cases ¶ 73,346 (E.D. Pa.).

13. *In re Multidistrict Vehicle Air Pollution*, 481 F.2d 122 (9th Cir. 1973).

14. *Buford v. American Finance Co.*, 333 F. Supp. 1243 (N.D. Ga. 1971).

15. *Graybeal v. American Savings & Loan Assn.*, 59 F.R.D. 7 (D.D.C. 1973).

16. *Eisen v. Carlisle & Jacquelin*, 417 U.S. 156 (1974).

17. *Hackett v. General Host Corp.*, 1972 Trade Cases ¶ 73,879 (E.D. Pa. 1970).

18. *Boshes v. General Motors*, J9 F.R.D. 589 (N.D. Ill. 1973). See also the rulings of the notorious U.S. Ninth Circuit Court of Appeals, e.g., *In re Hotel Telephone Charges*, 500 F.2d 86 (9th Cir. 1974); *Kline v. Coldwell, Banker & Co.*, 1975 Trade Cases ¶ 75,436 (9th Cir.).

19. E. Budd, ed., *Inequality and Poverty* (New York: W. W. Norton, 1967), at XXI–XXIII.

CALIFANO: The Washington Lawyer: When to Say No

1. J. Boswell, *The Life of Johnson*, vol. 2, ed. G. B. Hill and L. F. Powell (1887), at 47.

2. Reich, "Towards the Humanistic Study of Law," 74 *Yale L. J.* 1402, 1407–8 (1965).

3. *Code of Professional Responsibility*, Canon 7 (1969).

4. "It is not much of an exaggeration to say that the Washington lawyer has been almost a fourth branch of government for the past thirty years. His participation in the public policy process has taken many different forms—lobbyist, regulation writer, consultant, advocate, speech writer, witness, critic and crusader."—Mikva, "Interest Representation in Congress: The Social Responsibilities of the Washington Lawyer," 38 *Geo. Wash. L. Rev.* 651 (May 1970).

5. See generally J. C. Goulden, *The Superlawyers* (New York: Weybright & Talley, 1972); 38 *Geo. Wash. L. Rev.* 527 et seq. (entire issue devoted to "Inside Washington Law: The Roles and Responsibilities of the Washington Lawyer").

6. *In re Kelly* 243 F. 696, 703–704 (D. Montana, 1917).

7. Emmanuel Fields, Securities Act Release No. 5404 (June 18, 1973) *CCH Fed. Sec. L. Rep.* ¶ 79, 407.

8. Stone, "The Public Influence of the Bar," 48 *Harv. L. Rev.*, 1, 2, 5, 6–7, 10 (1934).

9. See Nader, "Law Schools and Law Firms," *New Republic*, Oct. 11, 1969, at 20; Green, "Law Graduates: The New Breed," *Nation*, June 1, 1970, at 658; *contra* Green, "The Young Lawyers: Goodbye to Pro Bono," *New York*, Feb. 21, 1972, at 29.

PERTSCHUK: The Lawyer-Lobbyist

1. *United States v. Harriss*, 347 U.S. 612 (1954).

2. J. C. Goulden, *The Superlawyers* (New York: Weybright & Talley, 1972); M. Green, *The Other Government: The Unseen Power of Washington Lawyers* (New York: Grossman, 1975); see also Zalaznick, "The Small World of Big Washington Lawyers," *Fortune*, Sept. 1969, at 120.

3. Kempton, "The Washrooms of Power," *New Republic*, Aug. 3, 1963.

4. See Canon 8 of the *Code of Professional Responsibility* (1969).

5. Brandeis, "The Opportunity in the Law," 39 *Amer. L. Rev.* 555, 558 (1905).

SMYSER: In-House Corporate Counsel: The Erosion of Independence

1. A. Blaustein and C. Porter, *The American Lawyer* (University of Chicago Press, 1954), at 46.
2. Carruth, "The 'Legal Explosion' Has Left Business Shell-Shocked," *Fortune*, April 1973, at 155.
3. J. Donnell, *The Corporate Counsel: A Role Study* (Bloomington: Indiana University Bureau of Business Research, 1970), at 30.
4. Hickman, "The Emerging Role of Corporate Counsel," in *The Life of the Law*, ed. J. Honnold (Macmillan [The Free Press]), 1964.
5. Donnell, *supra* note 3, at 83.
6. Swaine, "The Impact of Big Business on the Legal Profession," *ABA J.* 89 (1949).
7. *Carruth, supra* note 2, at 155.
8. Llewellyn, "The Bar Specializes," 167 *Annals* 177 (1933).
9. C. Curtis, *It's Your Law* (Cambridge: Harvard University Press, 1954), at 32.
10. Frankfurter, "Personal Ambitions of Judges," 34 *ABA J.* 747 (1948).
11. D. Boorstin, *The Americans: The Democratic Experience* (New York: Random House, 1973), at 56.
12. Swaine, *supra* note 6.
13. R. Hofstadter, *The Age of Reform* (New York: Random House, Vintage ed., 1954), at 158–59.
14. Llewellyn, *supra* note 8.
15. *Id.*
16. Brandeis, "The Opportunity in the Law," 39 *Amer. L. Rev.* 555, 559 (1905).
17. Wilson, "The Lawyer and the Community," 35 *Reports of the ABA* 419, 430 (1910).
18. Boorstin, *supra* note 11, at 417.
19. Curtis, *supra* note 9, at 32.
20. *Id.*
21. Quoted by Curtis, *supra* note 9, at 5–6.
22. Brandeis, *Other People's Money and How the Bankers Use It*, foreword by N. Hapgood (New York: F. A. Stokes, 1932), at 158.
23. Curtis, *supra* note 9, at 32.
24. Practicing Law Institute, *Managing Law Offices* 73 (forum transcript).
25. Swaine, *supra* note 6, at 170.
26. *New York Times*, March 7, 1974, at 37.
27. Hickman, *supra* note 4.
28. Blaustein and Porter, *supra* note 1, at 48.
29. EC 5-18.

RABINOWITZ: The Prosecutor: The Duty to Seek Justice

1. The most petty and perhaps also the most typical manifestation of this arrogance appears in a prosecutor's treatment of a defendant in a courtroom. The second circuit in at least seven cases in 1973 had occasion to consider this kind of prosecutorial misconduct: *United States v. Santana*, 485 F. 2d 365; *United States v. Drummond*, 481 F.2d 62; *United States v. la Sorsa*, 480 F.2d 522; *United States v. Fernandez*, 480 F.2d 726; *United States v. Miller*, 478 F.2d 1315; *United States v. Pfingst*, 477 F.2d 177; *United States v. White*, 486 F.2d 204. In most of these cases the appellate court affirmed convictions while criticizing the conduct of the prosecutor.
2. 373 U.S. 83 (1962).
3. 18 U.S.C. 793(e).
4. *Mesarosh v. United States*, 352 U.S. 1 (1956).
5. 407 U.S. 297 (1972).
6. For example, see A. Westin, *Privacy and Freedom* (New York: Atheneum, 1966); S. Dash, R. Knowlton, and R. Schwartz, *The Eavesdroppers* (New Brunswick, N.J.: Rutgers University Press, 1959). Periodical and pamphlet material on the subject is even more plentiful. For example, H. Schwartz, *A Report on the Costs and Benefits of Electronic Surveillance* (ACLU, 1971); Schwartz, "The Legitimation of Electronic Eavesdropping: The Politics of 'Law and Order,'" 67 *Mich. L. Rev.*

455 (1969); Lewin, "Facts About Wiretapping: Lewis Powell's Confusion," *New Republic*, Nov. 20, 1971; Note, "The National Security Wiretap: Presidential Prerogative for Judicial Responsibility," 45 *So. Calif. L. Rev.* 888 (1972).

7. Administrative Office of the United States Courts, Report on Applications for Orders Authorizing or Approving the Interception of Wire or Oral Communications for 1971. See also the appendix to the opinion of Mr. Justice Douglas concurring in *United States* v. *United States District Court*, 407 U.S. 297, 334.

8. Among the cases discontinued were *United States* v. *Sinclair* in the Eastern District of Michigan; *United States* v. *Rudd* in the Eastern District of Michigan; *United States* v. *Bacon* in the Southern District of New York; *United States* v. *Hilliard* in the Northern District of California; *United States* v. *Jaffe* in the Western District of New York; and *United States* v. *Smith* in the Central District of California.

9. *Coplon* v. *United States*, 191 F.2d 749 (D.C. Cir. 1951), *cert. den.*, 342 U.S. 926.

10. *New York Times*, Feb. 13, 1974, at 18.

MORRISON: Defending the Government: How Vigorous is Too Vigorous?

1. *Flast* v. *Cohen*, 392 U.S. 83 (1968).

2. *Williams* v. *Phillips*, 360 F. Supp. 1363 (D.D.C.), *stay denied*, 482 F. 2d 669 (D.C. Cir. 1973).

3. *Public Citizen et al.* v. *Brinegar*, No. 74-1621, D.D.C. Order of March 20, 1975, *appeal pending*, No. 75-1399, D.C. Cir.

4. *Public Citizen* v. *Sampson*, Civil Action No. 781-73, D.D.C., *revised and dismissed for lack of standing*, 515 F.2d 1018 (D.C. Cir. 1975).

5. *United States* v. *Richardson*, 418 U.S. 166 (1974), and *Schlesinger* v. *Reservists Committee to Stop the War*, 418 U.S. 208 (1974).

6. See Arnold, "The Power of State Courts to Enjoin Federal Officers," 73 *Yale L. J.* 1385, 1394 (1964).

7. 28 U.S.C. 1331.

8. 327 F. Supp. 238, 242 (S.D.N.Y. 1971).

9. *Williams* v. *Phillips*, supra note 2, at 1365. It was undoubtedly because of this decision that government counsel in the case which sought to declare unlawful the firing of Archibald Cox, and to have him reinstated as special prosecutor, did not raise the $10,000 question, since it is clear that Mr. Cox's salary would have far exceeded that in a matter of months had he been returned to office.—*Nader* v. *Bork*, 366 F. Supp. 104 (D.D.C. 1973), *appeal dismissed as moot*, No. 74-1260 (D.C. Cir. Aug. 20, 1975).

10. *Bivens* v. *Six Unknown Named Agents*, 409 F. 2d 718, 723 (2d Cir. 1969), *reversed on other grounds*, 403 U.S. 388 (1971).

11. *National Council of Community Mental Health Centers, Inc.*, v. *Weinberger*, 361 F. Supp. 897, 900 (D.D.C. 1973).

12. *Toilet Goods Association* v. *Gardner*, 360 F. 2d 677, 683 n.6 (2d Cir. 1966).

13. 501 F. 2d 887 (D.C. Cir. 1974).

14. *National Council of Community Mental Health Centers* v. *Weinberger*, 361 F. Supp. 897, 900 (D.D.C. 1973).

15. *Id.*, at 901.

16. Kleindienst, "The Federal Attorney's Position Within the Government," reprinted in 32 *Federal B. J.* 1, 8–9 (1973).

17. *Schlesinger* v. *Reservists Committee to Stop the War*, 418 U.S. 208, 232 (1974) (dissenting).

18. *Code of Professional Responsibility*, at 1.

19. E.g., F.E.C.-7-2: "The Federal lawyer is under the professional obligation faithfully to apply his professional talents to the promotion under law and applicable regulations of the public interest entrusted to the department, agency or other governmental agency of his employment." See 60 *ABA J.* 1541 (1974) for all F.E.C.'s and comments on them.

20. Two articles did deal with ethics legislation, but were concerned primarily with conflicts-of-interest problems in the traditional sense: Comment, "Texas Public Ethics Legislation: A Proposed Statute," 50 *Tex. L. Rev.* 931 (1972), and Legislative Note, "The Illinois Governmental Ethics Act—A Step Towards Better Government," 22 *De Paul L. Rev.* 302 (1972). One earlier article by a

former general counsel of the Navy Department, F. Trowbridge von Baur, entitled "Care and Feeding of Government Lawyers," 56 *ABA J.* 669 (1970), was concerned primarily with improving morale and finding new ways to attract competent government lawyers, but made no mention of the obligation of government attorneys to the public at large.

21. C. Fahy, "Special Ethical Problems of Counsel for the Government," Lecture at Columbia University School of Law, April 11, 1950, reprinted, 33 *Federal B. J.* 331 (1974): "Where both sides of a controversy are represented by counsel, as in court work, the zeal of each for his respective client, the zeal which accompanies advocacy of a cause, tends to create a balance. There is a delving into all relevant aspects of a case. The arguments pro and con are marshalled. In government work, most of which is not in court, this is often not available. The lawyer finds himself considering a matter as an advisor or as a judge without benefit of opposing briefs or arguments. His opinion is desired. A unique obligation thus arises."

22. Quoted by W. Safire, *New York Times*, Jan. 28, 1974, at 27.

RAVITZ: Reflections of a Radical Judge: Beyond the Courtroom

1. See *Johnson* v. *Louisiana*, 406 U.S. 356, and *Apodaca* v. *Oregon*, 406 U.S. 404, cases in which the U.S. Supreme Court on May 22, 1972, held that the states are not constitutionally required to follow two hundred years of precedents mandating that jury verdicts in criminal cases be unanimous.

2. See, e.g., *Life*, Aug. 8, 1970, at 26.

3. An *ex parte* injunction is a judicial order to prevent activity, and it is granted at the request and for the benefit of one party in litigation without notice to or an opportunity to contest the order by the adverse party or parties who are bound by the restraining order.

4. *Chrysler Corporation* v. *George Bauer*, Wayne County (Mich.) Circuit Court, File No. 155874 (1969).

5. For a keen insight into the role of government concerning murders by police in Detroit—the home of the infamous Algiers Motel case and the home of a Green Beret–style police squad—read "Detroit Under STRESS," a pamphlet published by From the Ground Up, 7316 W. McNichols, Detroit, Mich. 48221.

6. P. Stern, *The Rape of the Taxpayer* (New York: Random House, 1973), 14, 229.

7. C. Kelly, *Uniform Crime Reports* (FBI), 1972, at 2.

8. See Seney, "Our Criminal Law's Moral Obsolescence," 17 *Wayne L. Rev.* 777, 801 (1971).

9. National Commission on Product Safety, final report (1970), cited in 17 *Wayne L. Rev.* at 801, n. 18.

10. 17 *Wayne L. Rev.* at 801, n. 116. As my comrade B. P. Flanigan—a revolutionary poet—says, "Fisher Body makes dead bodies, regularly."

11. Credit for this phrase goes to the Los Angeles chapter of the National Lawyers Guild. I, at least, first saw the phrase in its newspaper masthead.

12. It has been reported that I am the first American judge to have ever sentenced someone to jail for having violated a Weights and Measures Act—acts that have long been on the books in probably every jurisdiction. See *Media and Consumer*, Vol. 1, No. 13, at p. 9, Dec. 1973. Research, however, indicates that in 1946 a California judge sentenced such a defendant to ninety days in jail. See *In Re Marley*, 29 Cal. 2d 525, 175 p. 2d 832.

13. *Detroit Free Press*, Nov. 10, 1972, at 1-B.

14. "Gentle People" is a poem written by B. P. Flanigan. It appears in *No Other Way Out*, published by Changeover Productions, c/o 7316 W. McNichols, Detroit, Mich. 48221.

NEWFIELD: The Ten Worst Judges

1. *Daily News*, March 20, 1974.

2. Dkt. # Q-19113-5, Nov. 15, 1971, at 5.

3. Dkt.# K-423612, Part AP-1, Brooklyn Criminal Court.

4. Dkt.# K-418044, July 11, 1974.

5. Dkt.# K-343085, K-340347.

6. *People* v. *Norton*, Dkt.# X-7461, April 7, 1972.

7. Indictment #4077/72, Bronx County, at 16, 28.
8. Indictment #2213/72, Bronx County.
9. Indictment #1829/72, Manhattan, at 354–57.
10. See, for more details, Mary Perot Nichols' article in the December 7, 1972, *Village Voice.*
11. SCI Report, April 8, 1974.
12. Dkt.# A-78627, Dec. 9, 1972.
13. Dkt.# Y-400173-4, Jan. 14, 1974.
14. Dkt.# X-307912.

SCHMIDT: Lawyers on Judges: Competence and Selection

1. Even at the Supreme Court level, critical evaluations rarely focus on the work of particular justices. For a recent example, however, see Wolfman, Silver, and Silver, "The Performance of Mr. Justice Douglas in Federal Tax Cases," 122 *Univ. of Penn. L. Rev.* 235 (Dec. 1973).

2. The council now has more than a thousand lawyer members and in 1972 it was admitted to full status as an affiliated local bar association with a seat in the American Bar Association's House of Delegates. In addition to its work in connection with the federal judiciary, it has provided blunt, public evaluations of state court judges seeking appointment or retention in office, based on the candid evaluations of lawyers. It has also been active in promoting reform of the legal profession and over a wide range of substantive areas of law.

3. The analysis by Beverly Blair Cook, Associate Professor, Political Science, University of Wisconsin, Milwaukee, concluded, among other things:

> The usefulness of this data on the federal district judges in Chicago has been checked for bias in responses by internal tests of validity and for inaccuracy of responses by external tests of validity. The questionnaire included 28 questions to evaluate qualities exhibited by the trial judges and two questions to allow a preference for the retention and/or promotion of the judges. The internal tests showed a close relationship between favorable answers on characteristics and on preference for retention, indicating a thoughtful consideration of judicial qualities in relation to the lawyer's vote of confidence. Ability to handle civil cases was positively correlated to recommendations for promotion and retention and negatively to recommendations against retention. Qualities which might be expected of appellate judges, including ability to handle complex cases, to keep informed of new legal developments, and to do adequate research and preparation, were more significantly related to the votes for promotion than retention. Moreover, the graphing of the negative evaluations by lawyers showed no large group in the sample which strongly disapproved of any judge. Rather, each graph curve was similar, in that increasing numbers of lawyers found a diminishing number of poor qualities for each judge. Moreover, the three judges most severely criticized by the respondents were of diverse political, ethnic, and other background characteristics.

4. *United States* v. *Dellinger,* 472 F. 2d 340, 388 (7th Cir. 1972).
5. J. C. Goulden, *The Benchwarmers* (New York: Weybright & Talley, 1974), at 115.
6. Rose, "The Quiet Revolution," *Chicago Sun Times,* June 5, 1974.
7. See President's Page, 58 *Ill. B. J.* 591 (1970).
8. *Konigsberg* v. *State Bar of California,* 353 U.S. 252, 269 (1957).
9. A second survey is being conducted for release by the end of 1975.
10. *Supra* note 5.
11. *Supra* note 6.
12. *Id.*

13. In 1975, the Chicago Council of Lawyers publicly expressed its "disappointment" with two of Senator Percy's nominations, saying they represented "a step backward from the high standards which have, on the whole, characterized Senator Percy's prior judicial nominations and which we believe should be applied in making appointments to these courts."

TUNNEY & FRANK: Epilogue: A Congressional Role in Lawyer Reform?

1. These laws and related court decisions are included in hearings before the Subcommittee on Representation of Citizen Interests, Committee on the Judiciary, U.S. Sen., on *The Effect of Legal Fees on the Adequacy of Representation,* 93rd Cong., 1st sess., Sept. 19, 20; Oct. 1,2,4,5, 1973; 1266–1536. (Hereinafter *Legal Fees Hearing Record.*) Note that 28 U.S.C. 2412 had been held to prohibit awards of attorneys' fees when suing federal officers unless such awards are specifically provided for by statute.

2. *Alyeska Pipeline Service Co.* v. *The Wilderness Society*, 421 U.S. 240 (1975).

3. *Argersinger* v. *Hamlin*, 407 U.S. 25 (1972); *Gideon* v. *Wainwright*, 372 U.S. 335 (1963). See also *Miranda* v. *Arizona*, 384 U.S. 436 (1966). But see *Michigan* v. *Tucker*, 417 U.S. 433 (1974).

4. *United Trans. Union* v. *State Bar of Michigan*, 401 U.S. 576 (1971); *United Mine Workers* v. *Illinois State Bar Assn.*, 389 U.S. 217 (1967); *Brotherhood of Railroad Trainmen* v. *Virginia* ex rel. *Va. State Bar*, 377 U.S. 1 (1964); *NAACP* v. *Button*, 371 U.S. 415 (1963). See Brickman, "Of Arterial Passageways Through the Legal Process: The Right of Universal Access to Courts and Lawyering Services," 48 *NYU L. Rev.* 595, 625 (1973).

5. State Bar of Texas press release (undated) concerning comments made by Senator John V. Tunney before the Harvard Law School Forum.

6. *Goldfarb* v. *Virginia State Bar*, 43 U.S.L.W. 4723 (U.S. June 16, 1975), #7470. See also Testimony of Mr. Bruce B. Wilson, *Legal Fees Hearing Record, supra* note 1, at 164–65.

7. For example, the limitation on attorneys' fees in veterans' cases has been handled by the Veterans Affairs Committee; the legal services program in the Office of Economic Opportunity was handled by the Labor and Public Welfare Committee, as was the legislation to create an independent Legal Services Corporation which was drafted as an amendment to the Economic Opportunities Act.

8. See Hourigan, *Today's Lawyer in a Changing Society*, American Bar Assn. Proceedings of the Third National Conference on Law Office Economics and Management 6 (1968); Special Comm. on Professional Utilization, American Bar Assn., *The Report of the Task Force on Professional Utilization* (1972).

9. *Legal Fees Hearing Record*, Testimony of Ms. Dolores Durham, at 40.

10. *Id.*, Testimony of Mr. and Mrs. Kenneth L. Kornher, at 10.

11. See, e.g., Gellhorn, "Public Participation in Administrative Proceedings," 81 *Yale L. J.* 359 (1972).

12. *Legal Fees Hearing Record*, Testimony of Mr. J. Anthony Kline, at 789–90.

13. S.2928, 93d Cong., 2d sess. (1974), introduced by Senators Magnuson, Moss, Tunney, and Kennedy, was unanimously reported by the Senate Commerce Committee and reintroduced in the 94th Cong., 1st sess., as S. 2069.

14. *Id.*

15. 29 U.S.C. 186, as amended by P.L. 93–95, Aug. 15, 1973.

16. Baird, "Charitable Deductions for *Pro Bono Publico* Professional Services: An Updated Carrot-and-Stick Approach," 50 *Tex. L. Rev.* 441 (1972). Reprinted in *Legal Fees Hearing Record, supra* note 1, at 1537–43.

17. Remarks to Ford Foundation Public Interest Law Conference, San Diego, Calif., April 16, 1974.

18. The most recent remarks on this subject were by Joseph Sims, assistant to the assistant attorney general, Antitrust Division, Department of Justice, before the Committee on Professional Ethics, New York State Bar Association, Rochester, N.Y., Aug. 21, 1974.

19. *Supra* note 12, at 789.

20. *Northcross* v. *Board of Educ.*, 412 U.S. 427 (1973); *Northcross* v. *Board of Educ.*, 489 F.2d 19 (6th Cir. 1973).

21. *Stanford Daily* v. *Zurcher*, 366 F. Supp. 18 (N.D. Cal. 1973).

22. *Hall* v. *Cole*, 412 U.S. 1 (1973).

23. *La Raza Unida* v. *Volpe*, 57 F.R.D. 94 (N.D. Cal. 1972).

24. *Lee* v. *Southern Homes Sites Corp.*, 444 F.2d 143 (Fifth Cir. 1971). Fees have also been awarded in a Native American claims case. *Pyramid Lake Paiute Tribe of Indians* v. *Morton*, 360 F. Supp. 669 (D.D.C. 1973). However, the decision was reversed on the grounds that the lower court's finding of statutory authority to award attorneys' fees was in error. Civil Action No. 73-2184 (D.C. Cir., June 28, 1974).

25. Fellers, "The Challenges of Supplying Legal Services," 60 *ABA J.* 45 (1974).

Index

Index